MARK PEDELTY

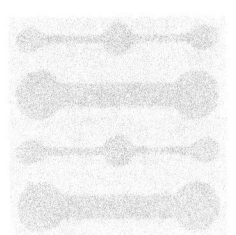

Musical Ritual in Mexico City

FROM THE AZTEC TO NAFTA

 University of Texas Press, Austin

"Aventurera" by Agustín Lara. Copyright © 1930 by Peer International Corporation. Copyright Renewed. Used by Permission. All Rights Reserved.

"Solamente una vez" by Agustín Lara. Copyright © 1941 by Promotora Hispano Americana de Música. Administered by Peer International Corporation. Copyright Renewed. Used by Permission. All Rights Reserved.

"Noche de ronda" by María Teresa Lara. Copyright © 1935 by Promotora Hispano Americana de Música. Administered by Peer International Corporation. Copyright Renewed. Used by Permission. All Rights Reserved.

"María bonita" by Agustín Lara. Copyright © 1947 by Promotora Hispano Americana de Música. Administered by Peer International Corporation. Copyright Renewed. Used by Permission. All Rights Reserved.

Some material in Chapters 10 and 11 was published previously in Mark Pedelty, "The Bolero: The Birth, Life, and Decline of Mexican Modernity," *Latin American Music Review* 20, no. 1, 30–58. Copyright © 1999 by the University of Texas Press. All rights reserved; and in Mark Pedelty, "Mexican Popular Culture as Development Discourse: An Intertextual History of Augustín Lara's 'Aventurera,'" in *Redeveloping Communication for Social Change: Theory, Practice, and Power*, edited by K. Wilkins, 119–134. Lanham, Md.: Rowman and Littlefield, 2000. Used by Permission.

Copyright © 2004 by the University of Texas Press
All rights reserved
Printed in the United States of America
First edition, 2004

Requests for permission to reproduce material from this work should be sent to Permissions, University of Texas Press, P.O. Box 7819, Austin, TX 78713-7819.

∞ The paper used in this book meets the minimum requirements of ANSI/NISO Z39.48-1992 (R1997) (Permanence of Paper).

LIBRARY OF CONGRESS CATALOGING-IN-PUBLICATION DATA

Pedelty, Mark.
   Musical ritual in Mexico City : from the Aztec to NAFTA / Mark Pedelty.—1st ed.
     p.   cm.
   Includes bibliographical references (p.   ) and index.
     ISBN: 978-0-292-72614-7

     1. Music—Mexico—Mexico City—History and criticism.   2. Music—Religious aspects.   3. Rites and ceremonies—Mexico—Mexico City.   4. Mexico City (Mexico)—Civilization.   5. Mexico City (Mexico)—Social life and customs.   I. Title.
ML210.8.M4 P43   2004
780'.972'53—dc22

2003018269

MUSICAL RITUAL IN MEXICO CITY

To Holmes and Jane Pedelty

Contents

Acknowledgments xi

CHAPTER 1 Introduction 1

Part I The Mexica: 1325–1521 3

CHAPTER 2 Tenochtitlán: 1325–1521 5
CHAPTER 3 Mesoamerican Resonance 25

Part II New Spain: 1521–1821 37

CHAPTER 4 Colonial Mexico: 1521–1821 39
CHAPTER 5 Colonial Resonance 70

Part III The New Nation: 1821–1910 83

CHAPTER 6 The First Century of Independence: 1821–1910 85
CHAPTER 7 Nineteenth-Century Resonance 107

Part IV The Revolution: 1910–1921 117

CHAPTER 8   Revolutionary Mexico: 1910–1921 119
CHAPTER 9   Revolutionary Resonance 131

Part V Modern Mexico: 1921–1968 137

CHAPTER 10   Bolero and Danzón during the Postrevolutionary Era 139
CHAPTER 11   Bolero and Danzón Today 180
CHAPTER 12   Classical Nationalism during the Postrevolutionary Era 203
CHAPTER 13   Classical Nationalism Today 216
CHAPTER 14   Ranchera during the Postrevolutionary Era and at Mid-Century 225
CHAPTER 15   Ranchera Today 238

Part VI Contemporary Mexico: 1968–2002 247

CHAPTER 16   Popular Music Today 249
CHAPTER 17   Conclusion 275

APPENDIX 1.   Theory and Methodology 291
APPENDIX 2.   Timeline 311
APPENDIX 3.   Discography 315
              Bibliography 321
              Index 335

Illustrations

Aztec teponaztli   17

Aztec huehuetl   18

Voladores in Chapultepec Park   28

Performers in a touring version of the Guelaguetza   31

Dúo Villey-Hinojosa   78

The Mexican Army Band playing in the zócalo at dusk   109

Orizaba, Conjunto Jarocho led by Martín Campos   112

Los Volcanes del Norte   132

Eugenia León at the Baile, Música y Canto de Iberoamérica concert   190

Master organist Victor Urbán   220

Ricardo Martínez of Mariachi Juvenil de América   244

The multitalented Pepe Loza   244

Trío Los Tres Ases   259

The Rollos and Rock and Roll   270

Acknowledgments

I would like to thank collectively all of the ethnomusicologists, musicologists, and musical historians cited here. This book would clearly not be possible without the lifetimes of effort that these researchers have committed to the study of Mexican music and culture. I am an indebted interloper, thankful to investigators like Mercedes Díaz Roig, Pablo Dueñas, Susana Dultzin Dubin, Juan José Escorza, Jesús Estrada, Rafael Figueroa Hernández, José Antonio Guzmán Bravo, María Herrera-Sobek, Alan Knight, George Lewis, Ana López, Marit Melhuus, Vicente Mendoza, Carlos Monsiváis, Yolanda Moreno Rivas, José Antonio Nava Gómez Tagle, Robert Parker, Esperanza Pulido, Susanna Rostas, E. Thomas Stanford, Robert Stevenson, Ignacio Paco Taibo, Lourdes Turrent, Eric Zolov, and the many others who have dedicated decades to Mexican musicology and cultural studies.

My sincere apologies to the musical researchers whose work I have accidentally overlooked. It was certainly not for want of effort. In order to gather relevant materials I combed through all available databases; spent years rummaging through shelves of new and used bookstores in Mexico City and the United States; and accessed library collections in Mexico City (Universidad Nacional Autónoma de México [UNAM] and National Library), Austin (University of Texas), Minneapolis (University of Minnesota), and others via interlibrary loan. I am certain that lacunae remain, and I look forward to filling them with the help of readers.

The authors cited above and the reviewers mentioned below have done much to make this book succeed where it does. To the extent that problems and mistakes remain, it is my doing alone. I would like to thank the following for reading sections and providing comments on this work: Daniel Goldstein, Patrick McNamara, Karin Wilkins, Daphne Berdahl, John Ingham, and the faculty members and graduate students of the University of Minnesota Department of Anthropology who read and critiqued drafts of the Agustín Lara material. I am grateful to Dorris Sommer and the members of the Social Sciences Research Council seminar on Cultural Agency in the Americas in Cuzco, Peru. They were both critical and constructive when I shared some of the most "vulnerable" material with them, greatly strengthening the work as a result. Thanks also to John Kelly, who provided valuable feedback as a discussant at the American Anthropological Association Annual Meetings in 1999. I would like to acknowledge the faculty and students of the School of Interdisciplinary Studies, Western College Program of Miami University, where this research was conceived and developed. The Miami University Latin American Studies faculty played a major role in the development of this project, including friends and fellow instructors Tom Klak, Raúl Ianes, Reed Anderson, Walter Vanderbush, and Sheila Croucher.

I would like to thank the following for providing financial support for this research: University of Minnesota McKnight Travel Grant, University of Minnesota Office of International Programs Travel Grant, University of Minnesota Summer Research Fellowship, Miami University (Ohio) Grant Programs, and the Phillip and Elena Hampton Grant.

I would also like to thank Adan Quan, who has provided me with significant insight into popular music during our discussions in El Salvador, California, Ohio, and Michigan. Likewise, thanks to Peter Redfield for his helpful critique, constant support, and solid bass-work. Carolyn Haynes has provided invaluable intellectual, emotional, logistical, and musical assistance throughout the project and continually reinforces my faith in the power of pedagogy.

I am especially grateful to Mabelu Pedraza for her invaluable assistance in Mexico and for her continued friendship. Thanks to Carlos Franco for his professional camera work. I'd also like to thank all of the staff, students, and faculty of the General College of the University of Minnesota for the help and encouragement they have offered during the final years of this project.

Above all, I would like to thank the musicians, fans, parishioners, and others who have shared their musical passion with me in Mexico City. Mexico City is one of the world's most fascinating musical communities. I owe a major debt to its people, which I cannot even begin to repay.

A big thank-you to my parents, Jane and Holmes Pedelty, for their support and proofreading. Finally, I would like to acknowledge the person who clears away my commas and proofs every page, my best friend, Karen Miksch.

> *If you want to see if a nation is well governed, listen to its music.*
> — CONFUCIUS (IN CASTELLANOS 1970:65)

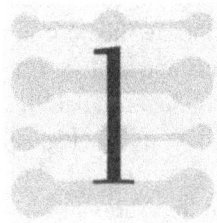

1 Introduction

Mexico City has been the cultural and political heart of the Mexican nation since the Mexica founded their capital there in 1325. In a matter of decades, the Aztec settlement grew into the metropolis of Tenochtitlán, an island city on Lake Texcoco. Although neither the ancient city of Tenochtitlán nor Lake Texcoco can be found today, traces of both remain, buried just a few meters below the surface of modern Mexico City.

Similarly, layers of time have created a cultural foundation for the modern city. The past can still be seen, felt, and heard in the capital. For example, on the *zócalo*, the main square of Mexico City, Mexico's entire musical history is performed every day. "Mexica" percussionists drum and dance in the square's cemented central part. Inside the Metropolitan Cathedral, on the northern edge of the zócalo, choristers sing colonial *villancicos*. Meanwhile, just outside the National Palace, to the east of the square, the Mexican army marching band plays the "Himno nacional," a vestige of the nineteenth century. These remarkable sounds are subsumed and incorporated into the city's soundscape, no longer a dominant cultural force but vital nonetheless as reminders of Mexico's past. Although pop, rock, and *música grupera* dominate the contemporary soundscape of the world's largest city, these more subtle echoes continue to resonate as well. We can learn a great deal by digging through these musical layers. With that in mind, this book presents an aural excavation of the city's musical history and a snapshot of its contemporary musical life. The goal is not just to detail past and present musical rituals, however, but to explore the inextricable relationship between the two.

Such research requires not only historiographic examination but also ethnographic analysis. Both methods are applied here. Each chapter narrates the development, execution, and social functions of the main musical modes of a given historical period. Each historical survey is followed by a chapter describing how the same musical forms resonate today. For example, Chapter 2 is about Aztec music and ritual observance. Chapter 3 focuses on the ways in which Aztec ritual music is performed today, nearly five hundred years after the Conquest. The rituals of the Aztec Empire have been radically transformed, becoming rituals of renewal and even resistance when performed in the present. The sacred *huehuetl* drum no longer provides the soundtrack for sacrifice but instead renews the spirit of middle-class office workers and college students gathered in the zócalo. The conch trumpet no longer signals the hour of bloodletting; it entertains throngs of tourists at archaeological sites. The slit-gong *teponaztli* no longer plays for rituals of state but instead enlivens archaeomusicological ensembles at the National Museum of Anthropology.

Catholic rites (Chapter 4) that once legitimated Spanish rule have likewise lost their social centrality, taking on new, often antithetical cultural meanings in the postcolonial present (Chapter 5). A similar fate was met by the profane *jarabe*, a ritualized dance that challenged the colonial hegemony of Spanish theocrats. The radical colonial dance became an official ritual of national identity after the first Mexican Revolution (1810–1821), only to fade into fossilized "folk" status after the next (1910–1921). The growth, florescence, death, and rebirth of the jarabe and other musical forms of nineteenth-century Mexico are examined in Chapters 6 and 7. Modern musical styles, from the revolutionary *corrido* to postmodern rock, are similarly detailed in Chapters 8–16. The book concludes with a spectacular ritual event, the presidential inauguration of Vicente Fox, a dramatic ceremony recapitulating 700 years of Mexican ritual history.

Each of the musical movements described here has experienced a fairly similar life-trajectory, moving from creative obscurity to social dominance, only to be replaced in the next era by other musical forms and ritual regimes. Although each assemblage of sound has been quieted through time, none has been silenced altogether. Echoes of the musical past continue to resonate in Mexico City's museums, theaters, concert halls, restaurants, and parks. To understand those echoes, we must return to the beginning, when a relatively small Aztec band first reached the shores of Lake Texcoco.

PART

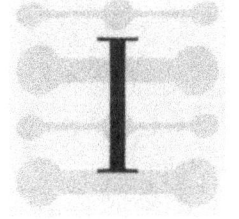 The Mexica:
1325—1521

I the master song composer,
I the singer beat my war drum
That its stirring call may waken
The dead souls of my companions.
— FROM "WAR SONG" IN
The Song of Quetzalcóatl (CORNYN 1931:149)

Tenochtitlán: 1325–1521

The Mexica were one of "twenty or so" Nahuatl-speaking or "Aztec" tribes who migrated into the Central Valley of Mexico (Smith 1996:4). They were one of the feared Chichimec or "barbarian" peoples who lived beyond the northern borders of the large Mesoamerican states. Their initial relationship to the more established Mesoamerican cultures was like that of the Huns to the Roman Empire and the Mongols to dynastic China. Like the Huns, they went from being hired mercenaries to being conquerors, defeating the same states that once sponsored them. Like the Mongols, they adopted the urban infrastructure and mythology of the larger civilizations they defeated. They conquered and acculturated.

The Mexica made their way to the Central Valley of Mexico from their homeland of Aztlán somewhere to the north. Despite being the last Aztec tribe to reach the Central Valley (about A.D. 1250), the Mexica would eventually rise to lead the Triple Alliance (A.D. 1428), a coalition formed with the neighboring city-states of Texcoco and Tlacopan. The Triple Alliance would gain control of a vast Mesoamerican territory, exacting tribute from less powerful societies and controlling trade in the region.

The Triple Alliance Empire, like all state civilizations, was maintained through a combination of military might, clientelism, and ideology. Complex myths and rituals legitimated the alliance's control of the region. Its mythology centered on a pantheon of gods borrowed from previous Mesoamerican empires, with the addition of a few of its own, including Huitzilopochtli (the god of war), Coyolxauhqui (his sister), and Coatlicue (their mother).

The Mexica claimed to be the direct heirs of the Toltec, the preeminent power of the Early Postclassic (A.D. 950–1150). It is from the Toltec that they borrowed the cult of Quetzalcóatl, a hybrid god combining the pre-Toltec Feathered-Serpent deity and an actual Toltec ruler. According to legend, the human Quetzalcóatl was a deposed emperor who opposed human sacrifice. According to another legend, for the Mexica he was a white god who would one day return from the East and recapture his empire. If the historical legend is to be believed (some claim that it is fiction contrived by the Spanish chroniclers), Emperor Motecuhzoma Xocoyotzin (Motecuhzoma II) interpreted the arrival of Hernán Cortés as the return of the Feathered-Serpent. Given that Quetzalcóatl was already a god-man hybrid, Cortés-as-Quetzalcóatl provided a sensible "historical metaphor" (Sahlins 1981) for interpreting the arrival of the alien interloper. Despite being sensible from a mythological standpoint, however, the Quetzalcóatl interpretation had disastrous human consequences.

Up to the point of the Conquest, Mexica mythology provided an excellent cultural map to success. Between the founding of their island-city Tenochtitlán in A.D. 1325 and their fall at the hands of Cortés two hundred years later, the Mexica created an empire. Little wonder that Mexica leaders favored the most literal interpretations of their mythological metaphors. History had provided manifest proof of divine favor.

In addition to mythological maps, the Mexica also used brute force, technological superiority, bureaucratic efficiency, and a system of production unlike any other in the world. Supplementing the sumptuous trade and tribute flowing into Tenochtitlán was the local chinampa agricultural system. Through a series of dikes and dirt-fill gardens placed in the midst of Lake Texcoco the Mexica managed to transform saltwater and sand into lush garden plots. Supported by these seemingly endless resources, over one million people were living prosperously in the Central Valley by the time Cortés arrived (Smith 1996:60).

Around 200,000 of these valley inhabitants lived in the island-city of Tenochtitlán itself. Millions more lived in the nearby valleys of what is today Central Mexico. Despite a relative lack of meat protein sources, the people generally ate well. By soaking corn in lime and combining tortillas with beans and other cultigens, even those without access to meat were able to achieve a complete protein enzyme package (Smith 1996:68).

Material organization, wealth, and brute force, however, do not of themselves make an empire. Myth and ritual were also important. Pedro

Carrasco explains that for the Mexica "there barely existed any human activity that did not require a corresponding ritual" (1994:237). The Mexica maintained a constant ritual cycle, closely tied to the seasons. In Mesoamerica, those seasons include the dry months, January through May, and the rainy period, June through October (November and December are transitional). Food production, war, and life itself were dictated by this annual cycle.

MEXICA RITUAL

Life in Tenochtitlán involved constant ritual performance, from daily rites in the domestic household to massive affairs of state, the great sacrifices. I focus on the latter here. In doing so, however, I do not want to lose sight of the fact that the Mexica, and all of the peoples of Mesoamerica, had just as many nonlethal rituals. While state functions were carried out with a level of shocking violence, smaller-scale rituals marking birth, marriage, death, and other community events were peaceful affairs, dramatically contrasting with the violent rituals of power (Smith 1996:134–143).

Likewise, we should not lose sight of the fact that the brutal ritual acts documented in the Aztec codices, ethnohistoric narratives, and archaeological remains were committed by and for Mexica elites. We know that many of the tributary peoples found these acts brutal and oppressive. Therefore, we may assume that many Mexica commoners also found these ritual acts of violence excessive, just as today the all-too-frequent acts of state-supported violence against lesser foes are widely protested. In fact, one possible interpretation of Motecuhzoma II's quick acquiescence to Cortés-Quetzalcóatl is that the emperor felt he had overstepped his ritual purview, having taken the rites of state to new heights of violence.

Just as extreme violence (Native American policies, slavery, colonialism) is merely one legacy and not the totality of United States social history, human sacrifice should not be viewed as the sole legacy of the Mexica. As Michael Smith reminds us, "the very same people who produced this sacrificial blood and gore wrote some of the most beautiful and poignant lyric poetry ever recorded" (1996:2). Aztec poems, such as the following fragment, "are monuments, as durable as stone, to the humanity of the Aztecs, and perhaps more indicative of the nature of their civilization than the sacrificial altars where their still-beating human hearts were offered to the Sun" (1996:161, 163):

8   The gold and black butterfly is sipping the nectar,
    The flower bursts into bloom.
    Ah, my friends, it is my heart!
    I send down a shower of white frangipani.

Yet it is also wrong to assume that ritual sacrifice was a capricious, culturally unsanctioned act of the elite. Instead of being seen as moral transgressions, these rites were viewed as moral imperatives. If at times leaders took this to excess, it is still clear that for many Mesoamerican societies humans were duty bound to sacrifice themselves to the earth and gods so that the cycle of life would continue.

In attempting to understand Mexica sacrifice, it is best to start with the perspectives of the Mexica themselves. The Mexica believed that the gods needed human blood to subsist. Sacrifice was more payback than taxation. For example, Tlaltecuhtli, the earth goddess (sometimes also represented in male form), was ripped apart to form the earth. She gave her flesh and blood to create land and continued to provide for the needs of humanity through cycles of bloodshed and fertility. Tlaltecuhtli is the womb and tomb of all life.

The origin myths of the Mexica speak of many gods who sacrificed themselves for humanity, thus establishing a "debtor relationship between humankind" and themselves (Smith 1996:204). The sun, music, and humanity itself resulted from the deities' deaths. Therefore, humans exist in a blood-debt relationship to Tlaltecuhtli and all of the gods. To deny them their blood feast would mean bringing an end to the fifth sun. Being just one reality in an ongoing series of worlds that the gods had created and destroyed, the fifth sun would also be snuffed out someday. The entire ritual cycle was designed to satisfy nature and the gods, which were largely one in the same. In so doing, humans could help maintain the seasonal cycle of life and delay the apocalypse of the fifth sun as long as possible.

Liminal or "in between" periods were considered particularly dangerous and required focused ritual attention. Failure to perform the correct ritual at the beginning and end of each cycle could result in disaster. This was true of the periods between days, between months (eighteen of them), and between the two seasons (wet and dry). It was particularly important to perform the "new fire ceremony" every fifty-two years, the length of a Mexica century. The new fire ceremony was performed in the evening on the last day of every century. All fires were extinguished, producing darkness and a sense of fear throughout the empire. As the century came to an end, priests lit a new fire on the chest of a sacrificial victim, ripped out his heart, and threw it into the fire. The priests then brought the fire to the center of the world, the Great Temple. All of Tenochtitlán could see the fire burning in the temple of Huitzilopochtli atop the pyramid (Carrasco 1987:139). When people saw the new fire, they knew that time and the fifth sun would continue. The new fire was then spread throughout Tenochtitlán and the empire atop the torches of young runners. In this way, each end was also viewed as a beginning—not of a new era, as in the Judeo-Christian sense of time, but of another movement in the ongoing cycle of existence. The Mexica thought of time in circular terms rather than as linear progression. The goal was to continue the current cycle as long as possible.

The needs of nature, not those of humanity, dictated the execution of Mexica ritual performance. The tens of thousands of sacrificial deaths that took place during Mexica rule were demanded by the natural world and the god-spirits of that world, not by the priests, emperors, and warriors who carried them out. Sacrifice was sacred. In fact, in many Mexica rituals the sacrificial subject (*ixiptla*) was treated as a god before his or her demise (Smith 1996:224). The sacrificial victim was viewed as a representative of that god, a sacred stand-in. In the Toxcatl ceremony, for example, a handsome young man was selected a year in advance for sacrifice to Tezcatlipoca. He was ritually cleansed, fed delicacies normally reserved for nobles, given four beautiful wives, worshiped, and in general treated like a god.

The *toxcatl tixiptla* led ritual performances throughout the year, involving singing, dancing, and conspicuous flute playing. Similar to flute march rituals elsewhere around the world (e.g., Murphy and Murphy 1985:113–121), the Toxcatl flute-march was most likely a phallic performance of male fertility and power, given the association with Tezcatlipoca. The sacrificial man-god ixiptla became a sacred surrogate, and in his death he would become a messenger to that most potent of all gods, indicating that all things were in order on the human plane of existence. The ritual presented a sophisticated virtual reality of sight and sound, reaching apogee at the moment of sacrifice. The divine victim would lead the dance and even choose the moment of his death (Guzmán Bravo and Nava Gómez 1984a:129). Plied with alcohol, treated as a divine being, and emotionally immersed in the ritual, these most privileged of the condemned could be brought to make such a choice willingly. They were at that moment the center of a cosmic drama, elevated through death. Theirs was the most honorable of sacrifices.

Of course, there were also other, more profane reasons for these rites. It is clear that human sacrifice satisfied the needs of the state as well as the gods. "These ideological concepts served to legitimate the dominant values of this expansionist warrior state," explains Johanna Broda, "and to motivate the subjects to act according to these values" (1987:64). By legitimizing power and the status quo, ritual not only gave "cohesion to social life, but also" made possible "the reproduction of the material conditions of existence" (1987:66–67).

The material conditions of existence in archaic states were directly related to the dominant mode of production: highly intensified agriculture. Gradual changes in population density in Mesoamerica led to ever greater and more segregated levels of stratification, increased informational and political hierarchies, enabled more intense forms of repression, required new disciplines, and fostered the forms of violence that distinguish states from nonstate societies. Allen Johnson and Timothy Earle present a compelling and synthetic explanation of the causes and contexts of state development in *The Evolution of Human Societies: From Foraging Group to Agrarian State* (1987). The rise of the Mesoamerican empires fits their model well. The levels of population density, subsistence intensification, political hierarchy, social stratification, and violence increased together, each mutually reinforcing the others. Archaeological evidence indicates a rise in each of these factors over time, culminating in the Triple Alliance, the state with most violent methods of control, the most hierarchical political system, the most stratified society, and the most intense and integrated economic system experienced in precortesian Mesoamerica.

The Mexica: 1325–1521

The Mexica state boldly performed its power through human sacrifice. Sacrificial victims came from the ranks of the slave castes and captured enemies from tributary states. Tributary leaders were invited to watch as their soldiers were put to death. The blood of their warriors streamed down the steps of the Great Temple (Smith 1996:227), producing an "acid and abominable stench" (Broda 1987:66). The message was clear: "Don't mess with the Mexica." The Mexica, believing themselves to be the rightful heirs of the Toltec and most favored children of the gods, saw these acts as not only acceptable but also sacred. That view was probably not widely shared, however, by the 55 provinces and 450 city-states under their control (Smith 1996:175–178).

In other words, ritual is polysemic. Different people interpret the same rituals and myths in divergent ways. The story of Huitzilopochtli, as told to Spanish missionary Bernardino de Sahagún (1950–1982, Book 3), serves as an illustration.

One day, Coatlicue, she of the Serpent Skirt, was sweeping out the temple atop Coatepec, the Serpent Hill. As she swept, a ball of feathers floated down from the sky. Distracted, Coatlicue placed the feathers in her shirt and kept on with her work. Later, when she went to take the feathers out of her shirt, she discovered that she had been impregnated and the feathers were no longer there. She was going to give birth to a great son, the god Huitzilopochtli.

Rather than rejoice, Coatlicue's 400 children, led by Coyolxauhqui, marched angrily to the summit with intentions of killing their mother. Coyolxauhqui, the warrior goddess, had convinced her brothers that their mother, Coatlicue, had dishonored them by sleeping with an unknown man and becoming pregnant. Coyolxauhqui led her angry brothers, exhorting them to climb Coatepec and kill their mother.

Just before Coyolxauhqui reached her mother, however, Huitzilopochtli was born, ready to make war on his rebellious siblings. Huitzilopochtli laid waste to them, saving the worst punishment for Coyolxauhqui herself. Huitzilopochtli dismembered his older, faithless sister, and then rolled her severed limbs and torso down the hill of Coatepec.

Huitzilopochtli gained honor by protecting his mother, while Coyolxauhqui became a symbol of the faithless daughter. The Mexica constructed temples to honor Huitzilopochtli, reenacting his heroic deed through ritual sacrifice of conquered enemies atop the Great Temple. As warning to all who would step outside of their subordinate state, the body of the enemy victim was lanced with arrows or the victim's heart was ripped out of its cavity. Often the victim was dismembered, like Huitzilopochtli's rebellious sister, and rolled down the pyramid steps until coming to rest on the Coyolxauhqui stone, a huge circular monolith memorializing the transgressions of the goddess (Matos Moctezuma 1988:34–35).

The conquistadors were made aware of this ritual tradition when several of their captured comrades were ritually sacrificed, dismembered, and flayed as they watched from shore. Later the Spaniards recalled the sound of "the dismal drum of Huichilobos [Huitzilopochtli] and many other shells and horns and things that sounded like trumpets and the sound of all of them was terrifying" (Díaz del Castillo 1956:436).

In fact, the Noche Triste, the "Sad Night" when the Spaniards were routed out of Tenochtitlán, was set off by the violation of a ritual act. Pedro de Alvarado, left in charge while Cortés was on the coast, violently disrupted a ritual honoring Huitzilopochtli. The surviving Mexica told Friar Sahagún that "when the dance was loveliest, and song was linked to song, the Spaniards were seized with an urge to kill the celebrants" (León-Portilla 1990:74). The conquistadors quickly moved to the center of the rite, "forcing their way to the place where the drums were played" (1990:76). Once there, they cut off the drummers' arms. The Mexica, outraged by the Spaniards' violent interruption of their most sacred rite, besieged them and eventually were able to drive them out of the city. Catching his breath on the opposite shore, surely even Pedro de Alvarado (nicknamed Tonatiuh, the sun god, by the Mexica) realized that he had made a grave error. Ritual was life to the Mexica.

The Huitzilopochtli-Coyolxauhqui myth and ritual clearly illustrate the Mexica belief that theirs was a sacred path. Performance contexts and methods indicate additional cultural and political dimensions, however. Among these is the obvious element of gender. Huitzilopochtli, the god-son, was closely associated with the sun-god, Tonatiuh; both are clear archetypes for the Mexica male. Huitzilopochtli was born for war, fighting in the service of his earth-mother, Coatlicue (it was quite common for multiple gods to take on overlapping domains, as in the case of two earth-related deities, Tlaltecuhtli and Coatlicue). Conversely, Coyolxauhqui was the female transgressor, trying to kill the good mother and her sacred brother. As is true in many cultures, the she-god Coyolxauhqui was associated with the moon and therefore the female cycle as well. Coyolxauhqui, the persuasive and powerful, had to be brought low, as did the enemies of the Mexica.

Obviously, Coyolxauhqui's defeat is a patriarchal metaphor. Woman, if fulfilling the roles ascribed to her, would be honored. Therefore, a woman who died giving birth to a son would earn a ride through the sky with Tonatiuh, the same honor given a fallen warrior. Woman the transgressor, however, was feared and reviled, viewed as dangerously powerful, as are all things liminal. Coyolxauhqui represented a form of power outside social control — one that ultimately had to be controlled by man, lest she remake the social order entirely.

Such myths represented idealized versions of the Mexica order. Similarly, in ritual performance, women were mostly accorded domestic and reproductive roles (Turrent 1996:53). Although women did serve as temple priests, this was itself a rite of passage, a means of ritually containing the danger represented by them as liminal beings making their way from adolescence to womanhood — a passage out of, and back into, the moral order symbolized by marriage (Smith 1996:220). Another role accorded to women outside the domestic context was that of the prostitute. Sometimes prostitutes were acquired by the Mexica as a form of payment from tributary states. These prostitutes operated openly in a regulated marketplace and were not reviled. This was an additional socially sanctioned role for unmarried women. Prostitutes were even occasionally honored, and more than one Mexica ritual required their participation (Turrent 1996:54). From slave and prostitute to emperor and priest, there was an assigned place and role for everyone in the moral order of the Mexica.

RITUAL TRAINING AND REGULATION

Ritual was an important means of political regulation not only for adult men and women but also for youth. Although the content of Mexica youth rituals is unique, the general process is not. Like most official adolescent rites of passage, Mexica youth ceremonies served to contain and redirect the potentially rebellious power of youth. From the perspective of power, the disruptive potential of libidinous youth must be contained and, if possible, redirected to serve the needs of the state. Entire institutions, from convents and armies to schools and prisons, have served that purpose. For the Mexica this work was accomplished in the *telpochcalli* (schools for commoners), *calpolli* (neighborhood schools), several special schools dedicated to individual deities, and *calmecac* (schools for nobles and exceptional commoners), where young boys became men, learning "military skills and values" (Smith 1996:170). These schools instilled a sense of "self-discipline, knowledge of history and the gods, and a respect for Mexican society" (Turrent 1996:48).

Tenochtitlán

The calmecac was a total institution. Life was "spartan and monastic" for its students (Kandell 1988:35). Every day they drilled in the physical skills required of warriors, the mental disciplines necessary for social leaders, and the spiritual beliefs that would unite them. At night the students' sleep would continually be interrupted for impromptu lessons. There were various levels of attainment, from the entering students who were forced to clean temples to those who became cantors and priests assigned to the service of specific deities (Carrasco 1994:282).

The educational process in the calmecac was the same as for any other rite of passage in a total institution: break down the entrants in order to expunge all that they had been as children and then build them back up into the type of people required by the institution and social order. This was as true for the calmecac as it is for the modern prison, school, football team, fraternity, and army. Mexica schools were designed to enculturate students completely through a strict pedagogy based on Mexica myth and ideology. As with most cultural institutions, the goal was to produce true believers. The calmecac also socialized students into accepting their prescribed roles as religious, political, and economic leaders ready to rule an empire. This was the top level of formal education among the Mexica. Just as modern school systems are stratified in order to train various levels of social functionaries — from Ivy League elites to tech school workers — Mexica schools effectively reproduced the social system through socially appropriate and culturally correct training.

The cuicacalli schools were specifically dedicated to the performing arts (Guzmán Bravo and Nava Gómez 1984b:97). Like the larger society to which they belonged, these schools functioned hierarchically. The *tlapizcatzin*, or "lord of the house of flutes," was in charge of instruction, and the *tzapotlateohuatzin* served as his assistant and substitute instructor. The *tlamacazcateutl* was the school principal, in charge of administration and discipline. There were also resident composers and a range of grade levels, including older students who attended to important ritual matters. The most skilled instrumentalists would go on to specialize, working with experts in their chosen instrument. A particularly skilled scholar-musician would be called *tla-mati*, the word applied to all people with significant knowledge in a scientific or artistic discipline.

Instruction for boys and girls who attended these schools was segregated, although they did prepare and execute certain rituals together. Friar Diego de Durán, a Dominican who spent much of his life studying Aztec culture, observed: "Young people took great pride in their ability to dance, sing, and guide others in the dances" (quoted in Smith 1996:273). They learned these skills through rigorous musical and religious training.

Durán noted that the Aztec practiced not only sacred musical rituals but also secular "dances of youth," which he and his fellow missionaries considered "highly improper" (Smith 1996:273). One dance of love and sexual expression had a special name: Cuecuechcuícatl, "the ticklish dance" (Castellanos 1970:57–58). Another was the suggestive "snake dance" (Guzmán Bravo and Nava Gómez 1984b:106). Similarly, a sacred rite of passage into marriage employed the use of feathers and "erotic choreography to prepare the young women to receive their husbands" (1984b:108).

The brunt of female education took place in and near the home, where girls learned the domestic arts. These arts were an essential part of the ritual cycle as well. For example, each ritual required a specific set of foods. Days before a major ceremony, women would grind mountains of corn meal for use in making tamales. A festival for Tezcatlipoca called for tamales filled with beans and chiles (Pilcher 1998:1); Huehuetéotl, the fire god, required tamales with shrimp and chile sauce (1998:1); and so on.

In other words, while women were generally not ritual leaders, successful ritual performances required their intensive labor. "The Mexica believed that women had the basic responsibility of feeding the men," explains Jeffrey Pilcher, "and men, in turn, took up the duty of feeding the gods" (1998:17). Just as the entire mythical cosmos of the Mexica began with and was based on gender dualism, their ritual life involved segregated yet tightly integrated masculine and feminine dimensions.

THE RITUAL SENSORIUM AS VIRTUAL REALITY

Mexica ritual specialists were able to draw on a nearly inexhaustible pool of resources. A phalanx of architects was employed to produce monumental structures reproducing the world of Mexica myth on earth. Tenochtitlán itself was designed according to ritual requirements. The island city contained a street grid system laid out to correspond with the cardinal directions (6.5 degrees east of true north). Four massive avenues and causeways led to the island, three of them leading to the Great Temple (Smith 1996:198). A short highway from the edge of the island to the temple traced the path of the sun from its birth in the East to the center of the world. The Tacuba causeway was also aligned along the east–west axis, connecting the Great Temple and Tenochtitlán itself to the mainland, thus tracing the path of the sun from its apex at the Temple Center to its death in the West (Matos Moctezuma 1988:44).

Tenochtitlán

The Great Temple was an explicit reproduction of Coatepec, the mythical hill where Huitzilopochtli defeated Coyolxauhqui during the Aztec migration. The architecture was so exact in terms of detail and scale that the ritual spectator did not have to function in the world of simile but rather experienced myth as a material metaphor. In other words, the Great Temple was not *like* Coatepec, it *was* Coatepec. A dismembered Coyolxauhqui lay in stone relief at the foot of the Great Temple/Coatepec. Stone snakes wound their way up the stairway of the "serpent hill," looking skyward to the temple of Huitzilopochtli and his amaranth-seed likeness. To borrow the terminology of Marshall Sahlins (1981), the Great Temple was at the same time historical metaphor and mythical reality.

The Great Temple was also a perfect set for the ritual drama. The temple complex reproduced the entire Mexica cosmos, not just the Coyolxauhqui saga. Alongside Huitzilopochtli's temple was Tlaloc's heavenly rain-temple. Together the two gods served as dualistic representations of the dry (war) and wet (agricultural) seasons, respectively. Further illustrating the hybrid cosmology of the Mexica, the cold, dead world of Mictlán lay to the north of the pyramid, with its skull racks and skeletal figures (Matos Moctezuma 1988:80–81). As the political, economic, and religious "axis mundi" of the empire, the Great Temple was the "meeting point of heaven, earth, and the underworld," serving as a "backdrop and stage for the theatrical presentation of myth, military policy, and economic order" (Broda, Carrasco, and Matos Moctezuma 1987:5).

The priests, who were charged with carrying out the ritual performance with theatrical precision, gave life to the architectural corpus. They filled the temple complex with dramatic movement, burning *copal* incense in giant braziers to add an olfactory dimension. Petroleum taken from surface wells near the Gulf of Mexico was also burned on occasion, adding an acrid odor to certain festivities (Guzmán Bravo and Nava Gómez 1984a:129). When ritual spectators entered this sensorium of otherworldly sights, sounds, smells, and impressions, they were immediately transported to the sacred border between heaven and earth. By the final days of the empire, only nobles were allowed to enter the complex, although much of the activity atop the great temple would still be clearly visible from outside the temple complex walls. Similar if less spectacular rituals would be carried out throughout Tenochtitlán for the commoners' sake. This practice of ritual exclusion probably only increased the sense of awe accorded to Great Temple rites.

Ritual allowed the Mexica to experience myth as practice. While carrying out their daily lives, people would be much less likely to experience the world of myth in that way or enact the mythical principles prescribed in their culture's metanarratives. Ritual performance allows myth to become actual practice, if only for a moment. Sight, smell, touch, taste, and sound combine to make myth manifest. In no culture is the world of myth fully incorporated into daily profane existence. That is one of the reasons for ritual. During the ritual act, we can at least approximate the world of myth. We can feel it in a visceral way, through the heightened sights, sounds, smells, and movements that define the ritual experience. Like the cathedral of New Spain, the zócalo of independent Mexico, and the mass-mediated spectacles of the twentieth century, the Great Temple was a place where the world of humanity could be projected onto a cosmic plane and reflected back in ritual.

THE SOUND OF SACRIFICE

It is somewhat inaccurate to use the Western term "music" in the Mesoamerican context. The Mexica term *incuicatlinxochitl* (flower-poem/song) may approximate the English term "song" in that it can refer to literary verse set to voice and instrumental accompaniment (Turrent 1996:59). In Mexica culture, however, the performing and literary arts were considered inextricable elements of a unified cultural practice (Stevenson 1968:5). There is no evidence that regimes of sound were considered "musical" in and of themselves or could be extricated from other performance arts.

The two most important instruments played in the Mexica ensemble were the teponaztli, a hollowed-out wood slit-gong with two tongues, and the huehuetl, a large log drum topped with a tight jaguar skin. Both of these instruments play two basic tones, leading one of the foremost musicologists in the field of Latin American studies, Robert Stevenson, to conclude that the teponaztli and huehuetl served as acoustic symbols of the Mexica's dualistic belief system (1968:29–30). Adding weight to Stevenson's argument is the appearance of what appears to be binary percussion notation in the *Cantares mexicanos*. Unfortunately, the *Cantares*—written about thirty years after the Conquest—provides the only recorded evidence concerning how these twin instruments may have been played by the Mexica.

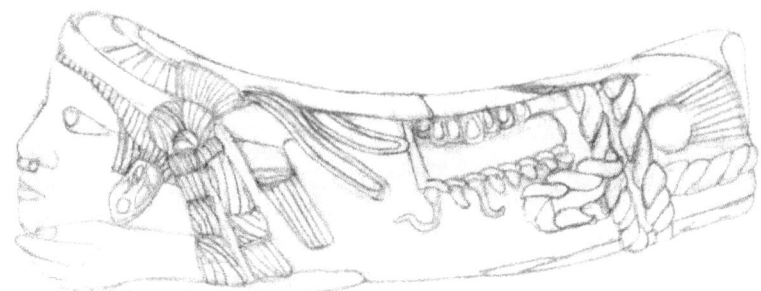

Aztec teponaztli. Drawing by Elizabeth A. Wakefield.

The teponaztli and huehuetl formed the core of the Mexica ensemble. They projected sufficient sound to fill the ritual space of the Great Temple complex and beyond. Their sound not only pervaded the territory of Tenochtitlán but the surrounding lake and countryside as well, as evidenced in Bernal Díaz del Castillo's terrifying account of his comrades' sacrifice. The teponaztli and the huehuetl each beat two distinct tones, mirroring and amplifying the tone of the victims' "palpitating hearts" (Díaz del Castillo 1956:436). It is clear in nearly all descriptions of Mexica sacrifice, whether in ethnohistoric accounts taken down by the Spanish or in Mexica glyphs and art, that one of the essential functions of the sacrificial ritual was to intimidate real and potential enemies into submission.

However, creating intimidation and terror was not a profane, covert motive. It was a central feature of Mexica religious belief and practice.

Aztec huehuetl. Drawing by Elizabeth A. Wakefield.

The Mexica: 1325–1521

Intricately carved images on Mexica huehuetls and teponaztlis link religion, war, and ritual. Two such carvings present very specific narratives detailing how captured warriors themselves were made to play music before being sacrificed (Stevenson 1968:20–22).

The gods Teponaztli and Huehuetl were sacrificed in the court of sun god, Tonatiuh, for the sake of the Mexica (Castellanos 1970:47). Before that twin sacrifice, there was no music, no joy, among humanity. It was an act of honor to play the instruments embodying these dual deities, and only right that debt sacrifices should be made in their presence.

The great drum's importance is also evidenced linguistically. Any large gathering of musicians, dancers, and singers was referred to as *huehuetitlán*, the "place where huehuetls are played" (Stevenson 1968: 43). To this day, a "venerable man" is referred to as a *huehue* in Nahuatl (1968:41).

On certain occasions the link between the instruments of music and death was made literal. Often sacrifices were carried out using the teponaztli directly, slung over the chest of the victim, who played it as he or she was led to death. Sometimes larger teponaztlis were used as ritual platforms. Sacrificial offerings would be strung out over the teponaztli so that the blood from their opened chest cavities could pour into the sacred vessel, satiating and repaying the instrument-god who had sacrificed his divine life to bring humanity music (Stevenson 1968:68–69). At other times, the ashes of cremated sacrifices would be placed inside the teponaztli.

Another ritual depicted on the side of a huehuetl involved *pochteca* (merchant) slaves, dancing to the tune of the teponaztli. The slave who best performed to the beat of the teponaztli would be sacrificed and eaten by the gathered pochteca in what Stevenson wryly refers to as an act of "conspicuous consumption" (1968:68).

Although sacred and central, the teponaztli and the huehuetl were by no means the only instruments employed by the Mexica. Stevenson (1968:30–85) and Susana Dultzin Dubin and José Antonio Nava Gómez Tagle (in Guzmán Bravo 1984:170–220) present two of the most complete and useful listings of precortesian instruments. Mexica orchestras included various membranaphones (percussion instruments created by applying a stretched membrane over other materials), including the huehuetl and a range of lesser drums. The Mexica Mixcoacalli (musical storehouse) included a number of aerophones, such as the conch shell trumpet (*atecocoli*) with which the hour of penitence and autosacrifice (self-cutting ritual) was signaled, wood and metal trumpets (*tepuzquiquiztli*), whistle-flutes (*chichtli*), ocarinas (*huilacapitztli*), and more melodic flute types (*cocoloctli*).

The Mexica also played a number of instruments classified as idiophones (instruments whose basic material produces a sound when struck). Foremost among these was the teponaztli. Another instrument of interest was the *tecomapiloa* or "hanging gourd" (Stevenson 1968:61). This was an instrument played exclusively by female priests, combining a small teponaztli with gourd resonators hanging from each end. Although it was definitely not the aboriginal marimba that Latin Americanist musicologists have long sought in order to give that instrument independent provenance in the New World, this modification would have produced an interesting range of percussive tones, creating a distinct sound for the corn sacrifices during which they were played. This was not a true marimba, however. It is generally accepted that the marimba was brought to the New World from Africa after the Conquest rather than invented independently in Mesoamerica as an extension of the unique tecomapiloa (Garfias 1983).

Mexica idiophones also included jingles made from a wide array of materials, such as the gold bells worn by Coyolxauhqui, whose very name means "painted with bells." Other idiophones included turtle and tortoiseshell drums (*áyotli*), bone rasps (*omichicahuaztli*) used primarily during funerary rites, copper disk gongs (*chililitli*), gourds or gourd-shaped rattles (*ayacachtli*), and a wide array of additional rattles, including tripod-base jars with rattling legs (*cacalachtli*) and phallic *omichicahuaztli* that were "dangled in front of a woman captive" representing the fertile Young Corn Mother, Xilónen, just before she was sacrificed (Stevenson 1968:38).

Mexica instruments were made of wood, animal skins, bones, plant materials, shale, clay, and metal. One can imagine the sound produced by these orchestras. When it was combined with the lithe movements of dancers, the scene would have been awe-inspiring. Conch shell trumpeters began most of these ceremonies by playing to each of the four cardinal directions. Each of these directions represented a primary child of Ometéotl: the Black Tezcatlipoca (the most powerful), Red Tezcatlipoca (Xipe Tótec), Blue Tezcatlipoca (Huitzilopochtli), and White Tezcatlipoca (Quetzalcóatl). This four-part manifestation or "unfolding" of Tezcatlipoca represents religious syncretism, the melding of the Mexica god Huitzilopochtli into the more ancient pantheon of Mesoamerica.

Huitzilopochtli himself developed through cultural concretion. Jonathan Kandell suggests that the Mexica borrowed their central deity from the Tarascans, who featured a hummingbird god (1988:27). The Mexica name Huitzilopochtli literally means "hummingbird on the left": when one faces the setting sun from Aztlán with outstretched arms, the left hand points in the direction of the promised land to which Huitzilopochtli would lead his chosen people. As the Mexica came into contact with the established city-states of the Central Valley, their favored deity would eventually take on traits associated with their more long-standing gods, such as Tezcatlipoca and Tonatiuh (Carmack, Gasco, and Gossen 1996:115), becoming increasingly warlike in the process. As the Mexica changed, so too did their gods and the cosmos within which they existed. The Mexica understood their historic rise as part of a divine plan, with Huitzilopochtli providing guidance. Only a complete and utter cataclysm could shake that faith, and even then the Conquest would seem to fulfill ritual prophecy rather than refute it.

RECONSTRUCTING MESOAMERICAN MUSIC

The Mexica considered their musical poetry to be "the wind of the gods, born in the house of butterflies" (Castellanos 1970:66). Each leader, in addition to being a forceful general, was also expected to be a poet-king. The most heralded of Aztec emperors, Nezahualcóyotl (*tlatoani* of Tenochtitlán's powerful ally Texcoco), was said to have authored no less than seventy moving poem-songs, ranging from themes of romantic love to human mortality (Castellanos 1970:68). Motecuhzoma Xocoyotzin was also considered a great poet-musician (Castellanos 1970:69). It must be remembered that song-poems were "obtained from paradise by securing their release from divine power," however, and that music-making required not only earthly efforts but also heavenly reciprocity to be considered complete (Bierhorst 1985:21). In other words, even the great tlatoanis were considered conduits of song rather than authors in the modern sense.

Tenochtitlán

Based on his translation and interpretation of the *Cantares mexicanos*, John Bierhorst challenges the common claim that Aztec leaders were often great poet-musicians, although he does not entirely exclude kings "from the ranks of composers" (1985:101–105). James Lockhart agrees that Aztec leaders do not "appear to have composed the songs we know in the form in which they have come down to us" (1991:121), although he leaves open the possibility that the legendary musical reputation of the Aztec tlatoanis is warranted. Because the "*Cantares* are saturated with royalty and high nobility," Lockhart "would be surprised if kings and lords did not compose songs both before and after the Conquest" (1991:121). To be considered a poet-musician obviously elevated the image of a leader. The arts were considered an essential element of political life in Mesoamerica.

Given that there was no written music beyond the relatively scant and obtuse notes in the *Cantares mexicanos*, little is known about Mexica musical arrangements. Nor is it clear how instruments were played. Knowledge of Mexica organology is mostly speculation on the basis of evidence from the archaeological record and instrumental reconstruction (Rawcliffe 1988:36). Even with the replicas on hand, it remains largely a matter of guessing how they were played (1988:43). Based on her replication and play of Mexica aerophones, Susan Rawcliffe suggests that perhaps "melodic contour or timbre was valued more than pitch or the kind of tonal organization we think of as scales" (1988:57).

E. Thomas Stanford notes that even in Europe during the Mexica era playing styles, arrangements, and ensembles differed greatly from place to place, despite more formal, written music and traditions. Therefore, he reminds us, "we will surely never know" what Mexica music sounded like (1984a:79). Stanford further warns us not to imagine that music of contemporary indigenous societies is somehow a direct channel to the past (1984a:79). The influential Mexican musicologist Vicente Mendoza once believed that was the case. Like many of his colleagues, Mendoza thought that if one could reconstruct the music of the conquistadors and then eliminate those elements from the post-Conquest music, it would be possible to find "residual" Aztec elements (1953:7). As he noted, however, time and again the hopeful belief in such cultural "survivals" has been crushed by closer historical analysis.

As mentioned earlier, we do have some knowledge regarding how percussion instruments were played. In addition to the binary system recorded in the *Cantares mexicanos*, there are a few other references concerning technique. The huehuetl, for example, was normally played with the fingers and not with a mallet. Two tones were produced, one near the rim and the other in the middle. Pitch may have been altered by tightening or loosening the jaguar-skin membrane. Therefore, it is possible that the instrument was tuned to match others, such as the teponaztli, which was carved in order to play two tones. Those tones ranged from a major second up to a perfect fifth, depending on the width of each wooden tongue. Based on a survey of extant teponaztlis by Daniel Castañeda and Mendoza, minor thirds seem to have been preferred (Stevenson 1968:64).

It appears that ritual song tended to develop in tone and complexity to parallel the narrative development of the ritual act. At the start, perhaps only one huehuetl would play (Stevenson 1968:48–49). By the time the priest plucked out the sacrificial heart or some other dramatic climax was reached, all instruments would be playing in concert. The *Cantares mexicanos* indicates this pattern for huehuetl play, including songs that built progressively from a lone huehuetl heartbeat to a climax of as many as ten drums playing simultaneously (Stevenson 1968:48–49). In addition to its ritual progression, the music was also probably played in repetitive mantra-like cycles, producing transcendent states in the ritual participants (Dultzin Dubin and Nava Gómez 1984:20).

Based on archaeological evidence, most musicologists argue that the Mexica probably preferred a pentatonic or "five note" system. Stanford (1984a:82) and others have noted that even with four-hole flutes the flautist can produce many more than five potential notes by means of half-stops and overblowing. This is a matter of speculation, however, and the tendency toward four-hole flutes surely indicates a pentatonic mode.

Polyphonic music would have been possible by combining flutes, but there is no evidence that the Mexica practiced it. Friar Sahagún speaks of myriad flutes played at the same time but not in tune with each other, at least not to the Western ear (Stanford 1984a:83). This may indicate that Mexica scales were much looser than the Western fixed scale or that it was not necessary for the flutes to resonate at harmonic intervals or that Sahagún, as a Spaniard with Western-trained ears, could not discern the musical patterns woven by Mexica flautists.

There is also no direct evidence that the Mexica played stringed instruments (Stevenson 1968:22). They certainly could have used their bows for such a purpose, although there is no archaeological or ethnohistoric evidence to indicate this. Instead of describing Mesoamerican music in terms of what it lacked relative to Western music—polyphony, stringed instruments, written music—it is more useful to think about its actual features and purposes. Mexica music was particularly rich, emphasizing subtle articulation of percussion, overlain with complex winds, tightly coordinated with ritual movement. At the center of this was one of the most privileged Mexica citizens: the musician.

Tenochtitlán

THE MEXICA MUSICIAN

The Mexica honored their musicians. It was an extremely precarious position, however: a flautist who blew the wrong note or the drummer who missed a single beat would profane the sacred ritual and thus invite disaster from the gods. The fifth sun could literally end on a bad note. Therefore, the offending musician was usually punished. Capital punishment was not at all uncommon for musicians who erred at key ritual moments.

There were also numerous advantages to being a professional Mexican musician. Mexica musicians "enjoyed great social prestige" due to their essential role in religion and political life (Dultzin Dubin and Nava Gómez 1984:19). The ritual calendar included a day dedicated to musicians and dancers, which inaugurated a series of celebrations that could last up to a month. In other words, music was associated not only with solemn spiritual rituals but with joyous celebration as well. In fact, the Spanish missionaries were almost as upset by these licentious celebrations as they were by rituals involving human sacrifice.

Although Mexica music was mostly a collective practice, exceptional musicians and dancers could gain fame and a very comfortable court life (Guzmán Bravo and Nava Gómez 1984b:89–90). A fragment from the "Song of Quetzalcóatl" (Cornyn 1931:74) provides a sense of the poet-musicians' role in Postclassic Mesoamerica:

And so I the singer gathered
Blossoms to bedeck the nobles,
Cover them with beauteous garments,
Fill their noble hands with flowers.
And in worthy song I lifted
Up my voice and glorified them
To the Author of Our Being.

Such words and images recur throughout the archaeological and ethnohistoric records, demonstrating the centrality of musical ritual in the spiritual, cultural, and political life of the Mexica.

3 Mesoamerican Resonance

The music of the Mexica still lives. Its spirit resonates in nearly every contemporary Mexican musical style, from mariachi to rock. This chapter focuses on performances that directly reference Mesoamerican ritual. The musical events I describe here range from museum exhibitions to midnight dances in the zócalo.

Clearly such events are performances. They are meant to be experienced by an audience. In fact, if no connection is made between creator, performer, and audience, they are considered failures. Yet these modern performances are also rituals: collective acts of remembering. They are meaning-making events that say just as much about the present as they do about the past (or perhaps more). As was true of the "original" Mexica rituals they reference, these rituals reflect, reproduce, and even remake the contemporary social order.

Unfortunately, often the closer we get to more familiar contemporary contexts the less we are able to see the ritual dimensions of a cultural performance. As David Kertzer reminds us, "our own rites, our own symbols, are the most difficult to see" (1988:184). We imagine that theatrical performances are more conscious acts of meaning-making than the ritual acts of the past, forgetting that such events always embed a range of collective, subconscious, and sublimated cultural values. We write off most popular performances as mere diversion and understand others, such as academic and museological demonstrations, as didactic representations alone, pedagogical acts rather than rituals in their own right. These modern performances are also rituals, however, illustrating, negotiating, and remaking the cultural values of producers, performers, and audiences.

Therefore, for the purpose of studying contemporary musical rituals "we do not need to make a distinction between ritual and performance" (Rostas 1998:85). When we watch a film, dance at a wedding party, or scream at a basketball game, we are involved in ritual every bit as much as the Mexica warrior involved in sacrifice. When members of a musical group put on Aztec garb and play Mesoamerican instruments for tourists in the zócalo, they and their spectators are involved in ritual just as much as those involved in the original historical rituals they reference. We must remember that those "original" Aztec rituals were also reflections of previous rituals—and so on. Cultural meanings and social contexts have changed drastically over time, but the importance of ritual to human social life has not.

MESOAMERICAN MUSIC AND MUSEOLOGICAL RITUAL

The Mexica: 1325–1521

Several groups perform precortesian music in contemporary Mexico City. Tribu is one of the most long-standing and well-known Mesoamerican performance ensembles. A. Agustín Pimental Díaz, the group's leader and founder, has performed for almost thirty years. Other members of the group have played for thirty, nineteen, and sixteen years. Pimental Díaz studied in the Music Department of the National Autonomous University of Mexico (UNAM) and is known internationally for his work. As the president of the Center for the Assistance to the Development of Ethnomusicology in Mexico (CADEMAC), Pimental Díaz is an accomplished archaeomusicologist and performer.

Tribu performs often. One of its performance sites is the National Museum of Anthropology, Mexico's largest and most important museum. Tribu plays for mixed museum audiences, including both foreign and Mexican tourists, Mexico City residents on occasional visits, and throngs of Mexican schoolchildren on fieldtrips.

Tribu's educational performances reference much of what is known about Mexica music. In order to bring the performance alive, however, the performers invest a great deal of creativity into their music. They exhibit an intimate knowledge of their instruments, having reconstructed each one by hand. A giant huehuetl dominates the stage, flanked by teponaztlis of various sizes and nearly the entire range of instruments described in Chapter 2.

The four musicians begin the concert by blowing into conch shells. The shells range in size and shape, allowing multiple tones and even a rudimentary chord structure to develop when all four are played together. While this does not mean that the Mexica employed such musical elements, the performance boldly demonstrates the possibility of harmony, polyphony, and counterpoint.

Each musician moves, in turn, to another instrument. One moves to a seated position behind a low drum, while slowly shaking seed rattles tied to his legs. Another takes up a small flute and pounds his foot to shake seed-pod rattles laced around his ankle. The third walks over to play teponaztlis of varying sizes for a marimba-like effect. The fourth starts to beat the giant huehuetl slowly, providing a lead beat for the others to follow.

By the end of the performance, Tribu will have played drums of widely varying sizes, whistles with low rattling sounds (containing ceramic pellets), turtle shells played with antlers, pan pipes, a thin slate rock "xylophone," rain sticks, and other Mesoamerican instruments. They add occasional chanting and some coordinated movement. (See Appendix 3: Discography for recordings by Tribu and other artists presented in the book.)

The effect on the audience is clear. Even in this short, fifteen-minute performance, Tribu is able to give the audience a sense of the dynamic potential of Mexica music and an introduction to the basic narrative structure of Mesoamerican ritual. Starting slowly and with relative calm, the music crescendos to a climax, as described in the Spanish chronicles and ethnohistoric accounts.

MESOAMERICAN RITUAL AS POPULAR ENTERTAINMENT

Upon exiting the National Museum of Anthropology, one often hears a huehuetl. The *voladores* or "flyers" present a Totonacan ritual throughout the day on a lawn across from the museum entrance. "Five minutes to the next show," shouts one of the performers. He calls it an *espectáculo* (spectacle or show). The huehuetl helps spread the message.

The site is ritually purified with copal incense as four flyers climb a giant pole. The four begin to twirl, slowly letting out rope, hanging upside down as their circle expands outward and downward. One flyer plays a small flute and drum throughout the flight, never missing a beat. Meanwhile, a grounded flyer walks around selling souvenir instruments and candy. Placing the ritual in a show format allows the voladores to commodify, and therefore maintain, their ancient rite.

Voladores in Chapultepec Park. Photos by author.

The Mexica: 1325–1521

MESOAMERICAN RITUAL AS THEATER

Just across Avenida de la Reforma, in another part of Chapultepec Park, a very different sort of performance took place in 1998. In the shadow of the Hill of the Grasshopper, for which Chapultepec is named, lies the Casa del Lago (House of the Lake, run by UNAM), where art exhibits are mounted and concerts and plays are performed each weekend for students and the general public. Among the plays presented there was *Cura de espantos* (Cure for Fears), an interactive play blending Western texts, Mesoamerican mythology, Mexica ritual, and participatory theater.

I attended *Cura de espantos* on Friday, January 23, 1998. It remains one of the clearest, most disturbing, and most meaningful memories of my musical fieldwork in Mexico. The performance took place on a dark and chilly night, starting late, as usual. A small crowd of us waited for the performers to finish their preparations, uncertain what we would be asked to do. The college students milled around in solid packs, deflecting their nervousness through loud conversations, ostensibly personal, but obviously meant to be heard by all gathered there.

The performers approached suddenly, lining us up into a pretend "boat," linking us together and placing hoods over our heads and eyes. We were told that we would be going together into the underworld to retrieve our "soiled and frightened bones." We were then made to march in silence. An occasional giggle by a college student would be met with severe reproach. Eventually we were silent, only able to move ahead with careful coordination. We had to touch each other. There was no choice; it was the only way to find our way in the dark.

We marched for a long time to the slow beat of the huehuetl. We were not told what underworld we would be visiting. Hades? Certainly the boat gave us that impression. Hell? Where else would the damned go? Mictlán, the Mexica underworld where Quetzalcoátl, in dog form, went to retrieve the bones from which humanity was first made?

Only a few shadows could be seen through the hoods, adding to the hellish effect. After a slow march down a long incline, we arrived. They took off our hoods. At first we were surrounded by dark but then were given candles to light our way. A series of ghostlike performances followed, mainly by young women, merging texts by William Shakespeare (*Othello, Hamlet, Macbeth*), the Marquis de Sade, Dante Alighieri, Pedro Calderón de la Barca, Isabel Allende, and Nahuatl poetry. We walked around the underworld, from place to place, performance to performance. Particularly impressive was a spirit-woman who burned with "envy" for a best friend who had stolen her husband. Even long after we moved on from her place in Mictlán, we could hear the spirit-woman's cold screams.

Another woman was engulfed with sexual desire yet had only a tree to satisfy her obsession. As we moved away, her desperate and painful orgasm caught up with us. Just as that sound reached our ears, we were met with a woman who committed suicide, overtaken with guilt. She was partly the spirit of Lady Macbeth, seeking to be "unsexed" for eternity.

That was merely the warm-up. We were next taken to our own stations, places to be alone with our sorrow and fear. In my peripheral vision I could see and hear a few others acting out, fully integrated into the spirit of the underworld.

Our spirit guides then gathered us back together. We came to a large fire and formed a dance circle. We danced around the flames, while a huehuetl played. Our guides stopped us and asked that we pair up. The head guide asked that we look deeply into each other's eyes, so that we could see each other and ourselves. My partner and I had a hard time. We were both clearly too shy for this sort of interaction with a total stranger. She was a short woman with a skeletal face. She seemed kind and as frightened of me as I was of her. I can only imagine the terrible image I presented in the firelight, a tall, bald gringo, looking like a skeleton in even the best light. Our individual fears fed the other's. By the time the guide asked us to put our right hands over each other's hearts, they were beating furiously.

We were asked to offer forgiveness to the other by throwing the weight of our sorrow to the fire. Next we were asked to do the same for ourselves and were finally given permission to look away. Then we reformed the circle, holding hands and dancing while the spirit guides brushed us with incense from smoking boughs. We were asked to hug "Mother Earth" before getting back into the boat. We began to march back to the living world.

Already it was clear that the participants' reactions varied widely. Some of us were deeply affected by the performance. Others, particularly many of the young, seemed angry and resistant. They started talking among themselves despite the remonstrations of our guides. A friend of the director danced to the music, moving near the dissenters and asking them to quiet down. Her enthusiasm was infectious.

Back at the Casa del Lago we climbed out of the boat and burned our "bones" (hoods) in order to purify them. We placed the burning bones in metal incense burners like those once used at the Great Temple. To conclude the performance our spirit guides threw flowers over us as we applauded their efforts. The postmodern performance produced a rare sense of communion among its audience-participants.

Cura de espantos was just one of several performances I attended that merged modern theatrical techniques and Mesoamerican ritual elements. On Sunday, February 22, 1998, for example, a dance performance entitled *Graniceros* took place at UNAM. *Graniceros* is choreographer and director Pilar Urreta's vision of the Mesoamerican healer. Graniceros is the name given to the shamans of Morelos, the state just southwest of the Federal District.

Graniceros can be men or women; as demonstrated in the performance, they inhabit somewhat of a third gender category. The performance focused on four shamans, each representing one of the sacred directions, a phase of the moon, and a specific attribute associated with

Performers in a touring version of the Guelaguetza, a Oaxacan celebration presented in the Mexico City zócalo. Photos by Carlos Franco.

the healer in question. Each of the first four scenes is dedicated to one of the four shamans. The fifth scene presents the ritual initiation of a neophyte shaman. The sixth scene represents healing and the giving of blood. The seventh is a cyclical epilogue, taking us back to the full moon and the first scene.

Urreta describes dance as "a ceremony where we discover the darkness and light of our interior worlds . . . a primordial ritual through which we celebrate life" (concert bill). Like *Cura de espantos*, *Graniceros* plays with both the introspective and collective dimensions of ritual. I was struck, when watching the dance, by how much better that form is at capturing the ritual spirit and totality of Mesoamerican music and movement than are the other Western arts, even when performed in a Western stage-and-audience mode. Indigenista classical music (Chapter 12), for example, falls far short in comparison.

MESOAMERICAN DANCE AS PARTICIPATORY RITUAL

The Mexica: 1325–1521

The most inclusive Mesoamerican rituals take place in the zócalo, the political and spiritual center of Mexico City. Susanna Rostas has written about two related movements represented there, the Concheros and the "Mexica" (1996, 1998). The Concheros are an archetypal example of syncretism. Like the Virgin of Guadalupe, they are a mixture of prehispanic and postconquest cultural influences. They dress in an interpretive form of Aztec clothing and play instruments that blend Mesoamerican and European features, such as the *concha* from which their name is derived. The concha is a stringed instrument formed out of an armadillo shell. The Concheros represent a melding of Christian and Mesoamerican religious principles, performing on Catholic saints' days and those associated with Aztec deities. Their most important ritual performance takes place during a fiesta in honor of the Virgin of Guadalupe.

Conversely, Mexica dancers seek to expunge all Catholic elements from their ritual performance. Unlike the Concheros, they do not enter churches during any part of their performance. As Rostas demonstrates so well in her work, their values and aims are quite distinct from those of the Concheros, which are based on a collective philosophy of "Union, Conformity, and Conquest." The first two have to do with collective identity, while the last has to do with conversion, not in a strict Christian sense but in terms of winning over the participants and observers to their communitarian ethos and philosophy. The Concheros hope that observers will one day become active participants in the dance. In other words, the Concheros dance to create a sense of inclusion.

In contrast, Mexica dancing tends to be frenetic, individualized, and competitive. Although they have adopted the Concheros' basic ritual design — a series of solo dancers in the middle of a circle setting the example for the rest — their dance styles are much less communitarian. Dancers often demonstrate extremely difficult maneuvers and steps that "lose" even the most seasoned group members. "Rather than animating the rest of the dancers," explains Rostas, the expert's "dance turns [other dancers] from being co-performers to disempowered strugglers" (1998: 99). This is in line with their philosophy, however, which is a "desire to assert the self rather than to deny it" (1998:99). The Concheros seek collective transcendence, whereas the Mexica are more of a political movement. Both groups include people from all walks of life, but the largest cohort of both groups is composed of middle-class urbanites, ranging from "people who have clerical jobs, to professionals, to those involved in the arts" (1998:87).

Perhaps a third set of dancers should be added: "Aztec" dancers and musicians who perform in the zócalo for money, using the Conchero ritual format. These performers are very aware of the touristic context within which they work, and so is their audience.

One of the most interesting critiques of such ensembles came in an unlikely venue, an *India María* film. India María is a demeaning representation of indigenous Mexico, highlighting a large, buffoonish Indian woman who, despite her ignorance and clownish behavior, somehow always comes out on top in the end. Before leaping to the conclusion that India María is, therefore, a subversive text, I suggest that the reader watch one of these films. They are on a par with blackface comedy in the United States. Racist and stereotypical images of indigenous peoples are played out, with only a thin veneer of empathy for the clownish heroine salvaging what is otherwise simple parody. Although other classes and groups are skewered in the process, the basic thesis remains: rural indigenous peasants are childlike simpletons. In one such film, *Las delicias de poder* (The Delights of Power), India María stumbles into political power, transformed from a representative of the rural electorate to a clownish demagogue (a clear warning regarding what would happen if "they" took over). India María is at first manipulated by the corrupt local elite, who use her as a means of gaining popular approval.

In one scene, India María is made to serve as an intermediary between the local people and a group of gringo businessmen interested in investing in the area. India María's local Ladino handlers stage a performance, which she subverts through her ill-mannered behavior. What is striking about the scene, however, is not the very typical plot but rather a play within the play. A postmodern Aztec ensemble performs for the gringos during the scene. Their leader is dressed in the same sort of flamboyant and stereotypical "Aztec" clothing worn by the zócalo performers, but his glove, hat, and hairdo signify that he is not just an Aztec dancer but also a Michael Jackson impersonator. As the ensemble plays, he performs what appears to be a mixture of the Yaqui Deer Dance and Jackson's moonwalk. The India María vignette is a clear slam against the zócalo dancers, their tourist audiences, and perhaps even official folkloric institutions like the Ballet Folklórico.

The India María critique presents one view of the zócalo dancers. Once again, however, I would argue against assessing such ritual performances by using the criterion of historical authenticity. Like the original rituals reflected in such acts, these modern amalgams are not diminished by their hybridity but enlivened by it. The office workers, teachers, students, and others making up the modern Mexica have adapted their vision of Mesoamerican ritual to fit their contemporary needs, as have the Concheros and even the tourist-oriented performers, just as the Mexica adapted Mesoamerican rites to fit their needs centuries ago.

The Mexica:
1325–1521

MESOAMERICAN MUSIC AS POLITICAL RITUAL

These performances could be categorized, with some injustice, into the following categories: museological, theatrical, spiritual, and touristic. Of course, these categories — and certainly the performances themselves — overlap. I conclude this chapter by describing a set of Mesoamerican musical ritual performances whose main purpose is to create political change. This is not to say that the performances listed above were not also political but rather that in each case their political intent is superseded by other didactic, artistic, spiritual, and/or marketing goals.

Mesoamerican images and rituals have been used toward political ends throughout Mexican history. In modern Mexico City, however, these uses are more referential than reverential. The rituals detailed here are performed by Ladino urbanites as an overt means of resisting or remaking power rather than by indigenous peoples themselves as part of a long-standing ritual tradition.

It is important to note that even the rural indigenous rituals, although also continuing Mesoamerican practices, have likewise been influenced by 500 years of colonial domination. Indigenous identities have been formed in dialectical relationship to the dominant culture and thus, like all cultures, represent unique hybrids. Everything from colonial religious practices to modern mass-mediated music has been incorporated into indigenous ritual and musical life. As an example, Simón Jara

Gámez, Aurelio Rodríguez, and Antonio Zedillo Castillo note that the nineteenth-century *habanera* had a strong influence on "danzas indígenas" of the twentieth century (1994:43). One need only travel in rural and indigenous Mexico to see this creative cycle of imposition, acculturation, appropriation, resistance, and reinvention taking place now, from the diverse global village of Tepoztlán, Morelos, near Mexico City, to the most remote village of the Chiapas highlands.

Nevertheless, throughout rural Mexico one can also view the continued resonance of precortesian Mesoamerican music, rituals, and culture in contemporary indigenous communities. Guillermo Bonfil Batalla refers to this as *México profundo* (1996). The term *profundo*, like the English term "profound," contains a double meaning: deep as in buried or sublimated and deep as in extremely meaningful.

This double meaning is particularly crucial to understanding the uses of Mesoamerican music in Mexico City. The urban Mexican must reach very deep into history and delve deeply into contemporary musical culture to find such indigenous strands. Such acts are probably more accurately understood as reinvention than as cultural reclamation or preservation. Yet there is nothing artificial about reinvented memories. As historical metaphors, they allow Mesoamerica to remain a living tradition, reborn in the present. Take, for example, the work of Mario Flores Urbán, a painter featured in an exhibit at the Journalists Club of Mexico City (dedicated to the memory of Frida Kahlo). Sentenced to death on September 16 (coincidentally, Mexican Independence Day), 1979, in Chicago, he became a prolific painter while in prison. The cause of Flores Urbán—who was fingered by a woman who, according to many, was protecting her guilty son—was taken up by the Mexican Consulate of Chicago and the Mexican government itself. The Mexican government contends that his trial violated the Vienna Convention, which stipulates that defendants have a right to be represented by their home country. He has not yet been executed.

One of Flores Urbán's paintings is entitled *Sacrifice* (1997), illustrating Mexica sacrifice. The reference is clear—that human sacrifices continue today, even if those in power have changed. Mesoamerican images like this are constantly used as historical metaphors for and political tools against power in the present. Los Angeles artist Mark Vallen's protest art is a prime example.

Not surprisingly, such images have been wielded most successfully in connection with the Zapatista rebellion. The Chiapas-based pan-Mayan movement has brought a renewed awareness of the political dimensions of indigenous existence. Although the overwhelming majority of Mexico City residents are neither Mayan nor Chiapan, many strongly

Mesoamerican Resonance

support the Zapatistas. This was made evident on January 12, 1998, when 80,000–100,000 Mexico City residents marched through the city and flooded into the zócalo to hear Zapatista spokespeople and others address the problems of rural Mexico. Among the speakers were survivors of the Acteal massacre, where forty-five of their fellow Tzotzil were killed.

On Saturday, January 24, 1998, another gathering took place at the zócalo, concluding a "March for Peace in Chiapas." The march began miles away, at the Angel of Independence. The marchers were buoyed by the beat of the huehuetl and teponaztli, among other Mesoamerican instruments. The drums were held aloft as a direct challenge to police in riot gear as flautists produced a loud cacophony of whistles, chirps, and broken melodies. The Mexica instruments provided a ritual interlocutor between urban activists and the rural indigenous peoples they support, a symbolic act of solidarity.

The activists' use of Mesoamerican music has much in common with other rituals described in this chapter. However, such ritual acts are also distinct from the more museological, touristic, theatrical, and participatory rituals of remembrance described above. Like the ancient performances they reference, such ritual acts are wholly "in play," directly integrated into the political life of the nation. The urban activists have converted the huehuetl and teponaztli — once the implements of power — into tools of resistance. Five hundred years of colonial occupation failed to silence the twin drums completely. Their hearts beat slowly and steadily, foreshadowing the birth of another sun.

PART II

New Spain: 1521–1821

4 Colonial Mexico: 1521–1821

Musical ritual was at the center of the Conquest. The Spaniards brandished musical ritual as a tool during their two-year campaign to conquer Mexico, and the Mexica responded with their own ritual arsenal. Like the contemporary Concheros, who refer to their instruments as "weapons" (Rostas 1996:208), musical ritual was an essential weapon for both sides. Cortés, who favored musicians among his ranks, put on a series of demonstrative musical Masses in order to awe and convert the indigenous peoples he encountered. The Mexica impressed the Spanish with equally spectacular ritual displays.

The Spaniards' early, peaceful stay in the city of Tenochtitlán involved a conspicuous back-and-forth ritual display as each side sought to learn about, and impress, the other. It was during one such ritual that the Spaniards—invited guests to the city—became open antagonists. Left in command while Cortés was off battling his own countrymen on the coast, Pedro de Alvarado made the fateful decision to attack the Mexica as they celebrated the Toxcatl ritual (León-Portilla 1990:70–82; Thomas 1993:383–393). Perhaps because the Toxcatl made reference to the god of war (it was a syncretic ceremony originally dedicated to Tezcatlipoca before its appropriation by the priests of Huitzilopochtli), Alvarado read the ritual as a declaration of war.

Fearing that the ceremony was a prelude to war, and perhaps spooked by the awesome spectacle, Alvarado let loose his troops and massacred all those in attendance. The Spanish began their onslaught by hacking off the arms of the huehuetl player, a ritual act in its own right. It is hard to imagine a more profane insult from a Mexica perspective. The war had begun in earnest.

The beginning of war did not spell the end of ritual. During the war, the Mexica played music to inspire their own troops and frighten the enemy into submission: "I am playing my huehuetl, I who hunt for songs to awaken and fire our friends whose hearts lie listless" (Stevenson 1968: 42). The Mexica performed conspicuous sacrifices within eyesight of their European enemies, using ritual in what modern war-makers refer to as "psy-ops" (psychological operations). The Spaniards, in turn, made silencing the Mexica drums a priority.

Fighting alongside the Spanish soldiers and musicians were thousands of indigenous allies, including Tlaxcaltecan musicians playing songs of war to intimidate the enemy (Stevenson 1986:81–83). One effect of this musical ostentation may have been to solidify the locals' belief that Cortés was Quetzalcóatl, for the Feathered-Serpent was a patron of the arts. It was Quetzalcóatl who originally created humanity by playing the music of the sacred conch (León-Portilla 1963:107–108). Other historical coincidences reinforced the view of Cortés as Quetzalcóatl. Like the Feathered-Serpent, Cortés was a powerful white figure "returning" from the East on exotic rafts to "retake" his empire.

New Spain: 1521–1821

Cortés actualized the myth of Quetzalcóatl in geographic space, marching from the east, and in so doing recreated a mythical and ritual path that would continue to serve that purpose for centuries. Twelve Franciscans made their way from Veracruz to Mexico City on the same road, barefoot, replacing Quetzalcóatl with Christ. The Conquest was similarly reenacted with the arrival of each new viceroy from Spain, not to mention subsequent invasions by the United States (1846–1848) and France (1862–1867), each time following roughly the same route of conquest. Many U.S. soldiers brought along Díaz del Castillo's record of the Conquest, imagining themselves to be modern-day conquistadors invading the "Halls of Montezuma." The Conquest has been replayed several times over, often taking the same ritual path.

As was true of Quetzalcóatl's original banishment, the reverse path served as a ritual antithesis of the Conquest. Cortés, Empress Carlota, dictator Porfirio Díaz, President Venustiano Carranza, and many other fallen leaders would over the centuries be forced to march the route back to Veracruz, ritually expelled from Mexico.

Before meeting that eventual fate, Cortés-Quetzalcóatl achieved remarkable success. Spanish attempts to silence the huehuetl succeeded in late 1521, when the invading army stormed onto the shores of disease-ravaged Tenochtitlán for its final assault. For the last time, the priests of Huitzilopochtli beat the drums from atop the Great Temple to rally the

Mexica. Unfortunately, their warrior ranks had been decimated by an effective naval blockade and an even more devastating smallpox epidemic. Two Spanish soldiers finally made it up the pyramid, a ritual replay of the Coyolxauhqui charge. This time, however, the ascent succeeded. Huitzilopochtli, who had once defeated hundreds of his own siblings in battle, could not defeat a like number of Spaniards. The invaders had steel, horses, dogs of war, and, worst of all, a devastating microscopic ally, smallpox. The Spaniards "cut down" the priests and tossed them down the stairs (León-Portilla 1990:99). In terms of myth and ritual, the Mexica's beginning and end shared an ironic resemblance.

RITUALS OF CONQUEST

Mexica song represented just one of thousands of Mesoamerican musical traditions. Hundreds of smaller bands, tribes, and states lived within and near Mesoamerica, each with its own distinct musical traditions. In fact, some of the most complex musical forms appear to have existed in the earlier Classic period (roughly A.D. 300–900). For example, archaeologists have discovered several complex compound flutes from that era (Castellanos 1970:51). These flutes have led some musicologists to make a claim for Mesoamerican polyphony (Stevenson 1968:4, 54) and perhaps even harmony.

The question of whether or not polyphonic music was present in Mesoamerica before the Conquest is still up for debate. However, there is no doubt that a complex array of instrumentation existed throughout Mesoamerica and that the greatest emphasis was placed on sophisticated rhythms and precision percussion. All Mesoamerican states emphasized coordination of music, dance, and ritual performance. Yet beyond that there was a great deal of diversity in instrumentation and technique. Even at the time of the Conquest, Mexica music represented only one genre among many Mesoamerican forms (Castellanos 1970:62).

The Spaniards quickly learned that it was impossible simply to convert the Mesoamericans to European ways. They would also need to work within the idiom of indigenous musical ritual. While the most disastrous episode of the Conquest had been set off by a Spaniard's brutal attempt to censor a Mexica rite, the most effective means of conversion would be to incorporate such rites into the Christian ritual cycle. By the 1530s the Spaniards were successfully converting thousands of Mesoamericans via "open-air theatrical masses to dramatize the Christian faith to the Indians" (Matos Moctezuma 1987:16). The Spanish missionaries also incorporated indigenous art styles into the ritual conversion process, including painted cloth *lienzos* that related biblical narratives (Matos Moctezuma 1987:16–17).

Cortés was very aware of the power of musical ritual and used it to his advantage. He ordered the celebration of a Mass each time his band encountered a village or city for the first time. This partly explains his predilection for musicians. Musicians were essential for performing the Mass, particularly the sort of ritual displays that Cortés needed to communicate his message of conquest and conversion.

Of course, I would not want to overstate the power of Spanish ritual. Clearly, ritual display alone did not humble the Mesoamerican cities, states, and empires into submission. Ultimately, it was the Spaniards' *Guns, Germs, and Steel* that won the day (Diamond 1997).

In fact, many colonial ritual displays appear to have been designed more to assuage the guilt and legitimate the rule of the Spaniards than to impress and cow those they would conquer. Foremost among these was the reading of the Requirement, a document mandated by the pope and Crown to legalize (in the minds of the Spaniards) the acquisition of new territories. Representing a three-way negotiation involving colonizers who sought bald conquest, church leaders who sought a more just treatment of the indigenous population, and a Crown that feared the potential power of colonizing rogues like Cortés, the Requirement today seems like an almost comical set of contradictions (Seed 1995:69):

> On behalf of His Majesty . . . I . . . his servant, messenger . . . notify and make known as best I can that God our Lord one and eternal created heaven and earth . . . God our Lord gave charge [of all peoples] to one man named Saint Peter, so that he was lord and superior of all the men of the world . . . and gave him all the world for his lordship and jurisdiction. . . . One of these Pontiffs . . . made a donation of these islands and mainland of the Ocean Sea to the Catholic kings of Spain. . . . Almost all who have been notified [of this] have received His Majesty and obeyed and served him, and serve him as subjects . . . and turned Christian without reward or stipulation and His Majesty received them . . . as . . . subjects and vassals. Therefore I beg and require you as best I can . . . [that] you recognize the church as lord and superior of the universal world, and the most elevated Pope . . . in its name, and His Majesty in his place as superior and lord and king . . . and consent that these religious fathers declare and preach . . . and His Majesty and I in his name will receive you . . . and will leave your women and children free, without servitude so that with them and with yourselves you can freely do what you wish and we will not compel you to turn Christians. But if you do not do it with

the help of God, I will enter forcefully against you, and I will make war everywhere and however I can, and I will subject you to the yoke and obedience of the Church and His Majesty, and I will take your wives and children, and I will make them slaves . . . and I will take your goods, and I will do to you all the evil and damages that a lord may do to vassals who do not obey or receive him. And I solemnly declare that the deaths and damages received from such will be your fault and not that of His Majesty, nor mine, nor of the gentlemen who came with me.

One must wonder if this might not have produced a laugh or two among those performing the empty act of reading a Spanish document to people who could not understand a single word. Yet, as Patricia Seed explains in *Ceremonies of Possession in Europe's Conquest of the New World, 1492–1640*, to the Spaniards it was a sensible act, borrowed largely from Islamic rituals of possession that they had been subjected to themselves (1995:72–99). Cortés was noted for his particularly faithful performance of the Requirement (1995:98–99).

Cortés occasionally took his love for musical ritual too far, however, as happened during his march south to punish the rogue conquistador Cristóbal de Olid. Olid started as one of his own men before breaking off to make an unauthorized bid to conquer Honduras, just as Cortés had done three years before in his conquest of Mexico. Angered by the betrayal, Cortés assembled a group of men to capture or kill Olid. To the consternation of his regular troops, he took along a band of musicians, draining limited resources to support noncombatants and superfluous equipment. After all, they were not challenging a group of indigenous people, who might be awed by their ritual prowess, but their own countrymen.

During that failed march all but one of Cortés' merry musicians were eaten by fellow soldiers. The company had run out of food. Even the surviving shawmer (the shawm is a double-reeded woodwind derived from the Arab *zamr*) later admitted that he had participated in this odd act of cannibalism. He ate the brains of the sackbut player (Stevenson 1968:223). Facing starvation, the same men who expressed horror at the Mexica leaders' ritual consumption of sacrificial flesh decided that it would be acceptable to sacrifice the musicians' lives and bodies to sustain their own.

Keeping in mind the caveat that ritual was at times perfunctory and possibly even deleterious for the Spanish, it is clear that it was also an essential weapon in the Conquest. Ritual worked because of cultural difference. The Spaniards brought to bear sounds (e.g., cannon fire), sights (e.g., richly decorated horses, pyrotechnics), and smells (e.g., gunpowder) alien to Mesoamerica. Such displays struck fear into Aztec emissaries, as intended.

Spanish ritual worked not only because of cultural difference, however, but also because elements struck a familiar chord. The Spanish and the Mexica had a great deal in common. For example, each was a state-level civilization "divided into social classes defined by their relation to the means of production . . . and their access to political power" (Broda 1987:63). This would mean that the two societies shared more with each other than they did with the thousands of Chichimec societies beyond the Mesoamerican frontier. Their large populations, intensified forms of production, stratified caste systems, massive wars, and ideological narratives would seem alien and unnatural to a Yaqui shaman or Shoshone hunter (Johnson and Earle 1987:31–38).

As natural as it would seem to a Mexica warrior or Spanish soldier to accept the uncontestable orders of a single, unapproachable monarch, most aspects of Spanish or Mexica life were alien to the people of the bands and tribal peoples living in regions of North and Central America outside the Mesoamerican domain.

Based on cross-referenced accounts, Pablo Castellanos concludes that even though the Spaniards found Mexica music and dance to be an affront, it was ultimately comprehensible. He explains that "high culture precortesian music appears to have communicated the same emotions to the Spaniards as to the indigenous" (1970:58). Melancholy music for the Mexica was interpreted as melancholy music by the Spaniards, and so on. This may have been due to the presence of nomothetic properties in the music itself, but mutually comprehensible social contexts may also have helped to translate such basic meanings from one empire to the other.

Furthermore, both empires considered music and art central to their exercise of power to a degree matched by few others. Musical ritual display was much less of a feature in English colonization, for example, perhaps because its goals were more exclusionary than assimilatory. Their extreme emphasis on musical ritual may have provided a cultural interlocutor for the Spanish and Mesoamericans, facilitating the process of acculturation.

Likewise, musical training was similar in the two societies. The calmecac, cuicacalli, and other schools were not unlike the educational institutions of the Spanish. Among the many similarities musically was the calmecac priests' "habit of calling the city to prayers at stated intervals" (Stevenson 1968:8). The Spanish friars also called their new penitents to prayer, having been influenced by both Roman Catholic and Islamic practices. While such disciplines would have seemed oppressive to the nonstate peoples of the New World, the state-disciplined bodies of Mesoamerica were used to such rigid daily regimens. In other words, although the Spaniards and Mexica were extremely different, there were nevertheless significant cultural interlocutors between them. Such similar beliefs and practices would provide important avenues for acculturation.

Of course, the resulting intercultural exchange was far from balanced. The Spaniards not only had the upper hand in such cultural negotiations but also had the upper gun. Therefore, what resulted from the process of acculturation certainly resembled the Spanish vision of the world more than any indigenous model (Lafayette Boilès 1982:75). Precortesian languages, clothing, religion, rituals, and music were radically transformed into something more acceptable to the Spanish. Even though the cultural life of New Spain would eventually begin to diverge from, and contest, Spain, such resistant cultural forms were themselves largely developed in a Spanish idiom. As Juan José Escorza notes, "it is not possible to conclude a military, economic, or political conquest without the indispensable complement of a process of acculturation," a process he refers to as "spiritual conquest" (1987:55).

This is not to say that all things Mexican and Mesoamerican were lost, even in the city at the heart of the empire. The Mexica continued to practice their sacred rites well into the colonial period (Turrent 1996: 119). According to Friar Durán, the same Mexica musicians who performed for the great sacrifices began serving as accompanists for the Eucharist (Turrent 1996:144). In other words, the musicians traded one ritual sacrifice for another. Similarly, adult Nahuatl singers were brought into the churches to sing while the first generation of neophytes underwent rigorous retraining.

Covert acts of cultural salvage took place everywhere, even in the center of the empire. As colonial officials issued orders to have temples razed, pyramids disassembled, and statues smashed, the conquered Mexica laborers buried images intact and stenciled glyphs of Aztec deities on the undersides of cathedral columns. Centuries later, many of these same artifacts would be resurrected as symbols of renewed opposition to Spanish domination (Matos Moctezuma 1987:20).

This process of covert cultural preservation was mirrored in religious performance as the defeated Mesoamericans merged precortesian and Spanish practices to form new, syncretic rituals. New Spain was a dynamic mélange of blended myths, rituals, arts, and cultures. The prime example of such syncretism is, of course, the Virgin of Guadalupe, a mixture of the Christian Mother of God and the Mexica goddess Tonantzín. Mexico's venerated Virgin, who first appeared at Tepeyac, the sacred home of Tonantzín, remains a testament to the power of people to create new worlds in the cultural borderlands. She was, and is, honored with lyrical references to tropical flowers and quetzal feathers, symbols associated with the Mesoamerican deities who preceded her.

Similarly, the Mexica concept of the soul, or *yolia*, would greatly influence the way that the neophytes (new Christians) of New Spain interpreted Christian myth (McKeever Furst 1995:17–22). Theirs was a more embodied sense of soul and salvation than that experienced by European believers. Similarly, the neophytes prayed to saints who took on Mesoamerican characteristics, performing rituals that merged precortesian and European elements.

This process was noted and begrudgingly accepted by the early colonial missionaries. Not long after the Conquest, Friar Durán noted that, just as each Tenochtitlán neighborhood once had its patron god and ritual feast day, each now had its patron saint celebrated in like manner, often on the same day (Turrent 1996:169). In the first years of the new city and colony, Christian saints and Mesoamerican gods were worshiped side by side.

Such practices lasted much longer in more remote parts of New Spain. Throughout the colony, however, the Christian lineup was clearly an extension of the Mesoamerican pantheon it ostensibly replaced. One must remember that Mesoamerican religions, like Christianity and all other world religions, were themselves developed through cultural accretion, substitution, conquest, and revolution. In that sense, the Spanish Conquest continued a cycle of conquest and cultural redefinition that had been going on for thousands of years in Mesoamerica, albeit with much more severe human consequences.

As was true of ritual and religion, the Conquest also did not spell the end of all precortesian musical practices. As an example, Guzmán Bravo and Nava Gómez offer the Cuicapicque, the Náhuatl musical composers of New Spain who practiced their trade well into the nineteenth century. They argue that the Cuicapicque were professional descendants of the court-based Mesoamerican composers of the Aztec world (Guzmán Bravo and Nava Gómez 1984b:89).

In fact, all of the professional positions in the cuicacalli music schools had their equivalent in the Spanish system. Therefore, for at least some of the Mexica who survived the Conquest, there would be commensurate professional roles waiting for them in the new system. Although their ability to function as music instructors would be diminished, the musical professionals of Mesoamerica would nevertheless find a place as practitioners. In fact, the Spanish order demanded it.

MISSIONARY MUSIC AND PEDAGOGY

The missionary orders were placed in charge of colonial enculturation (cultural training and education of indigenous individuals). In order to do this effectively, however, they unwittingly became agents of acculturation (exchange of cultural features between societies). In terms of early colonial musical training, the major missionary figure was Friar Pedro de Gante. A close but illegitimate relative of King Charles V, de Gante was one of the first missionaries to arrive in New Spain following the Conquest (Stevenson 1968:92).

Fittingly, de Gante and two other missionaries who arrived with him in 1523 were housed in a palace built by the legendary Texcocan leader and poet-musician Nezahualcóyotl. According to indigenous informants, Nezahualcóyotl had once constructed in that same palace "a great room where poets, musicians, astrologers, historians, and masters of other arts would gather and confer" (Guzmán Bravo and Nava Gómez 1984b: 101). The three European musician-theologian-pedagogues set off from that same meeting place in an attempt to create a dramatically new cultural foundation for the colony.

Although de Gante was difficult to understand in Spanish, due to a stutter, he nevertheless gained fluency in Nahuatl. He later described the language-learning process as one of the hardest undertakings he had ever experienced (Heller 1979:24). No doubt the struggle to learn about the Aztec and their language made de Gante more empathetic to their plight.

Using the tools made available through his Renaissance education in Europe, de Gante worked feverishly from 1523 to 1572 to convert and educate the Nahua (the name generally used for post-Conquest Nahuatl-speaking peoples). His main tool for both conversion and education was music. The following passage from a letter that de Gante sent to King Phillip II in 1557 demonstrates the proselytizing power of music (Stevenson 1968:93):

We were here more than three years, as I told you, without ever being able to attract them. Instead they fled from us. But by the grace of Almighty God I began to perceive their mentality and to understand how they should be dealt with. Their whole worship had consisted of dancing and singing before their own gods. When the time came to make sacrifices for victory over their enemies for the supplying of their daily wants, before killing their victims, they first must needs dance in front of the idol.

48 Upon comprehending this and realizing that all their songs were composed to the honor of their gods, I composed a very elaborate one myself, but the subject-matter was God's law and our faith that Christ was born of the holy and undefiled Virgin Mary. About two months before Christmas I also gave them some designs to paint on their dancing togs because they always danced and sang in costumes that bespoke happiness, sorrow, or victory.

When Christmas approached, we then invited everyone within ten leagues [thirty-five miles] to come see Our Redeemer's Nativity Feast. So many came that the patio, although very large, could not contain them. Each province had set up its own booths to entertain its chieftains, and even infirm persons came from a distance of seven and eight leagues, carried on hammocks, and others came almost equal distances, by water, to hear the singing.

New Spain: 1521–1821

In 1528 de Gante invited local leaders and other Nahua to celebrate Christmas in the atrium of the convent of San Francisco. They were allowed to wear their traditional ritual attire. There they played, danced, and sang "as in the ancient times" (Turrent 1996:189). In some ways, that decision marked a watershed moment in the history of Mexico. Rather than making use of simple terror, social extermination, and cultural replacement alone, the colonial policy of New Spain would also allow room for cultural negotiation.

Wisely, de Gante and his colleagues decided to start by educating the children, particularly after receiving a great deal of resistance from their parents (Turrent 1996:118, 122). Wide-scale conversion of the indigenous masses into Christian citizens of the realm would start with the training of individual children, particularly those of the Mesoamerican elite. De Gante organized a ritual march to inaugurate the new school. That day, four hundred neophytes symbolically left behind their natal culture to enter another. The new school was a total institution, much like the calmecac, meaning that the student's entire life was dictated by the economy, culture, and politics of the organization.

The missionary teachers also used musical ritual to demonstrate their success to colonial administrators. By 1530 a choir of neophytes was singing in the newly constructed cathedral in Mexico City (Oropreza 1996:44), placed on display by ecclesiastical school administrators who wished to convince the political leadership of New Spain that theirs was the best method of winning over Mesoamericans to Christianity and Mother Spain. From that point on, the cathedral became the center of colonial "musical life" (Estrada 1973:36). In fact, the school directly connected to the cathedral evolved into an institution specializing in musical pedagogy.

Music training was not a separate discipline but rather a central part of the curriculum. In order to reach his students, de Gante translated biblical themes into Nahuatl and set them to tunes familiar to his students, blending Mesoamerican and Spanish styles. Based on de Gante's pioneering success, Juan de Zumárraga, the first bishop of Mexico, instructed all missionaries also to use music in their work, referring to it as "an indispensable aid in the process of conversion" (Stevenson 1968: 154). Charles V made the same recommendation when addressing missionaries bound for the New World (Warkentin 1981:45). Cortés himself insisted that indigenous students be taught at de Gante's new school.

During the first years of colonial conversion, there was a proactive belief that Mesoamerican culture was compatible with Christian beliefs and Spanish citizenry. The missionaries even had papal sanction to retain "everything indigenous that did not conflict with Christianity" (Oropreza 1996:48). The music of New Spain and even contemporary Mexico cannot be understood without reference to that early openness to cultural exchange.

Composers in the new colony continued to foster de Gante's methods for musical syncretism well after the Conquest had concluded (Claro 1970:10). The music and the teaching of indigenous cacique Hernando Franco (ca. 1599) provide excellent examples. Franco's hymns dedicated to the Virgin illustrate not only syncretism but also the use of music as a didactic tool. In the late sixteenth century, hymns such as Franco's were used to teach Christian doctrine and appropriate behavior. Spanish clerics, particularly those directly in charge of education and conversion, continued to believe that "more than by preaching, the Indians are converted by the music" (Stevenson 1968:161). The indigenous people were thus transformed into Christian neophytes, a status and identity neither Mesoamerican nor fully Spanish.

As is true of all teaching, colonial teaching would not have functioned so well if it had not been a reciprocal process, at least to some degree. The Spaniards found it necessary to learn about their students in order to reach them. In doing so, they were also changed. No matter how much they saw themselves as the master teachers, it is clear that the more a Spaniard interacted with neophyte charges, the more radically he or she was changed. Sahagún, one of several friars to take a Nahuatl name, and his predecessor, de Gante, are just two of many examples.

This is not to say that these sixteenth-century Catholic missionaries became enlightened advocates of Mesoamerican peoples and cultures, except in a very relative sense. Nor was life pleasant for the tormented souls thrown into the new schools. Life in these institutions would have presented a severe disruption for Mesoamerican families, many of whom had already suffered great losses due to war and disease. However, they also experienced a level of cultural continuity. The one thousand students educated per year at de Gante's school, mainly sons of indigenous elites, led a life not unlike that of the calmecac. Religion, the arts, and labor were integrated into the daily round, instilling disciplines that reinforced the Spanish worldview and naturalized the new society's lifeways, while not completely expunging Mesoamerican conceptions.

Due to the success of these pioneering efforts in Central Mexico, later missionaries to the northern territories of New Spain would enact similar policies (Summers 1980), albeit with much less success (Warkentin 1981). Rather than representing a transformation from empire to empire, the acculturation process in the rest of the continent would involve attempts to incorporate small-scale nonstate societies into an empire almost overnight. The work disciplines, hierarchies, ideologies, and violent conscription of the colonial state were extremely alien to people who lived in these smaller-scale societies. Spanish institutions were even more of an imposition on them as a result. Likewise, the northerners' relatively low populations would be decimated still more by disease than the Mesoamericans had been, especially when the policy of *congregación* (congregation) was enacted, forcing people to live in small mission dormitories where the vectors of disease multiplied.

Furthermore, the missions on the Spanish frontier had to function as fairly self-sustaining economic units (Farnsworth and Jackson 1995). They lacked the support of the colonial infrastructure that readily sustained de Gante's more specialized and privileged mission school. For these and other reasons, the history of missionization in the North was one of rebellions and more violent forms of labor conscription than appears to have been the case in Central Mexico (Langer and Jackson 1995). The missionaries of Mesoamerica had a much easier task in some respects, because they were working with people long accustomed to the rigid disciplines and control of a state-bound life.

Instead of producing a new citizenry, therefore, the missions to the north were simply and unwittingly clearing the ground for Spanish, Mexican, and U.S. colonization of indigenous territories. Yet, even a century after secularization and the resulting disappearance of the missions in California, some of the descendants of the surviving neophytes could be heard singing the *alabados* and other songs taught as part of mission pedagogy (Koegel 1993:82–83). The missionaries' musical innovations became traditions, outliving the missions and colony itself.

In the center, Spanish institutions succeeded to a much greater degree, for better and for worse. Just as a primary rule of the calmecac and cuicacalli was "to teach the boys all the verses of the songs to sing, which they called the divine songs" (Sahagún in Stevenson 1968:104), de Gante successfully taught his charges to sing and play the Catholic liturgy. Like the Mexica themselves, de Gante believed that music was a direct conduit to God. A child of the Renaissance, de Gante felt that transcendence and redemption could be gained through joyful celebration of the liturgy. He and his colleagues saw the New World as their last and best chance to institute God's utopia on earth. Another reason for instructing neophytes in their own language was so that they would not be corrupted by the more secular Spaniards (Turrent 1996:146).

To that same end, the Spanish Crown issued laws forbidding Spaniards from living in indigenous communities, unless they could provide a good example (Turrent 1996:146). In other words, rather than merely disparaging their students as inferior, in some ways the missionaries viewed them as superior to their fellow Spaniards, who were seen as hopelessly corrupt. The conquistadors and *encomenderos* (plantation owners) indulged in popular secular entertainments, including styles of music unsanctioned by the church hierarchy. The missionaries, therefore, were waging their spiritual battle on two fronts: against Mesoamerican idolatry, on one hand, and European decadence, on the other.

Pedro de Gante's teaching set off a musical explosion, and in a relatively short time even the smallest town had its own complement of church musicians (Turrent 1996:129–130). There were an estimated one thousand church choirs by 1576 (Oropreza 1996:45). The demand for musicians and music instructors in the new colony was so great that even two of Cortés' soldier-musicians were able to set up shop as music teachers. One of them played the *vihuela*, a small, eight-stringed ancestor of the modern six-string guitar (Geijerstam 1976:27). Such stringed instruments, including the hand-held harp, were favored in the secular music of the time.

Many musicians and instrumentalists came to New Spain in the first decade of its existence, spreading throughout the conquered territory to teach their trade. Soon the neophytes were teaching each other music and crafting their own instruments. The *chirimía*, an oboe-like aerophone played with a double-reed, was one of the favorite instruments, as was a small pipe and drum combination (similar to that played by the voladores today). Like the pipe and drum combination, the chirimía became so closely associated with the indigenous musicians that many believed it to be of New World origin. Eventually, the musicians themselves became known as chirimías. The chirimías are still featured in various regional indigenous rites, often combined with the teponaztli as part of an "Aztec conjunto [ensemble]" (Chamorro 1982:171).

While there is nothing intrinsically Aztec about the chirimía, it is not necessarily European either. The instrument was introduced to the Spanish via conquest, brought to the Iberian Peninsula by the Moors (Chamorro 1982). The chirimía, therefore, is at the same time Asian, African, European, and American, as is so much of New World culture.

Following the Spanish Conquest of Mexico, chirimías were employed to provide music for the Mass. Midway through the first century of the colony, however, the Council of Trent (1545–1563) decided that the organ produced a more appropriate sound for the liturgy. That decision in turn led to an increase in organ production and increasing divergence between sacred and secular musical styles in the colony. Soon every major city boasted a grand cathedral, every one of which demanded at least one organ. New Spain quickly became famous in the New World for its organs (Fesperman 1984:107). Even the smaller cities and towns of the Crown's largest colony would boast their own organs by the end of the first century of colonization. The instrument became a central symbol and measure of each colonial city's connection to the empire.

The Council of Trent removed all percussive, blaring, and/or shrill instruments from church worship, so as not to upset the solemnity of the occasion (Chamorro 1982:170). It is important to note that those three adjectives—percussive, blaring, and shrill—were often applied in the missionaries' descriptions of Mexica music. In other words, it appears that the neophytes had adopted Old World instruments that fit with their own musical sensibilities. The repression of these same instruments by the Council of Trent, therefore, is a good indication that by the mid-sixteenth century the church (or at least the colonial administration) was growing increasingly less tolerant toward the integration of indigenous and popular culture into the liturgy. These instruments could still accompany outside religious observances and processionals, but they were not to be part of the liturgy itself. Officially, only the angel statuettes carved into the baroque churches would be allowed to retain their trumpets, vihuelas, chirimías, and other outlawed instruments (Guzmán Bravo 1986).

The Council of Trent's decision to move the more dynamic instruments outside the liturgy had important historical and cultural repercussions in New Spain. The new policy can be interpreted as a move against indigenous ritual enthusiasm and a sign that by the mid- to late 1500s the mission of the church had changed from spiritual conquest to maintenance of a well-established religious base (Estrada 1973:68). This and related edicts would literally move the popular religious experience outside of the official church and onto public squares. The public religious observances outside the cathedrals and in small pueblos throughout Mexico are largely the legacy of this ruling. The council's decision may have also pushed indigenous musicians from imitative to creative musical production, given that they were no longer as directly trained and overseen by Spaniards within official institutional contexts (Moreno Rivas 1989:53). This would give further impetus to the creation of distinctly local, Mexican styles of popular music. As would be true of the later Bourbon reforms, the Council of Trent's attempt to gain more colonial control may have had the opposite effect. In music as in all cultural politics, incorporation is usually more effective than simple censorship.

Within the confines of the church, however, the council's attempts largely succeeded. By the mid-seventeenth century, stringed instruments had largely replaced the instruments that colonial clerics had found shrill, returning the sense of peace demanded by the colonial leaders. *Bel canto*, languid arias usually accompanied by stringed instruments, was added to the colonial repertoire, continuing the trend toward more solemn and sedate liturgical music (Estrada 1973:35).

Even before the Council of Trent sent the "shrill" wind instruments and loud percussion into the public square, however, musical life was flourishing in the young colony. Toribio de Motolinía, a Franciscan who arrived in New Spain a year after de Gante (1524), claimed that composers "skilled in fashioning songs and ballads were everywhere in great demand" (Barwick 1994:350). By 1556 the number of neophyte musicians and instruments had grown to the point that church officials felt obligated to place strict limits on the types of instruments played during the liturgy, when and how they could be played, and by how many musicians. They feared that the musical exuberance of the locals was getting out of hand. Just as syncretic saints provided a means through which Mesoamericans could continue precortesian beliefs in new form, music provided an interlocutor for the neophytes, something that they could relate to, adopt, remake, and practice without completely losing themselves in the process. Having been denied the right to become priests by official edict, would-be religious leaders among the neophytes took to musical performance and teaching as their new channel for religious leadership. Furthermore, musicians were exempt from paying taxes in the colonial pueblos and cities (Chamorro 1982:170), as had been the tradition among the Mexica before them. Essentially, indigenous men received a tax credit for becoming musicians.

By the second century of Spanish colonization in Mesoamerica

(1600s), indigenous musicians were being named to key directorships, including the position of chapelmaster in the Oaxaca Cathedral (Stevenson 1979b). Music became a primary site of negotiation between the two worlds, just as it would later become a site of conflict with Spain.

And what of the man who helped begin this musical revolution? Turning down an offer to become archbishop of Mexico and several papal offers of ordination, de Gante preferred to remain a friar and teacher for the rest of his ninety-two years (Heller 1979:25). Although its results would vary over time, the enlightenment model that de Gante instituted would remain the ideal to be followed by all future Franciscan missions.

The musical missionaries played a complex role in colonization. On one hand, they were key agents in Spain's spiritual conquest of the New World. They were on the ideological front, proffering a religion whose basic tenets and practices legitimated colonial rule. On the other hand, they advocated the incorporation of indigenous people into colonial cultural life and favored the retention of all aspects of Mesoamerican culture that would not overtly challenge Christian precepts. They also provided a communitarian model for the new colony (Oropreza 1996:78) and fought on the behalf of indigenous labor against the brutal encomienda system (Escorza 1987:56). While the assimilationist model of the Franciscans was hardly radical, it was more enlightened than the policies of other Spanish colonial institutions and stands as a model superior to the "displacement, elimination, and cultural substitution" policies enacted during the Anglo invasion of North America (Butzer 1991:213).

Unfortunately, the relatively enlightened policies of de Gante would eventually be challenged from forces outside his Franciscan order. While Franciscans like Gerónimo de Mendieta bragged that "there is nothing that [the Mesoamericans] cannot learn to do," clerics in other orders felt that de Gante's pedagogical policies were wasted on the neophytes and that they should focus their teaching on less pleasurable disciplines (Guzmán Bravo 1978:350). The Dominicans, for example, "eschewed Latin instruction for Indigenous peoples" and "opposed the Franciscan college before the court of Charles V" (Harrison 1988:172). By midcentury, colonial policy began to turn away from de Gante's acculturation model toward a more "restrictive, conservative and controlling" plan (Oropreza 1996:80). By 1577 the Crown was issuing orders against "further inquiry into native history and religion" and even restricting the published ethnographic works of Sahagún (Oropreza 1996:80). Instead of an emphasis on the potential pleasures of redemption, the promotion of solemnity and earthly sacrifice became the order of the day. Although religious sacrifice rarely took on mortal force in the colony (excepting the occasional murders of the Inquisition and the deaths of resisters), everything from the castrations of male sopranos to monastic self-flagellation evidenced a belief held by the conservative wing of the church that physical pain could be a conduit for communication with the divine and a means of spiritual transcendence. These brutal physical disciplines also functioned to keep potential rebels in line with the will of a theocratic state, just as they had during the Triple Alliance.

SYNCRETISM AND ASSIMILATION

The colonial crucible created new rituals merging Spanish and indigenous practices, techniques, and sensibilities. For example, the traditional Spanish *autos sacramentales*—short plays with biblical themes— "were superimposed on *mitotes*, popular indigenous festivals" (Schmidt 1988:300). These hybrid performances incorporated the spirit of Mexica religious practice into the Christian ritual and mythological corpus.

Out of this process, new versions of the saints, martyrs, and Virgin Mother were born. Their evil opposites were recreated as well. The supernatural icons of the Old World gained new form in Mexico. A *copla* from one auto sacramental didactically introduces the Old World's archetype of feminine evil to the New World (Schmidt 1988:300):

¿Para qué comió la primera casada?	Why did the first bride eat it?
¿Para qué comió la fruta vedada?	Why did she eat the forbidden fruit?

However, the Eve of old would not be the same as the Middle Eastern or European versions. The mythical first woman of Europe became infused with characteristics of Mesoamerican goddesses, such as Coyolxauhqui. Similarly, La Llorona, the crying woman who roams the streets at night looking for "her lost children," reincarnated Cihuacóatl, an Aztec goddess. Hybrid feminine archetypes also developed merging historical figures and mythical archetypes, the most famous being Malinche, Cortés' translator and mistress. Malinche was transformed into a symbol of betrayal and deception in later centuries, in the Eve-Coyolxauhqui tradition.

Christian dichotomies of good and evil were imposed following the Conquest and then modified to fit the more dualistic Mesoamerican tradition (Robertson 1988:15). Figures like the hard-drinking, cigar-smoking

Saint Simón of Guatemala, burning Judases, and similar mythological characters were much less extreme in their evil or moral purity when compared to the European Christian canon and often had both good and evil attributes. The Latin American saints are much more like Mesoamerican deities than like their European namesakes in that regard.

DRAMA AND THE COLONIAL ENCOUNTER

The New World also influenced the Old in significant ways. Incredible social changes were wrought by the introduction of New World cultigens (tomato, potato, corn, tobacco, to name just a few) and cultural practices. The sexually charged sarabande dance of Spain, for example, provides evidence of New World cultural influence. Diego Durán believed the sarabande to be a direct descendant of the Mexica "tickle dance" (Stevenson 1968:225–231).

New Spain: 1521–1821

Likewise, themes of conquest and discovery were played out on the European stage, taking the form of dramatic plays (e.g., Shakespeare's *The Tempest*) and even opera (Maehder 1992). That tradition continued for some time in both Europe and later the United States as authors like John Dryden (*The Indian Emperour, or the Conquest of Mexico by the Spaniards, Being the Sequel of the Indian Queen*, 1667), Lewis Thomas (*Cortes the Conqueror: A Tragedy*, 1857), and Haniel Long (*Malinche*, 1939) created protagonists out of Spaniards and their perceived allies. The colonial composers and playwrights of New Spain likewise favored Emperor Motecuhzoma Xocoyotzin as protagonist. The Mexica leader was generally viewed as a sympathetic and tragic figure in the ritualistic dramas of New Spain, thanks to his ostensible alliance with Cortés (Kuss 1988:323).

The very existence of these previously unknown others caused colonists to rethink their world and selves. Every encounter with an "other" demands such a redefinition of self. That is as true for nations and continental cultures as it is for individuals. Thus, the colonial dialectic would remake Europe as well. The continent would become more cosmopolitan and, at the same time, brutal as it projected its own colonial savagery onto those it sought to control (Taussig 1987:74–92). New racist ideologies, later expressed in such movements as Manifest Destiny, scientific racism, and eugenics, would develop out of this continental encounter.

The most dramatic and catastrophic results of European colonialism, however, were experienced in the New World. The most horrific change was demographic. As much as 90 percent of the Mesoamerican population was decimated by disease, displacement, work conscription, and more direct forms of violence, facilitating cultural transformation.

RITUAL RIFTS

Cultural transformation took place on all levels. At the top, the Mexica state would be completely undone and replaced by a very different system. Despite sharing certain general characteristics as expanding agrarian-states, the Spaniards and Mexica were also profoundly different. For example, statecraft, social life, and religion were much more integrated in Mesoamerican civilizations. Conversely, the Spaniards, like other European states, had begun to bifurcate religious and secular governance, moving increasingly toward the latter. That is why the Spanish immediately went about constructing two new ritual edifices from the stones of the Great Temple. One would serve as the center of religious power (the Mexico City cathedral) and the other would become the seat of secular governance (the National Palace). To demonstrate their dominance symbolically, the Spaniards made certain that the new cathedral was slightly taller than the Great Temple it replaced. It is still the "largest Christian edifice in the hemisphere" (Stevenson 1979b:132). Conversely, the political functions of the state would be housed in the National Palace, just to the south of the spot where the Great Temple once towered.

Although religion and governance were in theory dual elements of a single theocratic state, there were growing tensions between the religious and political elements of the Spanish nation, state, and empire. These tensions were reflected, indeed performed, in the ritual arena. Throughout the colonial period major ceremonies represented turf wars, as bishops and viceroys contested their relative placement in processionals, marches, and, by extension, society. For example, in 1651 viceroy Count Alba de Liste broke into a sacred processional, demanding that he and his men bear the Eucharist, replacing church officials (Curcio-Nagy 1994:9). Fights and arrests ensued.

Many colonial rituals became sites of conflict and negotiation between secular and religious leaders. The state sponsored major celebrations to mark the arrival of each new viceroy, including bullfights and other spectacles (Estrada 1973:139). Likewise, the colonial government mandated massive mourning rituals whenever a Spanish monarch died (Barwick 1994:358). The church offered only token support for many of these state-sponsored events, whereas papal deaths and other church matters were marked with ostentatious display. Conversely, the clergy sponsored elaborate rituals during Lent, Easter, and Corpus Cristi, reminding an increasingly secular state that it was the church that served the higher power.

THE HEGEMONY OF OLD MUSIC IN THE NEW WORLD

Most trends in Spanish and European music made their way to New Spain. Among the musical styles transported from Spain was the baroque vogue of "polychoralism" (Stevenson 1987:76). As reflected in church design throughout New Spain, spaces would be created on either side of the central chamber for separate choruses to sing and play in counterpoint fashion over the heads of the parishioners. The same effect was accomplished with separately stationed instrumental *coros*, segregated into as many as four separate sections of the chapel. This "surround-sound" provided a heavenly sensorium to complement the gilded baroque design of the cathedral and pageantry of the Mass.

New Spain: 1521–1821

This sumptuous ritual style was particularly popular in the seventeenth century. If the Catholic response to the reformation in Europe was a didactic and aesthetic appeal to the senses, the baroque movement in the New World was perhaps even more extreme in its expressiveness and emotional appeal. New World composers, chapelmasters, and musicians took the baroque concept to its furthest possible extreme. This is sometimes referred to as "Ultrabaroqueism" (Moreno Rivas 1989:30).

The appeal worked very well in Mexico City. Englishman Thomas Gage, a Dominican, claimed that music was "so exquisite in that city" that people were attending Mass to hear it rather than "for any delight in the service of God" (Stevenson 1987:81). Music was so essential to the Mass that a chapelmaster could be fined whenever "a noticeable dissonance" intruded (Stevenson 1979b:171). While that punishment falls well short of those reserved for offending Mexica musicians at the height of the Triple Alliance, it does indicate how important music was to Catholic ritual in the colony.

Catholic ritual was, in turn, key to governance. Despite the growing rift between church and state, the state required a powerful ritually mediated ideology—religion—in order to maintain power. Nationalism would not replace Catholicism as the religion of state for some time. Therefore, religion dominated colonial discourse, so much so that even resistance would largely have to take place within rather than against it.

The same was true for music. As Juan José Escorza notes, "if in other aspects the spiritual conquest was never completed, in the case of music the triumph was barely less than total" (1987:59). The spirit of musical resistance continued, but it would mainly take place in a Spanish idiom.

MUSIC AS A FORM OF RITUAL RESISTANCE

Even in the initial decades of conversion and acculturation, signs of resistance were popping up everywhere. Juan Diego's claim to have witnessed the Virgin Mary at Tepeyac, an Aztec sacred site, was considered suspect for that same reason; clerics feared that Mesoamericans were simply trying to continue their old religion under Christian pretenses. Pedro de Gante and other missionaries were attacked for allowing the indigenous people to practice "the old pagan rites with nothing changed but the name of the patron" (Stevenson 1968:164). Many, particularly among the rival Dominican hierarchy, contended that the indigenous people could not be educated to the level that de Gante was (successfully) attempting to achieve. Spanish leaders worried that de Gante's school would become a breeding ground for an educated indigenous elite who might one day challenge Spanish supremacy (Turrent 1996: 140). It is perhaps no coincidence that Don Carlos de Texcoco, a cacique accused of heresy, was himself trained at de Gante's school (Turrent 1996:140). Don Carlos was accused of advocating a return to traditional religion and the abandonment of Christianity. One of playwright Juan Tovar's excellent historical dramas, *Las adoraciones*, revolves around that important trial (Tovar 1970).

By the mid-1500s colonial officials and clerics felt the need to rein in the musical and ritual exuberance of the indigenous neophytes, setting limits and regulating the type, style, and hours of singing, dancing, and playing. A church council called by Archbishop Alonso de Montúfar concluded that the Mesoamericans' explosion of musical festivity was more like the ritual practices they "delighted in during their days of heathenism" than like traditional Christian worship (Stevenson 1968:168). The neophytes contributed to a liturgical music that lacked "the rigidity and austerity" that characterized the Spanish Mass, inciting suspicion and fear among colonial elites (Mendoza 1953:23).

As was true of the music and ritual of New Spain, the colonial caste system also began breaking down. Even in the first century of colonial control, *mestizaje* (cultural mixing) was rapidly taking place, directly challenging the model of segregation and stratification that colonial planners were attempting to put in place. Among the many causes of this inevitable collapse were the *vagabundos*, poor Spaniards that Spanish officials attempted to keep from polluting the newly won souls of the indigenous people. Although free from political intent, various combinations of indigenous, Spanish, and African people were subverting the aims of empire simply by interacting with each other.

Nowhere was that mixing more evident than in Mexico City. In addition to being the center of Spanish power where "the decisive acts of colonial life were acted out," the capital quickly became associated with the sort of multiracial mixing colonial administrators had expressly attempted to avoid (Butzer 1991:214).

This unsanctioned mixing was represented musically. The villancico became the musical *lingua franca* of the city. Inventive villancicos were laced with phrases from various Spanish dialects, indigenous languages, and African American colloquialisms (Moreno Rivas 1989:39), a musical mestizaje that would eventually lead to the development of a national dialect quite distinct from the language of Castille.

The villancico, a simple poetry-song form, was an early precursor of later strophic forms in Mexico. Like the popular *bolero* of today, the villancico provided a simple template on which almost any message could be written, from Virgin devotionals to playful and profane prose. The villancico provided a structure that allowed great improvisation. Like the rappers of today, nimble minds like Sor Juana Inés de la Cruz were able to win rhetorical battles through lyrical improvisation. Villancico artists employed a "subversive and demystifying" sense of humor (Jiménez de Báez 1992:474). In the "Refrain from Santa Catarina," Sor Juana applauds the rhetorical triumph of the saint over arrogant "learned men" (Inés de la Cruz 1997:189):

¡Víctor, víctor! Catarina,	Victor! Victor! Catherine,
que con su ciencia divina	who with enlightenment divine
los sabios ha convencido	persuaded all the learned men,
y victoriosa ha salido	she who with triumph overcame
—con su ciencia soberana—	—with knowledge truly sovereign—
de la arrogancia profana	the pride and arrogance profane
que a convencerla ha venido	of those who challenged her, in vain
¡Víctor, víctor, víctor!	Victor! Victor! Victor!

Two centuries later, *yanqui* invaders were satirized with songs like *El mosquito americano* (Jiménez de Báez 1992:476) and other Mexican *décimas* (poetry and lyrics with ten lines), close kin of the villancico.

Starting another long-term Mexican trend, the colonial villancico emphasized voice and melody over instrumentation. That has been a hallmark of Mexican music ever since, particularly the music of urban Mexico. From the earliest colonial polyphony to modern rock, the most popular forms in the metropolis have tended to be those with the most active vocal range, with a distinct emphasis on lyrical prose (Schmidt 1988).

African Americans played a major role in mestizaje. They took an active part in the official musical activities of the colony, "singing in church choirs and providing musical entertainments outside" (Barwick 1994:358). Both free and enslaved African Americans took on such roles. In the mid-seventeenth century, the chapelmaster of the Oaxaca Cathedral directed a choir and ensemble that included at least a few of his own slaves, musicians who were paid for their churchly duties (Stevenson 1979a:182).

In 1609 the Mexican archbishop, a music aficionado with a penchant for rewarding talent, insisted that the salary of an enslaved male soprano be increased to reflect his exceptional talent. The man with "the singularly beautiful voice" gained enough money to buy his freedom six years later (Stevenson 1987:78). Eventually he earned more than any other musician working at that time and was ordained as a priest.

Church officials did not always welcome African American contributions. In 1648 the cathedral chapelmaster asked for the dissolution of a choir led by an African American director. The chapelmaster considered some of the choir's music "indecent" (Stevenson 1987:87). Veteran chapter members insisted that the popular choir director be retained, however, and won his retention despite the chapelmaster's complaints.

As for secular influence, regional dances like *la bamba* and *el huapango* developed out of an admixture of Spanish and African styles (Moreno Rivas 1989:45). By 1580 the black population in New Spain outnumbered the white population, as African slaves were brought in to supplement and replace indigenous labor (Ivey 1966:7). These slaves, having developed knowledge and talent in European trades, were even put in charge of indigenous towns and were often made foremen on work gangs. African Americans became associated with music early on, as they gathered in town squares to play their instruments, featuring styles of percussion that appealed to indigenous Mesoamericans as well. The musical mixing of indigenous and African American musicians raised great consternation among colonial officials.

The Inquisition took notice of the musical activities of African Americans in New Spain, noting that many of their rituals ostensibly held for the purpose of celebrating religious holidays were in fact excuses for secular musical celebrations. These events were filled with songs and dances accompanied by guitars, harps, and drums. Recorded in Inquisition records as early as 1669 (Saldívar 1934:221), such celebrations are obvious precursors to later *son* (whereas the names of other musical styles are only italicized when first introduced, *son* is italicized throughout, to distinguish it from the English word "son") and jarabe gatherings. During the colonial era, these unsanctioned acts caused great consternation among church and state leaders alike.

The inordinate amount of attention that the Inquisition paid to African American musical activities indicates that these musicians exerted a powerful influence on colonial life. African American street revelers went so far with their syncretic rituals as to play the huehuetl and dance around the Aztec Calendar Stone in the heart of Mexico City (Stevenson 1986:35). Such activities flaunted laws designed to limit ritual excess and cross-cultural interaction.

Several African American street musicians became well known, virtually above the law as a result of their fame. One of these was José Vasconcelos, a "Negro poet" who lived during the eighteenth century (Schmidt 1988:303). His improvised poetry was known throughout the city. Vasconcelos impressed the viceroy so much that he was asked to produce extemporaneous verse for the court. Despite that sponsorship, some of Vasconcelos' poems satirized the viceroyalty and other elites. He referred to Spanish rule as an "Octavian peace" and complained that the "Spaniards here have everything they dream of" (1988:304). Vasconcelos' surviving poems indicate a strong "class consciousness" and provide further evidence of "social unrest in the late colonial period" (1988:303).

Vasconcelos was also emblematic of the double life of Africans in the Americas. At the same time that his work was highly valued, Vasconcelos and his fellow African Americans were seen as outsiders by both the secular state and church hierarchies. They were a complicating threat to the dichotomous order of Spanish rulers and indigenous subjects imagined by the colonists. African Americans, although widely influential in terms of music and culture, were at the same time stigmatized for upsetting the already precarious balance between the New World peoples and their nervous overlords.

A number of mixed and African-led rebellions against the colonial government moved the colonial administrators greatly to curtail the importation and exploitation of African slaves. As the indigenous population rebounded from its catastrophically low numbers, African slaves became less necessary. In fact, import slavery was never very profitable in New Spain and may have caused more of an economic drain than a benefit. Spain did not control any of the major slave-exporting ports in Africa and thus had to pay foreign middlemen for slaves, draining capital from the colony.

As a result of all these factors, African Americans never became

New Spain:
1521–1821

viewed as fully Mexican. One of José Vasconcelos' poems represents a plea for such inclusion (Figueroa Hernández 1996:25):

Aunque soy de raza conga	Although of the Congo race
yo no he nacido Africano	I was not born an African.
soy, de nación, Mexicano	I am of the Mexican nation
y nacido en Almolonga.	and was born in Almolonga.

Vasconcelos was part of a growing popular class, those who saw themselves as largely outside the slowly dissolving colonial order. Nowhere was this dissolution more apparent than in the Corpus Cristi celebrations, the "largest annual festival to take place in the viceregal capital" (Curcio-Nagy 1994:3). So essential was this ritual to the colonial order that leaders even demanded its performance in 1692, despite the fact that the viceregal palace had been burned down in rebellion just the day before. That rebellion was thwarted by the ritual intervention of quick-thinking priests who rushed into the mob, holding aloft the Eucharist. In reverence for the sacred symbol, the rioters desisted; and by the next day the traditional ritual cycle resumed with the Corpus Cristi procession (1994:19). Even the homeless viceroy took part in the solemn ceremony, coming within spitting distance of the very food rioters who had demolished his palace the day before.

Position in the Corpus Cristi procession directly reflected one's place in the colonial hierarchy, from viceroy to street vendor. Every organization from the craft guilds to religious confraternities took part in the preparation and execution of the event. It was a tightly coordinated ritual spectacle, and music played a key role. Indigenous confraternities cleared the streets and spread sand and flowers on them to provide a clean surface for parading Christ's body. The city itself became the set for this most important and sacred social event.

The ceremony was not simply a show of unity and order, however. As indicated above, the dichotomous society that the Spanish wished to create—Spanish colonists and indigenous subjects—was crisscrossed and complicated by a number of hybrid identities and ethnicities. Power itself was split between Spaniards born in Europe and American-born Spaniards or *criollos*, who were beginning to contest the hegemony of the *gachupines* (Spaniards) by the second century of colonization.

Such class contradictions grew to crisis proportions in the eighteenth century, as reflected in the Corpus Cristi ritual. During the eighteenth-century Bourbon reform era, many indigenous elements were completely banned from the Corpus Cristi ritual (Curcio-Nagy 1994:16), not because of indigenous subversion but rather because of their conspicuous use by criollos. The Bourbon reforms were aimed at more effectively controlling the criollo classes of the colony (García Ayluardo 1994:82).

In order to understand the Bourbon obsession with ritual observance, it is also important to understand the larger reform movement of which they were a part. The Bourbon reforms were meant to modernize the Spanish economy, including that of the colonies. As part of that philosophy, religious excess and spectacle were viewed as deterrents to economic efficiency (García Ayluardo 1994:90).

As opposed to the protocapitalist principles of the Protestant nations, Spain retained a religious worldview that favored more feudal relations. Colonial-era Catholicism continued to promote values that reinforced an ecclesiastical state stranglehold on production, while promoting only the crudest forms of accumulation, as opposed to savings, investment, and growth. Yet the progressive Bourbons were trying to reform the Catholic kingdom in such a way as to make it more economically efficient and growth oriented. There was increasing recognition among Spanish leaders that they had reached the limits of crude accumulation. Territorial expansion was no longer possible, and simple resource extraction would not in itself fuel a productive economy.

With that in mind, Bourbon-era officials complained that festivals and religious observances in New Spain were culturally backward. What de Gante and his colleagues viewed as the colony's greatest success was now being represented as its greatest failure. "Whatever they earn by working," complained Hipólito Villarroal, "they spend on festivals and large dinners and drunken binges with which they celebrate these festivals, that really should be called bacchanalias rather than civilized and religious [celebrations]" (Curcio-Nagy 1994:18–19). In condemnation of what he and other Bourbon officials decried as an overly tolerant colonial policy, Villarroal also referred to the Corpus Cristi celebrants as "a crowd of drunk, miserable naked Indians wearing costumes" (1994:19).

As early as 1564 Spanish officials demonstrated concern that the indigenous participants were perverting the Corpus Cristi celebration to their own pagan interests. They began to regulate Corpus Cristi more closely to make sure that all of the elaborate floats entered into the procession were indeed related to the sacred event. Throughout the eighteenth century, however, restrictions on Corpus Cristi comportment became increasingly rigid until even the grand *gigantes*, large images of biblical and historical characters, were banned. Whereas early colonial officials viewed these figures as evidence of assimilation, they were now seen as symbols of resistance. The Bourbon officials recognized their parodic aspect. The gigantic figures of bearded conquistadors, Moors, gypsies, and Judases had once presented a relatively safe medium for critique, when all other forms of resistance were unthinkable. Yet the Bourbons banned even this more subtle form of resistance, closing an important ritual outlet.

Whereas enacting Corpus Cristi had once been the triumph of colonial acculturation and order, it was viewed as mere carnival by the end of the eighteenth century. Friar Motolinía one bragged that "if the Pope and Emperor" had witnessed the Tlaxcaltecan Corpus Cristi in 1538, "they would have been delighted" (Stevenson 1968:159). The Bourbons were anything but delighted with that same rite, as it had developed into parodic spectacle just two centuries later.

The Bourbon reforms and repressions were a case of too little, too late or perhaps too much, too late. Their reforms did little more than increase resentment of the empire, fueling the growth of revolutionary anger. The Bourbons tightened their grip on a crumbling empire, perhaps hastening its demise in the process.

Musicians were at the center of these rituals of resistance. In fact, the first strike recorded in New Spain was among the musicians of Mexico City. The striking musicians refused to play for the arrival of the Holy Inquisition after being stiffed for a previous performance (Turrent 1996: 153–154). Such musical "union" activity flared up several more times during the colonial era, usually over pay issues (Stevenson 1987:109). Even the first chapelmaster of the Metropolitan Cathedral, Hernando Franco, took part in a musicians' strike (Claro 1970:10). Many of the same musicians who played to the tune of power also orchestrated its resistance.

BACKLASH

Although the dialectic dance between colonists and the colonized would come to a head in 1810, colonial patterns of rule lasted for three long centuries. In other words, hegemonic assimilation, accommodation, and repression worked more often than not.

Colonial disciplines of incorporation and repression are well illustrated in the life of Sor Juana Inés de la Cruz. Sor Juana, a child genius born out of wedlock, was largely self-taught in terms of musical training. She gained her training in music theory through reading the work of European musicologists (Pulido Silva 1983:121). She and her sisters at the relatively liberal Convent of Santa Paula practiced the musical arts daily and led ritual performances. Because men were not allowed in the convents, choir directorships and other musical positions there were held by women. The convent was the only institution where such female leadership was allowed.

Sor Juana advocated liberal education for women and demonstrated with her very being that women could be as accomplished in the arts and sciences as men or more so. Typically, women were not provided with a formal education, and certainly not with training in the critical arts and sciences. Manifesting a concern for female education, Queen Isabel had personally requested that a team of female instructors be sent to educate indigenous girls in the domestic arts and Christian doctrine (Turrent 1996:126). However, female training was not to exceed those limited boundaries. Similarly, institutions developed in the eighteenth century that provided training in domestic skills and music, but only with the aim of making young women "more attractive as wives and virtuous women in the society" (Estrada 1973:57). There was a strict gender dichotomy, and neither sex was to violate the rigid cultural boundary separating masculine and feminine identities and domains. For the colonial Spanish, just as for the Mexica before them, the greatest insult one could hurl at a male opponent was to compare him to a woman (Robertson 1988:22).

This image of womanhood was too powerful to overcome, even for a person as talented and intelligent as Sor Juana. Her many friends and allies, including scholars like Carlos Sigüenza y Góngora, theologians, clergy, and viceroyalty, were ultimately too weak to contest these ideas and the machinations of one particularly dedicated misogynist, Archbishop Francisco Aguiar y Seixas. As a result, Sor Juana paid a high price for her challenges to the church hierarchy. She was literally silenced, having gone beyond the parameters of permissible discourse for a woman in that place and time. After her final rebuke, Sor Juana ceased writing poetry and song and instead dedicated herself to a suicidal form of nursing, working around the clock with plague victims.

THE END OF PARADISE

The paradise that de Gante and others imagined for the New World never came to be. The result was colonial dystopia rather than Christian utopia. Many of the indigenous people who did not fall to European steel or disease eventually succumbed in the encomiendas, mines, or other exploitative Spanish enterprises. Resistance was difficult to impossible for those first generations of conquest.

Even in key moments of colonial rebellion, resistance was largely contained. As noted above, food rioters in 1692 were halted merely by the symbol of the Eucharist. It is hard to imagine a better example of ritual hegemony. The downtrodden were made to share the basic cosmological premises and symbols of power. Therefore, even resistance took place within that idiom. By the last decades of the colonial regime, however, the ideological system was showing its age, and new possibilities were being imagined.

That breakdown in social control is well represented in the music of the era. While the criollos collected in covert meetings to discuss Enlightenment ideals, the lower classes gathered to perform forbidden dances and sing illegal tunes. People had been using song lyrics to get around official forms of censorship since the time of Cortés (Schmidt 1988:302). The songs of Bourbon-era New Spain elevated musical subversion to an art form. The "Chuchumbé," the most famous of these subversive songs, starts as follows (Rivera Ayala 1994:31):

En la esquina está parado	A Mercedarian monk
un fraile de la Merced	Is standing in the corner
con los hábitos alzados	Lifting his habit,
conseñando el chuchumbé.	Showing the Chuchumbé.

Another song, the "Tirana," continues that same theme (Rivera Ayala 1994:34):

En San Juan de Dios de acá	In San Juan de Dios over here
son los legos tan cochinos	The lay brothers are such pigs
que cogen a las mujeres	They grab the women
y les tocan los tocinos.	And grope their bacon.

Diverse crowds gathered in the urban markets and *pulquerías* (bars) of Mexico City to dance and sing these lewd songs. They heaped contempt on the colonial clergy, administrators, and merchants who had enriched themselves at their expense. These elites, in turn, considered the masses immoral by definition. The number of people in liminal categories (e.g., vagabundos and mestizos) grew throughout the colonial period, undermining the colonial order.

Condemned to hell by aristocrats, the masses of Mexico City simply appropriated the concept for their own. In his study of the lewd songs of late New Spain, Sergio Rivera Ayala explains that the street denizens "repossessed the concept of 'hell' from the official discourse in order to make it their own 'Holy Land,' a place where they could deliberately violate the norms of behavior" (1994:35). This work was accomplished in profane songs like "El pan de manteca" and "Pan de jarabe," tunes associated with an outlaw dance style. That same style would become the official national dance after the Revolution for Independence (Mendoza 1953:16). Another dance style, the waltz, became associated with France and, by extension, libertine philosophies (Stevenson 1964:2). People danced and sang these ritual songs as a direct challenge to both church and state.

These and many other songs and dances, preserved partly thanks to the Inquisition that censored them, demonstrate the extent to which covert parodies of earlier decades had developed into an overt assault by the end of the eighteenth century. "The word of God," explains Rivera Ayala, "was transformed into the word of the people" (1994:44). Whereas the Eucharist alone could stop a riot a century before, the symbolic infrastructure of sacred power was rapidly crumbling by the turn of the nineteenth century.

In addition to the Bourbon reforms, growing inequities between classes, and the rising expectations of a multiracial underclass, there were other reasons for the musical decadence of the eighteenth century. Samuel Claro notes that these included a shortage of musical training programs in the late colonial era, discrimination against native-born musicians, and an imposition of rigid European styles and methods at the expense of musical forms created in the New World (1970:12). Music and musicians, therefore, experienced the Bourbon backlash in very direct ways. With no official channel for training and expression, musical innovators were forced to work outside the walls of the cathedral, convent, and other ritually sanctioned spaces.

The colonial order, having been largely predicated on religious legitimation, also had to contest increasing secularization. Secular musical theater and opera started to take root in urban Mexico during the latter part of the eighteenth century. The first opera known to have been performed in the New World was written by a composer born and trained in New Spain, Manuel de Sumaya (or Zumaya in anglicized spelling; ca. 1678–1756). Like most musicians of his time, Zumaya received his training as a choirboy (Catalyne 1976:101). He was trained under the tutelage of Joseph de Agurto y Loaysas, a composer who, in his early days, had worked with Sor Juana Inés de la Cruz (1976:101–102).

Zumaya would no doubt gain a complete grounding in the Spanish trends of the day, including plainsong and polyphony, counterpoint and composition. He applied these lessons in the creation of innovative theatrical compositions, including entertaining autos performed on the streets, in the court, and in the church. Such autos were accompanied by and interspersed with various musical entertainments and invocations, much as would be the case for the *zarzuelas* (stage shows) of nineteenth-century Mexico and the *carpas* (tent shows) of the twentieth century. Musical interludes of the sort composed by Zumaya were "the only original contributions to stage music of the time" (Behague 1979:61). Such interludes were increasingly secular in nature. These secular interludes grew in size and proportion, eventually replacing the religious autos altogether.

Given his love for musical theater, Zumaya naturally took to the Neopolitan opera and borrowed a great deal from it. The musical influence of Italy would grow steadily from that point in Mexico, reaching its climax during the nineteenth century (Behague 1979:60). During Zumaya's day, the late colonial period, such operatic works required the backing of rich merchants and landowners. These "wealthy patrons assured performances that were appropriately sumptuous and festive" (Catalyne 1976:112). The secular bourgeoisie, which was mainly criollo, was slowly on the rise during the eighteenth century. Many of the criollo rich demonstrated their disdain for the gachupines by conspicuously favoring the arts and philosophies of other nations, including Italy, France, and the United States.

The colony's contradictions eventually proved too much for the declining empire to control. Wealthy and middle-class criollos rebelled, drawing upon the energy of the marginalized mestizo and indigenous masses. Naturally, the political transformation had revolutionary consequences in the ritual arena as well. Religious musical ritual would go the way of religion itself—certainly not lost, but no longer central to the maintenance and ideological legitimation of power. Although the church would rise up to contest the secular state on several more occasions in succeeding centuries—including the disastrous Cristero War (1926–1929)—after 1821 those in power would turn to secular music and ritual for ideological support.

5 Colonial Resonance

The traces of New Spain remain in Mexico City. Despite two centuries of earthquakes, revolutions, secularization, and modernization, the capital's culture and architecture still provide evidence of Mexico's colonial past.

For example, the ideological center of the colony, Catholicism, continues to dominate the religious world of Mexico. Nearly five hundred years since Cortés read the Requirement, demanding all Mesoamericans to accept the Catholic faith, Mexico is still an overwhelmingly Catholic nation.

Likewise, vestiges of the colonial caste system remain. Although Mexico has redefined itself as a mestizo nation, caste-like distinctions continue to thrive. To outsiders, treatment of mestizo and indigenous domestic, service, and factory workers by the mostly white Mexican elites often appears, for lack of a better term, "colonial." In fact, it is this extreme social inequality and caste-like control that makes Mexico so attractive to international investors. Foreign companies can get away with paying a pittance for labor that would cost a great deal more in their home countries.

Mexican history is as much a story of accretion as of revolution. A European empire was imposed on a Mesoamerican core. That empire forged a colonial society that, in turn, has been subsumed by a secular postcolonial state. The church that was central to colonial life and power has likewise receded from the center. No longer is power legitimated by religious principles. Yet religion remains an essential part of Mexican culture. The resonance of both religious and secular rituals can still be heard throughout Mexico City, taking on complex new meanings as their echoes blend into a modern cacophony.

THE MUSICAL MASS

The Metropolitan Cathedral still towers over the zócalo. Inside, parishioners can hear music written during the days of New Spain, including the works of cathedral musicians like Hernando Franco, Francisco López y Capillas, and Manuel de Zumaya (Catalyne 1976; Stevenson 1979b; and Barwick 1994). The power of the colony resonates inside the giant edifice, carried to the creaking rafters on the voices of dedicated choristers, embodied in revered statuary, and lovingly performed in every major and minor Mass.

A very special Mass took place in January 1998. The archbishop of Mexico City, Norberto Rivera, was named a cardinal, the second highest honor possible for a Catholic cleric. The celebratory rite took place in the Metropolitan Cathedral. Twelve prelates officiated alongside the soon-to-be cardinal. That number was surely not accidental.

Rivera and his elevated acolytes entered to the tune of a colonial-era string ensemble. The processional made its way slowly up the center aisle of the middle sanctuary. An acolyte walked before the archbishop, waving an incense burner. How easy it must have been to translate that practice to the Mexica, whose rituals also involved *incensarios* of all shapes and sizes, from small household vessels burning copal to Tlaloc's giant braziers burning a smelly petroleum-based fuel. As was true in the Great Temple, the unusual odor of incense signals to parishioners that the cathedral space is sacred and that what happens there is not only of this earth.

Rivera blessed the parishioners as he passed by, making the sign of the cross. The faithful reciprocated, crossing themselves as if to complete a spiritual circuit. Ostensibly about faith and other abstract mysteries, this ritual was also very much about magic. The parishioners hoped to gain something via proximity to this living saint. "He touched me!" said a middle-aged woman to her aging mother. There is an extremely tactile and visceral dimension to spiritual practice in Mexico — much more so than in the United States, where even Catholicism has been colored by the ascetic influence of Protestantism.

Rivera received heartfelt congratulations as he made his way up the aisle. Many of the women cried, and more than one touched his robes as he passed by. The same parishioners would scramble up the aisle the moment the call for communion went out. They were determined to take the Host directly from the archbishop, a man only twice removed from God.

The Mexican Catholic Church is extremely tactile, something very different from the ascetically surrounded Catholicism I grew up with in rural Iowa, where ritual and its sensory dimensions are reduced and simplified in order to fit into a mostly Protestant culture. For example, even though I was an acolyte for most of my childhood, I only remember using incense a few times during Mass. All ritual dimensions were diminished so as not to offend midwestern sensibilities. Conversely, the Mexican Mass is a rich bath of sight, sound, smell, and touch. The spare sign of the cross practiced in the midwestern United States becomes much more ornate in Mexico. The signer often touches his or her lips and perhaps even the chin, nose, and forehead. So, too, the scant "Peace be with you" handshakes of Iowa pale in comparison to the long embraces in the Mexican church. At this Mass, each of the twelve embraced Rivera, as if to transfer his mana to their own congregations. Touch is crucial.

At the end of the Mass, the members of the congregation burst into applause for their new cardinal. The exit processional was greeted with cheers, handshakes, and hugs. There was a palpable sense of rapture in the ancient sanctuary. Millions have been spent to lift the giant cathedral out of the sands of ancient Lake Texcoco, a task symbolized by a huge, silver plumb bob hanging down from the ceiling. Rivera's ascension has done even more to lift the spirits of the congregation. The parishioners reached over each other to make physical connection with him, hoping to take home his blessing. For them, such a blessing is a physical reality, not an abstract spirit. Yolia, the animating force of the Aztec, was similarly conceived, considered every bit as real as the organ it resided in, the heart (McKeever Furst 1995:10–70).

From the Mexican parishioners' perspective, one must use all of the senses, including touch, to feel the profound truth of the Christian spirit. This is embodied in the cathedral's most famous artifact, the "Christ of the Poison." The statue is given its own sanctuary in the front, where the most popular Masses are conducted. Its story is as follows.

Every day a devout priest came to pray at the statue, a dark image of the Messiah somewhat resembling the smaller "Black Christ" of Esquipulas, Guatemala. The faithful priest kissed the statue's feet every day before beginning to pray. One day the priest's rival decided to kill him by placing poison on the statue. The would-be murderer crouched in the background, waiting for his victim. The priest arrived at the usual hour, knelt, performed the sign of the cross, and leaned forward to kiss the statue's feet. The Christ figure drew his limbs upward along the cross, however, away from his faithful servant. The priest was saved by the statue's miraculous animation. Today people come from all over Mexico to see and touch the Christ of the Poison, which remains in its flexed position.

The Yopico Temple stood on the same spot five hundred years ago, facing the Templo Mayor. The Yopico priests honored Xipe Tótec, the "Flayed God," whose body, like Christ's, was mutilated for humanity's sake. Instead of robes, the Yopico priests wore stretched skins of sacrificed people. They wore their "golden capes" in reverence for the interconnected web of nature, agriculture, and human life (Markman and Markman 1992:205). Clearly, that ritual act was very different from those that occur today at the cathedral. Nonetheless, all of the rituals taking place in that sacred space over the last seven hundred years have shared a basic goal: transferring the blessing of an imagined world (Omeyocan and heaven) to the earthly realm. Ritual is the sacred intersection where that magic happens.

The cathedral is therefore a physical interface between heaven and earth. The Masses dedicated there help substantiate faith, making heaven seem real and realizable. Many parishioners referred to Rivera as a great spiritual leader, and one even called him a "saint." The word "chosen" was used repeatedly. The ascension of this living saint into the Vatican hierarchy provided evidence that their own faith would one day be rewarded.

Colonial Resonance

Such ritual reminders of redemption are needed by the faithful and sought after with great fervor. I was reminded of that when an image of the Virgin appeared in the Mexico City subway one day, bringing thousands of worshipers to look upon her. I saw her too. In fact, I was exiting the station not long after the Virgin Mother was first discovered. What looked to me like a large water stain became for the faithful incontrovertible evidence of her existence and all that she implies. Even amidst the sweat, smells, boredom, theft, and occasional violence of the Mexico City underground, the Mother of God is there, watching and waiting to bring all believers to their eventual reward.

I have to fight my temptation simply to reduce the Mass, the subway Virgin, and other religious events and beliefs to cultural "phenomena." I "believe" that these are systemic, ritual outlets for the frustrations of the poor, the sigh of the oppressed. Such an analysis is incomplete, however, and fails to explain the resistant dimensions of religion. For example, on the day of the Mexico City Mass, the bishop of San Cristóbal de las Casas, Chiapas, Samuel Ruiz, was officiating at a very different sort of Mass. The famous liberation theologian was blessing 1,500 Zapatista faithful embarking upon a political pilgrimage to Mexico City. Other believers were at that same moment demonstrating in Ocosingo, and others still were reclaiming a sacred Mayan site in Toniná. For them, religion is not a sigh but a shout of defiance. Religion is polysemic; it can repress or liberate, deflect or confront, hinder or assist the efforts of those who would like to undo the conditions of their oppression. It depends on the relationship of the rite to power and the context in which it is performed. Today the Metropolitan Cathedral sits in the shadow of power.

Clearly, the religious soul of Mexico is the Basilica of Our Lady of Guadalupe, on the edge of Mexico City, the site where Juan Diego first saw the apparition of the La Virgen de Guadalupe. The popularity of the "Patroness and Protector" of New Spain and later Mexico has grown with each century. Her witness, Juan Diego, was granted sainthood in 2002. Cardinal Rivera was a leader in the campaign to confer sainthood on the Mexican icon.

The most elaborate traditional Masses take place in the basilica, while snake healers and vendors hold court outside the church. The original cloak of Juan Diego, emblazoned with its miraculous apparition, hangs above the central altar of the basilica (naturally, the authenticity of the artifact is hotly disputed). To get closer, one waits in a line behind the altar to ride on a conveyor belt passing slowly beneath the sacred image. Millions visit the site each year to see the cloak, their faith greatly strengthened by the sight. It is a dramatic confirmation of a faith that was once completely foreign but is now deeply Mexican. The cult of Guadalupe is also one of the most enduring legacies of the colonial era.

POPULAR RELIGION

The unequal negotiation between Spain and Mesoamerica, the church and the indigenous people, was not simply resolved via syncretism. Much of popular religious sentiment was forced out of the church, starting with the Council of Trent's decision to ban unsanctioned instruments and practices. The popular religion still lives largely outside of the walls of the official church.

The popular religion is creative and varied. Whereas the modern imagination wistfully thinks of tradition as unchanging, conservative, and lacking in creative potential, nothing could be further from the truth. For example, rural villages have demonstrated incredible creativity in developing idiosyncratic rituals and continue to alter them as their social realities change. One example is the Misa Tepozteca (Tepoztecan Mass) in Tepoztlán, Morelos. That Mass incorporates local elements, featuring instruments that the town happened to have on hand when the ritual was developed, including a cow horn (first used to signal Zapatista troops during the 1910 Revolution), chirimía, guitars, and flutes based on prehispanic models. Like many local Masses around Latin America, the Misa Tepozteca constitutes a meeting place between the official liturgy and regional traditions (Leclerc 1966).

Despite such linkage between the official liturgy and local practices, there is nevertheless a clear segregation between the two. More solemn ceremonies tend to take place within the cathedrals, basilicas, and churches of the cities, whereas the more raucous rituals take place on rural streets. The revelers banished by the Council of Trent have continued their carnival in the streets and squares of Mexican towns and cities. In the official church, the purpose of music is to provide solemn support for the message of the Mass. Conversely, vibrant music and dance are central to the popular celebrations, the goal of which is not sober contemplation but rather spiritual transcendence through complete corporeal involvement. The urban parishioners sit, stand, and genuflect, a controlled and limited set of movements disciplined and directed by the officiating priest. In contrast, popular celebrants dance and sing, directed by communal tradition but much less controlled by the censoring force of the church.

Nevertheless, the official church now tends to support, rather than thwart, popular religion and ritual practices. Things have come full circle. The early colonial church inspired and even encouraged the growth of the popular religion via the work of missionaries like de Gante, only to clamp down on it by the mid-sixteenth century. Today the legacy of the colony lives on in the popular religion. Alabados (songs of praise brought by the Spanish and then remade by the locals) are still sung throughout Greater Mexico, including New Mexico, where the alabado thrives today (Stark 1983:117). Similarly, colonial villancicos gave rise to *las mañanitas*, still sung at birthday parties throughout Mexico.

Many of the practices mandated by the Spanish Crown and church remain integral elements of the cultural fabric. For example, the Spanish once required tithing of money and labor in order to build and maintain churches. *Cofradías*, local religious groups dedicated to continuing the religious ritual cycle, were officially enforced during the colonial period. They took on other functions, however, when the church barred indigenous leaders from becoming priests (Turrent 1996:192). Locked out of the official hierarchy, indigenous men took on cofradía leadership roles. Cofradías became a parallel religious infrastructure, influenced by but not synonymous with official Catholicism. Originally imposed as a foreign organizational structure, the cofradías became an integral part of popular religious life.

As a legacy of the popular religion founded during the colonial era, many small villages still spend an incredible percentage of their local income on religious fiestas (Turrent 1996:132). Whereas the Protestant capitalist, ascetic world sees such spending as wasteful, rural Catholics see this as a moral exigency. Such practices serve as social leveling mechanisms, distributing wealth and poverty more equally among the community. Whereas the traditional Protestant shows his or her *individual* worth and worthiness to enter heaven via frugality, traditional Catholics demonstrate their *communal* worth by collaboratively honoring God, the Virgin, and the saints with ostentatious ritual displays. In Mesoamerica, the debtor relationship between humanity and heaven is no longer paid in blood but rather through expenditures of money, labor, and musical energy.

SECULAR RESONANCE

New Spain: 1521–1821

New Spain also left a secular legacy. One of the hallmarks of colonial music was its extreme emphasis on voice. More people could be organized into choirs than into instrumental ensembles. The choir was an excellent disciplinary device, as it still is today throughout the Western world. The choir became a means of instilling colonial discipline and was therefore an essential element of colonial education.

That tradition lives on. There is a rich, living choral tradition in the capital. This is evident in events like the Choral Saturdays of the National Institute of Fine Arts (INBA). On December 2, 2000, I attended one of these fine concerts. The Child Singers of Tepotzotlán were singing that day, a choir created to "recuperate the choral tradition that existed in the viceregal period, formed by indigenous children" (concert bill). Tepotzotlán, the home of the choir, is not to be mistaken for Tepoztlán, the site of the Misa Tepozteca described above. Tepotzotlán is a suburb on the far northern edge of the Mexico City. A beautiful exconvent there has been converted into the National Museum of the Viceroyalty. The Child Singers of Tepotzotlán are associated with that magnificent institution. The choir was founded with explicit pedagogical goals in mind: to create a sense of "duty, punctuality, diligence, and the ability to work as a group" (concert bill).

The concert began on a somber note. The day before had been the Cambio de Poder (Change of Power) celebration; for the first time since the Revolution, a regime other than the Partido Revolucionario Institucional (PRI) was in power. That new regime was even more dedicated to neoliberal principles than the last. Therefore, public arts organizations feared a reduction in state support.

President Vicente Fox claimed that he was dedicated to reinforcing education, and musical education in particular, but the pedagogical arts community was nervous. "Despite changes in power," explained the event organizer, "we artists will always go on." Later he again referred to impending "changes," gesturing to the crowd and adding, "All of you teachers know how that is." Many of the adults in attendance nodded vigorously. A good portion of the audience was composed of music instructors from local schools.

The concert felt very much like a pedagogical exercise. Neither the children nor the audience seemed particularly inspired, although their talent was clear. Much of the concert seemed to contrast with the many professional concerts that I witnessed around town. A lot of that had to do with the audience, equal parts music instructors and family members. There is always at least a somewhat perfunctory air to the "school concert," wherever it is held.

In the back was an imposing set of teenagers, obviously there to fulfill a school assignment. They talked and took notes throughout the concert, clearly uninterested and uninspired by the music. There was one transcendent moment, however, when everyone listened with rapt attention. A little girl with a big voice sang Andrew Lloyd Webber's "Requiem." As she stared up at the ex-chapel's decaying ceiling, the concertgoers all watched and listened to every note.

The piece seemed dear to the hearts of the singers and their director alike. Earlier, when walking around the abandoned church, I saw the director drilling his young choir, rehearsing the "Requiem" with great care. This was clearly their signature piece. When they and their prize soloist sang it near the end of the performance, the distracting and distracted youths in the back suddenly stopped whispering, put down their notebooks, and listened. One of the rudest young men rose from behind a pillar and looked over the heads of the teachers, awed by the young girl who performed the solo. In a city with such an incredible home-grown musical repertoire, I found it odd that this popular piece would inspire such a reverential performance. Upon reflection, however, it made sense. Webber's work is itself a hybrid of the popular and classical, a creative integration quite fitting with the Mexican tradition. *Sones*, mariachis, boleros, and many of the most important musical forms in Mexico are likewise classical-pop hybrids. Furthermore, Webber's work is very melodic and romantic, defining features of Mexican popular music. The concert was also a reminder that, while some musicologists might labor to differentiate between local and foreign forms, musicians and audiences tend not to make such distinctions. For better or for worse, Webber produces music with global appeal.

A distinctly different sort of pedagogical exercise took place on a sunny mid-January weekend in 2002: a concert by Dúo Villey-Hinojosa. Tenor Carlos A. Hinojosa Franco and guitarist Isabelle Villey have performed together since 1974. Both teach and conduct research as faculty in the National Institute of Fine Arts (INBA). A small crowd gathered in the city center to learn about and listen to the duo's delightful renditions of secular music from the colonial era. Hinojosa introduced each song by providing historical and cultural background. He would then sing in theatrical fashion, when the song so warranted.

Many of the pieces, as Hinojosa pointed out, were theatrical in derivation. He noted that such songs were often played during *oratorios*, secular fiestas disguised as religious prayer sessions. When church or state officials came around, revelers would break into prayer, as if that were their purpose all along. "People would stop dancing and singing," explained Hinojosa, "and start praying." Such parties were similar to the later *jamaicas*, supposed charity events designed to provide cover for

Dúo Villey-Hinojosa. Photo by author.

bacchanalia. "These events were simply parties," explains historian Juan Pedro Viquiera Albán, "in which the principal entertainments were 'scandalous' and 'sacrilegious' dances such as: 'La llorona' (The Weeping Woman), 'El rubí' (The Ruby), 'El pan de manteca' (Shortening bread), or 'El pan de jarabe' (Syrup bread)," among many others (1999:123–127).

The Dúo Villey-Hinojosa illustrated the similar and in some cases identical melodies shared by colonial pieces and later folk *sones*. For example, the folksong "La lloroncita" takes its melody directly from "Los ympossibles," a song thought to have been written by colonial composer Santiago de Murcia. The audience marveled at the clear connections that Hinojosa Franco drew between the early colonial music and later Mexican folksongs.

Villey provided accompaniment on a vihuela with five double strings, wooden pegs, and baroque embellishments. Noting the small audience, Hinojosa stated, "It is sad that Mexicans don't take more interest in their history and culture." However, the audience made up for its diminished size with enthusiasm. Hardly a single adult left the venue without purchasing one of the duo's excellent recordings. Dúo Villey-Hinojosa's performance is a ritual of cultural preservation in the best sense. They are keeping alive a style of music and a musical history that might literally be lost if not for their efforts. Ironically, what was once popular is now preserved under the careful stewardship of classical musicians and musicologists.

THE GUELAGUETZA, FROM COLONY TO COMMODITY

Finally, no discussion of colonial resonance is complete without mention of the Guelaguetza. Although it occurs in Oaxaca and not in Mexico City, it is an obligatory reference in any book involving musical ritual. The Guelaguetza, which takes place on the two Mondays following July 16, originated in the colonial era. It is a celebration bringing together indigenous dancers and local villagers from throughout the region. The people of the Oaxaca area had long celebrated a fiesta to curry favor with Centéotl, Goddess of the Tender Corn. During that festival, offerings of food and goods were made to the goddess. The Carmelites renewed the Guelaguetza tradition in the colonial era, after locating a church on the same hill where the precortesian celebration traditionally took place. The ritual was revived in the 1930s as a way to bring tourists to Oaxaca.

The Guelaguetza is an incredible spectacle. Participating villages rehearse year-round and attempt to outdo each other with more dramatic dress, music, dance, and offerings than their rivals. Despite claims to the contrary, however, the Guelaguetza is far from an egalitarian community affair. Ticket costs exclude the great majority of the locals. Foreign tourists and middle-class Mexicans sit in the most expensive seats and thus receive the majority of the offerings cast out into the audience. The year I attended (1997), President Ernesto Zedillo occupied the center seat. Like a colonial viceroy, the great *patrón* graciously received a range of symbolic gifts from the village dancers, including baskets of fruit and live poultry.

There are even more powerful sponsors involved in the ritual spectacle. As my friends and I entered the grounds, a group of women handed out Coca-Cola hats. Walking back down the hill, after the Guelaguetza was over, beautiful young women wearing indigenous dress with "AT&T" sashes handed out informational brochures. The U.S. conglomerate had just been allowed into the Mexican market and was now openly competing with TELMEX (Teléfonos de México), the Mexican phone company. TELMEX, in turn, issued calling cards imprinted with pictures of pretty young Guelaguetza dancers. The old religions have given way to new faiths and practices, including commodity fetishism. That system is no less magical, with a machinery of the imagination able to transform large corporations like Coca-Cola and AT&T into cultural sponsors, symbolically reencoded in the personable figures of young indigenous women. Cultural capital can be bought.

New Spain: 1521–1821

The Guelaguetza serves as a reminder that ritual is never simply a referential echo of the past. The ritual past is transfigured to meet the cultural needs of the present and, in particular, the needs of ruling institutions. In this case, ritual magically mediates our relationship with large corporate networks, empowering them in the process.

RITUALS OF RESISTANCE

Capitalism, like colonialism before it, is more than ritual spectacle. It is a system of production predicated on the exploitation of many for the enrichment of a relative few (individuals, classes, and nations). Like the colonial system, therefore, the capitalist system will continue to engender significant dissent. This is particularly true for nations, like Mexico, where capitalism's advantages are the least evident.

Although most resistance to capitalism draws on modernist notions like anarchism and socialism, precapitalist—even colonial—concepts are also occasionally invoked. An excellent example was offered during "March for Peace in Chiapas" in Mexico City (Saturday, January 24, 1998). A musical group performed "El chuchumbé" at the zócalo, the culminating point for the march. The lead vocalist, intent on instructing as well as entertaining the protesters, explained that "El chuchumbé" was "banned by the Inquisition in the year 1766." There is "still an Inquisition in Chiapas," he continued. "Thus the struggle began and nobody is going to stop it," he added later, using "El chuchumbé" as an example of what can happen when people organize to oppose a colonizing force. He finished the set with the chant "¡Zapata vive!" to which the crowd responded, "¡Y la lucha sigue!" (Zapata lives . . . and the struggle continues).

Later that day President Zedillo restated his support for accords signed earlier between the PRI government and the Zapatistas, a grudging admission that his administration had not lived up to its obligations. He agreed that the accords needed to be reworked in the interests of peace, another positive nod to the protesters. Two hundred years after its birth, "El chuchumbé" was again sung with a sense of rebellious confidence.

Rock band Café Tacuba's "Madrugal" is another example of the political potential of colonial music and ritual. It is a beautiful piece of guitar music laced with harmonic vocal lines, but the words clash with the heavenly madrigal music. The song ends as the "cathedral disappears amidst smog and pigeon shit." The piece demonstrates an ironic antipathy for the symbols of the colonial city and culture, and even greater antipathy for the ravages of the modern present. However, composer Emmanuel Rangel's piece also demonstrates that the colony continues to live. Like the disappearing cathedral, the ghost of New Spain is still evident, if only in faint outlines and echoes.

PART

III The New Nation: 1821–1910

The First Century of Independence: 1821–1910

The Revolution for Independence shattered the "Octavian Peace" that controlled Mexico for three centuries. In the wake of the Spaniards' retreat, various internal and external forces fought to decide what form the new nation would take.

Spanish withdrawal had several musical repercussions. A marked decline in instrument-making took place in the nineteenth century (Guzmán Bravo 1978:355). Independence also created a severe decline in employment for Mexican musicians and a drop in their social status (Moreno Rivas 1989:29). Musicians played an indispensable role in the colonial social order. After independence, they were demoted in social rank, even stigmatized.

There was no musical post in colonial Mexico as important as that of the colonial cathedral chapelmaster. Men like Hernando Franco, Antonio de Salazar, Manuel Zumaya, and Ignacio Jerusalem not only oversaw hundreds of musicians but also served as composers, choir directors, instructors, and interpreters (Mora and Ramírez 1985:13). With the dissolution of the colony, even these vaunted musicians found themselves without adequate funding and power to fulfill their duties as musical organizers and leaders. With support from neither church nor state, most professional musicians began leading a more hand-to-mouth existence, looking for piecework rather than enjoying the constant and full backing that their colonial patrons had offered.

The end of Spanish hegemony also opened the door for competition from foreign musicians. Austrian Henri Herz, for example, drew upon the popular music of Mexico for his artful compositions. Both Mexican and European audiences applauded the Austrian composer's work (Carmona 1984:45). In fact, Herz took it upon himself to write a national anthem for Mexico.

Arriving in 1848, at the conclusion of the U.S. invasion, Herz found it odd that Mexico lacked an anthem. Attempts to agree upon such a theme had been taking place since the Spanish withdrawal, to no avail. His own attempts were likewise rejected. Many other foreigners entered the contest to choose a Mexican national anthem (Romero 1987:27–33). One of these, ironically a Spaniard, eventually succeeded.

Foreign musicians were able to take advantage of the musical vacuum caused by the fall of the colony. Independent Mexico was beset with social instability and a troubled economy throughout most of the century. The perpetually bankrupt state had little to spare for musical endowments. The church—taxed, divested, and cut off from prior sources of wealth—would likewise be forced to limit its sponsorship of musical activities. Despite the occasional rise of conservative political leaders who favored a larger church role in governance, secularization largely succeeded on the political level. Therefore, those musicians lucky enough to gain state support would need to work in a mostly secular vein.

Unfortunately, there was virtually no secular art music establishment in Mexico. For three hundred years, the church had largely disallowed the establishment of secular institutions. It had a virtual monopoly on the production of art music. Foreign and foreign-trained musicians filled this void.

The foreign invasion of newly independent Mexico was paralleled in other arts. Foreign directors, instructors, styles, and techniques continued to dominate the Academy of San Carlos, Mexico's famed art academy, despite independence. Rather than accelerate or improve domestic art production, the Revolution seems to have had the opposite effect.

The decline of the nation's art community did not begin with the Revolution for Independence, however, but rather during the Bourbon reform era preceding it (Moreno Rivas 1989:56). During late Bourbon rule, a great number of foreign musicians were brought in with the intent of "reviving" the dying musical life of the church (Mora and Ramírez 1985:14). As was true of the Bourbon reforms in general, that policy failed. What resulted instead was a steep decline in the musical arts and artists that would continue throughout the first half of the nineteenth century.

Mexico's art world eventually recovered, as did its musical community. The latter half of the nineteenth century witnessed the birth of new musical forms and exceptional talents, including Juventino Rosas and Felipe Villanueva. Mexican composers eventually gained "a new space" in independent Mexico (Moreno Rivas 1989:64). With the onset of independence, musicians were now "free" to sell their labor to the highest bidder. That individual political liberation would come at a cost, however. In order to get their work heard, it would now often be necessary to find a wealthy patron, whether in the government or in the private sector. The disciplines of conservative Catholicism were slowly giving way to the market-driven disciplines of liberal capitalism.

SEDITIOUS DANCES: THE JARABE AND WALTZ

Whereas the revolutionary transition initially inhibited the development of Mexican art music, it quite clearly benefited popular music and musicians. Genres banned during the late colonial era for seditious content, sexual overtones, and association with the insurgents suddenly became central to the new nation's emerging identity.

Foremost among these newly nationalized dances was the jarabe, including the *járabe tapatío*, a dance that would eventually come to symbolize *mexicanidad* both domestically and internationally. It is now known worldwide as the "Mexican Hat Dance" (Reuter 1981:10). *Tapatío* is the nickname given the people of Guadalajara. The jarabe became popular there during the latter half of the nineteenth century, first as a dance of the elite then eventually filtering down to the lower classes.

In fact, jarabes had been performed under other names at least as early as July 9, 1790. The July 9 performance took place in the Mexico City Coliseum. The viceroy banned all jarabes soon after that early performance. Nevertheless, people continued to gather in public squares and neighborhood fiestas to take part in the illegal dance, flaunting and challenging colonial law. In 1821 people celebrated independence with exuberant fiestas, conspicuously featuring the jarabe. Their freedom was symbolized in the lively dance, itself freed from colonial censorship.

The jarabe quickly spread throughout the country, branching into regional forms. In turn, some of these regional forms became elevated to national status. By the latter half of the nineteenth century, the jarabe tapatío was celebrated not only in Guadalajara but throughout much of Mexico. Emperor Maximilian and Empress Carlota, the Hapsburg conquerors (1862–1867), were said to have been big fans of the jarabe tapatío. It is still considered the "national dance" of Mexico today (Escorza 1990:6).

The jarabe tapatío is about sexual courtship and conquest. The woman, adorned in brightly colored *china poblana* dress, coquettishly avoids and then finally accepts the advances of her dance partner. The china poblana style was first adopted in the city of Puebla, as the name suggests. According to legend, the costume was first worn by a beautiful young woman from India. Impressed, her friends and neighbors in Puebla adopted the colorful dress style, and it spread from there. Incorporated into the jarabe, it has become the national dress of folkloric Mexico. Gabriel Saldívar notes that the dress style itself was most likely derived from Andalucía, Spain (1937:10). Like most things Mexican, however, many cultural influences—Andalusian, Pueblan, Guadalajaran, and perhaps Indian—are represented in the syncretic jarabe tapatío ritual.

Originally, the jarabe was danced by female couples, in order to avoid the wrath of the church. That gave way to mixed couples during the years leading up to the Revolution for Independence, a clear affront to colonial clerics (Saldívar 1937:7). An official edict against the jarabe in 1802 referred to the dance as an affront to "not only Christian, but also civic and natural law" (Escorza 1990:11). Although the jarabes use only metaphoric sexual references—such as courting birds in "The Dove"—the theme of human courtship, conquest, and consummation is fairly obvious. Recognizing its effrontery to the colonial church, the insurgents "took up the prohibited dance as their banner" (Guzmán Bravo 1986:145).

The jarabe is accompanied primarily by stringed instruments, including various types of guitars, the harp, and the violin. Manuel Ponce noted that "the music of our national dance" was designed to serve as "accompaniment for dancers and, definitely, was not designed to be listened to without dance" (in Esparza and Lluhi 1990:30). The dancers tended to be practiced experts (Stanford 1984b:50). Niceto de Zamacois, a Spaniard visiting Mexico, noted that everyone from senators to "the most humble vendor" would become "animated" watching the jarabe (in Escorza 1990:14).

The jarabe emphasizes major tones and simple harmonies. It is a joyful, cathartic ritual. The Dionysian dance strengthened Mexican resolve throughout the country's difficult wars with Spain, the United States, and France (Saldívar 1937:3). Today it is taught in nearly every grade school throughout Mexico. In many minds the jarabe is the consummate Mexican tradition, referencing much more than a nineteenth-century dance alone.

The jarabe was not the only dance ritual to threaten the Crown during the late days of the colony. The waltz gained the same infamy in Mexico City that it had much earlier in Europe. Tlalpan, a suburban area on the outskirts of nineteenth-century Mexico City (now part of the city itself), was known for its ribald waltzes, gambling, drinking, and singing. Spanish clerics abhorred the popular fad and were frustrated that many political leaders, including a viceroy, attended the Tlalpan dances. Although the waltz is of German origin, Spanish conservatives associated it with French libertines (Robles-Cahero 1989:41).

The *ilustrados*, members of the rising European and Mexican bourgeoisie, performed waltzes to challenge the conservative aristocracy. The waltz greatly offended theocratic officials. One Spanish prelate wrote that the waltz was "transporting the maximal corruption of disgraced France" to Mexico (Robles-Cahero 1989:41). José Antonio Robles-Cahero presents an intriguing analysis of Lorenzo Gerrero's 1815 diatribe. Robles-Cahero notes the role of women in the waltz, explaining that "the woman of New Spain had few vehicles to openly perform her erotic passions outside of the dance" (1989:46). In the waltz, however, women were ceded the same rights as men to express desires for "corporal pleasure and passion," which he believes may explain the "success of this famous and controversial dance" (1989:46).

What both the jarabe and waltz demonstrate is that the moral hegemony of the Spanish was definitely weakening in the final decades of the colony. The waltz became part of this culture war just as surely as the more popular jarabe did. The anarchic and carnivalesque spirit represented in the waltz and jarabe may have been almost as important as the strategic organizing of the insurgents. William Gradante notes that those condemning the waltz "might as well have been referring to 'jazz,' 'rock 'n roll,' 'punk,' or any other innovation in the domain of popular music" and adds that "the more vehemently conservative elements protest and resist a novelty the greater is its ultimate impact on society" (1982:38). The more the Spaniards clamped down on seditious ritual, the more popular it became.

SON

Another important musical movement took shape during the final decades of the colony: the *son*. It is best described as a "supergenre" involving three basic elements: (1) a combination of stringed instruments and percussion, (2) "the singing of coplas, rhyming stanzas of four, five, or ten lines that are generally octosyllabic," and (3) "the dancing of one or more couples" (Llerenas et al. 1993:5). The dancing takes the form of *zapateando*, graceful stomping on a wooden surface.

Although the *son* was brought to the New World via Mexico City, it eventually settled in the countryside. The distribution and diversification of the *son* is just one of many examples of an urban-to-rural diffusion of popular culture. The *son* would eventually be reduced to a folkloric curiosity in the city, while catching fire in the countryside.

Sones generally have simple themes and one-or two-word titles referring to a single person, place, or thing, such as "La llorona" (Huasteca), "La india" (Balsas), or "La venadita" (Jalisco). The first literary references to the word go back as far as the sixteenth century, and many coplas of contemporary *sones* go back at least that far.

Most *sones* were anonymously authored. Like the jarabe and prehispanic Mesoamerican music, the *son* refers to an entire ensemble of sound, dance, and literature rather than a musical style alone (Stanford 1984b:10). Like the jarabe, *son* dances often mimic the sexual act, further evidence that these twin styles might be at least partially derived from the same popular root. Gloria Carmona refers to that shared root as *tonadilla escénica* (1984:12).

Sones generally employ the "main harmonic patterns of Western music" and 3/8, 3/4, or 6/8 time. They often employ the *sesquiáltera* arrangement, notes arranged in two groups of three (two triplets in succession) or three groups of two (three half notes in grouped succession) (Stanford 1984b:27). *Sones* are sung almost exclusively by men. Within these general parameters, however, *son conjuntos* (groups) and styles are extremely variable and creative. The simple structure of the song style allows for a great deal of artistic freedom and cultural malleability. Thus the form survived, adapting to new social environments and incorporating changing ideas along the way.

The *sones* also demonstrate the continued role of Mexicans of African descent. Despite a sharp decline in relative numbers, African American musicians continued to exert strong influence. This is particularly evident in the *sones* of the Gulf Coast. *Sones* there are more rhythmically dynamic than noncoastal *sones* and much more Afrocaribbean in tone and texture. Fittingly, "Musician of Veracruz" by Edouard Pingret (1788–1875) features a Mexican musician of African descent playing three different stringed instruments at the same time, a testament to local musicianship (Esparza and Lluhi 1990:25). Clearly, Mexicans of African descent continued as icons of musical creativity and talent throughout the nineteenth century. It is also clear that, while the waltz settled into an upper-class niche, the *son* became Mexico's quintessential popular music style. All musical forms to follow, particularly the mariachi ensemble and *ranchera* song style, would owe a great debt to the *son*.

THE GROWTH OF SECULAR NATIONALISM

The "new liberal ideology" of the triumphant criollo class "would be expressed in grand romantic and patriotic themes" (Moreno Rivas 1989: 72). Revolutionary composers penned nationalistic songs like the following hymn for revolutionary martyr José Antonio Morelos:

Divina Guadalupana	Divine Guadalupe
con esos preciosos dedos	With your precious fingers
échale la bendición	Give your blessing
al señor cura Morelos.	To Father Morelos.

The revolutionaries fought under the banner of the Virgin of Guadalupe, while the gachupines adopted the symbol of the Virgin of Remedies. Therefore, the Revolution of 1810 became known as the "War of the Virgins." As María Herrera-Sobek points out, the Virgin portrayed in Mexican song is not a "frail, subservient, weak-hearted female" but rather a strong and motivating icon (1990:51).

Numerous factions and foreign powers attempted to fill the power vacuum left by Spain's expulsion. As was required for any respectable nineteenth-century army, each contingent featured a marching brass band. Mexican musicians were influenced by a succession of invading ensembles, from U.S. drum and bugle corps to the French foreign legion band. Partly inspired by the brass ensembles marching through their communities, every Mexican town would itself create a small *banda del pueblo* with a unique mix of instruments, whatever the local folk could attain and learn to play. One town's band might consist of a tuba, clarinet, trumpet, and snare, while the neighboring community might boast a conjunto of trombone, coronet, bass drum, and fife. Larger and more standardized brass ensembles formed in the capital.

The "Himno nacional mexicano" was the most important piece of brass-band music composed during the nineteenth century. Jaime Nunó, a Spaniard, composed Mexico's national anthem in 1853, using lyrics written by poet Francisco González Bocanegra. Nunó's anthem took first prize in a set of contests held to choose the national theme.

Nunó was a Spanish-born courtier of dictator Antonio López de Santa Anna. Santa Anna favored Nunó above all other musicians, naming the Spaniard a captain in his army and director of Mexico's military bands. In fact, it appears that he rigged the aforementioned contest in Nunó's favor (Romero 1987:88).

Having become associated with the dictator, Nunó and his theme fell out of favor during the subsequent presidency of liberal Benito Juárez. In fact, even conservatives rejected the hymn. They wanted to resurrect the Henri Herz anthem. Emperor Maximilian and Empress Carlota were said to favor Nunó's hymn, however. One would think such dubious support would have doomed his anthem. Instead, the song slowly gained currency among the populace in the decades between its selection by Santa Anna and later French occupation. Angered by the hymn's resurgence in the years following the end of French intervention, liberal officials denounced Nunó's hymn as the product of a foreigner. They noted that the French usurpers Maximilian and Carlota favored the Spaniard's anthem (Romero 1987:140); but not even Maximilian's support could defeat the song.

Meanwhile, Nunó was long gone. In fact, after the fall of Santa Anna, Nunó moved to Buffalo, New York, where he enjoyed a successful career as a composer, church musician, choral director, and teacher. If it were not for the resurgence of his song, life in Mexico would have been a minor footnote in the Buffalo obituary of Jaime Nunó, an immigrant piano teacher who greatly impressed the local community. Although Nunó felt compelled to flee Mexico, his song refused to leave. Instead, it moved into the lower strata, forging deep roots that could not be undone by any of the liberal, conservative, autocratic, or democratic rulers, no matter how hard they worked to undermine Santa Anna's arbitrary edict.

Despite all attempts to displace the anthem with more acceptable tunes, the song enjoyed overwhelming popularity by the early 1870s (Romero 1987:161). It would even be translated into Nahuatl. Attempts made as late as the 1940s to replace or alter the "Himno nacional" were met with public outrage, until finally the Mexican government wrote an official decree sanctioning Nunó's hymn as the national anthem, regulating its use, and prohibiting its alteration. As a result, this lengthy, dynamic anthem remains the official song of Mexico. Listening to the piece, one understands why Santa Anna and his people preferred it to all others. Whereas many people in the United States would like to replace the "Star-Spangled Banner" with "America the Beautiful" or "This Land Is Your Land" as the national anthem and official proposals to that effect are still floated from time to time, the anthem issue has long been settled in Mexico. It is a wonderful song.

The words of the Mexican national anthem clearly relate to the era in which it was written. From the first line to the last, it is about defending the borders of Mexico against foreign invaders. The hymn asks "Heaven" to "make a soldier of each son" and to stop those enemies who would "profane" the Mexican soil. It speaks of "patriotic banners soaked in waves of blood." The word *guerra* (war) occurs eight times in the anthem, more than any other word except *patria* (fatherland). The next most frequent terms, *sangre* (blood) and *cielo* (heaven), are used twice. It is a proud and rousing song aimed at uniting the Mexican people but also a symbol of the incredible insecurity caused by successive waves of foreign intervention, internal fracturing, and political instability during the nineteenth century.

During the U.S. invasion, for example, Mexico had to deal with not only a united and well-armed enemy but also lack of national unity. Regional *caudillos* refused to support a relatively weak central government. The government's inability to get these *patrias chicas* (little fatherlands) to unite long enough to defend the new nation caused it to fall relatively quickly to Yanqui invaders. The groundswell popularity of the "Himno nacional" may demonstrate that following this period of tragic intervention and internecine violence people were finally ready to consider themselves part of a single sovereign nation. By the latter half of the nineteenth century, there was a growing sense of identification with the "imagined community" of the Mexican nation (Anderson 1991). Spanish, U.S., and French invaders, while taking much from Mexico, at least left behind a unified sense of purpose and strong national identity. These common enemies united independent Mexico.

The Mexican national anthem is a bright and punctuated piece, a classic example of the genre. While the words are expressly Mexican, the music is international. The patriotic march is a hegemonic style, the obligatory formula through which nations musically identify themselves. Rather than choosing their own idiosyncratic musical styles, most nations have instead relied upon Western marching band music, a globally recognizable form. Paradoxically, the world's nations express unique identities through a single musical discourse. Fittingly, Nunó not only crafted Mexico's national anthem but also produced patriotic marches dedicated to his adopted home, the United States (Stevenson 1980a:109).

Despite his exit from Mexico, Nunó's name and fame were resurrected during his absence. This was not brought to the composer's attention until the Panamerican Exposition of 1901, held in Buffalo. The Mexican Army Band played the anthem on the street outside his house as an emotional appeal for Nunó to return to Mexico.

Although Buffalo remained his home, Nunó would make two final tours of Mexico (Romero 1987:166–167). The Spanish American was welcomed everywhere by local bands playing his "Hymn." Fittingly, in 1904 Nunó wrote and performed one more tune for Mexico, a march in honor of dictator Porfirio Díaz (1987:182). Upon his death in 1908, Nunó was at first buried alongside his wife in Buffalo and then reinterred in Mexico City next to González Bocanegra, the poet who wrote the anthem lyrics. Mexican president Manuel Avila Camacho presided over the ceremony.

In addition to leading to the creation of patriotic music, the birth of the Mexican nation also resulted in a profusion of nationalistic art. Foreign interventions and resurgent colonial conservatism encouraged this nationalistic outpouring. Painters began to produce nostalgic Mexica motifs and pastoral landscapes. Although still painted in European styles and techniques, these nineteenth-century artworks indicate a shift toward secular, national themes and away from the religious iconography of the colony. Foremost among these artists were the great landscape painter José María Velasco (1840–1912) and Rodrigo Gutiérrez (1848–1903), José María Jara (1867–1939), Petronilo Monroy (1832–1882), Leandro Izaguirre (1867–1941), and José María Obregón (1832–1902). The last five served as harbingers of the *indigenista* movement that would flourish in the next century. Perhaps the most pioneering painter of the age, however, was Félix Parra (1845–1919), whose critical depictions of the Conquest would have been unthinkable seventy-five years earlier. As opposed to colonial representations of Aztec savagery, Parra's work represents one of the first attempts by a formally trained artist to reinterpret the Conquest critically. A similar move toward secular nationalism took place in nineteenth-century theater, albeit rarely with the level of critical intent and daring shown by the aforementioned artists. Painters have long been the political vanguard in Mexico.

Musically, Mexico's stuttering process of nation building produced not only the "Himno nacional" but also a number of other patriotic tunes. These include lyrical pieces satirizing foreign interventionists and lauding local resistance efforts. For example, during the U.S. War of 1846–1848, a host of nationalistic songs were crafted in support of the resistance. "La pasadita," performed during both the U.S. invasion and later French intervention, describes the acts of foreign men cavorting with Mexican women, thus using the age-old metaphor of female violation to critique territorial intrusion (Schmidt 1988:306–307). The song criticizes both the foreign invaders and the Mexican elite, who are represented as "margaritas" who "speak English," thus equating the local rich to foreign usurpers (Escorza 1990:13).

The still-popular song "Adios Mamá Carlota" satirizes the French intervention in a similar way. The song turns the empress and the entire episode into a joke and point of pride, rather than the humiliating national experience it once was. "During the Reform Era," writes Carmen Sordo Sodi, "the canciones, jarabes, marchas, *sones*, mañanitas, and danzas very effectively contributed to the belittling of the invader and the empire and were a decisive factor for union and [national] identification" (1982:309).

Attempts were also made to enhance musical education in nineteenth-century Mexico. The Mexican Philharmonic Society was founded in 1866, an institution that laid the groundwork for the National Conservatory of Music, founded in 1877 (Behague 1979:97). For most of its early life, the conservatory was directed by musicians from Europe, further evidence that musical production lagged during the first century of Mexican independence. From the outset the conservatory had a uniquely progressive mission, however: to "provide honest distraction to the working classes of our society" (Carmona 1984:97). The postrevolutionary indigenista classicists of the twentieth century were not the first socially progressive and culturally didactic musicians of Mexico.

Most musical training was aimed at young men during the first century of the conservatory. While foreign opera divas thrilled local audiences, local women were still rarely allowed formal training. For nineteenth-century women, the practice of music was "mere adornment" (Carmona 1984:50).

The same gender inequity held true in the working classes. Mirroring the high-culture world, most popular music was played and sung by men of the urban working classes and rural peasantry alike. Among the remarkable exceptions were a few zarzuela singers and Angela Peralta, a Mexican singer who took both Europe and the United States by storm (Carmona 1984:87–110). Along with Nunó and Bocanegra, Peralta would become one of a small ensemble of musicians buried in the Rotunda of Illustrious Men.

Musical development for women was almost nonexistent. Yet even nineteenth-century men had relatively few opportunities for formal musical education and support. Every time social and political stability was achieved, often at the expense of basic freedoms, another political intervention, revolution, or coup would take place. For example, the triumph of Republicans over the French interventionists — a very welcome social development — caused somewhat of an artistic "recession" in the bankrupt nation (Carmona 1984:113). Ignacio Altamirano complained that even the most "eminent musician" of the era, no matter "how great his knowledge of harmony," was forced to earn a living by giving piano lessons (in Carmona 1984:118).

Altamirano's statement demonstrates not only the extent to which

Mexican musicians were struggling during the period but also the postcolonial bifurcation of music into performance vs. pedagogical tracks. Whereas colonial musicians viewed pedagogy and performance as virtually the same integrated practice—as had the Mexica before them—the nineteenth-century secular, liberal era would witness greater specialization and bureaucratization. Pure performance had become the desired avenue, while pedagogy became its poor stepchild.

This division of labor had everything to do with emerging class divisions. Professional art music performers began to provide essential cultural capital to the upper classes sponsoring them and were thus duly rewarded, while musical pedagogy became a middle-class profession. The classical concert was, and is, nothing if not a ritual of class distinction. Viewed from a colonial perspective, Altamirano's lament would have been incomprehensible. Providing music lessons was a priority for the colonial musician, no matter how vaunted his or her post. Given the relative stigma attached to piano pedagogy during the nineteenth century, however, it is remarkable that even the best musicians of the era were forced to become private piano teachers.

Due to the general lack of support for musicians, late nineteenth century musicians and composers needed to become extreme generalists. Juventino Rosas was one such man. He not only composed the world-famous piece "Over the Waves" but also created nationalistic marches like "Cuauhtemóc," presaging the indigenista movement. Rosas wrote and published salón pieces, light musical diversions for the urban middle and upper classes of Porfirian Mexico. Among these were some of the earliest published Mexican *danzones*.

Another great musician of the era, Felipe Villanueva, composed a number of well-received comic operas, waltzes, *danzas*, and mazurkas for piano. As a show of patriotism, Villanueva even dedicated a song to liberal leader Benito Juárez (Carredano 1992:73). Despite their proto-indigenista patriotism, Rosas, Villanueva, and other musicians of the late nineteenth century were still working almost exclusively in the European vernacular. The hegemony of European music was so strong during this epoch that even resistance tended to take place through foreign modes of expression. For example, in the National Conservatory a battle for control took place between the more conservative "Italians" who dominated the institution and the modernist "Group of Six," dubbed the "French," due to their musical interests. While championing their own work, the Group of Six, including Villanueva, favored the work of French, German, and Russian composers (Carredano 1992:61). Villanueva, as piano instructor, insisted that every student study Johann Sebastian Bach "or never attempt to play in public" (1992:64). Despite the rise of nationalist sentiments in the society at large, the world of art music was still decidedly focused on Europe.

Nationalistic sentiment would find its greatest expression in military band music and civic festivals. "Adios Mamá Carlota" was just one of many fashionable nationalistic themes played by the popular bands. It was composed and published by Vicente Riva Palacio, a political leader, newspaper editor, guerrilla fighter, playwright, and patriot. In addition to boosting the morale of the rebels during the latter days of French rule, "Adios Mama Carlota" became a patriotic anthem following the defeat of the invaders in 1887.

Such nationalistic imagery and sound not only supported the consolidation of the state but also served to legitimate the ascension of a new liberal democratic regime, the "Restored Republic" led by Benito Juárez. This era effectively ended with his death in 1872. After an intervening liberal administration, the Restored Republic in turn gave way to the dictatorship of Porfirio Díaz (1876–1911).

Often contrasted as opposites, Juárez the democrat and Díaz the dictator actually shared much in common ideologically. Both fostered liberal capitalist development and strongly opposed both theocratic conservatism and socialism. Around the world, capitalist development and the nation-state have tended to develop hand in hand, and Mexico is no exception. The "creole nationalism" of the late nineteenth century, illustrated in everything from nationalistic music to statuary evoking Aztec glory (Tenenbaum 1994:133), was not simply a spontaneous, popular outpouring of patriotism. As elsewhere, such hypernationalism evidenced the effective ideological efforts of an emerging capitalist class who worked to create a modern nation-state out of the disassembled patrias chicas left behind by the colony.

During their thirty-four-year reign, Díaz and his team of technocrats, known as *los científicos*, would greatly improve the economic infrastructure of the nation, further facilitating national development. With major investment from foreign nations, tens of thousands of miles of rail were laid, mining production increased dramatically, and hundreds of modern factories produced textiles, cigars, and other products. While new working and middle classes were created in the city, most Mexicans did not enjoy the benefits of this bonanza, however, and instead found that they were working harder to enrich foreign capitalists. In other words, the Díaz dictatorship created the perfect conditions for yet another revolution.

The Díaz dictatorship did more than create the conditions for revolution, however. Díaz actualized and consolidated the liberal capitalist vision, albeit without the political pretenses of bourgeois democracy. The economy was modernized, and great wealth was created. While promoting nationalist ideologies, Díaz was literally selling off Mexico to the highest bidder. Although very wary of the United States, he nevertheless allowed the sale of huge tracts of land to U.S. and European investors and allowed other foreign interests to control a large part of the Mexican oil, mining, and rail industries.

There was a wide gulf between the political-economic policies of Díaz and his claims. Managing such contradictions required heavy investments in political ritual (Beezley 1987; Esposito 2000). Ritual performances emphasized nationalistic imagery while attempting to sell the idea of capitalist internationalism. Using patriotic icons and fanfare, the Díaz regime tried to make the destiny of the nation appear dependent on successful industrial capitalist development. An official celebration marking the end of the nineteenth century demonstrates this ritual policy. The parade included twenty-three privately sponsored floats promoting various industries that were flourishing at the time (Morgan 1994:163). Patriotic icons, flags, and even costumed Aztecs were juxtaposed with symbols of modernization and industrial development. The implicit argument was that capitalist development would be in the best interests of the nation, the same basic pitch made today. This was in many ways the start of the modern capitalist era in Mexico.

The Díaz regime also needed to build a ritual argument for the role of international capital, no easy task in a country that had been beset by foreign intervention throughout the century. Symbolic of this interest, a float sponsored by the textile industry featured the flags of France, Spain, and Mexico. Given recent and distant Mexican history, this could easily have been interpreted by parade onlookers as a recitation of the nation's recent humiliations. Marching factory workers surrounded the float, however, a ritual tableau illustrating how Mexican national interests could be served by foreign capital. The sins of the past were to be forgotten for sake of an internationalist future.

Given the lengthy tenure of the Díaz regime, perhaps we can say that his ritual alchemy succeeded; but the Revolution that ended the dictatorship made it clear that the ideological marriage between national and foreign capital was never fully consummated. The lived experiences of peasants, workers, and even local elites contradicted the ideological claims and ritual performances of the Porfiriato. Eventually these contradictions were too much for the Díaz regime to manage. In the final instance, phenomenology trumped ideology.

CONTINUITY AND CHANGE

Mexico has experienced two great revolutions during the last two hundred years. First the Revolution of 1810 unseated the Spanish and ushered in a new nation-state. One hundred years later, the Revolution of 1910 unseated the last of the imperial dictators, book-ending a century of nation building. Yet historical periods are rarely so neatly punctuated. A focus on revolutionary conflagrations can cause us to ignore the social continuities bridging seemingly disparate periods and regimes. As demonstrated in Chapter 5, many of the identifying trends of nineteenth-century Mexico—secularism, internationalism, and capitalism—were underway in the decades preceding the Revolution. The Bourbon reforms, and local reactions to them, in many ways paved the way for the creation of a new Mexico. In that light, the Revolution for Independence can be seen as a punctuated part of social development rather than a distinct historical break.

Similarly, what followed the Revolution of 1810 was not a completely new society. Although the hated gachupines were expelled, their criollo offspring continued to benefit from the highly inequitable system of labor exploitation set into motion by the Conquest. The heavily capitalized and often anticlerical criollos took over what was left of the Spanish colonial infrastructure and made it their own. Rather than representing a revolutionary transformation, the movement from colonial to national rule can instead be viewed as a matter of more gradual social development.

The First Century of Independence

Nevertheless, new developments took place in Mexico's first century of independence. For the first time, merchants and proto-corporate organizations began effectively contesting state control of commerce. Before the Conquest, the Mexica had executed any pochteca (merchant) who became too wealthy. Similarly, the Spanish attempted to balance commercial, political, and religious interests, making certain that no sector achieved hegemony over the others. During the nineteenth century, however, secular commercial entities began to exceed the power of other political and religious forces. Capitalism, the religion of economy, slowly took root during Mexico's first century of "independence."

The 1810 criollo uprising was in part an effort by secular capital interests to wrest control of the Mexican political economy from a theocratic and monarchical state. Supported initially by a fractured peasant base, this nascent capitalism began to overdetermine affairs of state during the nineteenth century and effectively reduced religion to secondary status.

All of this can in turn be viewed as part of a much longer-term trend than a shift from theocracy to capitalism. The family had once been at the very heart of social power (in band societies) only to be replaced by the development of the local polity (tribal societies), an institution that was subsumed by the archaic state (Mesoamerican and Spanish). With the development of the early capitalist nation-state, the state itself slowly became a secondary ideological organ, subsumed within the larger body of global capitalism. All of these once-dominant entities—families, communities, and churches—are certainly still around, but they are clearly no longer the centers of power. In the new world and new state, the secular bureaucracy replaced religious hierarchy as the center of power. As the nineteenth century progressed, the state itself began to be subsumed by capital. The pochteca finally took control.

JUDAS AT THE JOCKEY CLUB

The New Nation: 1821–1910

One of the most interesting studies of ritual during the nineteenth century is provided in William Beezley's *Judas at the Jockey Club* (1987). European in origin, the Judas-burning ritual took on new meanings in Mexico. The Judas burning is, and was, partly a parodic ritual. Ostensibly part of the Easter ritual cycle, the exploding religious and historical figures allowed the faithful to work within an acceptable religious discourse, while at the same time criticizing power.

Beezley presents perhaps the best description and analysis of the Judas rituals, the history and complexities of which are beyond the scope of this book. To pick up just one of the themes, however, it is well worth discussing the political significance of Porfirian Judas rituals. In the early 1890s people of all social strata would explode Judas figures in lavish celebrations the day before Easter. The exploding figures contained everything from food and candy to silver coins and live cats, symbolizing abundance and life.

Negative reactions to one such performance, hosted by the elite Jockey Club in 1893, illustrate the political tensions and cultural contradictions of the time. The 1893 Judas ritual included a giant float crafted by Jockey Club members, who, according to one contemporary critic, "spent Holy Week in Judas' company" (Beezley 1987:110). The float included a giant balloon covered with coins. Four Judas figures rode in the gondola: a "mulatto," a butter salesman riding a pig, a guitar singer, and a beggar. The balloon was floated above the crowd and then exploded, sending its treasures down to the crowds gathered below.

Modernizers, liberal democrats and Porfirians alike, felt that the lavish Easter celebrations and other "deadly rituals" (Johns 1977:80–88) were "wicked" and an embarrassment to "all cultivated society" (Beezley 1987:111). Such celebrations were fiercely attacked as retrogressive displays and went into a period of quiescence.

The Judas celebrations were reborn with a vengeance during the final few years of the Díaz dictatorship. This ritual resurgence mainly took place in poor neighborhoods, however, becoming more overtly parodic and revolutionary. The Porfirians may have erred in removing elite sponsorship years earlier. What was once a precariously balanced ritual of appropriation and negotiation became a more direct form of confrontation in the hands of the disenfranchised.

Once again, history repeats itself. Under the reformist Bourbons a century earlier, such Saturnalian "religious" celebrations were similarly censored. A comparison of the two eras is instructive. Both the Bourbons and Porfirians viewed popular celebrations as excessive and regressive. The Bourbons saw the Judas burnings, Corpus Cristi, and other popular expressions as a threat to economic modernization and Catholic propriety. Similarly, the Porfirians felt that the raucous rites represented a threat to economic modernization and civic secularism.

What links the two acts of ritual repression is a fear of rising anarchy in the face of tightening governmental control. The popular festivals contained anarchic elements that those in power sought to contain and redirect in their favor. During the positivistic age of the Porfiriato, the humorous festivals of the folk "appeared to be nothing more than mockery, its playful ambivalence nothing more than disorder" (Beezley 1987: 124). Díaz and his fellow positivists sought to reorder the folk (1987:129):

> Whether people wanted parades or festivals, the Díaz government controlled the location—the Zócalo and its neighboring streets—for these displays of symbolic actions in Mexico's face-to-face, nonliterate society. Modern administrators paved these public places, controlled traffic on them, and finally directed their use during holidays. This was just one more restraint on traditional society by modernizers.

Today the zócalo is still a ritual battle site between a government that seeks to control the movement of dissenters and protesters seeking to expand beyond control. ("The demonstrators overflowed the zócalo" is a recurrent theme in opposition newspapers.) This is a legacy of centuries of ritual conflict at the city center. Revolutionary moments, particularly those of 1810 and 1910, have repeated this same dialectical pattern: waves of expression and repression mutually fueling each other. As leaders clamped down harder, popular movements became more subversive.

Such dialectics boil over into revolution when contradictions between official ideology and lived experience exceed the bounds of ritual containment. The Bourbons cracked down on previously legitimate forms of ritual expression, leaving no outlet for social frustrations at a time when they had reached the boiling point. The Díaz regime made the same mistake more than a century later.

RITUAL REFLECTIONS

Music reflected all of the aforementioned social developments. For example, the transition from a theocratic to secular precapitalist state is clearly evident in music. The sacred polyphony of "Ave Maria" gave way to secular tracts like "La carnival de México" and "El perico." Although religion was far from dead, it had clearly lost its centrality. The nineteenth century was the "crucible" of Mexican nationalism (Escorza 1990:6).

The first century of independence would produce a diverse array of new musical expressions. Opera, both tragic and comic, became the rage among Mexico City elites, paralleling the growth of the urban middle class (Carmona 1984:11). Italian composers, vocalists, and production companies were at the forefront of Mexico City's nineteenth-century opera scene. Therefore, the first operas written by Mexican composers were patterned along Italian lines. In return, Italian composers working in Mexico integrated local culture and history into their work (Carmona 1984:77).

Guatimotzin, by Mexican composer Aniceto Ortega (1823–1875), is one of the earliest and best examples. Ortega integrated nationalistic elements, specifically Aztec iconography, into his Italian-style operas (Behague 1979:98). In 1900 pianist and composer Ricardo Castro premiered his opera *Atzimba*, which similarly merged Mexican and European elements.

Perhaps the most influential Italian musical form during the nineteenth century was bel canto, a melodic song style that values "well sustained," subtle, and clear tones (Carmona 1984:103). Italian bel canto style would influence not only the art music of the era but also the popular music of the next. The twentieth-century bolero was partly an attempt to domesticate and popularize this nineteenth-century style. From its romantic spirit to clean, simple tones, bel canto would eventually become the refined, urban sound of Mexico, consciously experienced as the antithesis of more dynamic rural genres and styles. In fact, many *boleristas* of the early twentieth century were formally trained in bel canto style.

Although the most important influences in the art music of nineteenth-century Mexico came from Italy, Spain—as part of its colonial legacy—made the greatest contributions to popular music. The tonadilla escénica influenced the development of "sones, jarabes, canciones, coplas, trobos, corridos," and other styles of Mexican popular music (Carmona 1984:12). The extreme romantic sentimentalism of Spanish music in the 1800s is found in the popular music of Mexico during that century as well (Mendoza 1953:22). While the small middle and upper classes of the city were experimenting with Italian, French, and German styles, the working classes and rural peasantry were developing their own music, building on the Spanish forms that had dominated cultural life during three centuries of colonial rule.

French influence was felt most directly in Mexico City during the intervention of Maximilian and Carlota (1862–1867). French soldiers flocked to Mexico City theaters, which presented "vaudeville and Franco-Mexican spectacles" (Carmona 1984:87). Meanwhile, the high arts were directly influenced by the emperor and empress. Like most aristocracy of the era, Maximilian and Carlota demonstrated their cultural capital by playing piano and pianoforte for visiting elites in their magnificent Chapultepec Castle. They also sponsored concerts and theater events by the best available performers. Maximilian directly sponsored the Orchestra of S. M. Maximilian II (Carmona 1984:89). Despite the political expulsion of the French (and all their Hapsburg kin), French influence in the arts did not completely disappear during the following "Restored Republic" of Juárez and came back into vogue during the Porfiriato.

Mercedes Díaz Roig analyzes the qualities that allow a musical form to pass across national boundaries, including basic and comprehensible language, topical relevance, and familiar style (1987:616). Before music can pass between national cultures, however, substantial contact between those nations is required. Rarely does such contact take place on an equal plane. Although backward flows are always present, cultural influence tends to flow through channels of power, from colonial metropolis to colony. All world religions have been spread in that manner. Christianity, for example, was imposed throughout the world by successive waves of empire. Similarly, it is no accident that Spain, France, and the United States have been the dominant cultural influences in Mexico. Perhaps the only exception to the colonial rule is Italy, which had relatively little direct political or economic influence yet has contributed significantly to Mexico City's musical life.

After this description of some of the musical influences of Spain, Italy, and France, only one major influence remains unexamined: the

United States. The popular culture of the United States had a great impact on Mexico during the nineteenth century. Musicologists rarely mention those influences, however, perhaps due to lingering colonial wounds. Since Mexico survived the hegemony of Spain and intervention of France, it is now ideologically and psychologically safe to examine the legacy of those once great colonial powers. Not so with the United States, whose hegemony in Mexico remains at an all-time high. To examine U.S. cultural influences is perhaps seen as an insult to national sovereignty and pride.

For example, one of Carmona's few direct references to the United States in her study of the nineteenth century is to note that the war of 1846–1848 caused a pause in operatic production in Mexico City and that, following this catastrophic intervention and theft, the first national opera company was founded (1984:36). She further states that "light" entertainments were performed for the Yankee invaders (1984:36). Beyond these minimal references, however, little has been written about U.S. musical or ritual influence during the nineteenth century.

The New Nation: 1821–1910

Clearly, there has been U.S. cultural influence in Mexico, and Mexican influence was certainly felt in the United States. According to Robert Stevenson, during the nineteenth century, "American interest in Latin American political events stimulated a constant stream of sheet music publications" (1980b:73). Music composed for and played during the U.S. War of 1846–1848 was published and distributed throughout the United States. Music celebrating the U.S. conquest and various key battles became the rage of the day (Lemmon 1989:42). Even anti-gringo songs like "La pasadita" were published, albeit transformed in translation to a much less critical form (Stevenson 1980b:88). Reacting to the unjust invasion, which was criticized by leaders like Ulysses S. Grant and Abraham Lincoln, U.S. composers penned antiwar songs as well (although Grant did not oppose the war publicly, he expressed strong distaste and opposition to it in private letters and memoirs).

The music of Mexico was often pirated and sold in the United States during the nineteenth century (Stevenson 1980b:88–89). The late nineteenth century saw the first great wave of interest in Mexican music in the United States, as publishing houses from New Orleans to New York and Chicago printed music from Mexico. The Mexican Eighth Calvary Band "totally captivated" New Orleans in 1885 (Lemmon 1989:43). Movements of musicians and composers between the United States and Mexico indicate that a vigorous interchange was surely taking place throughout the century. Nonetheless, U.S. musical influence in Mexico has not been investigated in depth.

In sum, it can be said that newly independent Mexico, like all nineteenth-century nations, took part in an international exchange of musical ideas. Most of these musical concepts, at least in Mexico City, demonstrate some connection to musical and colonial centers in Europe. Romanticism was king throughout the first century of Mexican independence, leading some to call it "the century of bad taste" (Sordo Sodi 1982:299). Actually, the word most often used in Spanish is *cursi*, which connotes not only bad taste per se but also negative assessment of mass or "common" taste. This word would increasingly be employed to describe the romantic popular music of Mexico during the next century, applied quite often to the boleros of Agustín Lara, for example.

As for the romantic forms of the nineteenth century, Carmen Sordo Sodi claims that they "leave much to be desired" (1982:299). However, it is desire itself that explains the romanticism of the nineteenth century. After centuries of theocratic repression, secular Mexico allowed popular expression to take flight. The nineteenth century was a liminal period, when the convenient segregation between popular and official music broke down somewhat. For three long centuries, the Spaniards tried to maintain separate spaces for both, repressing the popular while fostering official liturgical musical pedagogy and practice.

During the nineteenth century, popular music heavily influenced official ritual discourse. The jarabe became a national dance just as other secular festivals repressed during the colonial era came out of hiding to color even the most important ritual affairs of state. Mexico City elites, while focused partly on Italian, French, and German performances, also took part in this popular outpouring. Mexican romanticism infused art music with a sense of the popular spirit as well. During the nineteenth century, the high and low arts intermixed in ways that would have offended previous colonial clerics and seemed distasteful to twentieth-century art music critics.

While collaborating in this romantic mélange of popular and art music, the elites also maintained distinct ritual spaces as well. The music of Joseph Haydn (Stevenson 1982b), Felix Mendelssohn, Gioacchino Rossini, Giuseppe Verdi, and Frédéric Chopin (Stevenson 1982a) provided a modicum of cultural capital to the new criollo elite. The same elites, however, largely rejected the efforts of local Mexican art musicians (Sordo Sodi 1982:301).

Even Mexican musicians and composers with advanced training were largely rejected by local critics. For example, the first Mexican opera, *Catalina de Guisa* by Cenobio Paniagua, was a critical failure, despite becoming a hit with the general populace (Sordo Sodi 1982: 301). Similarly, the cultural elite ignored romantic nationalist composers like Antonio Gomezanda (Velazco 1991), a precursor of twentieth-century nationalists. Such composers often had better luck abroad. Local elites were too focused on popular pretense and foreign fare to cede significant space to their own art musicians. The disputed capital did not allow for the development of a distinct music community during the first century of Mexican independence. Most creative musical development took place outside the capital, in the rural countryside. Like the many Mexican governments in exile during the nineteenth century, Mexican music was also often estranged from the capital.

That trend would continue during the Revolution to come. Mexico's last great Revolution (1910–1921) would unfold mainly on a rural stage. As such, its music would be that of the *campo* (countryside). Naturally, the musical repertoire of the Revolution of 1910 would include the still-popular rural *sones* described above. The archetypal music of the Revolution would be a different lyrical style, however: the *corrido*, a very old form remade for a very new era.

7 Nineteenth-Century Resonance

The musical rituals of Mexico's past resonate with variable intensity over time and space. Traditional ritual moments are set aside throughout the year for the purpose of reflecting upon the past. For example, annual festivals honor the ancestors (Día de los Muertos), the Virgin of Guadalupe, Christ's birth, and Christ's death. Just as the calendar is divided into greater and lesser periods of ritual reflection, so too the city is arranged into sacred spaces, where such reflection is encouraged, and profane spaces, where it is not. For example, the echoes of New Spain are louder inside the church sanctuary than anywhere outside. Conversely, as the initial era of independence, the nineteenth century resonates most clearly in the times and spaces reserved for secular state functions, such as the National Palace, the zócalo, and surrounding symbolic statuary like the Angel of Independence and the tomb of Benito Juárez. The foundational myths and moments of the Mexican state, rooted in the nineteenth century, are brought back to life in these secularly sacred spaces. Fittingly, nineteenth-century ensembles and songs, the brass band and national anthem, in particular, are featured in these reflective rituals.

Brass ensembles are still highly popular, perhaps the most audible evidence of nineteenth-century resonance. Band music is a living tradition in both the city and the countryside. To this day, almost every Mexican village features at least one such ensemble. In the city the brass band is a popular accompaniment to fiestas and political rallies, inaugurations and wedding parties, wherever a sense of gaiety or pomp is required. Although one contemporary pop form has evolved from the nineteenth-century brass band—*banda* music (see Chapter 16)—the original form is also alive and well. The same cannot be said for other nineteenth-century styles, such as the *son*. While the *son* is considered a historical folk form, brass band music is a living entity, practiced by amateur and professional musicians alike.

MARCHING THROUGH MEXICO

Imagine a walk through the heart of Mexico City, starting at Carlota's beloved Chapultepec Park and ending at the zócalo, a three-kilometer march. Among the many musical sounds one might experience are the following brass ensembles. Although I encountered them on separate days, their composite placement in a single walk helps to illustrate not only their vitality but also their selective use of space.

In Chapultepec, a small brass band featuring bouncing bass lines played on the tuba entertains children as they eat cotton candy and dance by the lake. Exiting the park and walking along Avenida de la Reforma—a street that Emperor Maximilian designed to mimic the Champs Elysées—we encounter a festival going on at the Angel of Independence. Children dance to the regional styles of Mexico, showing off to two thousand other schoolchildren who are gathered there for a demonstration (February 22, 1998). Brass music pours out of loudspeakers to accompany dancers in regional costumes, such as "Los chinelos" of Morelos. Sponsored by the National Union of Educational Workers (SNTE), the event is designed to demonstrate and foster national pride. Of course, there is a political purpose to the ritual as well. The union is using brass band music, a signifier of national pride and identity, in order to promote itself and the important work of its members.

Detouring into the Zona Rosa, we come upon a municipal police band playing for shoppers as they walk by or sip coffee at a local cafe. A crowd gathers, appreciative of the polished performance. Moving back out onto the Reforma, we turn right at Avenida Hidalgo and march into the Alameda, a large park and another favorite haunt of Carlota. We might imagine Carlota's courtiers lounging at the park, listening to a brass ensemble playing in the gazebo. Today, instead of the aristocracy, regular folk collect for a song or two and then move on. A few picnickers place their blankets on patches of green lawn, lunching on homemade *tortas* or Big Macs while taking in the free concert.

Crossing the park we reach Avenida Juárez and a grand monument to the hero's memory. We continue our march toward the zócalo, along Avenida Madero, named in honor of the man who sparked the Revolution of 1910. Hidalgo (the firebrand criollo leader of the Revolution for

The Mexican Army Band playing in the zócalo at dusk. Photos by author.

Nineteenth-Century Resonance

Independence), Juárez, and Madero — one hundred years of Mexican history in one short walk, accompanied by the tune of nineteenth-century march music. However, our walking concert is not complete until we reach a drum and trumpet duo playing for change near the zócalo and, a few blocks further on, an organ grinder and his aggressive assistant extorting money from passing pedestrians.

At the zócalo, it would not be at all unusual to hear the national anthem or any number of other nineteenth-century tunes. The most storied ensemble of Mexico — the army band — plays there every morning and evening while a giant flag is raised and lowered. Affairs of state are always accompanied by the "Hymn." It is the one song that finds all participants and onlookers, no matter how cynical, standing at respectful attention, singing: "Mexicanos, al grito de guerra . . ." Perhaps nothing symbolizes the Mexican nation better than these daily performances, recalling the troubled century during which Mexico first became a nation.

WOUNDS

Part of the living energy of the national anthem comes from the open wounds of intervention. The injuries of the nineteenth-century invasions have not fully healed, not only because so much was taken from Mexico but also because foreign institutions continue to exert such profound influence. Right-wing ideologues downplay the imperialistic dimensions of "free trade" pacts, while the Left continues to use images of imperialism to combat them. In that contentious environment, nationalistic songs and styles from the nineteenth century continue to resonate, recalling painful pasts and related contemporary problems.

Not all wounds run deep, however. Some interventions have faded into historical legend, the stuff of warm satire rather than cold anger. This is the case with the French intervention. Maximilian and to an even greater extent Carlota have become sources of popular entertainment rather than hated enemies. Recently the government spent millions to remodel the lavish Chapultepec Castle, improving the popular museum that features artifacts from the days of the emperor and empress. Crowds have flocked to the palace, curious about the lavish lives of their one-time usurpers. Satirical songs are still sung about the tragic couple, evidence that their insult is largely forgiven. Such treatment of the U.S. invasion is unthinkable.

A 1997 stage production of Vicente Leñero's *Don Juan en Chapultepec* exemplified Mexico's fascination with the French intervention. Fittingly, it took place in Chapultepec Park. The intimate play brings the audience directly into the domestic lives of Maximilian and Carlota, through the involvement of protagonist Don José Zorrilla. Zorrilla wrote *Don Juan Tenorio*, a play adored by Empress Carlota. In fact, she was said to have learned Spanish partly through repeated readings of his play. Zorrilla himself disliked the play and wanted to be remembered for his more subtle dramas.

Don Juan en Chapultepec presents Maximilian and Carlota as tragic-comic figures. Leñero's emperor and empress are young, deluded, and not terribly intelligent, although they have an earnest appeal that encourages the audience to empathize with their inevitable failures. By the time Carlota retreats into total lunacy, guided by Zorrilla's fiction, we feel for her. In the Chapultepec performance, Eugenia Leñero, the playwright's daughter, played beautiful Carlota to perfection. Welcomed into Carlota's castle, the audience cannot help but feel for the earnest young woman as she is cast out of paradise.

Such a performance of pity for the oppressor is unthinkable in the case of the United States, for several reasons. Foremost among them is the fact that the wounds of U.S. intervention remain unhealed. The language used by Diane Nelson to describe Guatemala's recent terror applies equally well to Mexico: continued U.S. involvement in the affairs of Mexico is *A Finger in the Wound* (1999). The amputation of the northern territories is still felt in Mexico, like a phantom limb. The United States cut Mexico in half in 1848 and has intervened repeatedly since (Ross 1998). Unlike the French intervention, these events will not fade into safe historical memory until the contemporary relationship itself changes.

Nineteenth-Century Resonance

BANDA DE TLAYACAPAN

The community bands play on. Tlayacapan, Morelos, boasts one of the most well-known village bands in Mexico. Almost every child in Tlayacapan is taught to play a band instrument as soon as he or she can hold it. In fact, several current band members are too young to hold their instruments and instead must rest them on their lap or a chair while playing.

The Tlayacapan band not only plays for local fiestas but is also hired by neighboring communities for special celebrations. It has even traveled outside the country to perform. When I saw the band play in Mexico City, it was preparing to travel to Arizona for a concert. It has become a national and international model for Mexican village band music.

The Tlayacapan band performances illustrate several major features of the form. Although the band is unusually large — it has thirty-two members, including director Carlos Santa María — it nevertheless demonstrates the wide instrumental variety and extreme experimental creativity of the small town band. No strings are present, only woodwinds and brass. The clarinets and drums together form a chirimía-like sound in many arrangements, a legacy of the popular colonial instrument ensemble. The band believes in improvisation and is less concerned with classical precision than with creativity and popular spirit. The tuba player explained that "we don't just play to play . . . music is an important thing, almost like life itself . . . it is the seed that is cultivated to continue our tradition."

The Nahua origins of the town are not forgotten, despite the adoption of nineteenth-century sounds. One musician explained that the band played "to dignify popular music and indigenous roots," adding that "it is unjust that they are killing our brothers," no doubt a reference to events in Chiapas. In other words, even the most Western musical forms have been incorporated into the local culture, appropriated from foreigners and then remade for local political and ritual purposes.

Although the band is dominated by men, there is no apparent sexual segregation according to instrument or position. The Tlayacapan ensemble includes six women and girls: a trumpet, alto sax, clarinet, French horn (a very small girl), trombone, and two oboes. According to the director, the band considers itself to be a "family, something we are very proud of."

Orizaba, Conjunto Jarocho led by Martín Campos, keeping the *son* alive in Mexico City. Photo by author.

The presence of the Tlayacapan band in Mexico City is indicative of the central role of the metropolis in the nation's musical life. Rural musical development and performance are greatly affected by the capital. Most rural forms, such as the brass band, filtered into the countryside only after entering through Mexico City.

Mexico City is not only the portal and filter for musical trends entering the country but is also often an arbiter as well. In order to gain national access and status, rural ensembles almost always need to impress gate-keeping institutions based in the capital. Viceroys, bishops, presidents, emperors, governmental ministers, wealthy patrons of the arts, record company executives, and television programmers have all in their time been responsible for selecting certain styles and ensembles for the national stage while rejecting others. The Tlayacapan band was performing on such a stage, arguing for its national worth. Such rituals of recognition have taken place for centuries, as rural ensembles of all sorts have come to play before the capital's cultural elite, who serve as arbiters of both musical quality and national identity. The selected ensembles receive institutional support and access to a national audience.

Clearly, reaching a national audience requires more than just live performance. To reach a larger national audience, a musician or ensemble needs to record the music and, if possible, gain airtime. Mexico City is where the more successful regional bands and performers must go to gain that level of institutional access. This is true for virtually all styles of music, even the marimba ensembles of Chiapas (Solís 1980:34). For example, record producers in Mexico City consider the marimba bands of Chiapas to be more authentic, and thus worthy of national distribution, whereas they tend to discount the local Mexico City ensembles. Naturally, Mexico City marimba players often resent the way in which Chiapaneco marimbas are viewed by the gate-keepers as "naturally" better than they are. The metropolis becomes the arbiter of both regionalism and nationalism, producing a relationship of dependence between rural musicians and cultural programmers in Mexico City. To gain national recognition, regional performers must make pilgrimages to the capital, as they have for centuries.

Brass bands that want to become known beyond regional borders must do likewise. According to one band member, the Tlayacapan band members play "so that our community maintains an identity." "Sometimes that means we must take meals with politicians," joked the musician, "some PRI, but that is OK." In other words, community identity is partly based on the group's relationship to the nation as a whole. Such metropolitan concerts are rituals of identity production and sites for the negotiation of what it means to belong to a given region.

The Tlayacapan concert was partly designed to drum up interest in Mexico City for the Tlayacapan carnival. "Come to the carnival and get out of the smog for a day," suggested the director. Tourism from the city has become an essential part of the economy of neighboring Morelos state. Many small towns like Tepoztlán and Tlayacapan in part depend on the urban tourists' pesos. At the same time, they fear urban encroachment, decadence, and pollution, both physical and spiritual.

The "Golf War" (Davison 1996) exemplifies this rural-urban dialectic and dilemma. Tepoztlán, Morelos, fought a long and bitter struggle

Nineteenth-Century Resonance

to keep metropolitan interests—in the form of the billionaire coalition Grupo KS, the U.S. corporation General Telephone and Electric (GTE), and the PRI—from building a golf course resort project that would have monopolized the town's water, labor, and economy. The town's struggle against global capital played out on the concert stage as well, reinvigorating the local musical scene as solo musicians and neighborhood bands took an active part in the resistance.

Local musicians and communities are inextricably connected to the metropolis, for better and for worse. Towns like Tlayacapan are not the isolated hamlets hyped in tourist brochures and travel guides. Townsfolk are quite aware of their relationship to the larger cities and world. "Specialists came from Minnesota to study our chapels," bragged one Tlayacapan band member. "We have twenty-six chapels, two fiestas per year in each, for a total of fifty-two fiestas in town, which is why we [the band] are so good: lots of practice."

The band, like the town, plays an essential if somewhat reticent role in the Mexican nation as a whole. The local ritual cycle has been amplified to provide the residents of the capital with a more "authentic" image of themselves as Mexicans. They visit the countryside to meet with family members and experience a sense of mexicanidad that is less ritually crystallized in the city.

As if to parody such urban projections of rural tradition, a group of dancing Tlayacapan children came out near the end of the concert wearing masks satirizing deposed leader Carlos Salinas, Partido de la Revolución Democrática (PRD) candidate Cuauhtémoc Cárdenas Solórzano, and foreign war correspondents. The reporters were represented in the single figure of a flak-jacketed white man with vampire-like fangs (a mask) and an imposing camera. The dance presented a colorful critique of metropolitan intervention. Such masked figures and rituals have been used throughout Mexican history "to imagine a world of local authority free from external control" (Harris 2000:250). Yet it is a dangerous ritual game and a precarious negotiation: the revolutionary potential of the ritual must be tempered, given the rural towns' dependence on metropolitan politics and pesos. Perhaps in recognition of this, the Tlayacapan dancers eventually reverted to Chinelos, local ritual figures which, despite their subversive origins, no longer signify such a critical stance.

Meanwhile, back home in the villages, music thrives. Living in Tepoztlán, Morelos, for three months, my wife and I were awakened several mornings at 6 A.M. by brass ensembles marching outside our window. They were headed toward fiestas in nearby neighborhoods or, in a few cases, initiating fiesta days in the local neighborhood. Community bands also play in the Tepoztlán town square. A mural there shows rich

U.S. golfers with devil horns fondling local women. The artist presents the same metaphor of violation employed in "La pasadita," which was sung in resistance to the first U.S. invasion.

Once again, the traditions, trends, and wounds of the nineteenth century are still alive. Rather than being places removed from modern space and time, as presented in tourist brochures, the small hamlets of Mexico are at the very center of struggle over Mexican identity and the nation's political future. Throughout the centuries, external cultural influences have been ritually reappropriated to serve local needs. That is certainly the case with Mexican marching band music. First brought to Mexican soil by a series of invading U.S. and European armies, it has been adopted and remade, becoming, among other things, a symbol of resistance and pride. Indeed, today there is nothing more symbolic of Mexican national pride than a brass band playing the national hymn. It links city and country, aristocrats and workers, socialists and neoliberals, around a shared discourse. In terms of musical ritual, it is perhaps the most important and enduring gift of the nineteenth century.

PART

IV The Revolution:
1910 – 1921

8 Revolutionary Mexico: 1910–1921

Until the Revolution, Mexico was a predominantly rural nation. Although great wealth was produced during the Díaz dictatorship, it flowed into the coffers of foreign companies, urban national elites, and, to a certain extent, the rising urban middle class. The poor were not invited to the party. The conditions of the majority—the rural peasantry, miners, urban working classes, and *los marginados* (the marginalized, destitute poor)—held steady or worsened. During the late Porfiriato, rural work conflicts at the Cananea mines (1906) and Río Blanco textile mill (1907) signaled the much greater conflagration to come. Eventually, a large base of campesinos and laborers would join the ranks of various caudillos, like Emiliano Zapata in the South and Francisco Villa in the North, to contest their common enemies.

However, the Revolution would start with a liberal caudillo, Francisco Madero, leading the way against Porfirio Díaz and his hated Rurales. The economic boom of the Porfiriato created a revolution of rising expectations among the poor and middle classes. The rich got richer and the poor watched the party from afar. As the director for the Tlacapayan town band explained, "The rich hacienda families would not invite us to their parties, so we invented our own music." Quite literally, peasants and workers were not invited to the Porfirian party. In 1910, 80 percent of the population still worked in the agricultural sector, yet 96.6 percent of rural households owned no land (Cockcroft 1990:91).

As was true of the Revolution for Independence, the Revolution of 1910 would not be led by disaffected peasants. Relatively well-off criollos sponsored the Revolution of 1810, drawing on a peasant base for firepower. One hundred years later, in the final years of the Díaz regime, local elites likewise went searching for a leader who would challenge Díaz while retaining many of his basic liberal capitalist policies. They needed to stop U.S. and European investors from siphoning off "their" wealth yet wanted to retain their own inordinate privileges. Díaz had been using investment from European companies, in particular, to balance out the constant threat of U.S. hegemony. The dictator viewed such foreign investment strategies as a practical road to national development. Many Mexican capitalists and landowners did not see it that way. Regional elites, in particular, were put off by the encroaching power of foreign capitalists like U.S. oil baron Edward Doheny and members of the British Pearson firm, who profited greatly from oil production, railroading, and ranching.

Local ranchers and capitalists found their leader in fellow hacendado Francisco Madero, a liberal who would challenge Díaz without threatening the caste-like system that guaranteed their continued prosperity. Many viewed the vegetarian Madero as an eccentric, but they also understood his political potential. Under the slogan "Effective suffrage and no reelection" (ironically, the same premise Díaz had used to attain power decades before), Madero led a movement to unseat the aging dictator. Díaz made Madero's work easier when he told a gringo reporter that his presidential career would end in 1910, at the conclusion of his current term. He later changed his mind, of course, but the damage was already done. Madero used the opening to lead a successful movement to unseat the dictator and reintroduce the vision of bourgeois democracy held by nineteenth-century liberals like Juárez. Madero and his fellow liberal caudillos formed a revolutionary force, drawing on the anger of displaced peasants and disenfranchised workers. Madero marched into Mexico City in 1911, victorious. "They have loosed the wild beasts," said Díaz as he left the country. "Let us now see who will tame them" (Kandell 1988:404).

These words proved to be prophetic. The resentment of the oppressed would not be so easily satisfied; nor would the elites remain united once their common enemy was deposed. The Revolution of 1910 would take a decade to reach its ambivalent conclusion (taking the transfer of power from Carranza to Alvaro Obregón in 1920 as the date of revolutionary consummation). One to two million people died during the Revolution, most of them poor peasants fighting in rural provinces. What they died for is not yet completely clear. While the plight of the poor did improve in many cases, the old problems of corruption and inequality persisted, while new forms of postrevolutionary poverty and oppression developed.

The Revolution:
1910–1921

The results of the Revolution are discussed in the following chapters. For now, suffice it to say that the revolutionary drama was not staged in Mexico City. It was a rural rebellion. Therefore, the central ritual drama was set in the northern deserts under generals like Villa and the mountains of Morelos, to the south, under the great Zapata. The people of the capital either joined the country folk in the fight or watched, read, and waited to see which army would come marching in next. If the lavish and ridiculous Centennial celebration was the last great ritual act of Díaz, the Revolution had no such definitive ritual moment to mark its end. A series of triumphant leaders — Madero, Victoriano Huerta, Villa, Zapata, and Carranza — would all have their moment in the sun. Each leader would at least once enter the capital to the sound of cheers and resounding brass, before exiting again, often under cover of silence. Meanwhile, the Revolution was happening elsewhere. The unreality of the capital was balanced by an all-too-real conflagration in the countryside, a cataclysm that would radically transform the nation in ways that no one at the time could possibly have foreseen.

The soundtrack for the revolutionary war was provided by marching brass. Every regiment, no matter how beleaguered, managed to have some martial accompaniment. Each general had his favorite anthem. It was said that Villa favored "La Adelita," a song first made famous by his military band. Even more important than the marching brass were walking guitarists who played corridos, long lyrical ballads that document actual events and tell the stories of real and/or legendary men (only rarely is the protagonist female). Such songs did much more than inspire and entertain the troops; they also informed the public and advocated the cause of a given leader. Although revolutionary regiments included corridos in their repertoire, they were more commonly played by itinerant guitarists loosely affiliated, if at all, with a revolutionary militia. These musicians kept the populace updated on revolutionary events through detailed song narratives, bending the news to match their own proclivities. The corrido became a form of both artistic expression and political communication. It remains the most important and lasting musical legacy of the Revolution.

CORRIDO ROOTS AND RITUALS

My remarks here concerning the corrido are limited, both because it was largely a rural phenomenon and also because a rich body of Anglophone literature already exists on the topic. While the denizens of Mexico City hunkered down and waited for the next triumphant caudillo to grace their gates, the people of the campo were engaged in an epic struggle to decide the fate of the nation.

The corrido documented the epic event, serving the same role in the countryside as newspapers did in the capital. This "newspaper of the folk" (Redfield 1930:186) kept a running tally on the battles just as balladeers had been doing for centuries, particularly in Europe. In addition to informing the folk, these often partisan ballads also helped rally the troops, giving a sense of greater glory to their sacrifice. As the war went on, the lofty goals of the combatants were often lost. Many were like the character Demetrio in Mariano Azuela's classic novel *Los de abajo* (The Underdogs), who finally admits: "I'll be damned if I know what it's all about" (1996:131). Fighting became a way of life, and by the end only the most idealistic believed that any profound positive change would result from the bloody quarrel. Given the high casualties and low rates of success on the battlefield, the corrido ritual became more and more essential to troop morale.

The Revolution:
1910–1921

It is impossible to think of the Revolution without the corrido. Never has a musical form been so intimately attached to a single historical event. However, the corrido was certainly not invented in 1910. Most musicologists agree that the style derived from old Spanish *romances*, songs that extend back centuries, well before the Conquest. The first recorded romance ballad written in the New World was scribed soon after the Noche Triste (Orta Velázquez 1981:13):

En Tacuba está Cortés	Cortés is in Tacuba
con su escuadrón esforzado,	With his squadron forced on,
triste estaba y muy penoso,	Sad he was and very pained,
triste y con gran cuidado,	Sad and with great care,
una mano en la mejilla	A hand on his cheek
y la otra en el costado.	And the other on his side.

Although the line, cadence, rhyme scheme, and meter are different, the basic narrative purpose is the same in this romance as in the later Mexican corridos. Early Spanish romances like this probably gave rise to the later corrido.

Celedonia Serrano Martínez disagrees. In his *El corrido mexicano no deriva del romance español* (The Mexican Corrido Does Not Derive from the Spanish Romance), he argues that "this popular genre is an original work of our people, created by them" (1973:227). While Serrano Martínez makes several good points in his detailed analysis, his work is more an argument by bold assertion than a clear explication of the corrido's origins. He continuously refers to the corrido as "our corrido," demonstrating that he considers the question of origins a matter of national pride.

The Mexican musicologists that Serrano Martínez critiques, however, see no contradiction between the corrido's Spanish origins and national pride. The corrido, like all cultural artifacts, is clearly derived from past and foreign forms but is also the creation of those who borrowed those earlier forms, reworked them, and made something new in the process. The corrido is a form of musical mestizaje, something qualitatively new created from multiple past influences, adapted, and augmented through performance in the present. Regardless of its derivation(s), the corrido is "the most authentic popular poetic genre that our people have created to sing their sentiments, celebrate their leaders, applaud their triumphs, lament their losses, and, in general, to conserve their traditions" (Serrano Martínez 1973:17).

Whether a derivative of the Spanish romance or best considered a wholly original form, the corrido is clearly derived from three traditional genres, the "epic, lyric, and narrative" (Herrera-Sobek 1990:xiii). The quatrain corrido tends to have an ABCB rhyming scheme: lines two and four of the quatrain rhyme. The corrido "Gregorio Cortez," analyzed by Américo Paredes in *With His Pistol in His Hand* (1958:64–67), is a good example:

En el condado de Kansas	A	In the county of Kansas
tal desgracia sucedió,	B	What a misfortune occurred;
mataron el Cherife mayor,	C	They killed the Major Sheriff,
dejando a Román herido.	B	Leaving Román wounded.

Other corridos follow an ABAB rhyming scheme. The following stanza is taken from "Defensa de Celaya y triunfo del General Obregón" (de María y Campos 1962:45):

Obregón ya en la Batalla	A	Obregón now in the battle
dispusó cinco sectores	B	Put five regiments
al derredor de Celaya	A	Around Celaya
mandó bravos defensores.	B	Commanding brave defenders.

The meter can vary as well. Note how in "Gregorio Cortez" the number of beats per line fluctuates between eight and nine. The same is true in the second example. There is no discernible pattern in either case. Meter in the corrido generally varies from eight to nine beats per line but is not restricted to that range. The four-line stanza structure, however, is an inviolable rule.

Performance context is everything in the corrido. Corrido performers engage in active dialog with their audience. Many corridos begin with a statement of humility on the performer's part, an introduction of self, and an introduction to the story that will be told. The story is related and then often concluded with either a clear moral or humorous farewell, depending on the nature of the event in question. The concluding stanza from "Corrido de Juan B. Galindo," an outlaw-turned-rebel in the postrevolutionary Cristero War, provides an example (Hernández 1989:195–197):

Vuela vuela palomita,	A	Fly, fly, little dove
les llevarás la noticia,	A	Take them the news
que ya Galindo está muerto,	B	That Galindo is now dead.
que ya está muerto de risa.	A	He is now dead of laughter.

The Revolution: 1910–1921

The "Corrido de Juan B. Galindo" contends that Durango's local hero escaped justice and concludes with a final bite at the Federales (Hernández 1989:195–197). Also note the AABA rhyming scheme—yet a third variant.

Perhaps the most interesting introductions and conclusions are those that qualify the nature of the knowledge related in the ballad. Often singers state that their version is based on what they have been told rather than on direct experience. In doing so, they act very much like news reporters divulging their sources. This demonstrates the *corridistas'* recognition of their public role as truth tellers. During the Revolution, the corridista was often the only link between local villagers and the nation.

REVOLUTION, RELIGION, AND THE CORRIDO

The corrido has been studied extensively, for several reasons. First, as a form most likely derived from a long tradition of European balladry, it has been around for centuries. Second, the corrido is a historical chronicle, "history created by and for the people" (Mendoza 1954:ix). Third, the corrido is not only or even primarily a musical form. Instead, it is literature. Robert Redfield, in his ethnographic study of 1920s Tepoztlán, entitles a chapter about the corrido "Literacy and Literature" (1930:170–193). The corrido is lyrical poetry set to very simple melodies and guitar accompaniment. Other instruments may accompany the corrido as well, but it is typically played and sung by one man. Harmony, when present, is almost always simple, tonic, and dominant.

Even today, the word *corrido* evokes the image of a lone man and his guitar singing to a small crowd in the village square. In a vignette from as late as the 1950s, Merle Simmons describes the corridista as "one of those rustic minstrels, also known as trovadores or cantadores, who travel from market to market singing their songs and selling cheaply printed copies of the lyrics to those who will buy" (1957:3). They sang not only about politics or war but also about familial impiety and moral retribution, not unlike the modern *telenovela* (Latin American soap opera). The corrido is nothing if not popular melodrama.

Redfield's fascinating study of Tepoztlán is one of the best contemporaneous descriptions of the revolutionary corrido. Immediately following the Revolution, the people of Tepoztlán began to memorialize the Zapatistas in song. The corridos helped produce and maintain the town's collective memories of the Revolution. Redfield called these "the real history-books of Tepoztlán" (1930:186). In a second chapter on the subject, Redfield argues that *el veterano*, the central protagonist of the postrevolutionary corrido, took on the same cultural role as *el santo*, the central figure in the sacred *alabanza* (traditional religious hymn). The revolutionary warrior had gained secular sainthood based on sacrifice and martyrdom (Redfield 1930:194–204).

Redfield provides further evidence to support Alan Knight's claim that the ostensibly antireligious state of postrevolutionary Mexico "did not neatly result in secularization" (1994:399). The Revolution simply added another set of saints to the pantheon. Knight refers to this as "revolutionary syncretism," the result of an "acculturating" process not unlike the colonial syncretism that took place following the Conquest (1994:406).

Zapata was the central saint of the revolutionary pantheon. In Tepoztlán, folklore held (and still holds) that the great general never really died in that treacherous ambush, as told in official histories, but that he was still alive and will "come back when he is needed" once again (Redfield 1930:204). Just as the postrevolutionary muralists unconsciously incorporated long-standing religious structures into their atheistic imagery, people in places like Tepoztlán continued to color their lives with mythical imagery largely drawn from religious tradition. The popular church did not meet the same tragic fate as the official church. As in Tepoztlán, rural folk all over Mexico poured their earlier religious zeal into new secular pursuits while maintaining syncretic traditions from the colonial and precolonial past.

GENDER ICONOGRAPHY IN THE CORRIDO

María Herrera-Sobek's *The Mexican Corrido: A Feminist Analysis* (1990) presents the most cogent argument concerning gender imagery in the corrido. As Herrera-Sobek makes clear, corridos represent women from a distinctly patriarchal perspective. She shows how the corrido draws upon long-standing female archetypes, including the good mother, the terrible mother, the mother goddess, the lover, and the soldier.

In other words, for all its newness—relating the events of the day through revolutionary prose—the corrido nevertheless tended to fall back on very traditional and conservative gender archetypes. In this and other ways, it is a truly mythic form. Based on these basic gender archetypes—*arche* meaning "beginning" and "types" or *typos* meaning "stamps" or "patterns" (Herrera-Sobek 1990:xiv)—the corrido re-presents patterns of culture that are fundamental to the Mexican worldview. Albeit about current events, corridos connote origin stories, communicating fundamental social values and providing a template for moral behavior. With few exceptions, moral transgression leads to death. Death in honor of the moral code, however, leads to musical immortality.

The Revolution: 1910–1921

With notable exceptions, corridos were, and are, sung almost exclusively by men. Notwithstanding the storied careers of Lydia Mendoza, the "lark of the border" (Gil 1992), and other exceptional women, the form has been dominated by men. Although the Revolution was itself also dominated by men, revolutionary roles were opened by and for women. In addition to supplying logistical support, many women also took up arms, and some even entered the officers' ranks. This is one of the most interesting differences between the Revolution of 1910 and the Revolution of Independence a century earlier. Although neither revolution would lead to a radical reduction in class disparity, poverty, and oppression, the modern socialist and anarchist ideologies that fueled the second revolution opened up certain opportunities for the subaltern classes. The fight for "land and liberty" did, to a limited extent, include women's rights. Conversely, although women were extremely instrumental behind the scenes during the Revolution for Independence, open advocacy of women's rights would have been unthinkable at that time.

Perhaps inspired by this potential for greater liberty, women greatly affected the outcome of the Revolution of 1910. If the corrido fairly represents the dominant cultural politics of the period, however, it is fair to assume that a good deal of masculine energy was also put into the task of containing that potentially revolutionary force. Revolutionary songs celebrating female participation present a double face, placing female heroines into the aforementioned archetypal categories rather than creating new roles for women.

Female participation is belittled through the application of cute nicknames, while male protagonists are given full identities as well as full first and family names. There is no better example of the backhanded compliments given *soldaderas* by male musicians than the classic tune "La Adelita." Although not really a corrido (it is a strophic verse and chorus song), "La Adelita" has become the archetypal corrido in the minds of most Mexicans. If they can recall the words to no other revolutionary song, people from Tijuana to Tapachula are able to recite the chorus of "La Adelita," if not the whole thing. The song has become the major musical artifact of women's participation in the Revolution. That chorus (with regional variations) is as follows:

Si Adelita quisiera ser mi esposa,	A	If Adelita wanted to be my wife,	
si Adelita fuera mi mujer,	B	If Adelita were my woman,	
le compraría un vestido de seda	A	I would buy her a silk dress	Revolutionary
para llevarla a bailar al cuartel.	B	To take her to a barracks dance.	Mexico

Who wrote "La Adelita" and whom the creator had in mind is a matter of serious debate (Herrera-Sobek 1990:108). Some say that Adelita was Villa's lover; others claim that the song predated the Revolution itself.

Whatever the origins of this classic song may have been, it is interesting to note the way in which the female soldier's role is reconceptualized. Rather than being a comrade, Adelita becomes a beautiful and potentially traitorous love-object. The singer warns of negative repercussions should she dare "be with another." Just as in the United States, where Rosie the Riveter was shoved back into the home after World War II, with the ideological support of mass media, the image of Mexican womanhood would be reconceived to fit a more traditional, male-centered understanding of gender propriety. In the typical corrido, women are objects rather than active subjects.

Nevertheless, Herrera-Sobek makes the claim that "corridos portray women in a less stereotypical mode than do artistic forms emanating from the ruling classes" (1990:14). She argues that the working classes have a more realistic view of women as working partners than do the more "ideological" songs of the elite. Herrera-Sobek provides an important, relativistic analysis of the corrido. She finds that, despite its inescapable "patriarchal ideology," the corrido has some liberating elements for women, including elements of "their power reflected in Guadalupe"

(1990:118). Although largely a patriarchal artifact, the corrido is also a site of cultural negotiation.

CORRIDOS AS POLITICAL RITUAL

Most revolutionary caudillos, from Francisco Madero to Francisco Villa, proffered policies that fell far short of the utopian desires of both their peasant base and the urban intellectuals who supported them. Only in the case of Zapata was there perhaps truly a one-to-one correspondence between a caudillo and his supporters. Zapata's rallying cry, "Land and Liberty," is emblematic of the close relationship between the leader's aims and those of his troops.

The corrido must be seen at least partially, therefore, as an attempt by the members of the base to imagine their leaders in a more perfect and heroic form. A Carrancista corrido illustrates the point (Vázquez Santa Ana n.d.:240–244):

Cuando Huerta se robó	A	When Huerta robbed
la poder de la nación,	B	The power of the nation,
Carranza se levantó,	A	Carranza rose up
contra la usurpación.	B	Against the usurpation.

Few people at the time felt that Carranza "rose up." Today many believe that he subverted the revolutionary potential of the more radical Zapatistas and Villistas. In corrido form, however, he becomes the nation's savior.

While radicalizing the image of liberal elites, the corrido may have worked to quell the revolutionary potential of the masses. As in all popular melodrama, the corrido assuages and manages revolutionary messages. It served as an anodyne supplanting revolutionary rhetoric with interpersonal intrigue. In the corrido, heroic outlaws like Juan B. Galindo are symbols of utopian desire—the triumph of the poor over the state—while more explicit socialist sentiments are, for the most part, removed.

The corridistas, like contemporary pop stars, circulated not just among the people but in circuits of power as well. They composed their prose in the shadow of local caudillos. Although their contact with power may have been nothing more than occasional concerts at a military encampment or regional headquarters, it was enough to keep the itinerant guitarists from going outside the local line. Heroic prose was safer than political rhetoric.

Likewise, the corridistas needed to appeal to a wide range of listeners. As in the case of contemporary pop, this limited the revolutionary potential of the form. A more generic, descriptive account, free of explicit political charge, would "sell" better in the village square.

In addition to those contemporaneous filtering mechanisms, historical filters have also influenced which corridos, and versions thereof, survived and prospered. There are precious few published Carrancista corridos even though he was more successful than Zapata or Villa in political and military terms. Subsequent political, intellectual, and artistic leaders, tapping into the popularity of Zapata and Villa, used Carranza as a foil in constructing their own melodramatic histories. Thus the Carrancista corridos disappeared, while the Villa and Zapata cycles prospered. Corridos for those tragic would-be-liberators of the North and South have been published and republished in countless venues, while corridos penned for lesser figures have largely vanished.

Specifically, the filtering mechanisms included publishing companies, recording conglomerates, and the Mexican government. Gatekeepers in these organizations decided which songs and performances would live on as published texts and recordings. The popularity of "La Adelita," for example, was enhanced by a recording made in El Paso, Texas. Even in this revolutionary era, when traveling troubadours held center stage, we get our first glimpse of the dominant ritual medium of the future, electronic mass media.

Revolutionary Mexico

The corrido performance was, and is, a form of ritual negotiation between musician and audience. It is also an intertextual dialog between musicians and texts. Supporters waged rhetorical wars through the corrido, sanctifying their patrons and often vilifying the opposition. One corrido answers another, contesting barb with barb, deflating claims of enemy bravery with evidence of cowardice and attempting to put a positive "spin" on events.

For example, several corridos tell the story of a battle between Villa and President Carranza's general, Alvaro Obregón, the future president of Mexico. Each version of the Battle of Celaya is told from either a Villista or Carrancista perspective (Moreno 1985:109–118, 147–154). Some tout the tragic bravery of the defeated Villa, while others deify Obregón. The Villista corridos emphasize how Villa was deceived by his one-time ally Obregón and the fact that his men were outnumbered. Conversely, the Obregonista corridos highlight the bravery of their caudillo, who won despite losing a limb in battle. In the Obregonista versions, the eventual president was destined to win at Celaya due to his greater intelligence and courage (de María y Campos 1962a:21–47, 1962b).

The corrido was not just a weapon in civil wars but also a way for Mexicans to express collective identities. For example, there are a series of corridos hailing Francisco Villa's midnight attack on Columbus, New Mexico, in 1916 and belittling the failed "Punitive Expedition" (1916–1917) sent by the United States government to capture him (Hernández 1986).

Corridos have served many of the same political and cultural functions north of the border (Villarino 1992). Corridos greatly influenced the development of the "cowboy ballads" of the western United States. More importantly, corridos have been used in Mexican American communities for over 150 years to develop distinct identities and enrich cultural life (Paredes 1976:21–109) and continue to be played by Tejano conjuntos (Peña 1985:149), banda ensembles, and *norteño* groups. Richard Flores shows how one corrido, "Los sediciocos," reflects not one but two such identities: "puro mexicano" and "mexicotejano," which is "a cultural form born from the ethnic margins of Mexican and American society" (1992:177).

In sum, the corrido can present any number of identities and themes, from the glorification of bandit heroes (Paredes 1958) and villains (Mull 1987) to songs of protest (Lewis 1992:60–67). Regardless of the thematic content, however, the corrido almost always presents its message with a sense of moral righteousness that is nothing less than "severe" (Garza de Koniecki 1992:591). It is perhaps that quality more than any other that marks the corrido as a predominantly rural form. In contrast, the urban music of Mexico tends toward moral ambivalence and polysemy. As the following postrevolutionary chapters make clear, Mexico City urbanites take nearly as much delight in ethical indeterminacy as rural audiences do in music with clear morals.

Following the Revolution of 1910, Mexico would move from a predominantly rural to urban nation. Out of the dialectics of the Revolution came a new world that none of the contending parties intended or imagined. People poured into the capital to escape a countryside ravaged by war. If the story of the Revolution was ritually mediated by the corrido—played out, reflected, and historically enshrined in its popular poetry—the story of Mexican music for the rest of the twentieth century would be played out mostly in the nation's center, Mexico City.

9 Revolutionary Resonance

One is much more likely to hear corridos played in small towns and villages than in the city. Only a few corridistas can be found performing regularly in the capital. Occasionally a guitarist on a street corner, in a restaurant, or in a cantina plays the classic corridos. Few professional performers strictly play the corrido, however. Nevertheless, amateur corridistas can be found throughout the barrios, playing mostly for families and friends.

Although most true corridistas reside in the countryside, there is a related class of musicians in the city. Itinerant musicians play in the Mexico City subway, bus system, and parkways. These guitarists are in some ways urban descendants of the rural troubadours. Although such musicians are as likely to play romantic pop ballads or boleros, most know at least a few corridos and slip them into their repertoire on occasion. One often encounters itinerant musicians while waiting for a train, sitting on a bus, or walking through the park. Many are blind and thus allowed to flaunt laws against solicitation on public transportation.

As opposed to the corridista of old, however, modern traveling musicians are forced to cram their music into a much narrower space and time frame. Navigating small subway cars, crowded buses, and busy sidewalks, they must be able to play their tunes between stops or quickly arrest the attention of passersby. This is no easy task—and a far different sort of performance than those executed by their revolutionary predecessors. The revolutionary corridistas held court on the street or in the cantina as people listened for hours. Today's itinerant musician must find a way to solicit the attention and pesos of moving audiences. Per-

Los Volcanes del Norte, corridistas in Acapulco. Photo by author.

The Revolution: 1910–1921

haps no type of music better illustrates the alienation of urban life in comparison to the rural countryside, at least when it comes to performance in the public space.

The subway and bus guitarists rush in and out before one gets a full sense of their traveling shows. They might have cans strapped to the front of their guitars or work in tandem with a collector, a small child or spouse. On a crowded train, one might catch nothing more than "Because time has cracks . . ." (a line from "El amor acaba," a ballad by Manuel Alejandro and Ana Magdalena) before the traveling performer again passes out of sight and sound. An onlooker may reach for a coin and plunk it in the can before exiting from the orange subway car. The old musician will continue this route all day or at least until shoved along by the police.

IS THE CORRIDO STILL CURRENT?

To experience the most profound resonance of the revolutionary corrido, one must travel to the countryside. The villages just outside Mexico City will do fine. Traveling over the southern mountains into the villages of Morelos, one finds a few corridistas still plying their trade. Most of these musicians have a day job, however. They play corridos for friends and neighbors on special occasions.

Some are professional musicians, traveling from restaurant to restaurant. Only a few such men are left, however, and they will not be playing much longer. I found such a corridista on my very first visit to Tepoztlán, Morelos. Or perhaps I should say that he found me. The man knows that gringos are often more likely to listen and pay for his performances than many local audiences are. I did so, grateful that he not only played but explained his art as well. The Tepoztecan corridista once needed to do nothing but play in the square or outside the general store. Audiences would come to him. These days he moves from restaurant to restaurant, hoping to find visiting tourists or day-trippers in from the cities.

I talked to a lot of Tepoztecans about the corridos. Most young to middle-aged folks knew little about them, other than having occasionally heard them sung by older relatives and neighbors. One elder Tepoztecan lamented:

The old men used to sing the [corridos] to each other on the street corners all the time. They would even compete, seeing who knew the most songs, and who knew the most lyrics to each song. Now hardly anyone knows the songs, except from songbooks. A lot of the people never even hear the corrido.

A younger relative of this same man, however, wrote music to inspire the people of Tepoztlán in their resistance to the development schemes of GTE and the PRI. Although the classic corrido no longer figures strongly in the repertoire of political performance, the tradition of political ballads is far from dead, having been taken on by *nueva canción*, folk, and rock (all of which are discussed in later chapters).

Despite the old man's lament, the corrido is not yet extinct even in the city. Although the corrido tradition is decidedly rural, the urban areas have their corrido traditions as well. In his 1930s study of the rural corridos, Redfield noted that in "the cities of Mexico such songs report dramatic crimes or accidents as well as the events of war" (1930:186). That tradition continued well past the postrevolution and continues today. *Neocorridistas* like Chava Flores and Oscar Chávez have kept the urban corrido tradition alive.

Flores gained fame as both a songwriter and performer and played his *neocorridos* on the nightclub stage, on the television screen, and in films like *La esquina de mi barrio* (1957). His songs provide a chronicle of the popular life of Mexico City, making the mundane seem magical. He was an honest and ambivalent critic, avoiding explicit political content in his lyrics for the sake of cultural reflection. For example, his song "Dos horas de balazos" is a corrido lampooning Hollywood films and stars. The chorus repeats the names "Tom Mix, Buck Jones, Bill Boyd, Tim McCoy" (Flores 1994:107). This song is a delightful parody of foreign influence and a reflection on the nature of modern mass mediation as well as a critical commentary on the way in which Mexican heroes of the Revolution had been supplanted by gringo movie characters. Urban neocorridistas in the tradition of Chava Flores can still be heard in Bohemian hangouts, in nightclubs, and occasionally on the street corner.

Political and art musicians of the city, performers like Tania Libertad and satirist Astrid Hadad, also occasionally pay homage to the corrido. Corridos continue to inform the public and serve as rhetorical weapons against the excesses of power. Issues locked out of local news coverage may find a place in the corrido. A series of corridos in the 1980s, for example, detailed the misdeeds of governmental figures like Arturo Durazo Moreno, Mexico City chief of police under President José López Portillo (Mull 1987).

In a less parodic and/or political vein, pop artists like Ana Gabriel occasionally toss corridos into their concert repertoires. I watched Gabriel sing the corrido "Valentín de la sierra" at a Mexico City concert. It is perhaps worth noting that this was one of the few songs her fans were not able to sing along with. The traditional corrido is no longer truly "what is current" in the contemporary city. When urbanites think of the corrido, they tend to think of something from the revolutionary past and rural periphery.

NARCOCORRIDOS

The corrido has gained renewed vigor to the north, in the form of norteño ballads and especially narcocorridos, which highlight the exploits of drug runners and gangsters who ply the dangerous narcotics trade between northern Mexico and the United States. Elijah Wald presents an honest and engaging exploration of the genre. Although clearly a fan, he admits at one point growing tired of the narcocorridos' repetitious themes: "big new cars, beautiful women, powerful friends, the hottest guns, the finest cocaine, another brave man shot, another friend avenged, another shipment snuck past the stupid gringos" (2001:149).

Given their repetition and simplicity, it might be hard to imagine why narcocorridos have such a committed following, at least in the North. The answer is provided in Wald's book. Narcocorridos mean many things to many people. They provide a means of engagement with current events, as did corridos of old, only this time the subject is a drug war rather than the Revolution. The narcocorrido continues the tradition of promoting brave underdogs and vilifying the powers that be, whether they are gringo border patrol agents or Mexican Federales. The

narcocorridos are also intertextual, drawing on the mythical power of
the old corridos and archetypes—Pancho Villa, "La Adelita," and the
brave vaquero—bringing a sense of romanticism to a complex, uncertain, and dangerous present. Horses become trucks, caudillos become
drug lords, and the enemies of old—Huerta's troops, Carrancistas, or
General John J. Pershing (the Punitive Expedition)—are replaced by
modern institutions like the U.S. Immigration and Naturalization Service (INS), otherwise known as La Migra. Narcocorrido narratives convert complex border realities into simple morality tales with heroes, villains, and fools, making myth of modernity.

Despite the renewed vigor of the corrido in narcocorrido form, the corridistas of old are a dying breed. In Mexico City the classic corridistas gave birth, and have since given way, to stand-up club performers like Chava Flores, political artists like Oscar Chávez of the new song movement, and norteño ensembles like Los Tigres del Norte, with their synthesizers and coordinated cowboy outfits. Classic corridistas have become historians rather than chroniclers of "what is current." Meanwhile, norteño corridistas keep the tradition alive, chronicling the bloody deeds of drug lords and law enforcement. Only occasionally do they break from the drug theme to deal with current news events, such as PRI scandals (Wald 2001:167–177) or the attacks on the World Trade Center in New York. Other styles of music, such as rock, are much more likely to chronicle and critique political developments in contemporary Mexico. Nevertheless, this centuries-old tradition may yet recoup its revolutionary role.

PART V

Modern Mexico: 1921–1968

10 Bolero and Danzón during the Postrevolutionary Era

The Mexican Revolution was fought under a banner of agrarian and electoral reform. Unfortunately, the Revolution's results were largely antithetical to the utopian intentions of its leaders. Zapata's and Villa's programs for agrarian reform went unfulfilled. In fact, the Revolution did much to accelerate urban hegemony over rural Mexico (Davis 1994:20–62). Instead of resulting in rural collectivism, the Revolution led to a radical increase in the pace of urbanization. Revolutionary battles caused incredible devastation in the countryside, sending hundreds of thousands packing for the city, looking for jobs.

After the Revolution, cities grew "like mushrooms after a rain" (Bonfil Batalla 1996:122). Mexico City grew "from 350,000 Christians at the turn of the century," explains Alejandro Aura, "until by the mid-twenties, it had 1,750,000 unbelievers who had left their native soil" and left behind many of their traditions (1990:27). These people came from their rural homelands to help construct what the great bolerista Agustín Lara lovingly referred to as "this capital of sin" (Kay 1964:144).

Most of the urban newcomers did not (and do not) arrive in Mexico City because of "pull" factors but rather because they were pushed out of the countryside due to lack of employment, food, and a meaningful future. Musician Juan Ramírez describes his fairly typical postrevolutionary experience: "We were always poor, my father was humble, and the Revolution left us even poorer . . . there was nothing to eat, the Revolution razed everything" (1995:13). Like millions in the Bajío and throughout rural Mexico, Ramírez had to move to the city, first Guadalajara and then on to Mexico City. "I did not like for my family to have to live in Mexico City," he lamented (1995:36). Relatively few chose their urban fate; it was chosen for them.

A new popular culture was needed for the reborn city. Previous forms like the corrido no longer spoke to the lives and needs of these urban neophytes. Bolero and its dance complement, danzón, did. Whereas the corrido told stories of lives lost and evil conquered, the velvet bolero offered instead bittersweet memories of love lost and evil enjoined, moral ambivalence and cultural relativism, modern catharsis. Carmen de la Peza completed an exhaustive content analysis of the bolero and determined that 98.43 percent of the Mexican boleros deal mainly with issues of romantic love (2001:57). Her book *El bolero y la educación sentimental en México* is required reading for anyone with a serious interest in the bolero. Based on her doctoral thesis at Loughborough University (1998), it is a rich and insightful study of the bolero.

The bolero is a slow, strophic musical style emphasizing vocal melody and a softened *cinquillo* rhythm (a five-beat cadence with emphasis on the last). The following excerpts from Agustín Lara's "Solamente una vez" and "Mi novia" provide a sense of the bolero's typical narrative style and subject matter, including the central themes of ideal romance, love lost, and bittersweet nostalgia:

Solamente una vez amé en la vida,	Only once I loved in this life;
solamente una vez y nada más.	only once and never again.
Una vez nada más en mi huerto	Only once the light of hope
brilló la esperanza.	shone in my orchard.
La esperanza que alumbra el camino	The hope that lights the path
de mi soledad.	from my solitude.
Mi novia es la tristeza.	My sweetheart is sadness.
Mi canto lamento de amor.	My song a loving lament.
Mi orgullo su rubia cabeza	My pride is your blonde head
y sus brazos la cruz de mi dolor.	And your arms my painful cross.

Boleros are about lament (e.g., "Lamento jarocho"), sadness (e.g., "Triste recuerdo"), and soft betrayal (e.g., "Dos palomas al volar"), replacing the rural corrido's bold promotion of great men, brave horses, enduring love, epic betrayals, and strong moral convictions. In short, the bolero was "a genuine hymn to desperation" for people who had been displaced from their rural homes (Monsiváis 1993b:114). Bolero provided both nostalgic catharsis and a new, modern orientation. Agustín Lara's "Noche de ronda" illustrates the bolero's strong sense of loss and longing:

NOCHE DE RONDA

Qué triste pasas
Qué triste cruzas
Por mi balcón

Noche de ronda
Como me hieres
Como lastimas
Mi corazón

Luna que se quiebra
Sobre las tinieblas
De mi soledad
¿Adonde vas?

Dime si esta noche
Tú te vas de ronda
Como ella se fue
¿Con quién está?

Dile que la quiero
Dile que me muero
De tanto esperar
¡Qué vuelva ya!

Que las rondas
No son buenas
Que hacen daño
Que dan penas
Que se acaban
Por llorar.

NIGHT OF THE ROUNDS

How sadly you pass
How sadly you cross
By my balcony.

Night of the Rounds,
How you wound me.
How you injure
My heart.

Moon that breaks
Over the gloom
Of my solitude,
Where do you go?

Tell me,
If you go on your rounds
tonight as she did:
Who is she with?

Tell her that I want her.
Tell her that I am dying
Of so much waiting.
That she should return now!

That the rounds
Are not good.
That they do damage.
That they cause pain.
And that they end
With weeping.

Bolero and Danzón during the Post-revolutionary Era

Like jilted lovers, the new city dwellers looked back to their rural campo with longing and regret, until even rituals like "Noche de ronda" were little more than memory held in song. Nicaraguan novelist Mercedes Gordillo picks up that theme in her book *Luna que se quiebra*. In a chapter entitled "Noche de Ronda," an old street vendor named Porfirio explains the concept of *de ronda* to Felipe, a young man who is searching desperately for a woman (or perhaps a transvestite) he has fallen in love with. "Noche de ronda" "is a mountain of things," explains Porfirio: "visits to places of the night, diversions, adventures, I don't know . . ." (1995:25).

Upset by the old man's explanation, Felipe sets off to find the object of his obsession. He finds a taxi, asking, "Do you know where women go when they are *de ronda?*" Translating the question into contemporary slang, the taxi driver understands him to say *de onda*, as in the popular phrase "¿Qué onda?" (What's up?). He takes him from nightclub to nightclub, but Felipe never finds the object of his affections. Perhaps his *mujer* does not exist. Perhaps she was a necessary invention, enabling Felipe, the (Nicaraguan) postrevolutionary, to continue his hopeless search for a love and time that never really existed.

Mexican postrevolutionaries also looked back to idealized prerevolutionary pasts. Looking back gave meaning to their urban lives and uncertain futures. Their ancestors had experienced time very differently, as a cyclical process. In contrast, the new metropolitans would live by the clock and orient themselves toward the future, showing faith in the ideal of economic growth and development. They would experience life as atomized selves and nucleated families rather than as extended communities. The rural ancestors considered the past a vital part of the present rather than a lost antecedent. They performed their vision of the past in a ritual cycle that would itself repeat, always leading back to the beginning. Conversely, urban refugees imagined the past in a modern, disjunctive mode: nostalgia. History was a lost time, a simpler time that simply could not coexist with the profane present. History became antithesis.

The bolero and danzón are nothing if not nostalgic. The newly urbanized masses of postrevolutionary Mexico used these musical styles and rituals to construct a new culture, drawing partly from invented memories of a world that never was. Looking to metropolitan icons like Lara as models of urbanity, the new city citizens imagined themselves to be distinctly different from their rural cousins and selves. Like the Mexica long before them, these Chichimeca (rural "barbarian") newcomers to the city formed fictional kinships with more long-standing urban societies and traditions. The Mexica performed ancient Toltec rites and borrowed their gods in order to stake a claim to urban membership. Similarly, postrevolutionary peasants-turned-urbanites appropriated nineteenth-century musical traditions like the Porfirian salón and danzón music to claim their place in the new city.

Nostalgia involves a sense of loss, forgetting, and failure, a belief that the decadent present has somehow betrayed a promising past. The Revolution produced such a betrayal. Instead of creating participatory democracy, revolutionary victors developed what Mario Vargas Llosa called "the perfect dictatorship" (Reding and Whalen 2003). Instead of taking part in economic collectivism, the Mexican people found themselves in a system of state-directed capitalism, at first under the dictates of Alvaro Obregón and Plutarco Elías Calles but eventually under the control of one of the world's most effective political machines, the Partido Revolucionario Institucional (PRI). Unable to effect utopian change on the material plane, the Mexican people of the postrevolution would have to dream a new revolution, first through forgetting the old Revolution and later through remaking it. The first step, forgetting, would take place in the salón, on the airwaves, and in other urban spaces far removed from the Revolution's fallow battlefields (the second step, remaking the Revolution, would take place through the ranchera, as discussed in Chapter 14). Bolero and danzón are as far removed from the social realism of the muralists as popular art can get. They are perfect rituals for forgetting past unpleasantries and creating new, ideal histories.

This is not to say that the Revolution had no material effects. The results of the Revolution were certainly revolutionary but hardly what the main body of rebel leaders and their peasant base had originally hoped to achieve. Rather than experiencing a clean break from Porfirian policies, postrevolutionary Mexicans were subjected to a liberal modernization program much like that put forth by the científicos during the Porfiriato. The new regime and single party system was much more sophisticated than the Díaz dictatorship, however. The postrevolutionary Mexican state and PRI machine used political-economic cooptation and ideological obfuscation rather than military repression to enact their modernist policies (Knight 1994). As Llosa's famous quote indicates, theirs was the more "perfect" of the two dictatorships.

However, the new Mexican state was much less successful on the cultural front. The architects of the future PRI hoped to promulgate an ideological popular culture based on *indigenismo* (Indianism) and antiimperialism. Despite the incredible aesthetic and didactic achievements of their campaign, their efforts remained largely at the level of state ideology. The great mass of Mexican people—the "popular classes" to and for whom the artists and intellectuals imagined themselves to speak—looked elsewhere for the art, music, and literature that would speak to their needs and desires. Mexican postrevolutionaries wanted art that more honestly represented their new lives or, better yet, that would allow them to escape and add magic to their potentially mundane urban existence. This new society needed a better "mirror in which to see itself" (Aura 1990:28).

Finding their lives, ambitions, and passions in neither past genres (e.g., rural corridos and *sones*) nor the designs of indigenista intellectuals and artists, postrevolutionary Mexicans often "saw themselves in the

Bolero and Danzón during the Postrevolutionary Era

songs of Lara" and other boleristas (Aura 1990:27). While elite artists and intellectuals were promulgating indigenista classical music (see Chapter 12) and folkloricism, seeking "experiences among the ethnically exotic" (Britton 1995:57), the masses were listening to bolero and dancing the danzón.

The bolero continued a romantic lyrical tradition going back at least five centuries in Mexico (Schmidt 1988:311). However, it also expressed something new. The bolero gave authentic voice to modern sentiments that neither the traditional forms of the past nor the state-sponsored artists could duplicate.

The new urbanites at first came to the bolero by attending inexpensive live shows in the carpas, brothels, and theatrical reviews and then, as the 1920s concluded, via radio and the dance hall. In the next decade, the bolerista trend would continue in film. The bolero, an urbane and cosmopolitan new sound and sensibility, formed the core of postrevolutionary culture and mass media. The music matched the era and the people, providing not only a nostalgic catharsis for paradise lost but a way forward as well.

Mexico City was not simply a decadent, urban grave for the displaced rural masses but also a land of precious opportunities for those with sufficient luck and desire. In this new environment, there was "now no one who watches you, who snoops on you, who judges what hour you arrive, what hour you leave, with whom you come or go, how long you wear your skirt, how high or low your neckline plunges, or how long your hair is" (Aura 1990:27). In other words, in addition to the high costs of urbanity, there were also significant benefits. The bolero and danzón celebrated urban freedoms, whereas other forms seemed to deny or repress them.

While looking backward to quasi-mythical points of origin, the new urbanites would use bold and melodramatic genres like the bolero, danzón, and their hybrid progeny (e.g., bolero-ranchero music and *cabaretera* or "cabaret" films) to provide themselves with a new cultural sensibility and orientation to the future. They embodied what Mexican anthropologist Néstor García Canclini refers to as "the utopian or searching aspects of culture," reflecting not just the material conditions of the present but also what the social collectivity "imagines beyond them" (1993:x). It was in the bolero era that this modern imagination began in earnest for the majority of the Mexican people. "When the violent phase of the 1910 Revolution was concluded," explains Henry Schmidt, "Mexico had undergone the most extensive revelatory experience in its history; whence its modern culture would develop in a way that would characterize the rest of the century" (1988:309).

HISTORY OF THE MEXICAN DANZÓN

The bolero's origins and evolution are closely linked to those of the danzón. Danzón originated with the English "country dance" in the seventeenth century and evolved while passing through "at least 6 countries in 3 continents" (Trejo 1992:9) to become Mexico's "waltz of the poor" in the twentieth century (Monsiváis in Trejo 1992:54). The danzón was carried to Mexico in part via the *bufos habaneros*, comedic shows performed by Cubans or in the Cuban style. Danzónes were played between acts and during breaks in the bufos.

The Cuban danzón also influenced the development of the Mexican *contradanza*, which in turn influenced the development of the Mexican danzón and bolero. "The Mexican contradanza," explains Guzmán Bravo, "is a direct ancestor of the bolero and danzón that would close a pole of unity between Seville, Havana, Veracruz, and Mexico City" (1986:145).

In addition to demonstrating a continued flow of cultural forms from Europe, through the Caribbean, and into Mexico, the danzón also provides evidence of continued Afro-American influence in twentieth-century Mexican music. The Mexican danzón, bolero, and, much more recently, salsa and *cumbia* are examples of cultural exchange between Mexico and its Caribbean neighbors. Although people of African decent and those claiming it are relatively rare in contemporary Mexico, the influences they set into motion during the colonial period continue to this day. Perhaps at no time was this musical legacy and influence more overtly celebrated, however, than during the postrevolution. Cuban bandleaders of African descent, like the great Acerina, were the toast of the town. Danzoneras led by or featuring Cubans were always in demand.

Bolero and Danzón during the Postrevolutionary Era

Popularized by the touring companies, the danzón as a musical form first became popular as salón music (private parlor gatherings) during the Porfiriato and was thus sold in the form of sheet music written specifically for piano. Danzón was practiced at the most exclusive clubs, including the famed Jockey Club (Jara Gámez et al. 1994:48). The Revolution democratized Mexican musical culture, however. Following the war, the middle and working classes of Mexico City appropriated such upper-class diversions for themselves.

The modern danzón, forged immediately following the Revolution, is most often an instrumental dance form. Although lyrical danzónes go back at least as far as 1879 (Jara Gámez et al. 1994:188), the danzón is more often executed solely as an instrumental form, featuring dynamic horns. The emphasis on horns demonstrates the influence of jazz. Also representative of the jazz influence are the names of early danzonera bands, such as Mexico Jazz Band and Jazz Band Jalisco (Jara Gámez et al. 1994:63–64). The fact that these bands used the English word "band" also clearly demonstrates the influence of U.S. jazz. Along with danzón, these popular *orquestas* needed to include other dance styles in their repertoire, including U.S.-style dance numbers. Such dance techniques were eventually incorporated into the Mexican danzón as well. In sum, the Mexican danzón represents a hybrid form influenced by musical styles and traditions derived from Europe, the Caribbean, and the United States.

It was in Mexico, however, that the modern danzón developed its most distinctive musical and ritual features. The brunt of that development took place immediately following the Mexican Revolution. The postrevolution was one of the most creative periods in Mexican cultural history, a hopeful time when modernity and high modern ideology reigned. Everything seemed possible.

Modern Mexico:
1921–1968

HISTORY OF THE MEXICAN BOLERO

While there is some debate over the extent to which the bolero branched off from the danzón, and when that may have occurred, the two were clearly already separate forms in nineteenth-century Cuba. By the time each left Cuba, they had diverged into distinctly different types of music, one a dance form, the other a song style.

The bolero arrived in Mexico in the first part of the twentieth century, via Veracruz and the Yucatán. These were the ports of entry for all things Cuban: tobacco, sugar, refugees, and music. The bolero's name is derived from the Spanish *volar* (to fly), demonstrating its derivation from an earlier, much faster and more frenetic Cuban dance music (Dueñas 1993:13–14). In Mexico, however, "the bolero was softened... made velvet: changed from rhythmic to melodic" (Ramos 1993:89). In the Yucatán, the bolero was played almost exclusively with guitars, complementing the regional *son* tradition. The bolero decelerated from a fast-paced dance in nineteenth-century Cuba to a placid song style in twentieth-century Mexico. The bolero also evolved into a slow, romantic song style in Cuba. Therefore, it is not clear exactly when, where, or how the transition took place.

Danzón and bolero took up very different roles in Mexico. In the modernized port of Veracruz, it was not bolero but rather danzón that became the rage, largely replacing traditional Jarocho (nickname for the people of Veracruz) dance styles. Young and old partners practiced this new dance in the zócalo, while well-healed dandies performed it at swanky beach clubs. Almost every bar with a bit of extra floor space provided room for couples to dance the danzón. It was a dance well suited to urban densities. Only tight squares, referred to as *ladrillos* (bricks), are required to execute its controlled, rhythmic movements. According to myth, the top of a sixty-count case of Moctezuma beer originally demarcated the ideal ladrillo. In truth, such a tight execution is nearly impossible for adult dancers of average size. Nevertheless, this urban legend demonstrates the emphasis that danzón aficionados place on control of space.

Although not the primary musical vehicle it became in the Yucatán, the bolero also flourished in Veracruz. The bolero provided relaxing musical relief during breaks between danzónes. Whereas the bolero became the featured form of popular music in Mérida and the Yucatán, in Veracruz it became a junior partner to the elegant danzón.

It was in Mexico City, however, not Veracruz, that the bolero took on its modern guise. Unlike most musical transformations, the bolero's modern makeover can be traced to a precise time, place, and event. The place was Mexico City or El Distrito Federal (DF), as it was becoming known. DF was the postrevolutionary nation's "emblem of modernization and progress," a place where the children of peasants abandoned rural traditions for sake of "the modern and highly pleasurable world outside the family" (López 1993:154).

According to one story, it was in that "pleasurable world" (quite specifically, in a brothel) that the modern Mexican bolero was born. It occurred during an encounter between Yucatecan bolerista Guty Cárdenas and brothel pianist Agustín Lara, who, at the time, was playing tangos for room and board. As legend has it, Cárdenas played his boleros for Lara, who was smitten. It is no accident that the modern Mexican bolero was born in a brothel. Brothels were important institutions in postrevolutionary Mexico, as indicated by the number of names invented to describe them (Aura 1990:15). If the hallmark of urbanity is decadence, then the brothel is its sacred center. Houses of prostitution offered a baptismal rite for young men and a confessional for the old. Prostitutes provided Lara with much of his musical inspiration. Featured in several of his songs, the prostitute would become a primary symbolic fixture in postrevolutionary popular life, music, and film (Monsiváis 1977:61–86).

Guty Cárdenas and other provincial boleristas provided Lara with a new musical style that he would effectively adapt to the urban milieu. Whether or not their brothel meeting really took place, the story is symbolic of a cultural exchange that certainly did occur. The provincial bo-

Bolero and Danzón during the Postrevolutionary Era

lero was adopted and adapted by Lara and other urban boleristas to fit their very different, metropolitan lives.

In the early twenties the most popular form of music in Mexico City was the tango, but it was quickly replaced by the bolero. The bolero carried a sense of foreign novelty (still somewhat associated with Cuba), as did the tango, yet it also featured a characteristically Mexican emphasis on lyrical melody, which the Argentineans' tango lacked. Lara thus abandoned tango and accepted Cárdenas' gift with great passion. He modified the form greatly, adapting the bolero to his cosmopolitan instrumentation, vocal limitations, and neo-Porfirian tastes. For example, Lara added gilded pianistic arpeggios to the bolero, signifying urban sophistication (albeit in a fairly simplistic and formulaic manner, perhaps due to his inability to read music and lack of formal training).

As a result of this modern makeover, the bolero became an interlocutor between provincial and urbane Mexico, between foreign and familiar popular cultures, and between the urban sophisticate's classical proclivities — signaled by Lara's use of piano, violin, and bel canto vocal techniques — and the popular styles of the rural masses, which had emphasized string instrumentation, including the harp, violin, and various forms of guitar. Lara's bolero was classical music for the masses. Whereas the tango remained an ephemeral foreign import, the bolero was quickly incorporated into the "cosmopolitan and metropolitan life" of Mexico (Kay 1964:140). Like the new urban immigrants who supported its rise to dominance, bolero was both a liminal hybrid and something qualitatively new. And "so was born the Mexican bolero in that 'questionable' place" (Dueñas 1993:149), the brothel, quickly replacing tango "with the same relentless force that rock 'n roll later replaced Lara's music" (Malzárraga 1993:25).

BOLERO AND DANZÓN AS URBAN RITES OF PASSAGE

In addition to demonstrating openness to foreign influences, the bolero also served as an interlocutor between past tradition and the modern era. The twin forms bolero and danzón were ritually adapted to serve the needs of the growing city and its millions of new citizens. Many new residents in the capital looked to the bolero and its close affine, danzón, for an understanding of how they were to comport themselves in the urban world. A vibrant ritual complex developed that served as an explicit guide to urbane behavior.

Bolero and danzón provided a cultural map for the modern world, emphasizing urban sophistication and control. As mentioned earlier, the danzón was to be danced within a clearly defined square, the ladrillo. One should never be so bold as to let one's knees pass through those of one's partner. The dance signals sophistication, reserve, and refinement. Featuring suits, tuxedos, "smokings," and evening dresses, the new styles were providing a costume for modernization that imitated the dress of Mexico's oligarchy.

Musically as well, people began imitating the sound and style of model modern sophisticates like Lara. They abandoned the wild cry of the rooster and other bold sounds featured in the rural music of the past (and the *charro* films of the future) in order to imitate the soft tones and subtle rhythms of the bolero. Just as music had once been the major tool of missionaries for acculturating and proselytizing indigenous neophytes, dance and music lessons became a central means for gaining cultural citizenship in modernizing Mexico.

Those who had participated in the rural Revolution, and particularly the youth who had become socialized as Mexicans during this violent epoch, were in particular need of such urban rites of passage. A range of public establishments thus came into being, most notably the dance salón, where young men and their female counterparts could go to learn about, and reinvent, an urban sensibility. Signs asked young men not to toss burning cigarettes on the floor, so as not to burn the ladies' feet. Rigid rules regarding the nature of the dance and dress were also enforced, signaling a more urbanized and "civilized" way of life for the ex-warriors. These "recent arrivals from the Revolution," explains Raymundo Ramos, "were looking for their place and equilibrium in the emergent middle class, their bravado calmed sexually in the amalgamation of Salón México" (1993:106).

Salón México also mirrored and instructed the class structure and comportment for the urban neophytes. Everyone "from workers to famous women" (Trejo 1992:67) came to dance at Salón México, filling the clothes-check with maid's breadbaskets, rebozos, and uniforms alongside the fur coats of glamorous film stars like María Félix.

The mixing did not stop with the new working, middle, and upper classes of Mexico; foreign elites like President Ahmed Sukarno of Indonesia and U.S. musician Aaron Copland enjoyed the modern aesthetics and urban decadence of Salón México. Copland's "El Salón Mexico" was born from his experience there in 1932. A fictionalized account involving Copland at the dance hall is presented in the 1995 remake of the 1948 film *El Salón Mexico*.

Yet, while Salón México provided a place where the feudal caste system might soften, the result was hardly carnivalesque surrender to the subaltern. There were four rooms in the salón, including three dance floors whose class affiliations were made evident in the culinary terms used to describe them: "butter," for the oligarchs and stars, "lard," for the emerging middle class, and "fat," for the working class. Fittingly, the fourth and final room was the "hall of mirrors." Places like Salón México served as laboratories of social experimentation from which the bolero's melodramatic tales of social climbing and moral decline would be derived, a trope that followed through into the distorted cinematic mirror of the cabaretera films of the 1930s, 1940s, and early 1950s.

The bolero, as a popular phenomenon, was partly an attempt by the lower and middle classes to approximate the sophisticated style of "the beautiful people" in the Mexican government, media, and business classes, who, despite their public nods to indigenismo, were busy forming exclusive suburban enclaves. In their hypercorrective attempt to appropriate the upper-class way of life, however, the popular classes invented something largely distinct from the object of their jealous affections. The working and middle classes' popular modernity was neither a copy of the foreign and domestic elite culture nor a simple extension of Guillermo Bonfil Batalla's romanticized *México profundo* (1996). What came out of this mix was a new Mexican culture, a modern hybrid. Like all living and dynamic societies, it was a mestizaje of borrowed and internally developed elements.

Although it is a modern amalgam, the bolero culture nevertheless evidenced a great deal of mexicanidad. For example, the bolero fits well into the time-honored genre of melodrama, a tradition that threads through Mexico's prehispanic ritual complex, colonial Christian liturgy, and the moral heroics of the revolutionary corrido. The postrevolutionary bolero and its accompanying rituals were, and are, no less melodramatic than their predecessors. The bolero, as ritual, projects a world of fantasy, motivated by the more profane realities of daily life from which it provides momentary escape.

In addition to their ritual functions, danzón and especially bolero also provided the "software" for a nascent broadcasting and mass-marketing apparatus. Mexico's modern media apparatus developed during the postrevolutionary era, producing almost overnight the sort of popular effects that just a generation before would have taken years, if not decades, to accomplish. For example, the corrido took centuries to evolve from the Spanish romance into a more Mexicanized ballad form, until eventually becoming the dominant musical style of rural Mexico during the Revolution (Mendoza 1997). Conversely, in a matter of years, the Mexican bolero was quickly transformed from a foreign import into a regional type (Yucatecan and Jarocho), into an urban bohemian interest, and then into a popular urban craze (in the Federal District) until, mere decades after first introduced to Mexico, it became a nationally and even internationally distributed musical phenomenon. Eventually, both the bolero and danzón became viewed as authentically Mexican musical forms, more associated with that nation in the global consciousness than with any of its other places of origin.

In a book on the Cuban bolero, Helio Orovio states that "México is the (adopted) fatherland of the bolero" (1991:12). Orovio notes that the bolero originated in Cuba but that "having enjoyed an extraordinary development it still lives in the land of Juárez" (1991:12). It not only began to live in Mexico but gained a new life and identity closely connected to the nation as a whole and Mexico City in particular. Walt Disney's *Three Caballeros* (1945) demonstrates the degree to which the bolero eventually came to be understood as a distinctly Mexican form, at least when viewed from a foreigner's perspective. Lara's "Solamente una vez," translated to "You Belong to My Heart" and sung by Dora Luz, is the feature song for the Mexico City segment of the Disney travelogue. The bolero was, and perhaps still is, the essential music of Mexico City.

Not long after Cárdenas and Lara's symbolic exchange, Mexico City became the "Mecca of the Bolero" (Dueñas 1993:12). Future boleristas need not be from Mexico City—bolero composers and interpreters continued to flow in from the Yucatán, Veracruz, and even Jalisco—but they had to move to the capital to make it on a national stage. The new popular music industry was highly centralized, making it absolutely essential for provincial musicians to move to the capital city if they wanted a chance at national success. This was not only the case for the boleristas of Mexico but for those of most other Latin American countries as well. The bolero quickly became associated primarily with Mexico and more specifically Mexico City. Whereas in 1924 the first Mexican bolero to be recorded—Armando Villarreal Lozano's "Morena mia" (1921)—was mislabeled as a "Colombian song" by its publisher, by decade's end six years later there would be no mistaking the Mexican bolero for anything foreign (Dueñas 1993:18).

Conversely, other "tropical" styles have failed to gain this linkage with mexicanidad. In fact, salsa music and dance are still experienced by foreigners and Mexicans alike as something largely alien to the national culture, even though they are extremely popular in Mexico. According to Figueroa Hernández, author of *Salsa mexicana: Transculturación e identidad* (Mexican Salsa: Transculturation and Identity), Mexicans generally "deny the possibility that someone born in our country would have the sensibility necessary to execute any of the afrocaribbean genres" (1996:12–13). Conversely, the bolero and danzón are viewed both internally and externally as authentically Mexican musical styles.

THE INFLUENCE OF U.S. POPULAR CULTURE

María Grever is among a handful of postrevolutionary boleristas who also deserve top billing. Although never achieving the lofty status of Lara, Grever had a successful career both in Mexico and in the United States, producing "cross-over" hits like "Yo soy feliz" (1918) years before Lara found fame. She produced one of the earliest danzón recordings and gave the world "Júrame," a "solemn and sacred ritual" of intimacy still sung worldwide (Gelpí 1998:206). Grever wrote songs intended for both Mexican and U.S. markets, including tunes for several Paramount films, before her death in 1951. Although she became a U.S. citizen in 1916, Grever asked to be returned to her homeland for burial. A 1997 film based on a Grever song title, *Por si no te vuelvo a ver*, revolves around a set of aging musicians who escape from their rest home in order to play another tour, an apt metaphor for the continued vitality of Grever's bolero compositions today. Another bolerista who had transnational impact was Consuelo Velázquez, whose "Bésame mucho" became a World War II hit in both countries and was particularly popular among U.S. soldiers abroad (Pulido Silva 1983:129).

Just as Mexico influenced the United States, U.S. influence was also felt in Mexico City's popular culture, manifested in food, film, music, and even the names of dance studios, such as "Hollywood" and "New York." One of the most popular cabarets in postrevolutionary Mexico City was "Río Rita," named after a Hollywood film by the same name. Río Rita was decked out in a style Armando Jiménez describes as "muy mexicanista" (1992:220), fitting the stereotypic images presented in the film. Mexican celebrities like the alluring Tongolele and great Mexican boxer El Chango (the Monkey) frequented the club. Another example is the famous Ba-ba-lú nightclub, named after Miguelito Valdés, a Cuban of Mexican ancestry who gained the nickname "Mr. Ba-ba-lú" while performing in the United States (Jiménez 1992:23). Of course, that same title would later be more popularized by and associated with the Cuban American performer Desiderio Alberto Arnaz y de Acha III, otherwise known as Desi Arnaz. Many other nightclubs in postrevolutionary Mexico had intercultural and intertextual origins as well. Examples include "Bagdad," named after a Hollywood film starring Douglas Fairbanks, Sr., and "Cuba Libre," which was named after a Coke-rum drink invented during the U.S. invasion of Cuba.

The intentional use of U.S. slang and terminology in the local lexicon became known as *pochismo*. Many postrevolutionaries looked to the

United States as a model for urbanity and modernity. Cabaret and comedy films of the era are dotted with pochismos, especially evident in the clever work of Resortes and Tin Tan, two comedian-singer-dancers who could expertly intersperse English phrases in any sentence or situation. The bolero and danzón were also part of pochismo culture.

Despite the government's attempts to inspire a more inwardly reflective culture, based on indigenismo and nationalism, popular culture in postrevolutionary Mexico City demonstrated an incredible degree of openness to foreign influences. The more the revolutionary government attempted to impose a nationalist ideology and popular culture, the more internationalist people became, at least in the decades immediately following the Revolution. It was the same basic dialectic as in the past. A government attempted to censor and redirect popular expression—as did the Council of Trent, Bourbons, liberals, and many other administrations throughout history—only to find that it had in fact produced an equal and opposite reaction.

MUSICAL FILM AND OTHER RITUALS

Bolero and Danzón during the Postrevolutionary Era

The bolero's quick movement from obscurity to ubiquity indicates that a major transformation took place in Mexican popular culture following the Revolution. The postrevolutionaries' experience of time had become something quite different from that experienced in el campo or even in Porfirian Mexico City. As explained earlier, the campesinos experienced time as a cyclical force. Natural forces, such as sunlight and rainfall, regulated their lives. In the city, however, time became more of a commodity, a thing to be captured, controlled, and consumed. The short, strophic, and immediately comprehensible bolero was the perfect music for time-pressed masses. Boleros are prepackaged bits of nostalgia that take little time or effort to consume.

Early mass media were central to the process of cultural modernization. While the bolero first flourished in live venues, the medium of radio developed at the right moment to transport the bolero to all of Mexico and beyond. The first major local station in Mexico City, XEB, had several boleristas on its staff, including and featuring Lara. The first nationwide transmitter, XEW, "The Voice of Latin America from Mexico," broadcast boleros from its inception in 1930. Lara and several other bolero musicians made up the inaugural complement of XEW, a station funded by U.S.-based RCA Victor.

Able to reach all of Mexico, Cuba, parts of the southern United States, and occasionally places even farther afield, XEW greatly affected the bolero's spread. Reaching Guadalajara and Havana instantly, songs no longer needed to move at the speed of human travel or trade. Therefore, not long after the agricultural term "broadcasting" was applied to radio by U.S. land grant colleges (Engelman 1996), XEW began metaphorically spreading the seeds of modernity throughout Mexico, connecting the entire country to the metropolis and making the capital a major processor, producer, and distributor of musical trends. Mass media made Mexico City the creative center of the nation's popular culture and, for the first time, a major cultural exporter.

Classical musician Manuel Ponce, along with most other classical artists and intellectuals, lamented the new medium's power: "I have been in an hacienda that is very far from the railroads, yet a radio is there, and the boys sing these 'sun-drunk palms' [boleros]; and, just like that, they have killed the vernacular music" (Pineda 1990:17). A new breed of musician, neither classical nor traditional, came into being "just like that" as well. Bakers (Emilio Tuero), painters (Luis G. Roldán), mechanics (Fernando Fernández), and brothel entertainers (Agustín Lara) were suddenly elevated to the status of cultural icons. Media monopolist Televisa (Fox 1997:37–52) evolved out of this early radio empire, and many of the children of these same workers–turned–radio stars would later inherit stardom in Mexico's highly nepotistic dream factory.

The film industry was undergoing significant transformation at the turn of the decade as well. At about the same time as XEW's inauguration in 1930, Mexico's silent cinema gave way to sound with the release of the film *Santa*. Naturally, Lara wrote the film's soundtrack and theme song. The film, based on a novel by Federico Gamboa, mirrors the typical bolero narrative: a corrupted provincial girl–turned–prostitute finds redemption in death.

The Mexican Golden Age ran roughly from the 1930s to the 1950s, although authors disagree on the exact beginning and end points. Rogelio Agrasánchez Jr. (2001) defines the Golden Age as 1936–1956, whereas Carmen de la Peza (2001) considers it to have been 1930–1959, and Gustavo García and Rafael Aviña (1997) define the era as 1936–1965. The movie posters presented in *Cine Mexicano: Posters from the Golden Age, 1936–1956* by Agrasánchez (2001) provide a good visual overview of the basic themes of cabaretera films and other Golden Age genres. Charles Ramírez Berg's introduction to this book provides an effective, concise grounding in the Mexican cinema's Golden Age (2001:8–22) as does García and Aviña's illustrated overview, *Epoca de oro del cine Mexicano* (1997).

Melodramatic themes would dominate the Mexican film industry during the Golden Age, when cabaretera films drew millions of Mexicans to the theaters. Through cinema, the Mexican people were continuing to learn about modernity while constructing their own. The "myth-fabricating machine was put into movement" (Ramos 1993:93), teaching a distinctly cosmopolitan philosophy, especially in its early years.

Film became "the most powerful influence" in the urban curriculum and "the first language of the urban popular culture" (Martín-Barbero 1993:144, 166). Bolero-era films featured the cabaret, a "moral hell and heaven of the senses" symbolic of Mexico City itself (Monsiváis 1993a: 145). Cabaretera films made loving display of the amoral pleasures possible in urban society as well as the horrors that could accompany them. In both the cabaret and the city, "all that is forbidden is normal" (Monsiváis 1993a:145). Moral absolutes were replaced by moral relativism, as cosmopolitan attitudes supplanted the communitarian strictures of rural and Porfirian Mexico. Despite concerted campaigns by conservative critics, the market and media would make only minor moves toward moral containment (Rubenstein 1998).

Whether film was the instructor or "great corrupter of the masses" during the postrevolutionary era, it was textually dependent on bolero music for its popularity (Dueñas 1993:11). Just as most of the earlier tent shows and reviews were based on bolero song titles, most cabaretera films were based on bolero themes. The boleristas themselves would take an active role in early Mexican cinema. Several boleristas played live accompaniment for silent films and nearly all played a part in later sound versions. Their film work included soundtrack composition and recording, "live" musical performances in cabaret settings, and even acting. These intertextual performances began a tradition that continues to this day in Mexico, as pop stars commonly double as film and television actors, particularly in telenovelas.

Although striking boleristas like Chela Campos and María Victoria were favored film icons of the bolero era, less attractive bolero interpreters also found roles in cabaretera films. The great Toña la Negra herself appeared in thirty-five films, despite having much less attractive physical features than many of her contemporaries (she often joked that she was one of the few singers Agustín Lara did not attempt to seduce).

Lara's film inspirations included "Aventurera," "Palabras de mujer," "Pecadora," and many others. As was true in the case of "Santa," these songs provided not only film titles but often themes and premises as well. Audiences would sing along when the title songs were played, turning cinema into a participatory ritual rather than passive entertainment. By the time the song "Aventurera" was sung in the film by the same name, the audience was ready to join in the catharsis:

Ya que la infamia de tu ruin destino	And now that the infamy of your ruinous destiny
Marchitó tu admirable primavera	Has wilted your admirable spring,
Haz menos escabros tu camino	Make your path less difficult,
Vende caro tu amor, Aventurera.	Sell your love dearly, Adventuress.

The 1942 film *Aventurera* would faithfully follow the song's narrative, a harsh story of a young woman's fall from grace at the hands of various urban underworld characters. Only after being raped, being forced into prostitution, joining a gang of robbers, rising to dance hall fame, resorting to blackmail, and manipulating a rich young man would she find a way back into the moral fold. This "most virulent of Sevilla's cabaretera films" features a much less ensconced misogyny and more overt violence in comparison to other cabaretera films (López 1993:158). Yet, as is true of all the cabaretera films, there is a thin moral narrative in *Aventurera* contesting the seductive aural and visual aesthetics, resulting in an ambivalent message regarding urban decadence.

In order to understand the cabaretera as ritual, it is necessary to know its basic narrative structure. *Aventurera* serves as a good example. It begins with an idyllic view of family life. Elena, an innocent young dance student, is showered with affection by her father while overly protected by her watchful mother. Yet — and this is the sin upon which the whole plot turns — the mother is caught kissing a friend of the family. This cuckolding betrayal is a clear example of the time-honored "terrible mother archetype" in Mexican popular fiction (Herrera-Sobek 1990). This unnatural act by Elena's mother sets off a tragic chain of events: the bad mother leaves, the good father kills himself, and innocent Elena is left with no means of making a living.

Fortunately, it would seem, Elena's "friend" Lucio finds her secretarial employment; but this is really a ruse intended to lure her into prostitution in a club owned by Rosaura, a fading yet charismatic beauty. Elena is served a drugged tea, raped by Rosaura's henchman Rango, and forced to become both a prostitute and a cabaret dancer. She quickly succeeds at both professions and soon rivals Rosaura in power, having derived cultural and financial capital from her seductive stage presence, dancing skills, and siren-like voice.

Elena finally goes too far, however, by directly challenging not only Rosaura but her customers and co-workers as well. Elena loses her job after clubbing a cabaret guest over the head with a wine bottle. Elena's victim was the same man who seduced her mother at the outset of the film. She makes him pay with a severe beating. The cabaretera audience is treated to the catharsis of popular justice, in addition to decadence. All sinners are made to suffer at least a little. In the end, only the voyeuristic audience remains unpunished.

Having beaten this unworthy customer, Elena flees the scene with Lucio, becoming his lover and thieving sidekick. While Lucio robs a bank, Elena waits in the get-away car. Rosaura discovers the plan, however, and tips-off Comandante Treviño, who is both the police chief and a loyal client of Rosaura's brothel. Lucio is captured in the act, but Elena escapes unnoticed.

Elena then returns to dancing. While watching her perform, a kind, wealthy, and handsome young lawyer from "one of the best families in Guadalajara" falls in love with Elena and proposes marriage. While considering the proposal, she discovers that her new fiancée's mother is none other than the infamous Rosaura. The madam has been living a double life, financing her upstanding family in Guadalajara with ill-gotten gains from the Ciudad Juárez brothel. Rosaura has symbolically violated the cultural soul of Mexico, the Bajío, by posing as *gente de razón* when she was in reality nothing more than an invader from the sinful northern borderland. Rosaura is a facilitator of Mexico's rape, a modern day Malinche who must be exposed and punished.

Yet by this point in the film Elena has essentially become Rosaura in order to overcome her. The audience has been allowed voyeuristic delight in watching that transformation and thus can be certain Elena will indeed marry the son in order to achieve security, money, and, most of all, revenge upon Rosaura. Elena furthers her revenge by seducing another of Rosaura's sons and exposing the bad mother to her children. Seemingly satiated, Elena returns to her dancing career at a rival cabaret, abandoning the man she has manipulated to achieve her horrible revenge.

In *Aventurera*'s complex collapse of victim and victimizer, the audience members are drawn further into the decadence than they might prefer, both as voyeurs and as saviors. As opposed to typical melodrama, the audience is not ceded a comfortable moral distance but must instead witness the sins of protagonists and villains alike. There is no absolute incarnation of "innocence and virtue" in *Aventurera*, no princess archetype whose "weakness calls out for protection and inspires the protective feelings of the public" (Martín-Barbero 1993:117). Elena — the closest thing to a protagonist — is also capable of very malicious acts.

As is true of many cabareteras, Elena goes too far into depravity, and with too much volition, to gain the absolute empathy of the audience.

Furthermore, the antagonists are made much too comprehensible to provide the viewers with the catharsis of unqualified loathing. Even evil Rosaura elicits some sympathy, having used her ill-gotten gains to raise, protect, and educate her sons.

Despite the violence, however, or perhaps because of it, these urban morality tales offer a redemption made that much more satisfying by the depths of decadence through which the audience is dragged. The city is a pleasurable hell, according to the cabareteras (and the boleros from which they were derived), but salvation is still possible in the end.

In *Aventurera* Elena's salvation springs from an unexpected act of mercy. After Lucio springs her from Rosaura's deathly grip, Elena stops him from killing the evil, knife-wielding Rango, taking pity on the beast who once raped her. This passing act of mercy for a mute, simple, and violent man results in Rango's moral transformation and his passionate devotion to Elena from that point on. He will repay her in the end by saving her life, facilitating her return to moral society.

Rosaura's son aids in Elena's salvation. Having discovered the truth about his mother, he forgives Elena and asks her to return. However, the evil Lucio finds the reunited couple, beats Elena's husband, and takes her away at gunpoint, proclaiming that he is going to force her to go to the United States. Elena begs him to release her, professing true love for her husband. Her Malinche mask is thus removed to reveal the violated Virgin inside. Once again, the cabaretera proclaims that redemption is possible, even in the worst of circumstances and despite the most horrible of sins.

In the end, Lucio agrees to let Elena go but pulls out his gun as she walks away. Before the tragedy can conclude, however, Rango intercedes, throwing a knife into Lucio's back. Elena's husband finds her on the street and embraces her, a surprisingly happy ending to this sordid tale. Elena, unlike the *femmes fatales* played by María Félix in films like *La devoradora* or *La mujer sin alma*, not only survives the tragedy but weathers hell in good stead. As Lopez indicates, the film is "virulent" and decidedly misogynistic. However, it is also full of redemption, a feature found in many cabaretera narratives.

Despite its Dante-esque vision of urban Mexico, *Aventurera* demonstrated to its postrevolutionary audience that there was room for mercy, forgiveness, and redemption in modern Mexico. Like the atheistic and moralistic muralists of the same era, filmmakers and songwriters were embedding elements of "Christian myth" (Martín-Barbero 1993:117) into their modernist narratives, adapting them to urban realities. The cabaretera signaled that moral life was still possible amidst the overwhelming decadence of the city.

The surface message of *Aventurera* (Elena as bad girl) provided traditional moral critique, while the sexual core of the cabaretera represented an amoral embrace of modernism. The theme of redemption, therefore, ritually mediated the poles of tradition (Christian morality) and modernity (secular ambivalence). The traditional dichotomy of virgin vs. prostitute was collapsed in the cabaretera in the figure of the virginal prostitute, women like Elena, *Aventurera*, *Santa*, and *Pecadora*. The fallen woman became a symbol for an ambivalent new age.

Traditional dichotomies were collapsing in the realm of postrevolutionary political economy as well. The war between capitalists and socialists resulted in a mutually unsatisfying yet politically effective compromise, embodied in the state-capitalist development programs of the PRI (Krooth 1995:186–215). Like the Malinchista-Virgin prostitutes of film fame, the state-capitalism of the PRI was recombinant, an unhappy marriage of neo-Porfirian policy and revolutionary rhetoric. On all fronts, it was an age of heightened ambivalence, exploration, and excess.

Aventurera is worshiped and reviled, rejected and desired. She is something very new, an icon representing both the extreme dangers and incredible opportunities of a modern nation. Aventurera is also something very old, a timeless duality. Like La Llorona, La Malinche, La Virgen de Guadalupe, La Adelita, and other real and fictional female icons throughout Mexican history, Aventurera represents a fearful projection of man's combined lust and fear. She is a weak being, defiled and denigrated. Yet at the same time she wields power over the lives and destinies of those around her, including all of the men who worship her. Elena represents a powerful and necessary "other" whose power must be appropriated and, finally, contained.

Nothing serves the purpose of cultural containment better than ritual. Rituals represent ideal models for society. For example, four centuries before the birth of the fictional Elena, Mexica sacrifice provided a sacred map legitimating the right of man to control woman. These rituals legitimated other political relations of domination as well, including master over slave, priest over penitent, and most importantly, the rights of the Mexica to exact tribute from their conquered foes. Yet perhaps the most explicit lesson in the mythical triumph of Huitzilopochtli over his sister Coyolxauhqui is the sacred primacy of man. The sexual power of Coyolxauhqui must be contained or destroyed in defense of Coatlicue, the good mother and, therefore, the good woman. Similarly, throughout the colonial era, Catholic rituals reproduced a gender caste system whose moral order was predicated on the control of female sexuality.

As illustrated in Chapter 4, the end of theocratic rule did not mean the end of ritual. To the contrary, independence gave birth to a host of secular civic rituals that, like those before them, instructed the masses on how they were to behave in relation to power. Ritual is partly an attempt to naturalize an ideal, mythical order, providing a template for social conduct on the human plane of existence (Doty 1986:28–29). Although the nature of power would change over the centuries, ritual would remain the pedagogy of power in the age of mass media.

As a purveyor of power, ritual not only must represent ideal orders and behaviors but must also provide warning against social deviation. Elena's story is a warning to those who might have considered deviating from their proscribed roles (good mother, honest man, etc.). In the Dante-esque cabaretera, transgressors always paid with their lives, wealth, or reputations. Conversely, those who conform to social standards were rewarded with eventual escape from the cabaret. Elena is an example of the latter. As the prodigal daughter, she was reincorporated into Mexico's postrevolutionary order because, although she became a prostitute and *rumbera* club dancer, in the end she willingly accepted her proscribed role as bourgeois bride and mother.

ENTERING THE AGE OF CONSUMPTION

As demonstrated in previous chapters, Mexico City had its own urban traditions before the bolero. Following the Conquest, most of those traditions were derived from Europe, a trend that became particularly pronounced during the Porfiriato. The city's nineteenth-century musical traditions included military brass marching ensembles, opera, waltz, schottische, polka, and various other styles of salón music.

The main drama of Mexico during the late Porfiriato and Revolution, however, developed in the countryside. The revolutionary corridistas survived by acquiring and mastering repertoires handed along via collaborative and anonymous chains of authorship. The first boleros were often composed anonymously as well. Enrique Galaz Chacón, for example, a pioneering composer of Yucatecan boleros, refused to sign his songs. "What does it matter to me if they put their signatures on my songs?" he asked. "The important thing is that they sing them" (Dueñas 1993:176).

Collective behavior was the norm for the corrido and precapitalist culture. The situation in the modern city, however, was very different. Composers like Lara survived by turning out high volumes of songs, clearly credited to their authorship. These songs were commodities that could be directly traced to a specific composer, whose services were compensated as a result. Now that there was an efficient means to mass-produce and distribute phonograms (the phonograph industry), as well as an effective and attractive system of mass marketing (radio and film), musicians could only survive and prosper if they could appeal to a community of corporate producers and consumers with easily recognizable song-commodities.

The first records had to be imported from the United States. However, the Victor Talking Machine Company eventually opened up a large record-producing facility in postrevolutionary Mexico, greatly increasing the availability of recorded music. Meanwhile, radio began using recorded pop songs to fulfill its most fundamental function: to sell the attention of listeners to corporate advertisers.

This new system of musical production, distribution, and consumption radically changed the relationship between musicians and audiences. Whereas previously a musician needed to develop real-time relationships with his or her audience, now it was equally if not more important to appeal to record producers and other corporate intermediaries. The world of music had become a system of commodity relations. Within the modern capitalist system, the relationship between musicians and audiences is not primarily mediated by the state, as was the case for the Mexica, New Spain, and nineteenth-century Mexico, but by an increasingly dominant institution: the corporation.

Naturally, the new capitalist system of musical production mirrored that of other Fordist enterprises. Inventions were patented, songs were copyrighted, and the separate tasks of authorship, production, and distribution were bureaucratically segregated. Whereas distinctions among writers, distributors, performers, and listeners were minimal before the advent of consumer capitalism, each task and identity was now systematically reorganized, separated, and ultimately alienated. The relationship and roles of musical producers and consumers grew particularly distant. The successful musician could produce his or her song commodities fairly rapidly (Lara was the king of commodification; he wrote at least 700 and perhaps as many as 3,000 songs). Mid-level producers contracted musicians to record their songs. Large record companies contracted with these producers and mass-produced salable copies of the musicians' records. Either these companies or other large record distributors marketed these song-commodities, creating a consumer base whose appetite for phonograms and films was nothing short of voracious. How far Mexico had come from the world of the itinerant corridista, in so little time!

THE BOLERO VS. PREVIOUS LYRICAL SONG STYLES

The corrido and bolero are not only different in terms of production, distribution, and consumption; they also differ greatly in content. The shift from corrido to bolero represented a move from heroic male protagonists in the former to anonymous, abstract, and quite often non-gender-specific subjects in the latter. Corridos communicated contemporary events, normally emphasizing the deeds of great men. Conversely, bolero's objects are usually either gender neutral or decidedly female. In both styles, however, the active subject role is decidedly male (De la Peza 2001:63). Men are subjects, women are objects.

Event narration, when present in the bolero, is much less historically specific than in the corrido and much more intimate and abstract. The bolero almost always expresses love or longing, yet rarely spells out explicitly from whom to whom. Thus, women and men performers can usually sing the same boleros, without needing to shift gender references in the lyrics.

Other comparisons are worth mentioning. Corrido narratives champion the traditional agrarian values of hard work, honesty, simplicity, morality, and patriarchy (Herrera-Sobek 1990:1993). When Obregón defeats Villa at Celaya in the famous corrido "Combates de Celaya," it is because of his masculine bravery, strength, diligence, and intelligence (Moreno 1985:109–118):

Les decía Alvaro Obregón:	Alvaro Obregón told them:
—Ahora lo vamos a ver,	"Now we are going to see,
hoy me matan o los mato	Today they kill me or I kill them
o me quitan el poder.—	Or they take away my power."

Good prevails over bad, justice over malice, Obregón over Villa. Good men are brave in the corrido, and brave men triumph. Patriarchy is ritually manifested through music.

In the bolero, however, the abstract protagonist is locked in existential combat with love, not war, and is more often the loser than victor. S/he is under the control of an ambiguous set of moral relations, existential fates, and urban forces, as in this song by Agustín Lara:

Farolito que alumbras apenas	Little street lamp that barely lights
mi calle desierta	My deserted street
¡cuantas noches me viste	How many nights you saw me
llorando lamar a su puerta!	Crying to call to his/her door!

In other words, patterns of authorship and subjectivity are reversed in the corrido and bolero. Corridos are anonymous and collectively authored ballads about real, well-known protagonists. Conversely, boleros are written and performed by well-known author-entrepreneurs whose songs feature anonymous and morally ambivalent protagonists.

The tradition of credited authorship goes back at least as far as 1521 in urban Mexico. However, it was rarely practiced in popular music until the twentieth century. The tradition of anonymous and communal authorship goes back much further. For the Mexica, "the names of musicians were not recorded" unless they were royalty; "music was regarded as essentially a means of communal rather than of individual expression, and therefore concerted rather than solo music was the norm" (Stevenson 1968:90). Although many art composers of New Spain and nineteenth-century Mexico signed their creations, anonymous and collective authorship remained the norm until the postrevolutionary era for Mexican popular music. The bolero era represented the first time that popular music would be habitually authored, signed, and copyrighted.

The bolero also continues certain long-standing lyrical traditions. It has a very simple and adaptable structure, not unlike the colonial villancico (Moreno Rivas 1989:35). The popularity of both musical styles resulted from the extreme malleability and simplicity of their lyrical structures. The simple rhythmic and melodic structure of the bolero, like that of the villancico, allows a variety of performance ensembles to play and sing it. Thus, Lara was able to take a string-based style and remake it for the keyboard, with relatively little difficulty. He produced boleros for other instruments and ensembles as well, such as the song "La marimba" (Solís 1980:35). The bolero has been adapted to a great number of musical ensembles over the last hundred years.

Finally, one other comparison is worth mention. The bolero was the first musical style in Mexico to incorporate a significant number of women musicians into its fold. Although a few of the most popular vocalists in nineteenth-century Mexican art music were women, popular music in Mexico remained almost exclusively a male domain until after the Revolution. Public performance by women was considered inappropriate, and their musical development was discouraged. That changed with the bolero.

Bolero and Danzón during the Postrevolutionary Era

AGUSTÍN LARA AND THE BIRTH OF MEXICAN MODERNITY

Provincial boleristas like Guty Cárdenas inspired Lara to abandon the tango for the sake of the bolero. That might have been the end of the story had the Musical Poet been able to sing. As Lara often explained later in life, he would have abandoned the piano and taken up guitar if only he had been able to sing like the musicians who so inspired him in his youth. Instead, he used piano improvisations to make up for his less than perfect singing voice. As soon as it became financially feasible, he began to hire others to do the singing.

It was Lara's lack of vocal skills, therefore, combined with a knack for piano improvisation (mainly gilded arpeggios) that moved him to reinvent the bolero. In addition to modified instrumentation, "Lara had a formula that he took advantage of intelligently, dividing his musical thoughts into phrases of four binary measures and separating the thirty-two measures of the traditional song in two sections of sixteen measures each, making it possible to move from the first to second with a change of tone" (Cabello Moreno 1975:186). Following this formula, he converted the bolero into a truly Mexican urban, modern, and popular phenomenon. These four qualities form Lara's identity as well. The story of his life charts the major transformations in Mexican society from 1897 to 1971. As such it is a life worthy of further examination.

Modern Mexico: 1921–1968

Little about Lara has escaped controversy, including his birth. He claimed that he was born in the small tropical town of Tlacotalpan, Veracruz, a hamlet known for its musical traditions (Salazar 1988:95). As illustrated in the film *Danzón*, the state of Veracruz is the heart and homeland of modern Mexican music, a place where the danzón and its sedate sister, bolero, cannot be contained solely within the walls of the salón or limited to the night but also burst forth into public squares and beachside cafes in broad daylight. During the postrevolutionary period, Veracruz was considered the antithesis of Mexico City: tropical, bright, and uninhibitedly romantic. Danzón became the central symbol of Veracruz's distinctive popular identity during this era.

From this soul of romance came the archetype romantic of the postrevolutionary era, Agustín Lara — or so he claimed. The people of Veracruz were certainly willing to believe it. The governor of the state gave a new house on the Gulf to their favored son. After all, Lara was perhaps the most famous Jarocho ever. The people of Tlacotalpan feted him on the occasion of his supposed sixty-eighth birthday (it was really his seventy-first; he lied about the year of his birth as well). They spared no expense to shower the aged bolerista with drink, dance, and song, partying until dawn in Jarocho style. Drunken old men with tears streaming down their faces told stories about the little Lara they knew three-quarters of a century before. According to several accounts, that fiesta was to be Lara's last moment of happiness.

What the people of Tlacotalpan did not know was that this man who claimed to be puro Jarocho was actually born to Porfirian parents in the dark heart of Mexico, the hated capital, DF. Lara was born in the place from which streams of day and weekend tourists had come to dirty their beaches, stain their reputations, and flaunt their cash for decades. According to one version, it was the Veracruzanos who first called the people of Mexico City Chilangos, the name of a bottom-feeding fish found in local waters.

It was another Chilango, journalist Jacobo Zabludovsky, who uncovered the truth of Lara's birth after discovering that he was born three years earlier than claimed, on October 30, 1897, on Calle Puente del Cuervo (today Columbia Street) in Mexico City rather than Tlacotalpan, Veracruz. Like Frida Kahlo, his neighbor, Lara spent much of his childhood growing up in comfortable Coyoacan. In fact, the first woman he "declared" himself to was Matina Kahlo, Frida's striking sister (Taibo 1985:29). Therefore, Matina could very well be the famous and anonymous "first love" Lara would later claim "to have loved with all his heart one time, the first time" (Kay 1964: 86). The Porfirian elite formed a fairly small clique, and the Laras were part of it. Who better than the cast-off child of a Porfirian doctor to bring salón music to the masses?

Lara loved to play with time and memory, offering up romantic and pure pasts in order to contrast them with the decadent present. This was true not just in his metaphoric use of time but also in his favorite plot vehicle, the fallen woman. Yet Lara did not return to the past with a moralist's intent for reform but as a modern aesthete, lovingly embracing the bittersweet present. He and his followers saw the postrevolution as a profane and secularized time. Unlike the moralists, however, the boleristas neither sought nor desired the return to Eden but rather used nostalgia and historical comparison as a means of self-reflexive exploration of the present. Unlike other musical forms of the time, the bolero was made for the present, a means of expressing emotions and attitudes concerning urbanity, decadence, and modern love. The Aventurera was not to be despised for her moral failing but worshiped and repaid "with diamonds" for her sacrifice.

Like everyone else, Lara had to reinvent himself to fit the postrevolutionary trope. Therefore, he chose the most pure of musical pedigrees. The people of Tlacotalpan, his adopted birth city, were renowned for their musical talents and celebrations. In truth, Lara learned to play piano by listening to his aunt and other Porfirians play in their Coyoacán salón. When Lara broke his arm roller-skating, it was patched by dictator Victoriano Huerta's personal physician. When it came to matters of urbanity, elegance, and sophistication—as illustrated in his flair for the arpeggio and all things French—Lara was a pure Porfirian. Like many famous moderns of his era, however, Lara faked the facts of his birth and childhood in order to create a more "authentically" Mexican identity. After all, during the Revolution "his French was out of fashion and, therefore, useless" for earning employment (Kay 1964:142). His pasty Porfirian identity needed mestizo peppering, and an Afrocaribbean component would work particularly well in that regard. That is what Agustín Lara gained in becoming Jarocho.

In taking on the Jarocho mystique and otherwise playing fast and loose with the facts of his past, Lara was joining other *capitalinos*, like Frida Kahlo, who changed her birth year to coincide with the start of the Revolution. Frida's on-again-off-again husband, Diego Rivera, also juggled his life record, falsely claiming to have taken part in both the Mexican and Russian revolutions, when in fact he sat them both out. Therein lay a great irony. Lara, Kahlo, Rivera, and many other intellectual, artistic, and political elites drew on traditional provincial Mexican identities to remake their own urban personas, demonstrating their modernity through extreme efforts to deny it. In traditional cultures, one is assigned an identity. In modern cultures, one is obligated to create one. Indeed, the elite moderns of the postrevolution experienced not only the opportunity but also the obligation to create their own identities. At the same time, the official postrevolutionary identity of Mexico was being cobbled together out of provincial campesino and indigenous cultural stereotypes. The new government, intent on political hegemony, officially embraced the ideology of indigenismo, in all its contradictions, and based its ideological claims on the premise that Mexico and Mexicans are a product of "The Three Cultures" (Spanish, indigenous, and African). Therefore, it was only fitting that individual capitalinos would draw on symbolic identities like the Jarocho (Lara), Tehuana (Kahlo), and revolutionary soldier (Rivera) to form their modern Mexican identities.

Unlike the muralists, however, Lara did not construct a nationalist political platform based on his playful appropriation of subaltern identity. In fact, he downplayed his revolutionary experience, making light of a very real life encounter with Villa's troops. Lara often told the story of how he attempted to enlist into Villa's army, only to be turned away despite having received military school training. According to the story, one of Villa's generals suggested that Lara, who weighed ninety-five pounds, might be better off seeking other employment. "I am very photogenic," the thin musician joked, "in x-rays" (Kay 1964:314). Perhaps this rejection is what led Lara away from political life and political art. He remained fiercely apolitical throughout his life.

Regardless of his reasons, Lara considered his fellow urbanites' appropriation of revolutionary campesino and socialistic rhetoric nothing more than an amusing affectation. The major intellectual and artistic politicos of his time, from musician Carlos Chávez and painter David Alfaro Siqueiros to their great patrón, education minister José Vasconcelos, all garnered great cultural and political capital via claims of solidarity with rural campesinos and indigenous peoples. In doing so, they were drawing from a stock of symbols and lives that could not be further from their own urban cultural practices and preferences.

Although Lara was willing to play fast and loose with his origins, he never felt the need to deny his modern existence. In fact, rather than deny modernity, Lara embraced it. This perhaps more than all else made him a truly popular figure for the millions who likewise felt compelled to face rather than sublimate their modern existence. In such a cultural moment and social environment, perhaps he can be forgiven for his creative play with the truth. After joking that Lara was, in fact, born in Guatemala, Aura puts this faked-birth controversy in perspective: "He was born where he was born; the important thing is that he belongs entirely to the order of our imaginary language, to our way of dreaming of things, of expressing our dreams, of pretending that we are the owners of the potential of being that which we dream of being" (Aura 1990:10). That is the soul of modernity. Lara's poetry provided a musical form for the collective dreams of millions who would likewise remake themselves in the alien confines of the city. In short, he was teaching the masses how to be modern.

LARA'S "MUJER"

Mujer, mujer divina,	Woman, divine woman,
tienes el veneno que fascina	There is mesmerizing venom
en tu mirar.	In your gaze.

The majority of Lara's "interpreters" (singers) were women, just as the majority of his songs were written about women. This was a major change from past traditions. Whereas women were secondary subjects in the revolutionary corridos, the postrevolutionary bolero focused almost exclusively, perhaps obsessively, on women. While the early Cuban and Yucatecan boleros also featured romance, it was Lara who turned the Mexican bolero into a "cult of the woman" (Kay 1964:146). Lara was quite simply obsessed with women. He referred to "woman" as "the most beautiful defect of nature" and the "the reason for my existence" (1964: 146). "The man who does not think of a woman," claimed *el flaco de oro* (skinny man of gold), "never can be inspired" (1964:15). In fact, Lara claimed that "hunger and love" were "the only motors" of his inspiration (Ramos 1993:108).

Lara's fictional women were in many ways combinations of the strengths and imperfections of the women he knew in real life. His life and work collapsed fact and fantasy into a single, seamless performance. Thus, when asked who inspired the song "Rosa," he would produce different answers, depending on who was asking the question. Once he claimed to have taken inspiration for the song from the fresh rose he kept at the foot of his dead mother's portrait. He told another interviewer that he was thinking of the "Rose of Tepeyac" (the Virgin of Guadalupe). Similarly, many of his song sirens seemed to be combinations of real, mythical, and fictional women blended together into one *mujer divina*.

Lara was never content to leave his images strictly in the realm of fantasy, however. Just as he created fictional goddesses for his songs, he also attempted to cultivate the perfect woman in real life. In several cases, he turned friends' daughters into special projects, paying for the best schooling and training. In at least two such cases, he married these "creations" once they came of age. Lara acted like a "modern Pygmalion" with his wives, and with women in general (Malzárraga 1993:26). He put one future spouse, Rocío Durán, through the finest schools and trained her in the ways of the urban bourgeoisie. After marrying Lara, Durán continued to call him "Papa," and she would often come by to see him in his declining years, despite their divorce.

Lara's perfect woman had "beauty, discretion, cleanliness, elegance, talent" (Kay 1964:58). Lara was raised by strong women, including an enterprising aunt named Profesora Refugio Aguire del Pino. He was attracted to the same sort of women. Lara praised talent and intelligence in "his" women. Yet, like many men, he was of two minds on the subject. In addition to strength and intelligence, he felt that the perfect woman was "even better if she is mute." As a fairly typical *machista*, Lara refused to let his wives, including María Félix, wear pants and was against women cutting their hair short. "I am a true liberal," said Lara, but he admitted that his liberalism ended at his own "doorstep" (Kay 1964:72).

Paco Ignacio Taibo (1985:10) describes El Flaco's fawning:

Those days there was standing guard in the house a Muse that took the place of the Muse-spouse that had abandoned the Musical Poet. Agustín wanted to change all the rugs so that the new Muse would not have to walk over the same floor coverings as the last Muse.

Obviously, there was a good deal of misogyny in Lara's fetishized representations of and behavior toward women. Alaíde Foppa argues that Lara is part of a "misogynistic tradition" (1993:130). In that sense his work is not very different from the corridista tradition. Yet there are also great dissimilarities between the boleristas' surrealist female fetishism and the corridistas' populist misogyny. The corridistas tended to reference and ideologically legitimate the subordinate realities of Mexican women more directly. They did so in a very straightforward and moralistic fashion (Herrera-Sobek 1990). Conversely, Lara and most other male bolero composers tended toward ideological obfuscation (Foppa 1993:134):

Naturally, [Lara] does not deal with the millions of women who wash dishes, change diapers, work in the factories, are fat or skinny, who grow old prematurely and support the domination—and sometimes the despotism—of a man who does not offer flowers, nor perfume, nor jewels, nor songs.

One can imagine that Lara might have defended himself by claiming to have spread a more enlightened romantic ethic to the rogues who would so brutally ignore their "Rosa," "Talismán," or "Sultana." More likely, however, he would see no need to defend himself at all. Lara was extremely comfortable with his prejudices.

Despite his machista pretense, Lara's wives and lovers treated him more like the unattractive, facially scarred, 95-lb. man he was than the powerful sophisticate he pretended to be. For example, ex-wife Yolanda Gasca staunchly defended her former husband against the critics, arguing that he was "the first protest singer of the century" (Gasca 1993:39). Her reasoning:

He wanted to provoke a change in the masculine consciousness. His desire was to break with the feudal morality of adoring virgins and enslaving them. Feminine liberation was initiated within the environment he developed.

This may indeed have been one of the unintended side effects of the bolero movement. Nevertheless, it is hard to believe that "feminine liberation" was truly Lara's greatest desire and motivation. His status as a "protest singer" is largely restricted to banal tunes like "Humanidad" and a few other antiwar tracts. As was true in the work of his *compatriota* Frida Kahlo, Lara's art is not large and didactic but instead deeply personal. This is certainly not to say that Kahlo and Lara were significantly similar; they were quite different in terms of personal politics and artistic aims. However, they share that one similarity; during an era when personal aesthetics were being shunned for sake of large, public, and didactic art, both artists chose to emphasize individual and interpersonal issues in their creative work. Women and men alike saw, and see, something of themselves in the personal romantic utopias created by Lara, just as people still identify with the human scale of Kahlo's portrait art.

Nonetheless, Lara had much more in common with Diego Rivera when it came to the question of women. Lara's real-life muses were far more complicated than his fictional "Mujer." Yet, like Rivera, he often treated both his fictional and factual women as goddesses and precious objects, to be treasured like fine art and to be traded as such. Lara's musical "Mujer" was "an object, sometimes like a doll, or, expressively, a toy" (Foppa 1993:122). In song, her skin was compared to crystal, porcelain, alabaster, light, flowers, silk, and marble, and her hair likened to sun and gold. A neo-Victorian, Lara saw women as the font of all beauty, moral purity, and truth as well as the central cause of men's moral transgressions.

It was perhaps this conflicted and ambivalent attitude toward women that led Lara to collapse the traditional oppositions — madonna vs. prostitute, Guadalupe vs. Malinche, La Virgen vs. La Chingada — into one. His female protagonists were, at the same time, pure and "Pervertida," strong and fragile, "Santa" and "Pecadora." The postrevolutionary intelligentsia found that move tasteless, and the church found it profane, but the masses experienced Lara's profane prose as a means of potential liberation. "Lara's popular songs," explains film historian Ana López, "embodied a fatalistic worship of the fallen woman as the only possible source of pleasure for modern man" (1993:159).

Once again, comparison with the corrido draws out the distinctive nature of the urban bolero. The rural corrido promulgated the "Eve mystique," a mythos that highlights "the woman's role in the loss of paradise for humanity" (Herrera-Sobek 1990:54). The Eve mystique becomes more complex in the bolero. The cabaret represents both heaven and hell, a place where fallen women become angels of deliverance, symbols of both the pleasures and terrors of the city. The "devouring vagina" (Herrera-Sobek 1990:55) of the Christianized corrido gave way to a more dualistic archetype in the secular bolero. The bolero presents a new version of the Mexica's devouring earth mother, Tlaltecuhtli, who was feared, fed, loved, worshiped, and reviled all at the same time. Woman is everything within the bolero narrative as well. Conversely, "Mujer" is secondary to the corrido, and she is rarely "mujer divina."

As mentioned above, the fallen woman of the bolero and related cabaretera films is far from the unsullied princess of the traditional melodrama. Nevertheless, there are a few semiotic similarities. Jesús Martín-Barbero explains how the princess "comes from above but has been debased, humiliated and treated unjustly," and that "more than one critic has perceived the figure of the proletariat in the condition of the victim, her 'loss of identity' and her condemnation to suffer unjustly" (1993:117). Perhaps for similar reasons, many women found resonance in the bolero's hybrid feminine archetype. While men could view "Aventurera" with a lustful and self-righteous sense of retribution (she has invited her own sexual debasement), women could read "Aventurera" as a strong woman who makes the most of a bad situation. Lara's music and the cabaretera films he inspired can be read both ways simultaneously. They are polysemic texts and thus never perform any simplistic ritual purpose. The men and women who listened to them, sang them, and watched them probably drew different, perhaps even antithetical, meanings from the same text.

Although the dualistic Tlaltecuhtli-princess model of "Aventurera" was certainly less than feminist, this new model for femininity greatly loosened the parameters for female perfection. Perhaps unintentionally, Lara produced an almost parodic version of traditional gender constraints. Gasca's feminist Lara, although inaccurate in literal terms, may nevertheless represent the female audience's interpretations of his work.

In addition to textual repercussions, Lara's work produced more immediate social effects as well. His strong predilection for women as subjects and singers resulted in new spaces for women as performers, recording artists, and actors. Lara's fetishistic focus on the "mujer divina" had the ironic effect of opening new spaces for women in a profession that had greatly limited their participation. Although this opening had already begun somewhat with the operatic divas and theatrical reviews of the nineteenth century, Lara's penchant for female vocalists greatly expanded women's participation in popular music.

Lara exhibited a playful, dada-like ambivalence to politics that made him a liberal bohemian legend and anathema to the revolutionary Left. "I have had many leftist friends," he once explained. "They have had the delicacy not to try to change me; nor did I attempt to change them" (Bruschetta 1993:48). He played for and even saluted General Francisco Franco but then dedicated a song to the staunchly Stalinist republican Siqueiros. Lara performed for General Rafael Trujillo of the Dominican Republic, on the occasion of the general's birthday, but then caused a scandal by publicly refusing to let his wife "Yiyi" (Gasca) stand for the guest of honor. As a modern Victorian, Lara believed that the moral essence of woman was above the political sovereignty of man. Furthering the scandal, he dedicated and sang the song "Mujer" to his beloved seated Yiyi, as the humiliated Trujillo looked on in shock. The song he chose, not surprisingly, had originally been written for and dedicated to a previous wife and muse, Angelina Bruschetta (Bruschetta 1993:48).

Lara was unwittingly at the center of many cultural and political controversies during the postrevolutionary era. The battle for cultural hegemony following the Revolution, explains Alan Knight, was "a three-way struggle, involving church, state, and people" (1994:415). Lara's popularity with that third element, the "people," greatly perturbed and frustrated the first two institutions, church and state.

Gender relations were an important yet politically sublimated element of postrevolutionary politics. Fairly significant changes took place in gender roles and relations following the Revolution, due to rapid urbanization more than to revolutionary political ideologies. In the world of popular culture, for example, women made important gains. Although women were treated as two-dimensional objects in Lara's popular poetry, they were also gaining significant representation as vocalists, partly for the same reason. Lara and most of his audience preferred female vocalists, like the great Jarocha Toña la Negra, who fit many of these songs better than male singers. Lara's sexist fetish ironically opened new performance spaces for women.

María Grever and the handful of other pioneers also created an important opportunity for women as composers of popular music. It was in the domain of performance, however, that women made the greatest gains during the postrevolutionary era. Along with the rise of the urban bolero came the rise of women as popular performers, both as live stage divas and as cinematic cabaretera icons. Ironically, that trend was greatly inspired by the great machista bolerista Agustín Lara.

LARA'S POLITICS AND CRITICS

Lara reached beyond the geographic borders of Mexico for inspiration. "The Mexican bolero," explains Pablo Dueñas, "is not conceivable without foreign influences" (1993:197). "Curiously," agrees Adela Pineda, "the search for a national urban popular music was found in Caribbean rhythms" (1990:18–19). Bolero's transnational constellation—Mexican romanticism married to Caribbean rhythms with hints of U.S. influence—in turn helped the Mexican bolero become a global success. Bolero helped fuel a U.S. fascination with Mexico during and following World War II, when Latin American popular music made direct inroads into U.S. charts. Lara and the other boleristas led this movement. "Perfidia" by Alberto Domínguez, for example, became a number one hit in the

United States in its original Spanish. Mexican music would also influence the United States indirectly, via Aaron Copland's "Salón Mexico," Cole Porter's "Jubilee," and others. Although best known as a corridista, Lydia Mendoza, "the Lark of the Border," popularized Tejano adaptations of Mexican boleros as well.

Translations and adaptations of Lara's Mexican hits sold well in the United States. Bing Crosby's version of Lara's "María Bonita," for example, sold two million records. "Solamente una vez" sold well as "You Belong to My Heart." Fittingly, given his global success, Lara was chosen to direct the orchestra at the 1959 Pan-American Games in Chicago. The orchestra consisted of fifty bands from throughout the United States. They played Lara's "Pan-American Hymn," providing him with "one of the most emotional moments" of his long life (Taibo 1985:86).

Lara's worldwide success is further evidence for Lise Waxer's claim that musical styles travel as "a flow of ideas and resources," rarely moving solely in one direction but instead developing via reciprocal and multidirectional exchange (1994:139). As Lara's work demonstrates, U.S. popular culture is much more indebted to Mexico than most people in the United States realize. And Lara's international fame did not end there—or even in France, Spain, and other Western nations. The song "Madrid," his loving dedication to the Spanish capital, sold very well when translated into Japanese. Likewise, the Norwegian and Russian translations of "Noche de ronda" sold very well. Lara's work was extremely successful in the Americas, Europe, and beyond.

The successful exportation of the bolero led to further stylistic changes. Over time the bolero began to lose its cinquillo rhythm, tropical syncopation, and 2/4 time to fit better into North American/European rhythm patterns and 4/4 time. This transformation happened quite clearly, for example, in Lara's music, leading Adela Pineda to argue that the bolero "stopped being an authentic expression of the marginal classes to become a more institutional cultural product" (1990:22).

The increasingly formulaic nature of the bolero does indeed indicate that it became more market-driven, as Pineda points out in her insightful analysis. Furthermore, as she claims, the main cause of this transformation may have been international market forces. It does not necessarily follow, however, that the bolero "stopped being an authentic expression of the marginal classes" simply because it adopted certain repetitive and formulaic codes (Pineda 1990:22). Popular or mass culture has always been distinguished by a ritualistic "aesthetic of repetition" (Martín-Barbero 1993:218–224), whether one is speaking of the traditional corrido or mass-mediated telenovelas.

Lara's boleros are extremely formulaic. The first sixteen measures are typically in a minor key, the last sixteen in major, followed by repetition of the last stanza. The latter innovation-turned-standardization was instituted by pioneer bolerista Galaz Chacón, however, well before Lara. Indeed, the simplification of boleros may have been more an outcome of their popularity in the middle and lower classes of Mexico than of their abandonment, as Pineda claims.

The bolero and the elegant danzón and melodramatic cabaretera cinema were basic *rituales de caos*, to borrow a phrase from Carlos Monsiváis (1995). Postrevolutionary popular culture provided an anchor within the chaotic cultural milieu of the city. Its nostalgic narrative was a bridge, linking a sense of the past (the simple, true, and moral love) with the present (an urban, unjust, and amoral defection represented by love lost). Those tandem themes, often combined in the same bolero and/or cabaratera narrative, dominate the form.

Unlike the "great majority of the poetry that was written in Mexico during those years," the bolero "did not run from the commonplace" (Gelpí 1998:202). In fact, as Juan Gelpí explains, the bolero "exhibits it, cultivates it, polishes it, and runs throughout it" (1998:202). While the high culture forms were hypocritically critiquing modernity, and ranchera was escaping it, bolero found romance in the "streets and avenues of the emerging modern city" (1998:202). The bolero represented an attempt to bring the potentially alienating world of the city down to a comprehensible, even intimate, scale. Boleros humanized modernity, replacing fear with pleasure.

As for the bolero having become an "institutional cultural product" (Pineda 1990:22), that is certainly the case. However, that is true of all music to varying degrees. As explained in Chapter 8, even the songs of the Revolution such as "La Adelita" depended partly upon mass-media institutions to gain widespread popularity. Before electronic mass media were involved, governmental organizations (e.g., schools) and church bureaucracies (e.g., missionary orders, secular clergy) heavily influenced the development and distribution of popular music. Nearly every schoolchild and adult in Mexico knows the words of "La Adelita" today, for example, partly because it was distributed and popularized in phonogram form following the Revolution, eventually becoming a means of ideological promulgation in grade schools. It should be clear after reading the previous chapters that every musical form is mass mediated to some extent, even if the mass medium is not electronic. All music is to some degree "an institutional product." The interesting question is not whether or not something is an institutional product but in what ways and to what extent.

Such accusations of alien influence are nothing new. The first Mexican boleristas, even the great Tata Nacho, were called *malinchistas* by the Mexican press for composing with the "foreign" cinquillo rhythms of the bolero (Dueñas 1993:19). In other words, the same feature that Pineda uses as the measure of the early boleros' authenticity was once viewed as evidence of its lack of authenticity and alien derivations. Not long after Tata Nacho was charged with malinchismo for composing with these "foreign" rhythms, however, the bolero's cinquillo rhythmic structure became familiar enough to be perceived as authentically Mexican by even the most nationalistic critics.

Once the musical controversy was set to rest, a new set of nationalist critiques developed, this time aimed at Lara's life and lyrics rather than the sounds he produced. Lara's global popularity made him an unavoidable target of frustrated nationalists. Opera singer-turned-bolerista Juan Arvizu called Lara "the most fertile, the most extraordinary, the most versatile, and, more than all else, the most international of us all" (in Mendizábal and Mejía 1993:59). The critics were less favorable and used Lara's international appeal against him. Painting his international success as evidence of malinchismo, one nationalist critic complained that Lara had "not written one Mexican song—*Aventurera, Pervertida, Cortesana, Pecadora*, etc., are the favorite names of Agustín Lara," adding: "He only leaves out *Horizontal* and *Harlot*" (anonymous critic in Kay 1964:206).

Despite his incredible popularity in Mexico, many "furious Mexicanistas accused Lara of being a malinchista, of preferring all that is foreign" (Taibo 1985:55). Lara, an admitted Francophile and Hispanophile, fueled the nationalists' anger by openly enjoying his international popularity. Honors were bestowed upon him by governments and civic organizations throughout the New and Old Worlds, and audiences listened to his music throughout Latin America, northern Europe, Japan, Russia, France, Spain, and the United States. Lara openly expressed a love for New York, visiting it at least fourteen times to enjoy the anonymity that its "cruel indifference" offered (Kay 1964:263). He was attracted to the West Coast as well by Hollywood film contracts. During one visit, Stan Laurel and Oliver Hardy, who eagerly sought out the company of Mexico's famous bolerista, showed Lara around town. Lara's reputation preceded him nearly everywhere he went.

While his internationalism would invite nationalistic criticism at home, Lara avoided the political contradictions of compatriots like Diego Rivera, who found himself rubbing elbows and greasing palms with Edsel Ford one day and debating socialism with Leon Trotsky the next. Well-heeled capitalists, particularly in the hated United States, often lured Mexican socialist and nationalist artists to produce under their patronage. Mexico's socialist and nationalist art was greatly subsidized by international capitalism.

As opposed to the subsidized socialists, a base of working- and middle-class Mexican fans supported Lara. These were the same people whom the Mexican nationalists claimed to represent, and they were very clearly enamored with the liberal bourgeois bolerista. While the nationalists required subsidies from the government and rich patrons to produce their didactic "people's art," Lara was suspicious of such patronage and refused almost any governmental connection. For example, when a government official asked Lara to write a song dedicated to the capital city in exchange for keeping his nightclub Manolo open later than the 1 A.M. curfew, Lara refused. He took a hit in his nightclub business rather than comply with the government (Taibo 1985:38). Similarly, when invited to play at a reception for incoming President Pascual Ortiz Rubio, Lara declined, instead staying home that night to write what would become one of his most popular songs: "Golondrina" (Mendizábal and Mejía 1993: 59–60). Granted, Lara was supported by a nascent and quickly expanding corporate media empire and not just by a groundswell of popularity alone. Of the various artists of the day, nationalist or otherwise, however, Lara was perhaps more popular (i.e., "of the people") than any other.

Whether motivated by politics, tastes, jealousy, or a combination thereof, many nationalists did everything in their power to convince "the people" that Larismo was an incorrect path. The following criticisms were typical (Dueñas 1993:197):

> Lara's music is an unmistakable manifestation of social decay. It is the same as certain shameful pains that engender visible pustules and toxic emanations. —JOSÉ LUIS VELASCO, POET AND WRITER

> [The] pernicious influence of this class of music will probably die in an "Intimate Hour." —ERNESTO CORTÁZAR, LYRICIST, WRITING IN 1933

> Some years have passed and the music of our beloved Agustín Lara continues to be popular with some of his songs now very famous throughout the world, the reason for which I ask, and many of us ask: perhaps the musical taste of humanity is degenerating? —MIGUEL LERDO DE TEJADA, COMPOSER

The critics had little effect, however. While the intellectuals and artists lobbed volleys of vitriol on Lara's work, even the Mexican Communist Party turned to El Flaco for popular inspiration, adopting "Mi novia" as their revolutionary theme:

MI NOVIA [LARA'S VERSION]

MY SWEETHEART

Mi novia es la tristeza;
mi canto lamento de amor;
mi orgullo su rubia cabeza
y sus brazos la cruz de mi dolor.

My sweetheart is sadness;
My song a loving lament;
My pride is your blonde head
And your arms my painful cross.

MI NOVIA [COMMUNIST PARTY VERSION]

MY LOVER

Mi novia es la lucha roja
mi canto, La Internacional;
mi orgullo, ser un militante
y morir por la Revolución.

My lover is the red struggle;
My song, the Internationale;
My pride, to be a militant
And to die for the Revolution.

In other words, the nationalists' attempt to save the popular classes from the ravages of poor taste and malinchismo failed. Lara became the "troubadour of the nation's soul" not despite his internationalism but perhaps because of it (Monsiváis 1993b:120).

Bolero and Danzón during the Postrevolutionary Era

The nationalists were not alone in their condemnation of Lara, however. Even during the height of the struggle between the Mexican government and the Catholic church, these "bitter enemies in their campaigns for cultural hegemony often agreed on the popular vices—drink, idleness, gambling—that needed to be extirpated" (Knight 1994:415). Lara could be added to that list. Atheist nationalists, socialists, and religious conservatives found common cause against his corrosive cultural influence. The "Laristas," stated businessman Roberto Soto, are "inebriating the public with these simple melodies and banal verses, fomenting vice-ridden music until evil triumphs, until the bad taste asphyxiates the good" (in Dueñas 1993:30). As evident in Soto's sentiment, issues of taste, morality, and perhaps even jealousy motivated the critics. The rumored all-night orgies, drug taking, and drinking in Lara's XEW studio further fueled popular fascination as well as governmental and religious censure.

The hegemonic vision of the day was what Alan Knight calls "developmentalism . . . the current of ideas that stressed the need to develop Mexican society and economy, above all by disciplining, educating, and moralizing the degenerate Mexican masses" (1994:396). "This current crossed both party lines and the great chronological divide of the Revolution," explains Knight. "It was enunciated by conservatives as well as liberals, liberals as well as Catholics, businessmen as well as ideologues, local officials as well as national leaders. It was, in short, a class project" (1994:396).

Perhaps nowhere are the limits, lies, and contradictions of twentieth-century developmentalism more effectively critiqued than in the 1999 Mexican film *La ley de Herodes* (Herod's Law). In that film a well-meaning, naïve, and impoverished PRI functionary is named *presidente* of a small village. As he attempts to modernize the village by adding a school and electricity, he is driven to corruption, and prostitution, by the exigencies of maintaining power. Similarly, for the PRI the ideology of development has formed a thin ideological patina over a much deeper ethos of governmental corruption.

As demonstrated in *La ley de Herodes*, prostitution was a central target of the developmentalists' campaign and perhaps their most obvious contradiction. At the same time that the developmentalists condemned prostitution and other vices, they were deeply involved in them. While the PRI and pre-PRI functionaries railed against Catholic hypocrisies (Bliss 1999:2), they were clearly behaving in like manner. Lara simply dared to name the game. He glorified rather than vilified the decadence surrounding him.

Nevertheless, this did not stop revolutionaries and conservatives alike from singling out prostitutes as key corrupters of the masses (Knight 1994). "Aventureras" became scapegoats, easy ideological targets in the moralists' campaign. Prostitution and the diseases it wrought, claimed the moralists, held back Mexican economic development (Bliss 1999:3). Naturally, Mexico City, "that hotbed of vice and immorality," was viewed as the center of sin and became ground zero in the state's battle versus vice.

In such a climate of moral panic and pogroms, Agustín Lara's popular odes to the prostitute were not just an affront to the religious powers but also a challenge to the developmentalist campaigns of the state. While the state's official policymakers and scientists put out proclamations declaring that prostitution was caused by the diseased and malfunctioning body of the prostitute, diagnosed as "hypovarian function" (Bliss 1999: 26), Lara was glorifying the prostitute as a modern-day "Santa," making parody of her supposed "sin." Although in both cases the prostitute remains a fetishized object of the male gaze, the boleristas' objectification was much more sympathetic than the repressive gaze of the postrevolutionary church and state.

During his presidency, President Manuel Avila Camacho permitted the Mexico City archbishop to establish an official "League of Decency," creating a united front of nationalist propagandists and religious conservatives against Lara. Jesús Flores y Escalante describes this movement as "the rebirth of the inquisition" (1993:101). It began in 1936, with a governmental censorship decree banning many of Lara's songs from use in schools and civic ceremonies. The decree was put into effect by the Ministry of Education, the same office that funded Rivera and other revolutionary artists. Several media businesses, presaging the latter symbiosis between the PRI and corporate mass media, also joined the movement against Lara, censoring the bolerista's music. In 1947 a new radio station, XEX, "the Voice of Mexico," completely banned Lara's songs from its playlist. Several Mexican radio stations banned "Aventurera" and several of his other songs. "Palabras de mujer" was banned for its passing mention of "God's desire." "Dulce aventura" was banned because of the line "to be spouses, boyfriend and girlfriend, and lovers all at once." While foreign governments and critics all over the world were lauding Lara, he was severely censored in his homeland. These attempts to limit his audience failed, however, frustrating the containment ideologies of both the Left and Right alike. The Mexican people embraced mass-mediated modernity, despite the traditionalists' and revolutionaries' best efforts against it.

The bolero held the center of the Mexican pop world until it was replaced at the top of the charts in the late 1940s and 1950s by the tandem forces of ranchera and rock and roll. Meanwhile, the bolero continued to produce new hybrids, such as bolero-ranchero and guitar-based *trío* groups, while exerting a strong influence on the development of Mexico's distinctive contemporary *pop* style.

It was during the postrevolutionary era that modern Mexico City was born. The capital developed its modern identity partly through the bolero and danzón. As demonstrated in the next chapter, bolero continues to play a central role in the musical world and ritual of Mexico City, while its elegant companion, danzón, has aged nicely, settling into a subculture of its own.

Bolero and Danzón during the Postrevolutionary Era

11 Bolero and Danzón Today

Danzón continues to play a role in the cultural life of Mexico City. Thousands of taxi drivers, teachers, and clerks escape their work life at night by dancing the elegant danzón. As represented in María Novaro's 1991 film *Danzón*, this subculture now largely consists of working- and middle-class urbanites who maintain a good deal of nostalgia for the postrevolutionary "Golden Age." What was once a sign of postrevolutionary modernity has become a reflective, nostalgic ritual reflecting an era when the city held greater promise.

Bolero culture was not completely killed off by the rise of ranchera and rock. In the Yucatán, for example, the bolero is still "alive, very alive" (Dueñas 1993:175). It is still a living phenomena in Mexico City as well, experienced nightly at piano bars, in nightclubs, and on the radio. The bolero has gained the status of a "classic" popular musical style in Mexico and Latin America as a whole, playing a role similar to jazz in U.S. cities (Gelpí 1998:210). It remains a sign of urban sophistication. As evidence of bolero's continued vitality, Agustín Lara's work continues to sell well throughout Mexico, Greater Mexico, Spain, and Latin America almost thirty years after his death.

In addition to being coded as urbane and sophisticated, bolero and danzón culture is experienced today as something intrinsically Mexican, thus romantic and sentimental. "The Americans are not so interested in love, right?" asked one bolero aficionado I spoke with. "They are more interested in practical things, true?" Having been officially redefined as Norteamericanos through the signing of the North American

Free Trade Agreement (NAFTA), many Mexicans are seeking ways to reconstruct and reassert a distinct national identity, rather than being reduced to second-class citizens in a newly imagined regional bloc. Calling upon the stereotypical construction of gringos as *frío* (cold) NAFTA technocrats, some Mexicans construct national identity in binary terms, viewing themselves as artful, passionate beings whose priorities lie more in art, spirit, and aesthetics than in business, material, and logistics. Danzón and the bolero are useful symbols in this identity dialectic.

Yet such simple cultural dichotomies cannot remain salient forever. Increased flow across borders has continued and accelerated the process of mestizaje or cultural "hybridization" between national cultures (Appadurai 1996; García Canclini 1995). One night, for example, I witnessed tables full of Mexican secretaries and Japanese businessmen sitting and conversing at a sushi restaurant in Colonia Cuauhtémoc while being serenaded by a Mexican *trova* ensemble performing Alvaro Carrillo's bolero "Sabor a mí." A large banner selling Jamaican rum flanked the ensemble, adding to the global mélange. It is a typical scene in contemporary Mexico City. The largest city in the world is also one of the most cosmopolitan.

Like most people in most places, Mexico City residents find such scenes and signs of globalization unremarkable. With continued exposure, people have the capacity quickly to naturalize and incorporate all that might appear alien on first encounter. Participants in this postmodern pastiche negotiate points of cultural stability despite the dynamic nature of their cultural universe. One way they do this is by reconstructing and reimagining the past as "tradition," stable, unchanging truths and values that persevere despite all evidence to the contrary. Music is helpful in that regard. It serves as a ritual sign of stability and becomes coded as tradition. We hear the music of our childhood and imagine that it is an unbroken echo from a time long before we existed. Music supplies evidence that—amidst all the cultural and personal change we experience—something larger and more fundamental remains unchanged. Of course, this is never completely true; traditions are always reinvented in the present.

The mariachi ensemble's ranchera tradition is an excellent example. As discussed in the following chapters, the ranchera "tradition" is in fact a fairly modern, hybrid invention. Nevertheless, it now serves as a sign of unbroken Mexican tradition, providing a cultural anchor in a turbulent time of change. Similarly, the bolero and danzón are now used to provide a sense of stability, a way of remembering a more innocent time of promise, a past reinvented in the present. The complications of the earlier era have been flattened and remade to fit contemporary needs and desires. Ritual tradition is a utopian mirror through which we can see our pasts reflected in more perfect form.

Although the cultural flow and integration of local, national, regional, and global cultures will eventually undo these seemingly fixed forms (Appadurai 1996:33), such reinvented traditions provide at least momentary hold. Amidst the blaring electric guitars, synthesizers, and drums are the more stable Mexican traditions: ranchera, bolero, and danzón. The modernity of the latter is no obstacle to their becoming viewed as tradition, just as the Mexica centuries before did not view their invented and borrowed musical rituals as contemporaneous inventions. Every age looks to past ritual inventions for a sense of stability and authenticity. The only other alternative would be to surrender completely to the centrifugal force of time, recognizing that the past, like the present, is always in flux.

However, the continued vitality of a musical form partly depends on the stability of the cultural and ritual forms to which it is attached. Mexico City still has its salons, park dances, and restaurant serenades, and the bolero continues to serve its purpose in those romantic ritual performance spaces. Without some social coherence, and even architectural continuity, ritual traditions could not continue to resonate.

Yet a popular musical form cannot remain truly vital without adapting to transformations in the popular culture. Bolero has retained that sort of vitality by changing along with Mexican culture, filling new performance spaces and taking on new meanings for successive generations of fans. The bolero has demonstrated such dexterity from the very beginning, adapting to new nations, new territories (e.g., rural and urban variants), and new performance contexts. Meanwhile, other musical forms have become more directly attached to specific institutions and/or ritual contexts, dying along with them.

The bolero continues to adapt and thrive in Mexico City. It is still sung in piano bars and other concert venues. It also continues to be a fundamental part of mass-mediated Mexican pop, in both "traditional" and greatly modified forms. Moreover, the bolero has found new and surprising ritual niches, in both parodic and, strangely enough, "folk" contexts. Unlike the neo-Mexica music, colonial forms, nineteenth-century styles, and revolutionary corridos previously explored, the contemporary bolero is still widely popular today by any definition of the term. Those earlier musical forms have settled into more circumscribed, subcultural performance spaces in present-day Mexico City, such as the zócalo, cathedral, museum, and other ritual spaces of historical significance. Their contemporary ritual power derives mainly from historical, traditional, and/or mythical reference. Conversely, bolero remains widely popular, in the sense that millions of people still actively seek it out and incorporate it into their lives. Bolero is a living cultural phenomenon, perhaps because postrevolutionary modernity is itself still alive. As opposed to the Mexica, New Spain, or the Porfiriato, no revolutionary conflagration has come to replace the modern present. Although modernity and its complements (i.e., capitalism, bourgeois democracy, state paternalism, and developmentalism) have certainly been tested and severely challenged, they remain the order of the day. In other words, the bolero still gives voice to the modern Mexican self and still responds to the collective experience of Mexico City.

Bolero's contemporary manifestations are explored throughout this chapter. There is no place better to start such an exploration than *Aventurera*, a postrevolutionary song-film text reborn in the present as musical theater.

AVENTURERA REBORN

The 1930s song-turned-film *Aventurera* was resurrected in the late 1990s as live musical theater. Performed at Salón Los Angeles, *Aventurera* marshals the talents of eight dancers and sixteen actors, many of whom are under contract with media giant Televisa. The Mexican Association of Theatre Journalists (Asociación de Periodistas Teatrales, APT) awarded the performance a special honor in recognition of its important contribution to local theater. I attended the play twice, in 1998 and 2000, interviewed the playwright, Carlos Olmos, and interacted with audience members in order to understand the cultural meaning of this popular performance not only as a form of entertainment but as a ritual act that has inspired hundreds of thousands to take part.

The 1998 version has been greatly modified. For example, the new *Aventurera* places greater emphasis on the role of police chief Comandante Treviño, providing a very obvious comical representation of governmental corruption in general and a not-so-thinly veiled critique of the PRI in particular. It is a polysemic attack, however, critical but evasive as jokes concerning the conservative Partido Acción Nacional (PAN) and left-reformist Partido de la Revolución Democrática (PRD) are thrown in by the ad-libbing Rosaura, played brilliantly by Carmen Salinas.

For example, when Treviño claims that a crowd is shouting "¡Te quiero! ¡Te quiero!" (I love you!), she corrects him, explaining that they are yelling "¡Culero! ¡Culero!" (Mexican slang for someone who is deceitful). In addition to being a strong insult, this is also a traditional chant heard at Mexican rock concerts, hurled at performers when they delay their entrance too long.

Most of the jokes in *Aventurera* are double-entendres. For example, during one performance Rosaura went on an ad-libbed diatribe against violence and crime in Mexico City. "All *violadores* [rapists] should be castrated," she proclaims boldly to her henchwoman, Buganvilla. "¿Los de Papantla?!" asks her shocked assistant, who mistakenly thinks her boss wants to castrate the "voladores," the venerated pole-flyers of Papantla. Buganvilla, Rosaura's transvestite enforcer, plays an unlikely straight man to the ribald Rosaura in Olmos' *Aventurera*. The contemporary play is far removed from the dark film on which it is based.

Adept at such wordplay, Rosaura is the audience's guide through the cabaret underworld, a smart and devilish woman who pokes fun at nearly everyone, including the political leaders of Mexico and the United States. "Fox says there is freedom of speech now," explains Rosaura. "Fine, I hope that our ex-president [Salinas] gets fucked!" She blames "El Pelón y Orejón" ("big eared baldy," a reference to ex-president Salinas) for the killing of PRI presidential candidate Luis Donald Colosio and for having tried to push the blame for Mexico's inflation onto his successor, Ernesto Zedillo.

There is another, unintentional reference to free speech in the play. The song "Señora" is sung by Buganvilla. In 1950 that same song was used to serenade the wife of a PRI leader (Pareyón Torreblanca 2001:15). The woman became infuriated, upset by the lyrics: "Señora, they call you Señora, and you are more lost than she who sells herself for necessity." She had the record removed from Mexico City jukeboxes. The performer who recorded the song, Chucho Manrique, was obliged to flee the country for three years. Author Roberto Pareyón Torreblanca informed the cast of this intertextual reference. They had previously been unaware of "Señora"'s political past life and meaning.

Whereas the madam and prostitutes are presented as intelligent and, in their way, honorable in Olmos' *Aventurera*, Comandante Treviño, the central governmental figure in the play, is represented as a clownish drunk, unable to understand anything but brute force. Like a grade-school bully, Treviño reacts with aggression to make up for his lack of mental dexterity. However, the clever Rosaura has no trouble handling the oafish comandante. In this version the madam becomes a woman of the people, practically a protagonist, despite having facilitated the rape and corruption of innocent Elena. It is as if a contemporary audience can simply no longer buy the idea that such an innocent can exist in the first place. Rosaura is not held in great disdain for her actions. She is what she is: a modern businesswoman keeping a small business afloat in a corrupt society.

As demonstrated by the "Señora" affair, there is a thin line between ritual fiction and nonfiction. Both are narrative texts informing the other. Such intertextual exchange was evident the second time I attended *Aventurera*. The wife of one of the six suspected killers of television star Paco Stanley served as the guest of honor. She was eventually invited onto the stage by Carmen Salinas to argue her husband's cause. She claimed, and many agree, that her husband was framed for the murder of the popular game show host. Her husband has since been released. This odd, real-life play-within-the-play was also a reminder that recent political dramas in Mexico have easily outdone anything fiction writers could concoct. From well-founded accusations that the exiled ex-president Salinas and his family members were involved in political murder, graft, and drug trading to a pan-Maya uprising led by a charismatic Mexico City intellectual, Comandante Marcos, the political murder of a Catholic cardinal, Juan Jesús Posadas Ocampo, and the recent election of a Coca-Cola executive to the presidency, there has been no shortage of drama on Mexico's political stage.

If the goal of power is to construct an uncontestable reality, one goal of political art is to deconstruct that reality. Although Rosaura's critiques are far from the sorts of deconstructive acts needed to coalesce audience resistance or guide opposition in any consistent direction, her satire does destabilize the sober fictions on which power in Mexico is based. One comes away from *Aventurera* with an unequivocal sense that political leaders in Mexico are corrupt and incompetent. Although such views are expressed very openly now, during the 1990s such critical popular performances were still relatively rare and perhaps unthinkable for Televisa functionaries. It is interesting that Olmos chose the apolitical triumvirate of postrevolutionary popular culture — danzón, bolero, and cabaretera — as his vehicle for social critique.

Olmos' work is emblematic of larger social trends. The PRI's development schemes have come under severe scrutiny on stage, in the streets, and even in the traditionally supportive corporate mass media. Seventy years of modernization programs proffered by the PRI have failed to convince the wider populace, including the urban middle class, that the answer to their problem is capitalist development. Although the ascendance of Vicente Fox's PAN government may indicate renewed hope for the promises of capitalism and developmentalist thinking, people have clearly lost faith in the PRI, the party that proffered such plans and promises for over seventy years.

Faith in the PRI has been continually diminished since the political revolts of the late sixties, continuing to falter along with their failed development and modernization campaigns. The oil boom speculation of the late seventies and the oil bust of 1982 helped further erode confidence in the party's development programs. Momentary blips of popular optimism notwithstanding (such as early optimism surrounding NAFTA), the development vision of the PRI and the idea of development in general have increasingly come under public attack. Promises of democracy and development were wearing thin long before Fox won his landmark election. Ethnographer Matthew Gutmann found that by the early 1990s "cynicism was already widespread in Santo Domingo [a barrio of Mexico City] with regard to the government's and the ruling PRI party's providing any kind of democratic hope for the future" (1996:259). This was true of nearly the entire city by 1997, when Cuauhtémoc Cárdenas of the PRD easily won the city's first-ever mayoral election. The Fox presidential victory was, of course, an even bigger loss for the Partido Revolucionario Institucional. Unquestioning faith in the PRI's development solutions has dissipated and may be nearing the point of complete exhaustion.

Olmos' *Aventurera*, therefore, is partly an attempt to look back and see what might be salvaged from the early days of Mexican modernity, when the PRI was new and hopes were high. In an interview (February 10, 1998), I asked Olmos to explain the political and historical dimensions of *Aventurera*. "[W]e have not advanced sufficiently politically, due to corruption," he explained. Therefore, he decided "to adapt the argument of 1940s life to the urban reality of today, including corruption," in order to show how little things had changed since then.

"I am from Chiapas," he explained. "[The Zapatista uprising] is a preoccupation on everyone's mind," as are "the elections, the PRI—that they could fall—narcotraffic, political assassinations, etc." Olmos argues that Mexican "theaters and films are full of nostalgia, because the current reality is so violent," and that even amidst the uncertainty and violence, "still, we have to go to the theater and movies . . . still, we dance the danzón."

Olmos admits a love for melodrama, "because it is the genre that the people like best." Like many Mexican authors, artists, and composers, he has enacted a cultural politics of engagement with popular media, embracing their inevitable contradictions and compromises, using them to achieve both entertainment and political ends. Olmos rejects the facile forms of distancing practiced by artists and intellectuals who see melodrama simply as "degrading" the sensibilities of the popular classes. Like

Martín-Barbero (1993:118), Olmos makes the case for political engagement with mass culture and artistic work within melodramatic forms.

Trying to work within, rather than in opposition to, mass culture, Olmos' *Aventurera* celebrates the "democratic" spirit of popular culture during the postrevolutionary era: "people went out to dance and mixed with prostitutes, with politicians, and with everyone." He places that democratic sensibility in opposition to the cultural and political exclusivity pervading NAFTA-era Mexico.

The fact that *Aventurera* is a distinctly Mexican text provides further political appeal in an age when the great majority of films and even live theater performances are foreign. Olmos cited *Beauty and the Beast*, *Fame*, and *A Chorus Line* as spectacles against which the Mexican theater industry cannot compete on the technical level. Other than *Aventurera*, there was nothing on the local scene around this time that could bring in as large an audience as these musicals. Bothered by the predominance of foreign plays in Mexico City, Olmos turned to Mexico City's cultural history and the "collective memory" that *Aventurera* represents in order to gain competitive advantage. It worked. Middle-class couples dressed in their finest pay the equivalent of ten U.S. dollars per seat to revisit the modern past, escape an uncertain present, and take part in reinventing the future. Nearly everyone sings along to the familiar songs that Olmos has chosen for his theatrical adaptation.

Aventurera is performed at the legendary Salón Los Angeles. The performance begins in the traditional manner, with the master of ceremonies shouting, "¡El que no conoce Los Angeles, no conoce México!" (Anyone who does not know Los Angeles does not know Mexico City.) The pageant continues, through both dramatic dialog and dancing. The action takes place among the tables, making the audience part of the cathartic ritual. As telenovela stars, the actors seem more familiar and more "real" than typical stage actors. For the couples that I sat with, *Aventurera* was nothing short of "a dramatic catharsis," just as Olmos intended it.

The contemporary *Aventurera* is a highly polysemic text, befitting what is once again a highly ambivalent, confused, and liminal era, when the political, cultural, and even sexual consensus of mid-century Mexico (the era of cultural conservatism that replaced the postrevolution) continues to dissolve. *Aventurera* provides both the comfort of nostalgia and a means of evaluating the present. In Olmos' words: "We are reviewing ourselves. It [*Aventurera*] is like being in a church." Olmos softened certain elements of the film, including the violence, while modifying other aspects in order to form a new critical narrative. Thus the henchman Rango has been transformed into the transvestite Buganvilla, a (wo)man who is at the same time both ultrafeminine and masculine. Just as the original film dissolved the sacred boundary between Virgin and prostitute, Olmos' play violates the sacred boundary between masculine and feminine. If the film challenged dichotomous notions of femininity, making Elena both Virgin (de Guadalupe) and whore (La Malinche), the contemporary play collapses dichotomous and essentialized notions of gender, making Buganvilla both man and woman.

Aventurera is equal parts reflection on the past, ritual escape from the present, and contemplation of the future. Ultimately, it has succeeded because, as Olmos intended, it is "narrating something important" to the Mexican audience.

THE PIANO BAR

Aventurera is unusual in its blend of live theater, music, and dance, but it is certainly not the only ritual forum in which the bolero and danzón still thrive. As mentioned above, bolero and danzón are performed throughout the city. In this section I describe a few of the bolero performances I have witnessed over the last four years while conducting fieldwork in Mexico City.

The piano bar is the quintessential site for contemporary bolero performance. A pianist by the name of Hernán plays the bolero several nights a week at one such nightspot, which I will call the Blue Moon. Often joining Hernán there was a medical doctor who was an amateur singer. I got to know him during my first visit to the bar. Upon entering, I was met with the usual polite query: "A cup [a drink] or dinner?" "Dinner," I replied. I sat down and began listening to Hernán and the doctor perform. In the piano bar, such performances are extremely casual, more like a group of friends gathering around a piano than a concert. Piano bar patrons are invited to sing. Rarely do they address an audience, and rarely is there an audience paying much attention to them. It is more of a social scene than a performance per se.

After hearing the doctor sing Lara's "Talismán" and "Mi novia (es la tristeza)," I requested and received a rendition of "Noche de ronda." The doctor knew all the words to the song and sang with great passion. After singing several other songs, the doctor joined me for a drink and conversation, in which he described singing the bolero as his "hobby" and his "life."

I am not certain if he was aware of it, but the good doctor was fulfilling a time-honored tradition in Mexico. There have been many famous doctor-musicians in Mexico. Aniceto Ortega del Villar (1823–1875) was both a gynecologist and master musician (Kuss 1988:323). Ortega del Villar wrote a successful opera about Cuauhtémoc and published marches that were enjoyed by both Juárez and his hated enemy, Maximilian. One of his marches became known as far away as Western Europe. In fact, the Prussians played it as they entered Paris (Sordo Sodi 1982:302). Contemporary bolerista and musical historian Pablo Dueñas is also a surgeon. Yet another accomplished Mexican musicologist, Dr. Gabriel Saldívar y Silva, began his musical studies after completing five years of medical school. Likewise, one member of Mexico's well-known nueva canción ensemble Los Folkloristas is also in the medical profession, working as a veterinarian (Heath 1987:17). Boleristas are often drawn from nonmusical professions, indulging their passion for the bolero, which ennobles and enlivens their more mundane daytime lives as doctors, mayors, waiters, taxi drivers, and laborers (a listing of just a few of the professions practiced by bolero aficionados I have encountered in Mexico City).

The doctor at the Blue Moon has retained full amateur status. His avocation for the music propels him out of the house and into this quiet little urban refuge whenever he feels the need to sing. He feels that need quite often, having been through a divorce and several subsequent partners whom he refers to as "girlfriends." He asked me where I lived. I was living in Ohio at the time. "I have been to Columbus," he said, referring to the Ohio capital as "beautiful."

The doctor exemplifies the bolerista attitude toward time and life. In the bolero consciousness, all things can be remade into bittersweet memories of loves lived and lost. All that is relatively flat and lifeless (such as Columbus, Ohio) can be reanimated in the musical mind. "To remember is to live," sang the good doctor, perhaps imagining a perfect love, time, or place. A good bolerista augments memory through musical performance. Bolero is a filter, a ritual means of purifying the past, thus ennobling the present. The bolero is a recreational ritual as a means of relaxation and, more literally, as a tool for re-creating the past to fit contemporary needs and desires.

Various Mexico City precincts present bolero concerts and danzón dances. One such series, Boleros en Coyoacán, was well attended in 2000. On Sunday, July 23, for example, an audience of 600 turned out. The audience was made up mainly of older folks, several of whom brought along grandchildren. The master of ceremonies began the concert by asking couples to "hold hands and remember those days." The performance included a wide selection of songs, including works by Alvaro Carillo ("Sabor a mí" and "Un poco más"), Armando Manzanero ("Contigo aprendí" and "Somos novios"), and, of course, Agustín Lara ("Nadie," "Piensa en mí"). The older members of the audience were entranced, singing many boleros word for word, while many of their young charges were annoyed by the "old people's" music. One woman sitting in the back had to reprimand her grandson for booing. The bolero and danzón have greater youth appeal when updated, mixed into more contemporary pop repertoires, or performed as art-house parody. For those who remember bolero's Golden Age, however, the classic performance styles are greatly preferred. More than one older person has complained to me about pop renditions of the cherished songs.

One of the most interesting bolero subcultures in contemporary Mexico belongs to the avant-garde playwrights, songwriters, and musicians associated with Bar Hábito and similar urbane art houses. Eugenia León, Astrid Hadad, and a small clique of Bohemian neoboleristas have used bolero and danzón to craft new political aesthetics. Combining the apoliticism, hypermodernity, and urbanity of the postrevolutionary mu-

Eugenia León at the Baile, Música y Canto de Iberoamérica concert. Photo by Carlos Franco.

sic with biting, satirical, and political lyrics, they have given new life to these aging styles. Liliana Felipe's neo-danzón piece "Que devuelvan," sung by Eugenia León, provides a brilliant case in point. Indicting the members of the Salinas administration for "the arrogance of their modernity" and blaming them for Mexico's current predicament, the song repeatedly states that Mexicans are the "victims of neoliberal sins." Felipe and other Mexico City performance artists are using a postmodern aesthetic, combining modern styles with discordant lyrical messages, to challenge the government and neoliberal ideologies.

León presents an interesting study in postmodern musical politics. She is an important feminist political leader and icon of feminine sexuality, a combination rarely attempted, achieved, or allowed in the United States. An article written for the Latin American feminist magazine *Fem* clearly shows this political dualism, a conscious part of León's art and politics. Entitled "The Pleasure of Being Eugenia León," the article is based on an interview in which she features her views on politics and the political importance of music. León was a representative of the Latin American delegation at the 1995 Beijing Conference on Women and has performed for audiences the world over. She claims that music offers one means of expressing the need for "liberty, justice, and democracy" in the world (Díaz Castellanos 1996:13). The *Fem* article and photos present León as sensual and strong, a sort of ultrafemininity very different from U.S. feminist representations. Guadalupe Díaz Castellanos ends the article by thanking León for "her red dress and black satchel," offering compliments to her hair and "great lips" as well. The interview is in keeping with the spirit of Eugenia León's music and politics. León critiques power while celebrating pleasure, making her work distinct from the puritanical politics of the U.S. Left and feminism, where commitment is more often signaled by abject seriousness. León works within the conundrums of oppression, exploring and expanding what it means to be a woman in a sexist society. Jean Bethke Elshtain has argued that when it comes to gender there "is no way *out* but there are several ways *in:* by going back to the texts and offering readings that track the ambiguities and ironies of our gendered identities" (1989:132). She could very well be describing Eugenia León's work when she argues for feminist scholars to "return with skeptical eyes to powerful texts and open them up to newer modes of interrogation" (1989:132).

Not only do the words of León's and Felipe's danzones and boleros demonstrate a sort of political playfulness, but the use of these forms represents a conscious attempt to work within, and expand, popular notions of propriety. León and Felipe politicize the popular, pulling its normally sublimated political elements out to the surface for all to consider and take pleasure in.

LIVING LARA, LOVING POP

Artists like León, Hadad, and Felipe are saving the bolero from the fossilization that tends to befall music as it ages. Too often, older forms of music are given the stigmatic label of folk "tradition" (i.e., something that school kids are forced to memorize and dislike). Ironically, by being kept from the categorical death of "folk music" or "traditional music," the bolero has been able to remain a living tradition in the way that other forms from the past have not. As noted below, however, the dangerous label of "tradition," and even "folk," is beginning to be applied to the bolero, perhaps signaling the beginning of its decline.

I have argued that the bolero allows us a glimpse into a period when a new, modernist orientation toward time first took hold of the popular imagination (see Chapter 10). This urbanized and modernized cultural orientation expressed itself through nostalgia for the Porfirian past combined with a licentious embrace of the sexual and social freedoms made possible in the present and a sense of optimism for the future. The postrevolutionary future seemed, at least for a short while, to be open to the democratic desires of the newly enfranchised masses. This sense of confidence and optimism can be heard in the experimental sound of the bolero and danzón.

As the promise of modernity has faded through successive waves of political failure and social disillusionment, Mexican popular culture has become less open to the promises of modernity and, perhaps, more retrospective than prospective. Therefore, the past and its music have been mined recently for clues as to how one might go about reimagining the future.

Lara has been resurrected as part of this critical, retrospective, and revisionist trend. As the Mexican bolero's patriarch and popularizer, Agustín Lara is increasingly viewed as a symbol for the postrevolutionary era. From the Agustín Lara Theater in Mexico City and the various monuments in Spain dedicated to his name to the sizable Lara CD sections in stores across the United States, there is great evidence of his continued widespread cultural impact, not only in Mexico but throughout the world. For example, at a recent retrospective spectacle in the zócalo, the Vicente Fox inaugural Verbena (public celebration) of December 1, 2000, Lara was one of only a handful of Mexican musicians and artists directly referenced. During the music, slide, and laser-light show, an image of Lara with singer Pedro Vargas was displayed, while the opening lines of "Mujer" were played over the sound system. Even Mexican rock stars such as the Jaguares cite Mexico's Musical Poet as inspiration.

Of course, Lara's continued fame could be overstated, and there certainly is generational fall-off. Evidence of this includes a recent game show (May 24, 2000). On *A ganar con Omar* (Win with Omar), a set of teachers and students alike could not identify the composer of "Santa." Nearly anyone from the elder generation would have known it was Lara. Lara remains popular; but, quite naturally, the depth and breadth of that popularity have changed over time. His followers have changed from fans (a large and relatively undifferentiated audience) to aficionados (a more specific type of audience composed of knowledgeable listeners who take a more active interest in bolero as a genre and Lara as an artist). Bolero is analogous to U.S. jazz in that regard.

Several contemporary pop icons have continued the Lara legacy, including Luis Miguel, Lucero, Ana Gabriel, Angela Carrasco, and Daniela Romo, among others. For example, Miguel brought Lara's "Noche de ronda" back to the charts with his 1997 release of a CD completely dedicated to the bolero. Many bolero aficionados and music critics are ambivalent about Miguel's work, however. The most insightful analysis is offered by Carlos Monsiváis, who notes the contradiction between Miguel's dynamic high-volume delivery and the intimate nature of the classic bolero lyrics he is singing (1995:193–197). For better or for worse, new generations have been brought to the bolero through Miguel's recordings and pop concert performances.

Other pop stars, less directly referential, have adopted various elements of postrevolutionary bolero without singing boleros per se. Lucero is an example. Because of her clear, smooth voice and movie-star looks, older folks view Lucero as a throwback to elegant bolero divas like María Victoria and Verónica Loyo. Younger audiences, particularly young girls, view Lucero as an ideal type as well: a world-traveling pop model leading the telenovela lifestyle. Lucero's recent marriage to another pop crooner, Mijares, became a popular television event and video hit. Taking up residence in Acapulco, Lucero and Mijares are fulfilling the Agustín Lara/María Félix tradition quite well.

Ana Gabriel, whose strong, throaty voice is more akin to that of great ranchera vocalist Lola Beltrán than to the velvet-toned boleristas, nevertheless includes several boleros in her extensive repertoire. Gabriel's mariachi version of Lara's "Solamente una vez," for example, was a popular hit in the 1980s. Her 1998 return to Mexico City, at a Valentine's Day charity concert, featured several bolero-style songs. Most of Gabriel's audience were able to sing along word for word.

Mexican pop stars still include the romantic bolero in their repertoires. Even when not performing true boleros, Mexican pop music demonstrates bolero influence in the form of romantic, nostalgic, and bittersweet lyrics, very much in keeping with the bolero tradition. Contemporary Mexican pop melodies are still typically accompanied by Afrocaribbean rhythms, an association first formed with the bolero.

Likewise, Mexican pop performances often bear distinct markers of the bolero tradition. Mexican pop stars frequently don tuxedos and ball gowns to execute *música romántica*, a category of popular music that has evolved fairly directly from the bolero. Although such contemporary pop songs and performances rarely fit the technical criteria that define the bolero as a distinct musical style, they nevertheless demonstrate its influence.

Ironically, when Gabriel, Miguel, and other contemporary stars include actual boleros on their CDs and in their performances, this is now represented as a nod to Mexican tradition. Almost without fail, contemporary pop performers present boleros as homage to the past, and audience members repeatedly describe the performances in nostalgic terms as well. After the Gabriel concert, one fellow audience member noted that the pop star sang in a Mexican manner, "the way they used to." The man made unfavorable remarks about other contemporary Mexican performers, who are "trying to be gringos." Pop rock, he argued, is the music of "Americanos" and sounds inauthentic when performed by Mexicans, just as "they" (gringos) would sound inauthentic trying to execute a bolero or ranchera tune. Even those too young to remember the postrevolutionary era — that is, most people currently alive — often describe bolero in reverential terms, as a link to the Golden Age of song and film.

Others are more critical in their reflections. For example, the members of an impoverished family band play on the street in Mexico City's high-rent Zona Rosa, skillfully working "Triste recuerdo" (Sad Memory) into the set, fully cognizant that the private meaning of their music is being lost on the largely foreign and Mexican elite passersby. They perform the bolero with a sense of ironic disdain for the present more than nostalgic reverence for the past. A boy passes around the hat with a wry smile, mouthing "Sad Memory" to no one in particular, because practically no one but he and his family understand the bittersweet meanings of their performance. In this case, as in the Bar Hábito performances, bolero is transformed from romantic text into social-realist critique. Such work is intended to raise the audience's awareness of, and anger at, social contradictions more than to assuage their modern frustrations. It is music as catalyst rather than anodyne.

TANGO VS. BOLERO

The bolero and tango are occasionally compared, having been popularized during roughly the same era. Indeed, the two styles share certain traits, such as melodramatic lyrics and a strong sense of modernist nostalgia. An analysis of their differences, however, can tell us much about the differences between Mexico, the adopted home of the bolero, and Argentina, the home of the tango. Two tango performances help to elicit the comparison.

One such concert, in a Coyoacán cabaret, was performed for an audience largely consisting of intellectuals, artists, and college students. During conversations before the event, I noted a great number of people demonstrating and performing their knowledge of tango to others around them. Many would drop the names of their favorite tango artists to impress conversation partners with their knowledge of the high-status style. Rather than being an indication of the tango's popularity, the scene demonstrated the generally foreign nature of the tango for most Mexicans. Something that is widely understood does not require such conspicuous performance. Indeed, tango is a form of conspicuous consumption in Mexico, as in the United States. It garners cultural capital for the listener. Conversely, a popular ethos pervades most bolero concerts. It is an inclusive ritual of the working and middle classes rather than an exclusive rite of identification for the intellectual and upper classes.

Another tango concert, Tangos con Libertad, was aimed at a more popular audience but also demonstrated the foreign feel of the Argentinean art form. It was a free Sunday concert in Chapultepec Park. An Argentinean male keyboardist-vocalist and a female vocalist provided a well-rehearsed program to an appreciative but unusually reserved Mexican crowd. Most of the Argentinean jokes seemed to escape the audience. The music itself failed to inspire audience engagement. As opposed to the typical bolero review, there were none of the rhythmic movements, gestures of recognition, conversations referencing a favorite song or composer, or singing along that I had come to expect at Mexican concerts. This stands in contrast to Mexican bolero, ranchera, pop, and rock concerts, where audiences tend to be extremely participatory. The tango audience members seemed to appreciate the Argentinean art form; however, they stood outside it rather than considering it their own.

One thing that differentiates more Mexicanized musical styles from the tango is the use of voice and rhythm. Mexican popular music tends to use more vocal dynamics, particularly taking advantage of the throat, whereas tango relies on classical European singing techniques such as singing "from the diaphragm." The sound should be clear, producing an unobstructed resonance from the body's various air chambers and passages (emphasizing the lower air chambers versus the sinus cavities). While some bolero, particularly early bolero, is also based on these principles, there is much greater emphasis on personal idiosyncrasy and vocal dynamics in bolero—and Mexican music as a whole—than on clarity of tone. One can gain an appreciation of the difference by comparing the sound of the great ranchera vocalist Lola Beltrán with any tango diva. Less stark, yet revelatory, is the distinction between boleristas like Toña la Negra and the typical tango performers. Mexico's popular vocal styles are much more dynamic and less disciplined by the strictures of classical European vocal performance traditions.

The Mexican bolero and Argentinean tango also differ in terms of their nostalgic sentiments. To be certain, both are extremely modern nostalgic forms. The tango's ratio of bitter to sweet, however, leans decidedly more toward the former when compared to the Mexican bolero. The first lines of the tango "Nostalgia" by Cadimaco Cobian provide a glimpse into the lamentful longing typical of the form: "I want to drown my heart in drink so that I might extinguish an insane love." A sense of desperate longing and sadness pervades the tango, providing profound catharsis for the listener.

Although also about lust, love lost, and longing, the bolero almost never reaches such depths of despair. The bolero's lyrical longing has a whimsical edge. The difference may be a reflection of the two national cultures from which these musical styles are derived. As evidenced in other cultural Mexican artifacts — the sugar skulls of Día de los Muertos, the Judas figures of village festivals, and the playful works of Diego Rivera — it is customary for Mexicans to make light of nearly everything, no matter how grave the stakes. The most serious tragedies are turned into melodrama and sweetened with large doses of carnivalesque humor. The bolero has adopted just such a sensibility. The tango, albeit melodramatic and bittersweet, still takes itself too seriously for a culture that has elevated satirical reproach to an art form.

LEARNING THE DANZÓN

If the bolero is memory inscribed in song, the danzón is memory put to movement. Groups of older dancers still gather one or two nights a week at Mexico City dance halls throughout the city to remember collectively a time when danzón was new and all things seemed possible. Similarly, every weekend the Cuauhtémoc Delegation of Mexico City sponsors an afternoon concert dance in the Plaza de la Ciudadela, providing a much safer alternative to night travel to the salons.

Hundreds of people meet in the plaza every Saturday to practice the danzón. Most of the participants are older, working-class dancers who have been practicing the danzón for their entire lives. It shows in the way they move to the music as if by instinct and know exactly when the rest periods will arrive for each song. They have danced the steps to each song so many times that their performances appear effortless. The men are able to communicate passage from the *base* (the basic ladrillo) to *va y ven* (movement forward and back in a line) and on to *el paseo* (a circular movement) with slight changes of pressure on their partners' lower backs. It is a truly beautiful scene.

In addition to the *jubilados* (retirees) that grace the square, several younger and middle-aged couples show up each week to practice the danzón as well. Some of these learned the danzón from their parents and have continued the tradition. Others are just now learning the danzón, getting a jump on what is commonly viewed as a dance for retirees. Rows of danzón neophytes line up on the west side of the plaza to take lessons from more accomplished dancers and professional instructors.

There are also several children in the plaza each week. Some are paired with older partners, perhaps a grandfather or uncle, who instruct them regarding the basic steps of the danzón. Teens are scarce, however, clearly too "cool" to be caught doing something so unabashedly romantic as the danzón. However, occasionally young *rockenrolleros* will stop and watch as they pass by the plaza. They will occasionally even sit and hold hands while watching their elders indulge a passion for the dance.

Perhaps no one receives more attention in the plaza, however, than the few teenaged and twenty-year-old couples who arrive each week to dance. Most of the couples in this category are competition-level dancers. They combine training with youthful grace, providing a glimpse into what the majority of the dance crowds may have looked like when danzón first exploded in postrevolutionary Mexico. Even the aging ensembles playing in the plaza — like Danzonera Cinco Estrellas and Danzonera Mexicuba — cannot help staring at the youthful dancers, perhaps seeing their past in reflection.

After observing the scene and chatting with some of the dancers over a series of weekends, I wanted to gain a deeper sense of the danzón. Reading and watching can only take one so far. Therefore, I went to a dance school and acquired a teacher (I will call her María). She taught me the danzón over a three-week period during the summer of 2000. María has the patience of her namesake. She worked tirelessly to teach this gringo to move from the hips, and my failure in that regard was certainly not for want of effort on her part. Despite my lack of dance skills, however, I was able to learn many of the basic steps. María developed routines for "Salón Mexico" and "Teléfono a larga distancia," which we danced in order to break the monotony of simply repeating the same steps over and over.

Why was it so difficult for me to learn the danzón? It is partly due to the fact that I lack the physical grace for any dance. I felt like the character Conchita in the Resortes film *Baile mi rey*, who was turned down for lessons because she lacked "grace."

In addition, I lack the requisite mental state and cultural disposition.

It is difficult for me to direct another person. I was raised on rock music, which is distinctly different from the danzón, in terms of both movement and cultural ethos. Rock is about dissonance, rebellion, and anarchy, whereas danzón is about accommodation, discipline, and dualism. Yet the struggle to adapt my body politics to the danzón helped me to understand the goals of the dance. As opposed to rock, which attempts to fight against all forms of ideological and spatial circumscription (thus falling prey to many), danzón makes the most of limited space, accepts it, and revels in it. Danzón disciplines bodies, celebrates and gracefully ritualizes contact so that movement is not only possible in the small interior spaces of the city but also beautiful and even pleasurable. Danzón is a negotiation and compromise between individuals and collectives, between men and women, and between people and the urban spaces they inhabit. Danzón domesticates the urban space, making it serve collective needs. I certainly have not come to master the dance, but my lessons did give me a better sense of what the dance means to those who have done so.

I learned that in the danzón a man should direct with firm, yet gentle pressure at both points of contact. The resulting movement should be smooth, even, and slow, unlike the rapid moves associated with salsa or the abrupt shifts of rock. The danzón is all about gentle flow and sophisticated urban restraint in contradistinction to rural exuberance. Even within a single province, Veracruz, there are greatly contrasting dance styles in the city versus the countryside. Whereas the rural Jarochos of Veracruz tend to *zapatear* (loudly, yet gracefully, stomp their heels on a wood floor or platform), urban Jarochos dance the soft and elegant danzón. Although such rural/urban distinctions are no longer as salient as they once were (García Canclini 1995:207–212), in the practice of the danzón one witnesses the resonance of a postrevolutionary moment when they meant everything.

"People think danzón is an easy dance," explained María when we first met, "but they don't realize how difficult it is." Danzón is about subtlety and flow, less demonstrative than the melodramatic tango, more restrained than nearly any other style of popular dance. It is a complicated mix of egalitarian restraint and distinction. One is not supposed to stare into the eyes of one's partner, nor call undue attention to other dancers. Thus, when I took a friend along to witness the plaza dance and show her a few basic steps, nobody stared or laughed at the awkward gringo helping the Mexicana learn the danzón. The unwritten rules of the danzón prohibit such a judgmental gaze. Everyone in the danzón is part of the family, as demonstrated by the traditional introduction: "Hey, familia, este danzón dedicado a . . ."

In addition to my first attempts at learning the danzón, I have also sung boleros in various locations inside and outside Mexico City with a guitarist or pianist, usually only after the other patrons cleared the room. It is in such moments that I begin to gain a more profound sense of what these styles mean to those who love them. But it is little more than a beginning. I have certainly not gained the sort of expertise that dancer-ethnographer Julie Taylor gained, for example, in her study of the tango (1998). I do hope to continue gaining a more profound sense of what the danzón and bolero mean to those who have dedicated their lives to them. Ethnography is learning.

MUJER DIVINA FROM OBJECT TO AUTHOR

Among the lessons I have gained from learning to dance the danzón and sing the bolero is the importance of gender issues in both. The danzón and bolero are, among other things, gendered pedagogies. Given the centrality of gender to these postrevolutionary rituals, it is fitting to end with a discussion of the recent success of women in the field of popular music and their relationship to the postrevolutionary traditions illustrated above.

One of the most interesting bolero performances I witnessed during my fieldwork was a concert following the December 1, 2000, Cambio de Poder, a ritual marking the turnover from the PRI to the Partido Acción Nacional (PAN) of the Fox administration. For two full days following the inauguration of Fox, the city government, controlled by the Partido de la Revolución Democrática (PRD), sponsored a counter-concert. A banner on the PRD stage proudly proclaimed that *El corazón de México late a la izquierda* (The heart of Mexico beats on the left). Musicians from the world of nueva canción (Tania Libertad, Chavela Vargas, Pablo Milanes) and rock (Eli Guerra, Julieta Venegas) headlined the two-day concert, with a 500-piece mariachi ensemble thrown in for good measure.

One of the headliners was Eli Guerra, a rising folk rock star. Guerra has garnered critical praise not only for her music but also for challenging the major corporate labels by independently producing her work. Like many contemporary rock stars, she has also been a strong supporter of indigenous rights and causes. At the concert in the zócalo, she dedicated a song to the Tarahumara, an indigenous society in northern Mexico. At the Cambio de Poder concert, Guerra entertained a throng of young rockenrolleros with an a cappella rendition of Grever's "Júrame." She introduced it as a "song by another Mexican woman who also wrote her own songs." After presenting "Júrame," a loving nod to her musical heritage, Guerra called the crowd's attention to her "friends carrying a banner for the promotion of sexual diversity." Through such clever and subtle juxtapositions, Guerra created a seamless link between past and present. She made no call for a revolutionary break, as demanded by the traditional Left. Nor did she attempt to present postmodern pastiche. Hers was not the "I'm-clever-look-at-me" sort of performance that we have come to associate with political art but a direct, honest, and artful expression lacking in such artifice. Guerra's honest style of political introspection appealed to the young crowd.

Guerra's performance was a soft sell in comparison to the work of León, Felipe, and Hadad. Instead of drawing constant explicit references to political leaders and events, she used indirect reference and more subtle aesthetics. Performances like Guerra's signal perhaps yet another stage in the development of political pop, one less carnivalesque in its reference to the past, more respectful of the musical ancestors, more interested in musical aesthetics, more directly tied to political movements, and less obligated to political pretense than previous generations of political artists.

The performer following Guerra, Julieta Venegas, also represents this subtle shift in pop politics. As Venegas sang her melancholy anthem "Recuerdo perdido," a young woman standing by me hung her head and sang along, acting as if she were at a Mass offering the profession of faith. To that girl and others in the audience, the performance seemed to be a ritual of liberation, potential and real. Their engagement with Guerra and Venegas is profound. Words like "love," "soul," and "feeling" dominated my casual conversations with their fans.

As I look back at this and other musical events I have witnessed over the past few years, it is clear that the most striking change in the recent history of Mexican musical ritual is the rise of women performers and, more recently, composers. Although largely unnoticed in the ethnomusicological and sociological literature, the rise in popular music for and by women is remarkable. Female audiences now sing the words of songs crafted by women. If they often lament the patriarchal present, they do so in their own voices rather than relying solely on the borrowed prose of male composers.

A review of concert billings in the Mexican newspaper clearly demonstrates that the female musician is becoming less and less of an exception to the rule. Quite unlike the situation lived by María Grever, Sor Juana long before her, or the Mexica priestesses before her, women no longer perform alone within overwhelmingly patriarchal ritual arenas. Although the ritual context may still be largely patriarchal, the women performing there are less and less alone onstage. The space for women's performance is expanding rapidly.

Yet, in addition to creating alternative spaces, many women performers are also clearly making argument for inclusion in the Mexican mainstream. The bolero is useful in that regard. The bolero has made a transformation over time from national threat to national symbol. It is now viewed, in Mexico and throughout the world, as an authentically Mexican musical style. Therefore, the selection of the bolero by many women musicians is probably not accidental. The bolero provides an aegis of authenticity, invoking popular conceptions of nationhood and citizenship. Just as the bolero was once incorporated into the nation, the neoboleristas are themselves working toward greater representation in the national popular culture. Although such incorporation represents a host of potential problems, contradictions, and limitations for women, it also presents certain opportunities.

As I survey my field notes, the increase in the representation of women's voices and music stands out as the most significant single change between contemporary and past ritual performances I have studied. Most major musical rituals continue to demonstrate the inordinate ideological access of political, economic, and cultural elites to the public space. In that sense, musical ritual remains somewhat static. Only the names, formations, and legitimation of power have changed. Ethnic and class elites continue to dominate ritual discourse to a highly inordinate degree. Not so in the case of gender, however. The unjust gender pedagogies of the past are being challenged to an extent that would have seemed remarkable just decades ago. It would appear that women are increasingly becoming the authors and subjects of popular music rather than serving solely as the ritual objects of song.

As Marit Melhuus and Kristi Anne Stolen argue in *Machos, Mistresses, Madonnas: Contesting the Power of Latin American Gender Imagery*, "discourses on gender and gender inequalities contain a certain potential to order other discourses" (1996:4–5). That has certainly been the case during the history of Mexican music and ritual. Transformations in gender discourse and ritual have tended to mirror, or even presage, transformations in other social discourses (e.g., politics, religion, economy). Given the primary role of gender as an ordering principle throughout Mexican history, perhaps women's increased presence in musical production roles reflects and portends positive change in gender politics throughout Mexican society. The fact that the bolero has become a tool in that transformation stands as one of the more delightful ironies of contemporary Mexican music. The recent opening for women in popular music, initiated partly by Lara's fetishistic focus on women performers, has been greatly expanded by generations of women pop artists since. The history of the bolero traces the transformation of "Mujer" from musical object to active subject. In studying the continuities and disjunctures between eras, this gender shift stands out—perhaps above all other trends—as a distinguishing feature of the modern era.

12 Classical Nationalism during the Postrevolutionary Era

Most scholars interested in postrevolutionary popular culture have focused on the political artists of the era, notably muralists Diego Rivera, David Alfaro Siqueiros, and José Clemente Orozco. These artists have been both lauded and lambasted for their ideological collusion with, and resistance against, the postrevolutionary state (Britton 1995; González Cruz Manjarrez 1996; Kandell 1988:443–484). However, painters were not the only artists involved in the postrevolutionary campaigns. They were joined by nationalistic composers like Carlos Chávez and a host of writers, directors, and choreographers (Sevilla 1990) supported by Mexico's postrevolutionary government. These were the artists and "intellectuals who assumed the task of constructing and justifying the revolutionary project" via public works on a grand scale (Bonfil Batalla 1996:108).

The new government promulgated a complex ideology based on socialist rhetoric, anticlericism, hypernationalism, mestizaje, and indigenismo. Whereas the mestizo had once been marginalized and stigmatized by regimes that feared racial mixing, the postrevolutionary government promoted the idea that all Mexicans were descendents of "the three cultures" (European, African, and indigenous). José Vasconcelos, the minister of education, underwrote the work of hundreds of nationalist artists and musicians. It was he who first referred to Mexicans as "the cosmic race." For the first time, mestizaje became sanctioned as the official doctrine of Mexico and not a culturally and psychologically sublimated reality.

The government also adopted indigenismo as its official ideological stance. Symbols of the pre-Columbian past were enlisted in order to create a new sense of national identity. Indigenista policies demonstrated greater respect for indigenous communities. Such policies still promoted assimilation, however, rather than cultural coexistence.

The emphasis on European, African, and, especially, Native American roots left only Asian Mexicans outside the official fold, a group that would therefore bear the brunt of overt discrimination on several occasions during the twentieth century. For example, revolutionary caudillo Francisco Villa committed atrocities specifically aimed at the Asian population, and official governmental actions were often no better. Even those officially recognized in the new ideology continued to face severe racism. Mexico's indigenous population, while officially embraced by government rhetoric, continued to suffer severe repression at the hands of the indigenista government. As a result, the Cristero rebellion against the postrevolutionary government received strong support in many indigenous communities, despite the fact that the government was operating under an indigenista flag.

Mexico's postrevolutionary regime attempted to create a "new man" and a new society. Ritual would be employed in order to make that happen. Brigades of young volunteers marched into rural Mexico at the behest of postrevolutionary presidents and governors, in "a campaign of dechristianization by means of education and mass propaganda, including speeches, songs, civic ritual and anti-clerical satire; and the repression of worship" (Bantjes 1994:266).

"Anti-clerical satire" calls to mind the Revolution of 1810. Such satire was no longer aimed at power, however, but instead promulgated by it. Secular ideologies were developed to make the Mexican masses conform to the modern order. Holdout communities were viewed as backward, ignorant, and in need of reeducation. Once again, among the central targets of the modernization campaign were the indigenous people. Indigenismo was largely promoted by secular urban elites; it was a movement that often led to further impositions on indigenous communities rather than to their liberation.

As is true in virtually all nation-states, ideological concepts of nationhood and national identity would be used in Mexico to legitimate and obfuscate the workings of state power. Under the guise of justice and reconciliation, a new urban elite extended its power and reinforced its privilege. The Porfirians were swept out of power only to be replaced by another set of bureaucrats and business leaders. Although the rhetoric of indigenismo, nationalism, and socialism was occasionally put into practice — the progressive regime of Lázaro Cárdenas (1934–1940) being by far the best, and last, example — for the most part the postrevolution laid the foundation for state-sponsored capitalism rather than a more egalitarian system. The new state-managed capitalist system would inordinately benefit the rich and a new cadre of corrupt political bureaucrats at the expense of marginal, working, and middle classes. Well-intentioned artists and intellectuals unwittingly laid down an ideological smokescreen for the new state-capitalist regime. Taking the new government at its word, many believed that the Mexican state might truly embrace economic egalitarianism and political democracy. Classical musicians took leading roles in that hopeful movement, only later becoming disillusioned with the ironic outcomes of the Revolution and the postrevolutionary system it spawned.

NATIONALISM AND INDIGENISMO IN THE CLASSICAL MUSIC OF THE POSTREVOLUTION

Manuel Ponce (1886–1948) was one of the first truly nationalist classical composers in Mexico. Ponce "drew from all types of Mestizo folk music (corrido, jarabe, son, huapango, etc.)" in order to produce compositions that would be embraced by both Mexican and international audiences (Behague 1979:125). He believed that "despite their foreign origins" the folk music works of the early twentieth century contained "the seed of our idiosyncrasies, the melancholy of the indigenous, the picaresque qualities of the mestizo, and the proud sentiments of the European" (in Pulido Silva 1986:44).

Classical Nationalism during the Postrevolutionary Era

Yet, in addition to being folkloric and indigenista, Ponce's work was also an extension of nineteenth-century salón music, very much in line with his European training. He is best considered a "romantic nationalist," a bridge between the prerevolutionary and postrevolutionary eras, rather than a musical revolutionary per se. However, Ponce was instrumental in forming a Mexican school of classical music. His compositions provided an early model, and his direct training greatly influenced the postrevolutionary generation.

The members of that new generation did more than venerate and incorporate mestizo folk music—they fully embraced the ideology of indigenismo. The leader of the indigenista classicists was Carlos Chávez. He argued that indigenous music expressed "what is deepest in the Mexican soul" (Behague 1979:129). Chávez blended a growing knowledge of contemporary and pre-Columbian indigenous music with European techniques, scales, and instrumentation (Moreno Rivas 1989:139–140). Pieces such as *Xochipilli* (1940) and his masterpiece, *Sinfonía india* (1935), best represent his musical mestizaje. Such pieces show that in attempting to capture the essential spirit of Mexico Chávez managed to create something qualitatively new as well. Aaron Copland, a good friend of the Mexican composer, noted that his work, although possessing an "Indian quality," is "at the same time curiously contemporary in spirit" (in Behague 1979:141).

In showing surprise that something with "Indian" qualities could also have a contemporary spirit, Copland demonstrates the tendency to equate Indians with the past. These were not simply the sentiments of an untutored gringo. The same basic assumption motivated the Mexican indigenistas as well. Like many anthropologists of that era, postrevolutionary composers viewed their work as cultural salvage and salvation. As accomplished ethnomusicologists, they viewed themselves as cultural saviors and political allies of the indigenous people.

The Copland quote also correctly demonstrates how Chávez was creating music for the "modern man" (Copland in Behague 1979:141). Like the regime that paid his bills, Chávez was borrowing from marginalized identities and a mythic past in order to advance a modern project. This did not counter his own claims, for Chávez was critically aware of his modernist tendencies. Although he incorporated Mesoamerican instrumentation, the pentatonic scale, folkloric rhythms, and what he viewed as indigenous intervals (including open fourths and fifths), his work still fits well into the modern classical music world. José Antonio Alcaraz writes that Chávez was at the same time inspired by both "the song of indigenous fishermen and the skyscraper" (1996:26).

The groundbreaking work in electronic music by Chávez shows his fascination with modern technology and trends. Perhaps the ballet *Caballos de vapor* (Horse Power) is his most interesting work in this regard. Using sets by Diego Rivera, the work contrasted the human, tropical world of Mexico with the inhuman, industrialized world of the United States. This same dichotomy is seen in many of Frida Kahlo's paintings and diary entries. In *Self-Portrait on the Borderline between Mexico and the United States* (1932), for example, Kahlo places herself in the middle, between the organic earth, plants, and Mesoamerican sites of Mexico to the left and the cold industrial technology of the United States on the right. The same theme runs throughout postrevolutionary art, from Rivera's *Man at the Crossroads* to Orozco's *La katharsis*. While canonical Communists like Rivera believed technology could go hand in hand with liberation, however, Orozco showed the machine crushing humanity and dominating desire, a more anarcho-socialist sentiment. Yet both viewed the United States as a mechanical imperialist force. *Caballos de vapor* likewise represents Latin America as an organic alternative to the gringo *Homo technicus*.

Chávez attempted to produce music "national in character but universal in its groundwork"—a music that would "reach the majority of the people" (Behague 1979:130). Therefore, he borrowed from indigenous and folk musical traits, injecting greater dynamism, diatonics, percussion, and repetition into his work. Repetition was perhaps the greatest indicator of his interaction with folk music, strophic song structures being the hallmark of popular, traditional, and folk music. In fact, there are those who argue that classical music, although often positively contrasted with the formulaic principles of the popular, is usually structured by the same principle of repetition (Miranda-Pérez 1990:282). Chávez made it more overtly present, celebrating rather than downplaying the inherent repetitiveness of musical discourse.

Chávez borrowed directly from folk forms, a type of experimentation that was taking place in the United States and Europe as well. Rather than developing standardized and universal principles of music, the onus of the era was to uncover and develop connections between music and national cultural identity. Yet Chávez was not a simple populist. "Only when Mexican music reaches artistic quality," he argued, "does it become national art" (in Behague 1979:131). In other words, Chávez and many of his contemporaries saw themselves as both the students and instructors of the folk. These musicians would borrow from the genius of the people, while attempting to educate them in return. To that end, Chávez presented occasional concerts for union workers during holidays and free concerts for the general public.

Chávez believed that the main goal of the revolutionary musician was the "education of the public" (Saavedra 1989:82), combining vanguardist Marxist and high-culture capitalist ideologies into a unified project of "education and propaganda" (Moreno Rivas 1989:129). Therefore, although he was a folklorist of sorts, Chávez was far from a romantic relativist. He was certain that only through the mediation of the "great masters" could folk forms become "art" (Saavedra 1989:84). In other words, Chávez saw his role as raising the assumedly underdeveloped consciousness of the masses. In that sense, the postrevolutionary indigenistas were following in a centuries-old Mexican tradition: cultural betterment through musical training. Such musical reform movements took place throughout the colonial era. In the years following the Revolution of 1810, Mexican musical leaders also "became conscious of their active role in institutions that would maintain the teaching and diffusion of art music" (Carmona 1984:19). After the Revolution of 1910, this missionary outlook manifested itself in revolutionary rhetoric, but much of it came from the same elitist impulse as earlier musical reform movements. There was, and is, a constant fear of popular degradation in the Mexican classical tradition.

Chávez directed the National Conservatory (1928–1934), the National Symphony Orchestra, and the Instituto Nacional de Bellas Artes (INBA) during his distinguished career. In each of these posts, he encouraged the study of Mexico's folk music and rigorous training in classical European musical techniques. Chávez was enfranchised by the postrevolutionary regime and, as a result, practiced a politics of extreme contradictions. He was both in power and against it. Chávez was accused of being dogmatic and authoritarian by some, even compared with the Stalinist painter Siqueiros (Alcaraz 1996:21–22).

Like Rivera, Chávez continued to work for the government long after others in the Left recognized and condemned the regime's dictatorial tendencies, corruption, and capitalist orientations. Although ostensibly providing opportunities for musicians to create more authentically Mexican art music, Chávez has been accused by some of holding back musical creation in Mexico. His "egotism," notes Leonora Saavedra, "prevented him from endorsing any currents in Mexican music that did not flow through him" (1989:77). Chávez fits the profile of the classic alpha intellectual, certain that his path is correct and that others must follow it. He felt that he could and should stand in judgment of those who might deviate from the correct musical path.

The contradictions of elite indigenismo and nationalism did not end at home. One of the most interesting aspects of the postrevolutionary artists and intellectuals in the nationalist camp was their tendency to move back and forth between imperialist metropolis and home turf. While paving a nationalist path for Mexico, Chávez "supremely valued the approval that musical powers in the United States consistently gave him and did everything possible to cultivate and continue it" (Saavedra 1989:77).

While the connection between the masses and classical nationalists was somewhat tenuous, it is clear that the latter were well connected to foreign classical audiences and sponsors. Just as the muralists found themselves devoting much of their time to work in the United States, the classical musicians of the postrevolution enjoyed significant support from U.S. organizations, capitalists, and audiences. For example, when the organizers for the Aptos, California, music festival came calling to offer the post of musical director to Chávez in 1970, they were told to look for him in New York, where he was living at the time. Upon accepting the commission, the noted composer replied that he would be briefly away from his New York home the following week in order to conduct the Houston Symphony but that he could begin work on the California festival thereafter (Parker 1994:178). Chávez had composed a commissioned piece the year before for the Aptos festival and would successfully serve as musical director for four years, from 1970 to 1973 (1994:186).

As demonstrated in the case of Chávez, Mexican nationalism had an extremely strong transnational appeal; and the funding and support of international audiences exerted a seductive pull on many Mexican nationalists. Chávez wrote his "most 'nativist' work, the *Sinfonía India*, in New York City" (Hess 1995:6) and spent the last days of his life in his New York home, drawn by its musical pleasures. He believed that international travel was good for music and musicians and that intercultural exchange would enhance the music of each nation (Alcaraz 1996:93). Like many of the nationalist artists of the day, Chávez received his early training in Europe (Hess 1995:5).

As Alcaraz argues, there does not appear to have been a major contradiction for Chávez between international practice and his nationalist ideology. However, it is clear that members of the postrevolutionary nationalist movement maintained at times an acritical orientation toward their musical practices and ideologies. Chávez and his orthodox compatriots enacted a modern project that tended to essentialize the state. He argued that identification with the state was "natural" (in Saavedra 1989:85), certain that the state could and would become the means for liberating the working classes. Likewise, simplistic nationalist conceptions of imperialism distracted the postrevolutionary Left from examining other forms of international domination. Obsessed with the acts of powerful states, such as the United States, the Left was not always as cognizant of the transnational capital flows that were beginning to dominate global discourses, including music. Transnational capitalism, in tandem with homegrown counterrevolutionary movements, would move the nation toward more conservative administrations during the midcentury. The nationalist and socialist artists of the postrevolutionary era often underestimated the forces of conservatism domestically and capital globally, while overestimating their own power relative to that of the state.

Even institutions that the nationalists engendered, such as INBA, have demonstrated the conservative power of supposedly liberating state institutions. INBA, while fostering the development of a vibrant national art community, has also worked as an ideological gatekeeper. Many a performance has been denied previously promised funding for moving beyond acceptable ideological parameters. In short, Chávez and his peers created a nationalist movement that lacked introspection. The result was a sort of celebratory nationalism that discouraged internal critique and at the same time failed to challenge power directly.

Among the students Chávez mentored were the "Group of Four"—

Blas Galindo, Daniel Ayala, José Pablo Ayala, and Salvador Contreras — four exceptionally gifted musicians who would take postrevolutionary nationalism in new musical directions. Of these, Blas Galindo gained the greatest fame. Like his mentor, he held the post of National Conservatory director. Of Huichol lineage, Galindo produced some of the most beautiful and plaintive music of the era, reincorporating romantic elements rejected by his revolutionary mentors. Galindo's "Poema de Neruda," for example, is a loving, subtle string homage to the master poet's "Me gusta cuando callas" (I like it when you become quiet). Per its title, I have never seen a piece induce a more contemplative state in an audience. In producing such music, with somewhat less of a social mission in mind and greater attention to aesthetics, Galindo managed to create a very personal, intimate, and introspective connection to his audience.

Galindo, as a classically trained indigenous composer, was viewed not just as an extension of the nationalist-indigenista movement but also as a symbol of its fruition (Ruiz Ortiz 1994:12,23). Critics saw an authenticity in Galindo's work that they traced back to "remote corners" of Mexico's past (Ruiz Ortiz 1994:24). This circular thinking did not box Galindo in. Refusing to be simply a product of the nationalist vanguard, he experimented with modernist techniques that had little connection to Mexican nationalism and later settled comfortably into a fairly conventional classicist mode.

Before doing so, however, Galindo produced some of the most profound folkloric music of the twentieth century, including the "Sones mariachi" (1939). Galindo penned that song for presentation during the "Twenty Centuries of Mexican Art" exhibit in New York, under the insistence of his mentor, Chávez.

As happened in the art world, "a dynamic group of avant-garde composers" took off in radically new directions in the 1950s and 1960s (Behague 1979:147). For more than thirty years before that break, nationalist, folkloric, and indigenista musicians had attempted to promote a revolutionary message with government sanction. The results were understandably complex and contradictory. The ideologies they supported and worked under were at the same time both revolutionarily new and fundamentally conservative. Nationalism was revolutionary in the sense that for the first time the Mexican government was truly taking more direct control over the country's political and economic future. Culminating in the nationalization of the oil industry by Cárdenas, these gains were substantial, especially in light of the inordinate control that had been ceded to foreign companies by the Díaz regime.

Furthermore, the ideology of indigenismo, while far from ideal, at least provided indigenous peoples with greater legal and cultural recognition. This stood in contrast to both the conservative and liberal regimes of the previous century, the first of which preferred to maintain the indigenous communities' subordinate position in the traditional colonial order, while the second viewed indigenous communities as an impediment to modernization (despite the fact that the greatest liberal leader, Benito Juárez, was himself Zapotec). Although the postrevolutionary regimes adopted some liberal tendencies, they gave greater recognition to the rights of indigenous peoples. However, the dechristianization campaign struck at the very heart of many indigenous cultures. Catholicism was not an epiphenomenon in such communities, a mere colonial add-on; it was central to their identities and social lives.

The postrevolutionary government and its ideological triumvirate of socialism, nationalism, and indigenismo were fraught with contradictions. While the new nationalism was supposedly based on equality and justice, the reality was greatly different. The Porfirian elite had not been replaced by a more egalitarian regime but by another set of elites. Social stratification was not undone or even greatly ameliorated. To the contrary, social inequality and cultural distinctions increased and became more complex. New classes of capitalists and workers emerged in the postrevolutionary era, making the more feudal relations of earlier eras seem simple and somewhat benign in comparison. Likewise, although mestizaje was the official ideology, racial hierarchy and discrimination continued. "The cosmic race" was led by people who demonstrated greater phenotypic connection to the Spaniards of old than the "new man" or mestizo they promoted. Despite ideological pretenses to the contrary, the cult of whiteness continued as a legacy of the Conquest. As Henry Schmidt explains, European culture "would be officially dethroned, although in nonpolitical contexts it would remain as pervasive as ever" (1988:309). Urban elites, living Euro-American lives of privilege, made great careers on symbolic capital drawn from the ideologically elevated, yet materially deprived, indigenous and mestizo masses.

Classical Nationalism during the Postrevolutionary Era

Whereas earlier regimes promoted ideologies based on more direct legitimation (e.g., ordination by the gods), the postrevolutionary regime fostered an ideology that hid more than it revealed. A brief comparison with past ideologies is instructive. Aztec ritual, myth, and ideology boldly claimed that the Triple Alliance was in power, as ordained by the gods. That truth was made manifest via military success. This simple system of ideology and social power was mutually reinforcing. The Aztec did not deny their power and intent but rather openly legitimated it through myth and ritual.

Similarly, New Spain was a theocratic state. The rule of heaven was made manifest in the Spanish Empire. The Spanish made this legitimating ideology clear in the Requirement and other theocratic rituals. Following the colonial era, the nineteenth century was a period of anarchic contestation, only partly resolved by the Díaz dictatorship. The more complex ideologies of democracy and capitalism developing in the United States and Europe were slow to develop in Mexico, due to infighting and interventions. Nineteenth-century regimes continued to promote mainly straightforward forms of legitimation based on personal charisma and overt force.

After the Revolution, however, a more complex and modern ideology was enacted. Socialist aims and pretenses were combined with state-capitalist practices to produce a set of ideological discourses that not only legitimated but also greatly obfuscated the nature of state power. In the modern, postrevolutionary era, such ideologies were elevated to art forms. Rivera preached communitarian democratic-socialist philosophies while supporting a government that was marching toward dictatorial capitalism.

Modern Mexico: 1921–1968

And so it went in the world of music as well. Chávez et al. were ritual specialists of a highly ambivalent and liminal era. Like the muralists, they embodied the best impulses and worst affectations of the age. These high priests of the modern state provided a message of hopeful populism following the catastrophic Revolution. At the same time, they unwittingly lent support to a fundamentally antidemocratic state, run by a hypocritical elite. Unfortunately, state patronage was a requirement of classical music production throughout the twentieth century. The costs of training musicians, organizing them into ensembles, and mounting performances are prohibitive without state support. Only with such patronage can a composer or musician hope to have his or her work heard. It is almost impossible to imagine such a musical complex not being tied to the destinies and disciplines of the state.

However, it is more than a matter of financial exigency. The classical nationalists' attempt to enlighten the masses started from a fundamentally flawed premise: that classical music could appeal to the masses if they were properly educated to understand it. Obvious class chauvinism and ethnocentrism aside, it is unlikely that classical music could ever appeal to a large popular audience. Classical music is largely defined in contradistinction to popular music, making popular classicism an oxymoron. As classically trained musicians, the postrevolutionary populists did not speak in the popular vernacular. In fact, most of the music has no words, a basic requirement for most popular music. There are essentially two types of popular music: for singing along and for dancing. Barring words, there must at least be movement. The popular is about sensorial integration and homology. Conversely, the classical concert is about discipline (or, in class-based language, "refinement"). The members of the classical audience are securely planted in their seats with their ears fixed on a complex of sound. The ritual is largely devoid of significant visual or kinesthetic sensation. Opera and ballet notwithstanding, classical music as ritual lacks the freedom of movement, variability, and extemporaneous potential associated with popular music.

Thus the classical populists were fighting a losing cause from the start. No matter how much they would incorporate elements of the huapango, jarabe, or son, theirs would remain *música culta* rather than *música popular*. The popular audience does not accept such discipline but rather demands more direct and active participation in the musical ritual. The classical concert is a ritual of class discipline and identity. The popular music event must always incorporate the carnivalesque at some level. Popular ritual is also always a negotiation between the aims of power and subaltern interests to escape normal social bonds and boundaries. Those elements are largely missing from the classical repertoire.

Therefore, the classical nationalist movement was more an internal, elite dialog than a conversation with the popular classes. There is no doubt that these classical products resonated more with the Mexican populace than did the classical music of Europe or the United States. The popular resonance of postrevolutionary classical music was still relatively weak, however, compared to more accessible forms like the bolero, danzón, and ranchera.

Classical Nationalism During the Postrevolutionary Era

REVUELTAS: THE ICONOCLAST

Of course, just as the great socialist painters of the era had radically differing political views, so, too, the musicians of the day disagreed with each other; and several refused simply to line up in the nationalist indigenista camp. Many were ambivalent from the beginning, and some were openly in dissent by the end of the postrevolutionary era.

Ironically, several of the dissenters had the most authentic indigenous and folk pedigrees. For example, the great Mexican composer Silvestre Revueltas was not even considered "to be a nationalist" by his peers (Alcaraz 1996:39), perhaps because he developed an antipathy for dogmatic nationalism and nationalists. Revueltas was much more an overt and unashamed internationalist than his peers. He attended college in Texas and later became directly involved in the Spanish Civil War.

Even though Revueltas laid less official claim to indigenismo, his music is perhaps more evocative of the sounds described by missionary ethnographers when they first encountered Mesoamerican cultures than of those of the indigenistas. Various movements of his *La noche de los Maya*, for example, are dynamic, discordant, percussive, and even unsettling to the Western ear, as its composer obviously intended. Revueltas himself was known for his "sarcastic wit" (Cardon 1991:15), which is evident in the way he plays with the listener's emotions. Like the movies for which Revueltas composed, his works fill one with a sense of foreboding, anxiety, and hope for a climatic resolution that never seems to arrive. Revueltas produced the ritual music of modernity, while drawing on Mesoamerican inspiration. Often composing for the cinema, he borrowed the spirit of one visual medium (Mesoamerican ritual) for use in another (film).

Revueltas' rival Chávez also attempted to experiment with film scoring. Despite correspondence with Walt Disney and other attempts to find a sponsor, however, he was never given the chance to put music to film. This may have deepened his antipathy to Revueltas. In fact, Chávez had originally planned to score the classic film *Redes* but was passed over for the assignment (Parker 1984). Revueltas created the *Redes* soundtrack instead, cementing his renown as a film composer. Despite their differences, one finds "the synthesis of an art that is at the same time national and modern" in the work of both these great rivals (Tello 1992:12).

They arrived at that synthesis in very different ways, however. Revueltas did not come to his art via the typical academic route but rather through listening to local bands and musicians in his home state of Durango. While Chávez was being trained by masters like Manuel Ponce and Pedro Luis Ogazón in the city (Moreno Rivas 1989:129), Revueltas was learning in the rural countryside, the place where the aforementioned masters turned for inspiration. In other words, Revueltas did not need to look to el campo for inspiration, because he was raised there. It was a central part of his musical identity.

Paralleling their muralist brethren, the postrevolutionary classicists maintained a heated internecine rivalry. As opposed to his more canonical colleagues, Revueltas showed a complete disdain for music critics and academic musicologists (Manuel Enríquez in Revueltas 1989:13). Although he integrated folk and national elements into his work, he rarely made the sort of overt academic references that color the work of Chávez and his followers. As a largely "self-taught, talented Bohemian," Revueltas shunned classical training and definitions in his life and work (Revueltas 1989:14). He expressed "incredible disdain" for his own fame (Revueltas 1989:101) and commonly criticized those, such as Chávez, who drew a line of distinction between art music and popular music (Moreno Rivas 1989:186).

Revueltas enjoyed being a conundrum to those around him, and, like "some of the most spiritual people of the Century," was an atheist (Peter Garland in Revueltas 1989:17). Unlike Chávez, he expressed an extremely negative attitude toward the trappings of civilization and modernity. Rather than being a vulgar Marxist awaiting the next inevitable step in the evolution of the workers' state, Revueltas felt that "'civilization' is distilled shit, bottled in law" (1989:117). Perhaps a musical parallel to the painter Orozco, he was an ambivalent socialist, given more to anarchism than to canonical communism.

Revueltas' writings paint the picture of a passionate, political, and self-reflective composer. He questioned the value of producing "a series of sounds and lines" while people were starving and dying. Revueltas eventually concluded that art could indeed be "useful." Rather than leaving it there, however, he asked if "that is perhaps merely a way of consoling myself, of defending myself?" (1989:94). The very fact that he was asking the question distinguishes Revueltas from many of his contemporary allies and rivals. For most other classical musicians of the day, the postrevolutionary era was not a time for introspection and political action; it was a space for self-certainty and modern optimism.

13 Classical Nationalism Today

One day on the way to a concert at the National Conservatory of Music I met a man whose daughter dreams of becoming a classical musician. She is a violinist. Her story is perhaps emblematic of the current state of classical music in Mexico. Her father, a taxi driver, works hard to put his children through school, taking only occasional days off for concerts and holidays. His daughter's accomplishments make him extremely proud, giving his work and life greater meaning. He is a patron of the arts in an age when governmental support has withered. Generations of Mexican musicians and their families have likewise sacrificed inordinate time and money to achieve musical educations. Except for the era of postrevolutionary largess, the great majority of musicians have lacked access to state patronage during the last two hundred years. For much of the nineteenth century and part of the twentieth, the aspiring musician required the support of family members willing to sacrifice their time, money, and future in order to see a talented child succeed. Such was the case for nineteenth-century composer Felipe Villanueva, perhaps the greatest of his era. Villanueva's impoverished family did everything in their power to earn him a formal education (Carredano 1992:23).

The situation is similar at the turn of the twenty-first century. The state lends little support to aspiring musicians, requiring them to seek patronage elsewhere. It is currently a period of reorganization in Mexican classical music. Foreign works dominate the concert schedule to an inordinate degree, with perhaps a few postrevolutionary pieces thrown in for local flavor. Alcaraz complains that the concert halls have been converted into "museums and crematoriums" and that Mexican classical music needs a rebirth like that provided by Chávez and the nationalists after the Revolution (1996:100). He believes that such a rebirth can be brought about through experimentation with both new and old, domestic and foreign influences, the same formula followed by the postrevolutionary pioneers.

CLASSICAL MUSIC AS GENDER RITUAL

The most promising current developments seem to be in smaller, experimental ensembles. Naturally, the postrevolutionaries, with their didactic interests, favored compositions and performances on a symphonic scale. Musical creativity is more dispersed today. While symphonies still perform, one is much more likely to catch a classical string quartet at the National Autonomous University of Mexico (UNAM), a small choral ensemble at the Palace of Fine Arts, or a piano recital one block away in the banquet room of the National Art Museum.

As is true in the world of pop music, the most striking development in contemporary classical performance is the increased participation of women. From large concert venues to smaller salón presentations, a large number of women can be found in nearly every ensemble. As an indication of future trends, the number of women in musical training programs is rapidly increasing. It appears that Mexican women are increasingly choosing to become classical musicians. This could be evidence of what sociologists call "decamping." Young men may be less likely to choose music careers as the profession becomes less prestigious and salaries decline. However, it is just as likely to be evidence of a rise in women's professional expectations. In either case, the gender shift bodes well for music.

Among the finest musicians I experienced while conducting this fieldwork is María Teresa Frenk. Frenk, a pianist, is "rescuing some of the nationalists' work that had been forgotten" (Frenk, speaking after a concert on February 17, 1998). The pianist performed in the banquet hall of the National Museum of Art, a building that once served as the Díaz Ministry of Communications. Frenk provided intimate translations of several postrevolutionary pieces. As described in Chapter 12, those works were originally designed as large-scale, didactic art in an era of modern flamboyance and optimism. However, Frenk allows such pieces by Chávez, Revueltas, Ponce, José Pablo García Moncayo, Galindo, and other postrevolutionary giants to speak more softly in an uncertain present.

Shorn of pomp and volume, the soulful spirit and musical nuances of the pieces come through in a way that larger ensembles simply cannot duplicate. María Teresa Frenk thus follows in the tradition of her *tocayo* (namesake), María Teresa Rodríguez, another outstanding pianist of the twentieth century. Chávez considered Rodríguez to be his best interpreter on the piano (Pulido Silva 1983:126).

Another excellent pianist is Eva María Zuk. I witnessed one of her concerts at the Old College of San Ildefonso on a stormy night in January 2002. Zuk played to an appreciative crowd in the city center. As she played, one could imagine the ghost of Frida Kahlo dancing on stage, teasing Diego Rivera, as she did on that very spot in 1922. Rivera was painting his mural *Creación* on the back wall and proscenium as the precocious Kahlo watched him work. Kahlo demanded that the "Frog Prince" (Rivera) assess her work and generally made a nuisance of herself until he did. Eighty years later Zuk looked at Rivera's female figures before starting each piece, as if she too could see Rivera and Kahlo sitting atop the scaffold, taking in the concert. The scaffolding has long since been removed, but the beautiful mural remains. In art, as in music, the postrevolutionary era continues to color the present.

Trained in Venezuela and the United States (Juilliard), Zuk has performed and won awards throughout Latin America, the United States, and Europe. In addition to her European repertoire, she is considered one of the finest interpreters of the works of Mexican composers Felipe Villanueva and Ricardo Castro.

Perhaps this gendered division of labor—men composing, directing, and playing for the big concert venues, women performing in the intimate salons—is not accidental. Over time, men have tended to dominate the larger public arenas, like the Palace of Fine Arts, while women have more often performed in intimate spaces, like the Old College of San Ildefonso. Such divisions were at their most extreme during the colonial era, when most public performances were out of the question for women. Therefore, women developed private musical spaces, within the home, court, or convent, beyond the censure of men.

Despite the advance of women in all contemporary classical niches, the classical concert remains an engendered ritual, reflecting and reinforcing the traditional roles of men and women as they operate primarily in public vs. private domains. It remains to be seen whether or not the movement of women into the public musical sphere will transform that space. Meanwhile, the proliferation of the smaller ensembles and public salón concerts may also indicate the feminization of Mexican classical music.

CLASSICAL MUSIC, CLASS, AND NATIONALITY

The reduced number of large classical concerts has much to do with the aforementioned withdrawal of governmental support. Yet most large concerts are still subsidized by the government, with additional corporate support and high ticket costs contributing as well. The talent is derived largely from the Conservatory and UNAM, both of which also remain key concert venues. As governmental support diminishes, private foundations are playing a larger role. Mexico is becoming more like the United States in that regard. To the extent that affordable concerts still exist, this is mostly due to private support.

One musical foundation is named after Manuel Ponce. Its concerts take place, appropriately, in the Sala Manuel Ponce, a small concert room in the beautiful Palace of Fine Arts. Among the concerts I witnessed there was the UNAM choir on February 1, 1998. The concert was typical in that very little music of Mexican origin was offered, as was true for the entire Ponce series that year. Mexican classical concert music is largely in an interpretive rather than creative mode at the moment. In fact, I chose to attend classical concerts based mainly on their potential for Mexican content and had relatively little to choose from as a result. This is perhaps another major difference between Mexican popular and classical music at present. While domestic production of popular music is booming, and being exported at an exceptional rate, domestic production of classical music seems to be in somewhat of a lull.

Classical Nationalism Today

Meanwhile, the tradition of free and inexpensive concerts that began during the postrevolution appears to be coming to an end. This has had a clear effect on audience composition. The small but enthusiastic working- and middle-class audiences won during the postrevolutionary era seem to be relegated increasingly to free student concerts, while professional ensembles and orchestras become the exclusive domain of a relative few who can afford the rising ticket costs.

The decline of governmental support for the arts has had a deleterious affect on concert attendance and redefined the audience in ways that mirror the situation in the United States. Philharmonic events, even at the UNAM, often cost over $10 U.S. ($5 in the balcony), an unthinkable fee for most Mexicans. Conversations in English and other languages are peppered throughout the audience, testament to the elite and foreign composition of the audience. One afternoon I was treated to a UNAM Philharmonic concert, including an exquisite interpretation of Blas Galindo's "Poema de Pablo Neruda," three minutes and forty-three seconds of bliss. Sharing the moment was a crowd of fairly wealthy Mexicans, a few members of the NAFTA middle class, and several foreigners like myself. The spark of hope that fueled the postrevolutionary fires of Chávez and his pupil Galindo is now little more than a warm glow. Yet the quality of such performances cannot be challenged. The National Symphony Orchestra, Mexico City Philharmonic Orchestra (OFCM), and UNAM Philharmonic Orchestra (OFUNAM), among many others, are maintaining the tradition of excellence in Mexican classical music.

The Mexico City Philharmonic Orchestra presented a very special concert on January 13, 2002, to mark the unveiling of the National Auditorium organ. After years of disuse and a multi-million-dollar restoration, the pipe organ was back in operation. Mexican maestro Victor Urbán would do the honors of playing the massive instrument for a nearly sold-out auditorium crowd. Urbán is a direct link between the present era and postrevolutionary Golden Age, having studied under many of the Mexican masters mentioned in Chapter 12. I was seated directly be-

Master organist Victor Urbán. Photo by Carlos Franco.

low Urbán and the organ, an excellent vantage point from which to witness the master's pedalwork.

The audience was larger than normal due to the location, purpose, and relatively low cost of the concert. To my left a middle-aged man wearing street clothes hummed along during the concert, either oblivious to the fact that such behavior is considered inappropriate in a classical venue or unwilling to bow to such convention. On my right was a set of smartly dressed older women, clearly comfortable in the classical concert setting. All were equally impressed with the performance. Loud "bravos" were shouted from my right while hearty, full-handed clapping came thundering from my left.

The concert was more than a demonstration of appreciation for organ and organist; it was also a political act. At the beginning of the concert, after the musicians were seated and tuned, the local musicians' union representative emerged with two others holding a banner calling for the local government to meet its economic obligations to the philharmonic. It was reminiscent of the first musicians' strikes at the Metropolitan Cathedral, hundreds of years before. The union rep complained that the philharmonic members had been promised a wage increase, but none was forthcoming. He asked for the support of the audience in the union's struggle to achieve just compensation. Many members of the audience booed and hissed the union representatives and shouted for them to get offstage. Gradually, the boos were replaced by supportive applause. Most people seemed not to know what to make of the plea, however. A woman behind me stated, "Why do they have to bring politics into it?" By the time the first violin and director were in place, the political plea was forgotten, buried beneath wild applause. Urbán's entrance several pieces later met with even greater fanfare. Following the concert, a man brought a flag to the stage and tossed it to the director, who draped it over the dais. Resounding applause and shouts of "¡Viva México!" followed and finished the ritual.

Classical Nationalism Today

There are distinctly Mexican touches to all the classical concerts I witnessed during this research, regardless of the program. First, concertgoers tend to filter in gradually, well after the concert begins, and feel free to leave at practically any time. This is, of course, taboo in the United States and Western Europe. Second, although most programs are drawn mainly from the European masters, the Mexican concert often begins or ends with a single piece written by a Mexican composer. Unfortunately, these two customs occasionally cancel each other out. Many people arrive after the Mexican piece has already been played, thus missing out on the experience.

A third tendency is to lavish on nearly every ensemble wild ovations and shouts of "bravo!" seemingly regardless of the quality. Almost every concert is followed by at least one encore, whereas in the United States and Europe such reactions tend to be reserved for only the most accomplished performers, and even then with much more reserved enthusiasm. Part of that energy seems to come from the audiences' appreciation of the brave efforts made by both student and professional musicians to continue playing despite dwindling financial support. A few fellow audience members explained their appreciation in those terms. They view classical musicianship today as an act of heroism. What once were rituals of state largess have become critical statements concerning state neglect for the arts.

Based on informal discussions with fellow audience members at various classical venues, I discovered that a great number of them were related to the musicians on stage. That was especially true in the small to medium-sized concert venues. This also explains the effusive nature of the audience reactions. Mexican classical music has become somewhat of a subcultural form made by and for a very definable social network and for very specific cultural reasons. One of those reasons is educational advancement. Learning classical music is a route toward incorporation into the professional classes, if not directly into the classical music world itself. Classical concerts with absolutely no connection to educational institutions are relatively rare in contemporary Mexico. Classical music remains in part class training, a means of gaining the requisite cultural capital to demonstrate one's worthiness to enter the professional classes. Musical education is at least in some small part a class-based rite of passage. Of course, it is also much more than that.

The boisterous demonstrations of support from the audience are matched by dignified restraint on the part of the musicians themselves. An example of this came during a salon piano concert by Dúo Arcaraz. The father-son team performed in the Pinacoteca Virreinal de San Diego (Museum of Viceregal Art), a church turned art museum. The duo played for a typically small but highly appreciative audience. The pianists were flanked by a set of massive colonial paintings, including the dramatic and didactic work of colonial master Miguel Cabrera (1695–1768).

Unfortunately, the wooden floor beneath the pianos appeared to be almost as ancient as Cabrera's paintings. One of the pedals began to produce a noticeable squeak each time José Luis, the father, depressed it. Rather than react in anger or embarrassment, however, the elder Arcaraz subtly glanced down at the offending pedal and began to use it as a sort of impromptu rhythmic device. The final song of the program thus gained an occasional seemingly purposeful "squeak," each time played with the same intensity and duration. On this and many other occasions I witnessed a Mexican musician making the most of the resources on hand, using skill and inventiveness to turn limitations into something interesting and new. Much of the best of Mexican music, indeed music in general, is born in such conditions. In that instance, as in the majority of classical concerts I have experienced in Mexico City, the small audience made up for its diminished size by providing a warm and enthusiastic response to the duo's wonderful performance.

DIGNITY, BEAUTY, AND ELEGANCE

This ethnographic interlude concludes with another narrative vignette. One day as I sat eating lunch in Coyoacán plaza—a bohemian and upper-middle-class enclave of artists, intellectuals, and professionals located near the university (UNAM)—I watched as a flautist played for an appreciative audience of one, a three-year-old boy. The boy stood upon his chair, enthralled by the impromptu street concert. Meanwhile his parents chatted, oblivious to the music.

The boy's parents, like many Mexicans in the professional classes, are hard to distinguish from their U.S. counterparts. Perhaps, as in this case, the only giveaway was the degree to which their clothing and other goods were orchestrated into a fully coordinated ensemble. Only the most stereotypical "yuppies" or "preppies" in the United States achieve such a state of coordination in costume and demeanor. The thin ranks of Mexican professionals, conversely, tend to demonstrate their social rank in a more overt and public manner. Telenovelas, while certainly stereotypical, nevertheless hold some truth-value in the way they represent the professional classes of Mexico. This family could have stepped right out of *Los ricos también lloran* (The Rich Also Cry), *Mi destino eres tu* (You Are My Destiny), *Laberintos de pasión* (Labyrinths of Passion), or any number of other Mexican telenovelas. They demonstrated a remarkable ability to ignore the street musician, as if there were more than a metaphoric wall between them.

Classical Nationalism Today

The well-groomed parents talked and sipped coffee as their little boy listened to the flautist, totally transfixed. The musician was just three feet away, on the other side of a small barrier separating the sidewalk café from the sidewalk itself. There was a sort of purity in the performance typical of the form. Although music has certainly become a commodity in Mexico as elsewhere around the world, it also thrives outside of market contexts, in the open air of the plaza, on street corners, and in the home. The classical nationalists contributed a great deal to Mexican music, but their mission of rescuing music from the market was both unsuccessful and perhaps unnecessary. Despite the upper-class appropriation of certain music forms, and the market-logic driving pop music, musicians continue to make music for reasons that go well beyond money and prestige. This Coyoacán flautist was one of hundreds of examples I encountered during my fieldwork in Mexico City.

As I thought about music, markets, and such things, the mother and father of the young savant decided it was time to leave. Failing to acknowledge the flautist in any way, let alone compensate him for entertaining and educating their child for several minutes, the mother plucked the little boy from his chair and off they went. The flautist simply turned and left in search of another audience. This vignette serves well as allegory. Many talented classical musicians perform today in Mexico City, usually for small yet enthusiastic audiences. Together, they and their audiences manage to create exceptional art despite the increasingly difficult conditions under which they must labor.

14 Ranchera during the Postrevolutionary Era and at Mid-Century

The term "mariachi" is most often used in reference to a specific type of musical ensemble rather than a single style of music. The mariachi conjunto consists of violin(s), trumpet(s), guitars, and various guitar variants, such as the *guitarrón*, vihuela, and *jarana*. People also occasionally use the term in reference to the styles of music typically played by mariachis, however, as in "mariachi music."

The type of music most commonly played by mariachis is called *ranchera*. Ranchera is a melodramatic style of music developed during the twentieth century, popularized through nostalgic radio programs and pastoral films featuring horse-riding heroes. Ranchera subgenres include cry-in-your-beer laments, romantic serenades, and proud geographic anthems, all sharing the extreme emotionalism that distinguishes the form. In this chapter, the term "mariachi" is used in reference to the ensemble and musicians (mariachis). The term "ranchera" is used to refer to the musical style that has been adopted and popularized by the mariachi conjunto.

Ranchera and bolero coexisted throughout the postrevolutionary era. The true Golden Age of ranchera came during the middle of the century. By mid-century ranchera had taken over top billing as bolero settled nicely into second position, transformed into a string-based style, called trío. However, ranchera and bolero are not completely separate forms. Ranchera was highly influenced by the bolero. In fact, during the postrevolutionary period much of the mariachi repertoire consisted of "bolero-rancheras," boleros adapted to mariachi instruments and techniques.

Ranchera gained its greatest popularity during the mid-century period. Although eventually knocked from top spot on the sales chart by rock and pop, ranchera continues to be extremely popular and is considered the quintessential musical style of Mexico.

REMAKING THE REVOLUTION

People continued to flood into Mexico City throughout the twentieth century, adding new and ever more impoverished settlements over what used to be Lake Texcoco. The rural refugees are still reminded of their lakebed location every time a hard rain comes, turning their barrios into thick swamps.

Meanwhile, many of the earlier refugees from the Revolution settled in, improved their lives, and proliferated. Their children have known only the city. Their experience of rural Mexico may involve just a few visits to the countryside, pilgrimages to attend fiesta days and meet distant relatives. Some never go beyond the city limits. These entrenched urbanites have a mental image of rural Mexico mediated mostly by film and television.

By the late forties and early fifties, most Mexico City dwellers were born in the city itself; and their attitude toward urbanity, history, and modernity is, naturally, quite different from that of their parents. They are more accustomed to urban existence and, perhaps for that reason, more romantically inclined toward the revolutionary past and rural life. Their parents knew better than to imagine the Revolution as an age of good vs. evil. They knew full well that rural life is far from pastoral bliss.

Conversely, their urbanized children began to imagine the rural past as the antithesis of their urban present. These later generations were rightfully proud of their parents' and grandparents' bold struggle to overthrow dictatorship and institute a more just and democratic society. Rather than sharing anarchist and socialist sentiments of the early revolutionaries, however, the mid-century generations tended to think in romantic and melodramatic terms, of good people overcoming bad despots. Ranchera music and charro films encouraged them to do so and helped fuel a nostalgic reworking of the Revolution, rural existence, and Mexican national identity. As the etymology of the term implies, in Spanish and English, to "re-collect" or "re-member" (*re-cordar*) is to put the past back together. The past is never put together as it was, however; we cobble it back together in new ways, through ritual, ideology, and collective forgetting.

The angst of urban existence engendered a wide audience for ranchera music and charro films. The charro is a gallant horseman. The term is often mistranslated as "Mexican cowboy" in the U.S. literature. If anything, it is the reverse. The U.S. cowboy is a later offshoot of the long-standing charro tradition, whose practice of ranching, roping, and riding goes back much further into antiquity than the nineteenth-century U.S. icon. The cowboy borrowed a great deal from the charro, including the ballad tradition, but the historical charro is not greatly indebted to the U.S. cowboy (although during the 1940s and 1950s U.S. cowboy movies clearly did influence Mexican charro films).

Ranchera's conservative reinterpretations of rural and revolutionary life gained popularity at the expense of the bolero and its cinematic complement, the cabaretera. The latter became a secondary, urban phenomenon, while ranchera music and charro film took over the Mexican imagination. Like mid-century cowboy movies in the United States, charro films were largely conservative, both politically and culturally. The question of cultural politics is discussed later in the chapter. First, it is important to look back at the historical origins of the mariachi ensemble and ranchera music for a sense of how this modern tradition developed in Mexico.

THE HISTORICAL DEVELOPMENT OF MARIACHI AND RANCHERA

Many people, both in Mexico and in the United States, think of the mariachi ensemble and ranchera music as the quintessential Mexican musical style, a tradition. Therefore, it is. What makes a tradition is not so much its longevity in current form — for traditions are rarely as static as we imagine them to be — but rather the collective act of imagining them to be so. If there is general agreement that something is a tradition, then it is a tradition, whether it was invented a decade ago or centuries before. Indeed, the mariachi ensemble as we now know it and ranchera music are largely modern inventions. Despite their central place in the Mexican national imagination, mariachi and ranchera should be understood in the context of their modern development and use.

Three major influences combined in the development of ranchera music: the "traditional" mariachi ensemble, charro-style films, and the bolero. From the first, ranchera borrowed instrumentation, clothing, and repertoire. However, the modern mariachis are far different from their predecessors on all three counts.

The style and constitution of the first mariachi ensembles may be indicated in the name itself. One explanation for the Mexican term *mariachi* is that the title was derived from the French word *marriage*. According to that story, the first mariachis were Mexican musicians playing for French and French-styled weddings and celebrations during the 1860s intervention and on through the following decades. Despite the withdrawal of Maximiliano and Carlota, French foods, fashions, and culture remained the rage in Mexico, especially during the Porfiriato.

E. Thomas Stanford disagrees with the French derivation theory. He argues that the word *mariachi* is a combination of the name "María"—once a generic designator for any Mexican woman—and the Nahuatl *che*. Thus it shares an etymological root with the Nahuatl term *malinche*. Because the Nahuatl had no *r* phoneme, they interpreted the Spanish name "Marina" as Malinche (Stanford 1984b:20). Stanford also contests French derivation based on the fact that the mariachi trumpet was added to the ensemble much later than the era of the French intervention and thus the modern mariachi could not be beholden to French inheritance (1984b:33). Stanford's analysis seems to conflate two issues, however: (1) the evolution of the mariachi conjunto and (2) the origins of the name. Indeed, the conjunto has long been in flux, as explained below. The French could still have influenced the term and some earlier manifestations of the conjunto, despite the fact that new instrumentation was added later.

Hermes Rafael claims that mariachi is a Mesoamerican tradition and gives much less credit to foreign influences (1983). He argues that the term is derived from a word in the language of the Coca people of central Jalisco. Rafael is seeking a distinctly Mexican derivation. However, there is little in the instrumentation that indicates indigenous influence. Yet it would appear that his argument, in line with Stanford's etymological reasoning, is at least partially correct. In 1852, a decade before Maximiliano's intervention (but not before French influence as a whole), a priest in Jalisco used the term in a written document, complaining that the "mariachis" were disrupting holy days. Another priest, this time in Guerrero, referred to a *mariache* musical ensemble in 1859 (Jáuregui 1990:15–18). The latter supports Stanford's linguistic claim, although it is odd that Stanford's "original" word, *mariache*, would be applied in Guerrero years after the supposedly evolved form, *mariachi*, was used in its Guadalajaran "birthplace." Meanwhile, the phonetic similarity to the French term—and the fact that French influence predated the French intervention—makes it impossible to throw out the once-popular hypothesis completely.

Furthermore, there is a European, classical tinge to mariachi that differentiates it from the *sones*—a formality and technical quality in performance and sound that might suggest French influence or at the very least some classical influence (perhaps from nineteenth-century salon music?). Unfortunately, no one is privy to evidence that would settle the debate, and a combination of these cultural influences is certainly possible. Therefore, I prefer to leave the problem of origins as an open question. What is most important is that mariachi developed in Mexico and has become the quintessential Mexican musical art form.

Etymology aside, it is clear that much of the instrumentation and musical style of mariachi is heavily influenced by European music, as is nearly all music in the New World, from Canada to Chile. The early mariachi ensemble contained mainly strings: a harp (eventually dropped), guitars, and, added not long thereafter, the guitarrón (a large six-string guitar, whose strings are usually plucked in octave pairs, adding deep bass support). Later, mariachi ensembles grew to include violins (usually two), the vihuela, and sometimes the jarana (small guitar).

As late as the 1950s, the musical style and even the instrumentation were still developing into the form we experience now. It certainly did not spring wholesale from a widespread rural tradition, as indicated in the modern charro-style films. For example, Juan Ramírez, a musician raised and trained in the rural Bajío, had to learn to play in a mariachi ensemble after moving to Mexico City. Despite decades of playing trumpet in the Bajío, it was not until he reached the capital in 1950 that he took up the mariachi life. According to popular belief and the myth-making media fueling it, mariachi music was ubiquitous in the Bajío during that time, inescapable for any local musician. Early film and television programs like *Noches tapatías* made it seem that everyone in the Bajío participated in some way in this long-standing musical "tradition"—cinematic exaggeration at its best.

Embarrassed by his lack of knowledge of mariachi music, and wanting to tap into its cinematically enhanced market power, Ramírez joined the mariachi union in the 1950s, went back to Guadalajara to learn his "native" style, and then returned for a "conquest of the capital" as a Garibaldi Square musician (1995:58). "From the mariachi," he explains somewhat whimsically, "I obtained enough money to conclude the educations of eight professionals [his children]" (1995:61). Although Ramírez certainly did not gain the kind of wealth won by the charro dons and divas, his story demonstrates how talented mariachis in Mexico City could earn a decent living during the mid-century. His life story indicates how this long-standing tradition was also a contemporaneous trend, pieced-together and revised rather than simply borrowed from past tradition.

The most important step in the punctuated evolution of the mariachi came decades before Ramírez adopted the form, however, with the advent of radio in the early 1930s. Although mariachi had been recorded as early as 1908, in Chicago, it was live radio broadcasting that most transformed mariachi playing style and ensemble composition. Because string music did not carry well on early audio equipment, trumpets were added to the mariachi ensemble. Having been popularized through mariachi radio programs and recordings, brass was soon demanded at live concerts as well. Mariachi trumpeters usually play basic harmonies, simple thirds. Unfortunately, they do so much more loudly than their string colleagues. Therefore, to keep the trumpets from drowning out the strings, more strings were added, increasing the size of the typical conjunto.

The same thing happened decades before in *son* ensembles, only with another instrument. The introduction of the modern six-string guitar drowned out less vociferous stringed instruments such as harps and especially violins. The adoption of the modern guitar had a "devastating effect over the traditional conjunto," causing the "violins to atrophy" (Stanford 1984b:19). Of course, a new equilibrium was established by adding more violins and violin solos, just as more strings would later be added to the mariachi ensemble to compensate for the addition of brass. Ritual traditions, especially when it comes to matters of musical instrumentation, change constantly.

In sum, the advent of electronic mass media was essential to the development of modern mariachi. Whereas radio and recording technology halted the spread of marimba music (Garfias 1983:211), it had a more positive effect on the mariachi conjunto. Radio extended the geographic reach of mariachi while greatly modifying the nature of its composition and performance.

Radio also caused a fundamental shift in the way popular music was produced and consumed. In order to be heard through early radio equipment, instrumental ensembles needed to introduce louder and more percussive instrumentation. This not only affected mariachi but may partly explain the success of Lara's piano-based boleros as well. The piano, unlike the guitar, carried quite nicely over the early airwaves, while early string-based boleros did not. In other words, early electronic technology greatly transformed musical ensembles and popular tastes. Not until the mid-century trio movement would strings make a significant comeback in the bolero. By then recording and broadcasting equipment had evolved enough to carry the more subtle sounds effectively.

The modern mariachi ensemble still bears the stamp of its media-mandated transformation. I have asked many people in both Mexico and the United States to tell me what constitutes an "authentic" mariachi ensemble. The trumpet is often the first instrument mentioned and is almost without fail included high on the list. People are generally surprised when I tell them that this traditional element was first added for the sake of modern broadcasting. While Mexican and U.S. ethnomusicological, sociological, and anthropological literature is replete with condemnations of commercial mass media for having killed off tradition (Bonfil Batalla 1996:123), in this case it was a key instrument in its formation. After all, what is a mariachi ensemble without brass?

Mid-century ranchera greatly invigorated and modernized the mariachi tradition. Names associated with this popular movement include José Alfredo Jiménez (Gradante 1982), Pedro Infante (León de Infante 1961), Lucha Reyes, Javier Solís, Jorge Negrete, and Lola Beltrán. By the late 1940s these men and women had largely supplanted the great boleristas. The hard-drinking (and behind-the-scene bohemian) Jiménez became known as El Hijo del Pueblo, a media icon for an urbanized nation that still wanted to think of itself as revolutionary and rural (Gradante 1982). From the sombrero to poncho, the ranchera movement took the basic symbols of rural Mexico and enlarged them, almost to the level of caricature.

Ranchera during the Postrevolutionary Era and at Mid-Century

Although ultimately driven by the same modern, urban impulses, ranchera is in other ways antithetical to the bolero. The bolero adopts some of the smooth tone and flow of nineteenth-century bel canto, while ranchera takes on the incredible dynamism of rural Mexican music. The ranchera ritual — on stage, phonogram, and film — is a medium of collective catharsis, an outpouring of anger, rage, grief, and joy, often within the span of a few minutes. In this way, ranchera captures the spirit of the traditional Mexican fiesta, for there "is nothing so joyous as a Mexican fiesta, but there is also nothing so sorrowful" (Paz 1985:49–54).

The emotional tone of the ranchera allowed it to be viewed as something uniquely Mexican. Despite also demonstrating some foreign influence, ranchera became much more completely associated with Mexican national character and nationalism than the bolero. Whereas U.S. crooners eagerly borrowed much from their Mexican bolero counterparts such as Lara, ranchera presents a vocal style, range, and dynamism that "most Anglo-Saxons would avoid even when singing in the bath" (John Roberts in Gradante 1982:53). Ranchera was, and is, a ritual of national identity, whereas the bolero has become a ritual of urban identity, abstract romanticism, and internationalism. They share much as music but differ greatly as ritual forms.

CULTURAL CONSERVATISM

Perhaps the last major step in the mariachi's musical evolution was the addition of the *requinto* guitar, an instrument first popularized by bolerista Alfredo Gil, a trío star of the late 1940s and 1950s. The use of the requinto spread into mariachi partly due to its popularity in bolero trío ensembles like Los Panchos. Once again the two forms, bolero and ranchera, were not simply opposites but managed to share a great deal. In fact, some of the more enterprising musicians of the 1950s played in both trío and mariachi ensembles, and it is the rare mariachi ensemble today that does not include at least a few bolero standards in its repertoire.

However, ranchera more effectively resonated with the ideological and cultural sentiments of post–World War II Mexico. This is clearly illustrated in the charro films. The nostalgic desire for (largely imaginary) rural ways dominated the cultural frame — no longer enamored with the newness of urban places, sounds, and styles — shoving aside the sense of urbane modernity embodied in bolero dress, style, and behavioral codes. Therefore, the smartest move any unestablished musician of mid-century Mexico City could make was to exchange a tuxedo or evening dress for a charro costume. Many did, turning "nationalism into a great show" (Monsiváis 1993a:144). One such showman was Jorge Negrete, who dropped his operatic past and bolero career to become the top charro icon of the ranchera movement.

Ranchera is a social realist genre. Rather than evoke an abstract or ethereal sense of love or longing, ranchera song and film narratives often deal with definable characters, living in actual places, taking very specific actions on behalf of the people. Ranchera protagonists, including the singers themselves, represent the people. They sing songs of collective regional or national pride. Ranchera is, in this way, a complement to the corrido.

Yet, at the same time, ranchera is a form of fantasy. It is about a Revolution that never happened, or at least not in that way. It is about great men who overcome overwhelming odds to thwart the nefarious deeds of evil *hacendados* (hacienda owners) and about actual places on the map, remade to fit this heroic narrative. In sum, the ranchera is social realist melodrama.

Ranchera classics trumpet pride of place and nation, as in the bold "Soy de San Luis Potosí" or "Ay Jalisco no te rajes," fulfilling the political objectives that had been attempted since independence: to create national unity from the patchwork of patrias chicas that dominated Mexican cultural life for centuries. In other words, electronic mass media were accomplishing in mid-century Mexico what the printing press and other state apparatuses had long been attempting: to build a modern nation. Now people from Chiapas to DF, Mérida to Baja, were singing ranchera hymns to San Luis Potosí, Jalisco, and the like as if the patrias chicas in question were their own. Of course, this in itself did not a nation make, and (as demonstrated earlier) other events and developments such as the U.S. invasion had previously helped coalesce the national consciousness. However, modern mass media and their ideological content—especially ranchera music and charro films—greatly reinforced and accelerated the process of nation-building.

The typical rural hacienda setting of the charro films also served as an abstracted symbol of the entire nation. The hacienda is owned at the beginning by a corrupt hacendado; it will take the intervention of a ranchera-singing charro to dislodge the unworthy leader. The strong, moral, misunderstood, and often falsely accused hero of the people inevitably earns the affection of the female protagonist, who, in turn, serves as symbol of the local pueblo. This provincial princess is usually subjected to the evil hacendado's untoward affections. The male protagonist must liberate her, and her people, for things to be set right. Good triumphs, and order is restored.

In other words, rather than call for a revolutionary overthrow of the hacienda hierarchy itself, the films instead call for reform, the replacement of a bad patron with a good one. Clearly, the Revolution is reinvented in the charro films. The good charro (PRI) forms a moral order, replacing the bad and antiquated hacendado dictatorship. The nagging incompletion and contradictions of the Revolution are painted over in the ranchera-charro complex. PRI's postrevolutionary rule was thus legitimated in these films and songs, and the fundamental corruption effectively obfuscated.

Ranchera music and charro films are, like all melodramatic and ideological forms, full of basic stereotypes. A plaque in an exhibit at the National Museum of Popular Culture read: "El mariachi: Entre la tradición y el estereotipo" (Mariachi: Between Tradition and Stereotype). Just as the postrevolutionary bolero was modernity for the masses, the charro complex presented an equally accessible nationalism. Ranchera music and charro films rode a wave of patriotism in the mid-century. Therefore, while classical "musical nationalism declined in Mexico" (Behague 1979:147), stereotypical, nationalistic imagery was on the rise in popular music, film, and television. Nationalistic images, some of them borrowed from the artists and intellectuals of the postrevolution, were finally being integrated into the popular culture as the postrevolutionaries once intended (but not in the way they intended). Perhaps this is evidence of a cultural lag effect, or else a "trickle down" from the elite to popular classes. Regardless, this new nationalism took hold of the popular imagination just in time to legitimate a regime whose programs were largely antithetical to the intentions of the postrevolutionary intellectuals and artists. In dialectical fashion, postrevolutionary socialists unwittingly laid the ideological groundwork for a conservative, undemocratic, and capitalist state, just as the revolutionaries before them unintentionally accelerated urbanization via their war for rural justice. The best-laid plans . . .

The PRI's main ideological goal was not unlike that of all postcolonial regimes: to knit together a nation from greatly distinct regional traditions. "Within regional diversity," explains Pineda, "they looked to create a national unity through which the people would newly identify as Mexican" (1990:4). The charro stereotype was perhaps the first nationally accessible icon truly to resonate in that fashion, becoming a mutually comprehensible symbol of the nation. This explains the central place of mariachi in most Mexican cultural and civic ceremonies, from the Mezcal fair in Oaxaca to Cinco de Mayo celebrations and parades in northern border towns.

Once again, mass media were essential to this process of nation-building. What nationalists had largely failed to do during a century of secular ritual cultural programming the mass-media complex accomplished fairly rapidly. Mariachi and related cultural forms, coded as long-standing tradition, provided a national identity, cultural consensus, and stock of symbols for the renewed popular nationalism of the 1950s and beyond. The rural revolution was remade in fairly apolitical form, domesticated and put to work for the PRI.

Of course, the charro-ranchera complex was not solely or even primarily responsible for the renewed success of nationalism, but it did provide a great deal of the ideological imagery. My intention, however, is certainly not to dismiss ranchera music as a spurious cultural form. It is deeply loved for many reasons, not the least of which is the incredible artistry and sophistication of the mariachi ensembles. Indeed, the mariachi ensemble is one of Mexico's most valuable contributions to world music. The fact that its development has certain ideological implications, and has been in a large way a product of mass mediation, does not detract from the mariachi's cultural status and quality as a musical form. It should be clear by now that all popular music, practically by definition, involves the interests of power. As with all prior forms, mariachi performance is both a tool of power and site of resistance. Furthermore, like all other art forms, mariachi cannot be reduced simply to its ideological elements. There is perhaps no sound so beautiful and unique in Mexico as that produced by the mariachis.

Given its ideological implications, however, many Mexican cultural critics are at best ambivalent when it comes to ranchera music and the charro film trend. Carlos Monsiváis describes the Golden Age film era as "the conquest of credibility with its credulous audience, gained by idealizing provincial life and the rural world, demonizing and consecrating the urban environment, exalting machismo, transforming social defects into virtues, defending conservative values to the bitter end (verbally at least) and putting on a pretense of attacking the 'heterodox' attitudes assumed in the attempt to win back audiences to the box office" (1993a:140). Thus, he claims, "the achievements of Mexican cinema have been sociological rather than artistic" (1993a:140). His point is extremely well taken. Cabaretera and charro films can also be viewed as double prongs in a campaign to condemn urban vice. Cabaratera films are morality tales concerning the outcomes of urban vice. Meanwhile, charro films extol conservative cultural values through ideological projections of rural life.

As documented previously, the rise of ranchera came during a time when the government was attempting to crack down on what it viewed as popular vice. Vice was elevated to the level of fetish in the postrevolutionary bolero, cabaretera films, and nightlife itself. By the late 1940s, however, popular decadence had run its course. Curfews were imposed, limiting nightlife after 2:00 A.M., putting a significant damper on the bohemian subculture behind the bolero movement.

Such restrictions must be understood as the fruition of a larger and more long-term movement. The postrevolutionary regime worked hard to change the moral character of Mexico. It instituted "secular anniversaries" concerning historical triumphs as well as celebrations honoring "the Day of the Mother, of the soldier, of the race, of the tree, of the Child" (Knight 1994:407), all of which were intended to supplant the religious ritual calendar. The supposed socialists also tried to work against the vices inherent in unrestrained capitalist consumption. Children pledged allegiance to the new nation and swore to give their lives to "combat the three mighty enemies that our nation faces, namely the Clergy, Ignorance, and Capital" (Knight 1994:411). Educators would measure their success based on the number of civic and even anticlerical rituals that their students performed in a given year. When Lázaro Cárdenas nationalized the oil industry, this provoked a ritual outpouring, as teachers "paraded phalanxes of children through the streets, flags waving" and everywhere children became involved in fundraising for the "petroleum

Ranchera during the Postrevolutionary Era and at Mid-Century

debt" (Knight 1994:414). These state-supported rituals were, in turn, directly contested. Well-organized movements like the Cristeros and Catholic Action waged open and covert warfare, while in the home "devout mothers competed with liberal fathers" (Knight 1994:417, 422) to undo the secular lessons.

Although the children of the revolution would reject many of the somewhat superficial anticlerical and socialist principles taught them by the state, they would nevertheless learn the lessons of modern development. The three-way struggle of church, state, and capital would largely be resolved in favor of a hegemonic consensus among the three. A ritual space would be maintained for both the secular and religious sectors. Meanwhile, the major organization and practices of power were to be found in a developing state capitalism. The enemies of the state in 1930s Mexico were "Clergy, Ignorance, and Capital" (Knight 1994:411). However, by the 1950s, the state had clearly decided to assuage the former and give in to the latter. The mid-century antivice movement was the residue of those earlier culture campaigns, shorn of secular socialist rhetoric, symbolic of the new church-state détente.

The conservative turn would triumph by the 1950s, after traditional and revolutionary developmentalists reached their accord. The accord was not so much a settlement between the various power factions as recognition of their mutual failure. Rural villagers "refused to obey the dictates and exhortations of the radical government in the 1930s" (Knight 1994:443). That resistance was based largely on religious conservatism. Yet this too would be challenged by necessity. Beset by poverty and propelled by the integration of a "developing" nation, many of these same rural resisters "obeyed instead the imperatives of the capitalist market of the 1940s and 1950s" (1994:443) and moved to the city, producing yet another wave of postrevolutionary exodus from the provinces.

Revolutionary socialism, if enacted more in earnest, would have contested the interests of capital. Religious conservatism, if practiced faithfully, would have undermined the capitalist ethic. Instead, what came out of the postrevolutionary dialectic was a sort of unsatisfactory détente, a state-directed capitalist system that mainly enriched the oligarchs and urban middle classes. Meanwhile, a permanent political class was formed, under the aegis of the PRI, which maintained power through effectively enfranchising certain sectors of the working and middle classes. That system would go largely unchallenged until 1968 and to this day remains the major mode of power in Mexico.

While perhaps not quite as violent or extreme as the reactionary conservatism of the United States during the same decade (1950s), the conservative trend in mid-century Mexico threw a wet blanket over the postrevolutionary party. Those who saw the postrevolutionary era as a space for modern experimentation — whether Communist libertines like Rivera and Kahlo or cultural anarchists like Agustín Lara — were forced to witness this national retrenchment and the end of their utopian dreams. Mexico was headed toward a more sober form of modernity, less open to its cultural potential, and even more fearful of its moral effects.

RANCHERA: BETWEEN ART AND IDEOLOGY

Ranchera is not the traditional, organic expression of national pride some believe it to be; nor is it simply a "prefabricated" mix of machismo, alcohol (Reuter 1981:14), and retrograde conservative ideology others would make of it. Instead, ranchera is a ritual point of negotiation in the ongoing struggle over Mexico's revolutionary legacy. As described earlier, ranchera music and charro film ritually reflect the conservative nationalism that eventually triumphed in mid-century Mexico.

Yet mariachi, the root source of ranchera and charro, is far more than an ideological artifact. Mariachi reflects some of the deepest moral beliefs and values of the Mexican people. One need only experience a mariachi session in a neighborhood restaurant or fiesta to come to that conclusion. Mariachi is a uniquely Mexican contribution to world music. It has evolved into much more than popular entertainment; it has developed into a folk ritual (Burr 1992), a classical musical style, and an art form.

15 Ranchera Today

The mariachi ensemble continued to evolve throughout the century and continues to adapt to different performance contexts. Ensembles range from small, four-member conjuntos to temporary orchestras with more than five hundred musicians organized for special concerts and public celebrations. In this chapter I describe a few typical performances.

Academic accuracy requires that I include both the bad and good in this description. The good news is that mariachi ensembles and their music are thriving. Unfortunately, no analysis of Mexico City mariachi is complete without reference to Plaza Garibaldi, and no description of Plaza Garibaldi is complete without mention of its precipitous decline.

TROUBLED TIMES IN PLAZA GARIBALDI

The mariachi center of Mexico City is Plaza Garibaldi. For generations, Mexican families and tourists have gone there to hear the finest mariachi bands. For a small fee, an ensemble will play people's favorite ranchera ballads, while they sit on a bench with their children or drink a shot of tequila at one of the restaurants ringing the square. Until fairly recently, it had been an obligatory stop for all visitors to the capital, Mexican and foreigner alike.

Sadly, the plaza has lately become associated with robbery, assault, prostitution, and drugs. Tourists are warned away from it, and even many capitalinos now avoid the area. Mexico City, like any large city, is a fairly dangerous place if one does not take the necessary precautions. It is very unfortunate that one of those precautions, for both locals and foreigners, is to avoid places like Plaza Garibaldi until they become more secure. As a result, the festive crowds of the past have dwindled down to a few families by day and a not-so-familial crowd of revelers at night. As Alma Guillermoprieto documents in *The Heart That Bleeds*, there were few places more depressing than the mariachis' Garibaldi Square in the 1990s as it traded on past glory (1994:239–242).

Perhaps the plaza's decadence indicates a decline in mariachi popularity in the city. Or maybe it has been a reciprocal process: the less popular the mariachis become, the more space opens up for illicit activities. Regardless of the reasons for the decline, it is, for the time being, no longer a place where most people can bring their daughters for their Quinceañeras or where young lovers can go for moonlight serenades.

Whatever the cause, Plaza Garibaldi has been in a severe slump for years. The Mexican Mariachi Union (UMM) has represented the Garibaldi mariachis since 1943. It recently called for a reduction in its ranks, stating that the plaza is "overpopulated" (*Excelsior*, Sunday, June 3, 2001: 7-E). While the claim is that the number of mariachis has risen too quickly, it seems fairly clear that the number of listeners at the plaza has also fallen off. Fortunately, the police have increased their presence at Plaza Garibaldi, leading some to predict a mariachi renaissance in the city center. I hope that the Mexico City government, despite what would seem to be more pressing human concerns, will nevertheless take steps to rejuvenate the plaza. One cannot overestimate the symbolic value of Plaza Garibaldi to Mexico City's cultural life and identity.

I do not take the decline of Plaza Garibaldi as a sign of weakening interest in the mariachi, however. Dispersed throughout the city in restaurants and (safer) public places, there are thousands of mariachi ensembles thriving and plying their trade. In the Bajío, the birthplace and spiritual home of the mariachis, the music is as alive as ever. For several nights I visited a set of open-air restaurants in downtown Guadalajara, Mexico's second largest city and the heart of the Bajío. I watched mariachi bands play late into the night there for recurrent waves of revelers. Likewise, mariachi thrives to the north and is the signature form of Mexican music in Greater Mexico. In fact, the farther north one moves from the capital, the more other forms of Mexican music dissipate and are replaced by mariachi bands and *grupero* conjuntos, which are the basic symbols of *música mexicana* in the diaspora.

POP MARIACHI

Most pop musicians genuflect at the national altar of mariachi and ranchera at least once during their career. In many cases they simply reproduce their synthesizer-driven pop ballads as mariachi tunes for special albums and performances. Likewise, tight spandex and miniskirts are exchanged for charro and charra outfits. Mexican pop artists demonstrate their love for *patria* (the fatherland) through these mariachi makeovers, in the same way in which they use bolero to illustrate a sense of urban sophistication. The mariachis give automatic authenticity to what might otherwise be considered malinchista pop, and it is an almost obligatory career move for the Mexican pop diva at some point in her career. Ana Gabriel, Lucero, Daniela Romo, and many others have mariachi compilations and have presented mariachi-style concerts. Paulina Rubio parodies this tendency in her video and song "El último adiós." The blonde icon sings in a seedy nightclub, fronting a mariachi band while wearing a revealing pop costume. The contrast between the pop-wear and mariachis is either a striking statement concerning pop appropriation or, conversely, a critique of mariachi's sacred status. It is not clear which, if either, of these points Rubio is making, yet it is nonetheless a bold visual statement.

When I talk to music enthusiasts in Mexico, particularly those over forty, the conversation almost always turns to condemnations of pop. Particular disdain is reserved for those who "profane" more traditional forms, such as bolero or mariachi. "Why don't they stick to their own music?" complained one woman I met at a bolero concert, referring to contemporary pop renditions of Golden Age boleros. Clearly, such pop appropriation is not performed in order to woo bolero and mariachi aficionados. Instead, these more canonical forms serve as a stock of symbols that pop musicians can draw on in order to enliven their work as well as an important source of cultural capital to link them to their nation. Constantly traveling the world, perhaps making a home base in Miami, Florida, a Mexican pop star might do well to don the charro outfit once in a while for a little homeland legitimation.

Despite the apparent artificiality of pop mariachi, however, it seems to be a fairly genuine expression on the pop artists' part. After all, these pop musicians were raised with mariachi and appear to love the music enough to spend significant time crafting ranchera albums and concerts. Pop artists like Lucero ultimately gain very little from their nationalistic nods. The mariachi compilations are often among their weakest-selling albums. Mariachi is at least partly a labor of love for these pop stars turned mariachis.

Of course, there may be additional motivations. Perhaps such pop stars do not want to appear or feel too un-Mexican in their pop. Or is this just one more character that Mexican pop stars can take on to remain everything to everyone? Indeed, one of the interesting distinctions between pop stars in the United States and in Mexico is that Mexican pop icons not only are allowed to take on significantly disparate character personas and musical styles but are obliged to do so. One day Lucero is the sexy siren, the next a charra, and the next an elegant bolerista. Only the rare U.S. pop star, such as Madonna, plays with shifting character-roles to the same extreme. Conversely, Mexican pop stars continually shift from one image and genre to another. Graciela Beltrán is a banda queen for one album, a pop balladeer the next. Daniela Romo sings with the mariachis then belts out a show tune. Romo makes more costume changes in a single concert than many U.S. pop stars do in a year. Whereas U.S. audiences might find such style shifts disorienting or inauthentic, Mexican pop audiences delight in the versatility and playfulness of their quick-change artists.

There appears to be a gender dimension to the shape-shifting pop. Male pop stars, like Luis Miguel, are accorded less leeway for change or, put in positive terms, are perhaps less obligated to change their musical personas. Men are supposed to be fixed and constant, whereas women are expected to transform themselves constantly, like the moon in its changing visage. Female performers are allowed, or required, to shift playfully among various character guises, while male pop stars are to remain seriously attached to a given style and genre (such as pop-rock, salsa, etc.). Male stars are often considered effeminate when they indulge in the shape shifting expected of female pop divas.

Mariachi purists dismiss pop mariachi as a bastardization of the art. Viewed as a salutary nod to the cultural power and beauty of the "real" mariachis, however, pop mariachi can be more easily appreciated. Yet the soul of mariachi is found far offstage and away from the cameras. Mariachi lives in local bars and restaurants, at wedding parties, Quinceañeras, and street festivals. In these familiar contexts mariachi is a ritual that bonds families, communities, and ultimately the nation.

FAMILY

Ethnography is tricky business. On one hand, ethnography is an enculturation process. Therefore, ethnographic research produces a more profound sense of cultural familiarity than more objective (read "distant") methodologies and greater cultural insight as a result. On the other hand, familiarity can also lead to a loss of wonder. Cultural phenomena are soon taken for granted by the ethnographer, even if these same practices seemed bizarre, beautiful, or profound before he or she entered "the field."

During my first major fieldwork project, in El Salvador, I discovered that a similar problem exists for war reporters (Pedelty 1995). The seasoned war correspondent becomes inured to violence, having seen too much, and becomes integrated into the local culture well enough to ignore the basic realities that still bear reporting. He or she passes the poor, hungry kid on the corner everyday, without taking notice; ignores the well-armed military police posted throughout the city; and comes to expect those in power to control the electoral process. The foreign correspondent documents the emanations and machinations of elites rather than the root causes and consequences of war. Therefore, sometimes it takes the arrival of "parachute" journalists to remind more permanent, culture-bound corps reporters of the unusual, unique, and perhaps newsworthy elements of the local scene from the perspective of an outside audience.

Ethnographic fieldwork can be like that. The fieldworker can begin to habitually experience, and thus take for granted, elements that are culturally commonplace. That is one reason why we take field notes, to remind ourselves of what was once remarkable. Unfortunately, even before I began this project, I had become accustomed to hearing and seeing mariachis all over, particularly in restaurants and public fiestas. It was the music of Mexico City itself, and in particular Mexican pop, that first drew me to this topic. Having decided to explore the subject of musical memory and ritual, I began systematic exploration, starting with the music of the Mexica. Looking back at my notes, I clearly ignored the omnipresent mariachis, even though I was enjoying their music throughout my research, as I had for years before I started the project. Like many Mexicans, I took mariachi for granted. I would request my favorite ranchera tunes from wandering mariachis at a streetside cafe while sitting with a friend or writing up my notes from the day's events. Yet I did little to document those mariachi moments.

Nevertheless, mariachi has left a profound trace in my memory as I think back over all of my musical experiences in Mexico. Like anyone who has lived or traveled in Mexico, I have listened to mariachis in restaurants and parks from Tapachula to San Luis Potosí, Veracruz to Guadalajara. Guadalajara is their legendary birthplace, and one can still find the itinerant troubadours at hundreds of restaurants in Mexico's second largest city. They also play day and night in the Plazuela de los Mariachis. Many kilometers south, on the border with Guatemala, mariachis in Tapachula's restaurants signal that one has made it to Mexico. In the northern cattle country, mariachis proudly proclaim, ¡Soy de San Luis Potosí! (I am from San Luis Potosí). Even in Veracruz, the capital city of danzón, mariachis play in public squares and private homes, drawing a connection between family, region, and nation.

In Mexico City, mariachis compete fiercely for the attention of Garibaldi visitors, serenade diners at restaurants that serve *comida típica* (traditional Mexican cooking), and welcome tourists as they arrive at luxury hotels in the Polanco district. Mariachis can be hired for Quinceañeras, birthdays, and retirement parties. In fact, "Mariachi" is one of the most common offerings under "Musicians" in the yellow pages. Whereas formal concerts are fairly rare, mariachi remains the sound of choice for family events and community fiestas.

At the local restaurant, a proud father asks the mariachis to play "Mi golondrina" for his daughter's Quinceañera. She blushes, sitting at the end of a long table, apparently embarrassed, but loving the attention her brothers, sisters, cousins, friends, aunts, uncles, and grandparents are giving her on this special day. That same night, at a fiftieth wedding anniversary celebration with immediate family the husband embarrasses and delights his bride with a mariachi rendition of the bolero "Bésame." Decades of secret meanings are communicated between the two, while the rest of us delight in the surface significance of the man's performance. It would be unimaginable to have any other style of music accompany such important life occasions.

Regardless of their multinational origins and mass-mediated modifications, the mariachi ensemble and ranchera style have united to form perhaps the most authentic Mexican national tradition, a collective expression of national identity. Obviously, there are ideological elements to the music, manipulated and managed by the state and other powers. Nevertheless, mariachi is also an honest expression of national identity at its very roots, an art form and cultural practice that must be respected and appreciated and not merely dissected by musical historians, ethnomusicologists, and ethnographers.

More than one mariachi I spoke to expressed displeasure with the way academics and reporters represent mariachi. They have read high-culture criticisms and academic analyses, none of which resonate with their lived experience. Mariachis play each night for a pittance to appreciative audiences. Their music holds great meaning for themselves as musicians and communicates important messages to their audiences. For example, when I took a photo of Ricardo Martínez, a member of

Ricardo Martínez of Mariachi Juvenil de América. Photo by author.

The multi-talented Pepe Loza. Photo by Carlos Franco.

Mariachi Juvenil de América, one of his older bandmates asked me "not to say anything bad about mariachi."

Indeed, one would have to work hard to find valid criticisms of their work. Mariachi Juvenil de América is a talented ensemble. One night I marveled as the group's members cast aside their typical set to play an impromptu list of requests from the audience. To their surprise, Cecilia Infante, Pedro Infante's niece, appeared in the audience. Urged on by friends and the rest of us gathered there in the bar, Infante sang with the band. She demonstrated a vocal range and depth reminiscent of her famous uncle. Mariachi Juvenil de América was equally impressive. Although the group is made up mostly of musicians in their twenties, they were able to transpose pieces instantly into Infante's preferred key. They either knew the requested pieces or were able to improvise brilliantly.

Originally representing a move toward conservative nationalism, mariachi has since settled into the national consciousness as an authentic musical symbol of *lo mexicano*. No matter what musicologists and other critics might say about its mass-mediated origins and nationalistic conservatism, mariachi is now an "authentic" popular tradition. New acts such as California's Nydia Rojas (Saldana 1997) and Ysenia Flores have provided new popular life for the form. Meanwhile, more long-standing mariachi artists like Vicente Fernández and Pepe Aguilar, as well as world-famous ensembles like Mariachi Vargas de Tecalitlán, continue to perform for significant audiences. Mariachi is aging well, remaining vital as a living ritual at all levels of society, firmly rooted in the family and community life of Mexico. If the bolero is Mexico City, mariachi is Mexico.

PART

VI

Contemporary Mexico: 1968–2002

16 Popular Music Today

In the late 1950s rock and roll came along and surpassed both ranchera and bolero in sales. By no means have pop and rock gained total control over the popular market, however. Older styles have continued to garner significant attention, and música grupera has a faithful following in Mexico City. *Grupera* is a term given to large synthesizer-driven bands that play a distinctly Mexican style of music. Whether they are technically dedicated to cumbia, merengue, banda, norteño, salsa, or some other style, these groups tend to have a look and sound that sets them apart from the conjuntos of other nations. For example, Control, a Mexican grupera-style cumbia band, is unlikely to be mistaken for a Colombian cumbia conjunto.

Although the term *grupera* is sometimes reserved solely for norteño groups, it is also often extended to any large Mexican pop conjunto. In addition to the typical drums, guitar, and bass, the grupera conjunto is distinguished by accordion and/or accordion-like synthesizer sounds, brass and/or synthesized brass, and acoustic and synthesized percussion that helps identify the music as belonging to a given pop category (e.g., norteño, banda, cumbia, merengue, salsa). Before delving into the main subjects of this chapter, pop and rock, it is important to discuss the musical styles associated with the grupera conjunto in Mexico: norteño, banda, and tropical.

NORTEÑO, BANDA, AND TROPICAL

Musical styles associated with northern Mexico have many fans in the city. However, banda and norteño styles (including narcocorrido ballads) are much more popular in rural and northern parts of the nation than in Mexico City and cities farther south. Norteño conjuntos include groups like Los Temerarios, Los Tigres del Norte, and Los Bukis.

Norteño bands are as popular in the United States as in Mexico. After all, many of the conjuntos are originally from Greater Mexico and find their biggest audiences at concert venues in San Antonio, Dallas, Houston, Phoenix, Los Angeles, and Chicago. Norteño music is often recorded and produced in the United States for distribution throughout the United States and Mexico.

Many Mexican immigrants to the United States come from the northern provinces of Mexico and the border territory. They have taken their musical tastes along in their travels to *el otro lado*. Such music is coded as authentically Mexican in immigrant communities, whereas much of Mexican pop and rock is viewed as having more foreign derivation and implications; it is "gringo" music. Such a tendency to favor the most apparently authentic musical forms is common in all diasporas. That which is coded as nationally authentic, regardless of its origins or history, is placed in contradistinction to the local, dominant culture. Issues of resistance, tradition, nostalgia, and identity are performed through such music. Clearly, rock and pop, no matter how popular in Mexico itself, would not perform those functions very well in the Mexican diaspora.

In Mexico City, however, norteño is viewed as somewhat foreign, not in the sense that it comes from another country but rather that it is the music of another region and culture. Norteño concerts are often poorly attended in the city. They generally take place on the outskirts of the city and are barely mentioned in newspaper schedules, *Tiempo Libre* (the weekly Mexico City events guide) listings, or other public advertisements. As with country music in the United States, the popularity of norteño fluctuates from year to year; and certain bands, like Los Tigres del Norte, are always a large draw. In 1999, for example, Los Tigres packed the zócalo with as many as 150,000 fans. Although the grupera acts are fiercely proud of their northern origins and home base, conquering the capital is still viewed as a proud feat, worth recounting back home in the northern states (Wald 2001:298). Yet for most norteño bands in most years such conquests of the capital are out of the question.

Norteño has its ardent supporters in the capital, but many Mexico

City residents view it as a curiosity from the North rather than a style of music representing their own sense of local and national identity. A norteño concert I witnessed in Mexico City involved one of the biggest names in the business, Los Temerarios. The most noticeable feature of the concert, held at the giant Mexico City speedway, was its relatively low attendance. I was able to wander up to each of the three stages, around the stands, and around the speedway grounds throughout the concert. That was not possible at the Rolling Stones concert, which had sold out the same venue a few weeks before. Mexico City rock legends El Tri opened the Stones concert to a cheering mass of Chilangos. The rockenrollero crowd dwarfed the later norteño contingent.

Los Temerarios played to a relatively small crowd of norteño devotees at the speedway, some originally from the city, others transplants from the North. The more enthusiastic participants I spoke with almost all came from states north of Mexico City. To bring the Chilango crowd into the norteño theme, vendors sold cowboy hats outside the speedway. A group of women ahead of me playfully donned new hats and put their thumbs in their belt loops, mimicking stereotypical norteño poses. The concert was a performative, playful experience for many of the Mexico City residents in attendance instead of being an event that fit naturally into their urban lives. They were playing cowboy, rather than experiencing a deeply felt connection to the norteño musical subculture.

The announcer began the concert by explaining to the crowd that this was "the national" music of Mexico, clearly feeling a need to promote it as such. The warm-up band then blasted into a set that included Spanish versions of the Carpenters' "Top of the World" and the Eagles' "Take It Easy." The bandleader kept shouting "¡Viva México!" while performing the gringo tunes.

Norteño, like country music in the United States, is associated with rural Mexico. It is also similar to country music in that it is viewed as a regional style. Conversely, pop, rock, and *música tropical* have been deterritorialized and globalized, much less associated with any given region or nation. To conclude the analogy, norteño is probably about as popular in Mexico City as country music is in New York City. It has its fans and a few radio stations, but its popularity is limited almost by definition. Norteño, as evidenced by the name, is so strongly associated with the North that many bands playing in the norteño style outside the region find it necessary to place "del Norte" in their names. In Chiapas, for example, one can find Los Zapatistas del Norte playing gruperastyle corridos to entertain the Ejército Zapatista de Liberación Nacional (EZLN) faithful (Wald 2001:5). Similar "del Norte" conjuntos exist throughout southern Mexico.

Banda, also associated with the North, is the contemporary heir of the village band tradition. Featuring bold brass, especially tuba, banda is to norteño what bluegrass is to country music. Many view banda as the more artful, experimental, and perhaps playful side of the northern música grupera movement. Don Cruz Lizarraga (1918–1995), who formed Banda El Recodo in 1951, was one of the first to transform the traditional village music of northern Mexico into a modern pop style. The movement continues apace, with groups like Banda Gauchos traveling in northern Mexico and the southwestern United States to play for fans who dance "La quebradita" with passionate devotion. Banda is a vibrant musical subculture throughout Greater Mexico (Simonett 2000).

Meanwhile, Graciela Beltrán has translated banda into a pop form that appeals to wider music markets. Her example illustrates another grupero tendency. Few women play or sing in grupera bands. The few bands fronted by a female singer tend to be listed under her name or to give her separate billing. In addition to Graciela Beltrán, examples include norteña stars Ana Barbara, Jenni Rivera, and Priscila y Sus Balas de Plata. The female-fronted grupera bands are also often viewed by fans as the more pop-style bands.

Banda has enthusiastic followings in the United States and northern Mexico. There are smaller pockets of banda devotees in Mexico City. Many of the people who find norteño music off-putting, with its more formulaic, synthesized horns and drum tracks, enjoy the experimental artistry of the banda conjuntos. The tuba, or its synthetic equivalent, carries the bouncing baseline in polka style. Unlike the deadly serious machista romanticism of the norteño-style grupera sound, banda's carnivalesque tuba and trumpet seem less rooted in a specific cultural archetype. One need not be a norteño, for play or for real, to jump into the banda festival.

Música tropical, pop music associated with the Caribbean and Latin America, is also very popular in Mexico City. The phrase *música tropical* has two general meanings in Mexico. First, it is a cover term for salsa, merengue, bachata, cumbia, and other popular Afrocaribbean styles. However, it is more common to use the name of the specific style to refer to a song or band that clearly represents one of these Afrocaribbean categories. An aficionado of Colombian cumbia, for example, would use the specific term *cumbia* and not *tropical* to describe his or her musical interest (cumbia is relatively popular in Mexico, perhaps because of its innovative use of accordion). Record stores often lump cumbia with other Caribbean and Latin American styles in the tropical section.

The term *música tropical* is also used to describe music played by Mexican grupera conjuntos and pop stars who integrate Afrocaribbean elements into their music. The addition of conga, claves, and other Caribbean percussion in the otherwise typical grupero conjunto might allow it to be designated *tropical*. Listeners in the Dominican Republic, Puerto Rico, or Colombia might not recognize it as such, but Mexican audiences view these grupero-tropical hybrids as música tropical.

How popular are grupera sounds in Mexico City? Radio broadcast data for 1995 acquired by Carmen de la Peza indicate that "música tropical–grupera"—including norteño, banda, and tropical—received 18.9 percent of total radio airtime in Mexico City (2001:178). These combined grupera styles garnered a fairly distant second place to rock, which was broadcast 39.3 percent of the time.

POP IMPERIALISM?

Having noted the parallel popularity of other styles, I focus for the remainder of the chapter on Mexican pop and rock. There is a definite identification between rock and Chilango identity. As briefly mentioned in reference to the bolero, El Chilango is a derogatory title given to the Mexico City citizens by other Mexicans. Many Mexico City people have taken on the title, wearing it proudly. El Tri's rock anthem "Chilango incomprendido" demonstrates this connection, as does Café Tacuba's "Chilanga banda." Numerous other songs and works of fiction identify El Chilango with El Rockenrollero.

Pop, rock, and accompanying rituals directly reference issues of power and hegemony in contemporary Mexico. Such rituals immediately raise questions concerning the power of the global culture industries in general and the influence of the United States in particular. Many lament what they see as the gringoization of Mexican music. It is viewed as a symbol of U.S. hegemony in Mexico, strong evidence of cultural imperialism.

That argument has a great deal of merit. Just as the Triple Alliance, Spanish, and subsequent regimes have greatly influenced the development of popular music in Mexico, the United States now casts a long shadow, as does global capitalism. Mexico is no less immune than other nations to the marketing techniques of the contemporary culture industries, many of which are based in the United States. Pop and rock are ritual entry points into U.S. culture and language.

Mexican popular culture presents several challenges to the cultural imperialism thesis, however, not the least of which is its continued ability to borrow, transform, and export what it receives from outside sources. Just because a culture borrows from others does not mean that it is entirely dependent on the "lender." Every nation, particularly the United States, is influenced by other cultures.

Similarly, despite its receptiveness to outside cultural influence, or perhaps because of it, Mexico remains a major producer and even exporter of cultural commodities. Mexico is not only a consumer of mass media but also home to some of Latin America's most important culture industries. Mexican telenovelas remain in demand throughout the world. For example, as of 1992, the Mexican telenovela *Los ricos también lloran* was the most popular show ever aired on Russian television, earning 70 percent of the viewing audience (Baldwin 1995:286). Telenovelas sell throughout the world, as do Mexican pop songs. The Mexican culture industries merge foreign and national influences to produce new hybrid cultural forms. Mexico's media mestizaje appeals to cultural consumers both inside and outside the country.

Another problem with the cultural imperialism thesis is the conflation of nation, content, and corporation. It is not nations such as the United States that extend mass cultural influence but rather corporations. These corporations, such as the "big six" music distributors, are based in but not beholden to or solely representative of any single national culture. Their reach and market share extends beyond national boundaries to encompass "90 per cent of the gross sales of recorded music worldwide of albums, singles and music videos" (Burnett 1996:2).

Granted, the media content produced and distributed by the global culture industries does tend to favor rich nations and their consumers to a highly inordinate degree. Such nations present the most lucrative market and generally serve as home base for these industries. This does not explain why people throughout the world desire to purchase and consume their products, however. There is a transnational appeal to the cultural products of the global culture industries.

Why is that the case? The answer would take us well beyond the scope of this book, but I would venture a few guesses based on my observations of pop and rock performance in Mexico. First, as mentioned above, these musical styles are viewed as entry points into U.S. and global cultures. Just as learning English is a means of economic advancement for Mexican professionals, global pop and rock provide a degree of cultural capital to Mexican youth. They are seductive rituals of power in that sense. Second, youths who see traditional culture as constrictive, as do youths around the world, often turn to the dominant global signifiers of cultural rebellion: pop and rock. That was certainly the mood, if not literal expression, at the Mexican rock concerts I witnessed. Pop and rock are experienced, rightly or wrongly, as rituals of liberation.

A third point is that pop and rock are not necessarily "foreign" to

Mexico. Much of Mexican pop and rock is produced locally. Ironically, the penetration of the global culture industries may have had the opposite effect of what was feared by the nationalists. Rather than merely flooding Mexico with foreign cultural goods, instead the global distributors have often looked to local areas for new products and markets. For example, the music of Chilango rock legends Café Tacuba and El Tri is distributed by Time Warner, a global company based in the United States. Such local groups were once locked out by local media monopoly Televisa, which has tended to favor safer and more derivative pop-rock acts, whereas global distributors have welcomed them.

The concern over corporate ownership of public media is valid, but displaced when put in the language of cultural imperialism. To a certain extent, no media industry is ever truly local. Only the wealthiest individuals and institutions own media enterprises, whether one is speaking of Mexican-owned Televisa or Japanese-based Sony. Only much smaller enterprises could ever possibly represent local interests. The issue is not so much one of national origin as of corporate scale. Furthermore, no corporation, no matter how large or distant, can simply foist an alien vision of the world on local markets. There must be some local appeal to the cultural content.

A fourth and final challenge to the cultural imperialism thesis begins with the question "What is culture?" If culture is a bounded thing, a unit of shared meanings and identities, then perhaps the national culture of Mexico is violated by the penetration of foreign media. Yet not all culture is national. Culture is a process, involving a shared stock of symbols. Therefore, no culture is sacrosanct or inviolate. We all belong to many cultures, musical and otherwise. It is clear that Mexican audiences consume media with seemingly foreign content. It is not clear that such content is so terribly alien to the Mexican audience, however, any more than that it really belongs to audiences in the United States, Europe, or elsewhere. Mexican rock audiences do not experience *rocanrol* as a foreign ritual, any more than a predominantly white audience in rural Iowa thinks about the fact that its rock rituals have been derived largely from southern black blues culture, European musical conventions, or other "foreign" influences. Culture is too fluid for such ownership to be established, recognized, and maintained for long.

What seems foreign in one decade feels familiar, perhaps even natural, in the next. We reconceive our hybrid environments as holistic, natural, and authentic experiences, regardless of their lack of antiquity or foreign origins. U.S. and Mexican rock fans may not share national citizenship, but they can be said to share cultural citizenship as part of the global rock audience. In other words, not all cultures are national, and there is nothing sacred about national culture distinctions. Transnational and global cultures have existed for centuries and are not necessarily threats to local cultural integrity.

Are global media imperialistic? Perhaps, but such control is no longer a matter of imposition by states. Systemic cultural influence is now carried by more mobile and powerful institutions: corporations. In 1999–2000 the combined revenue of the top three U.S. corporations—General Motors, Wal-Mart, and Exxon—exceeded the gross national product of Mexico, and the combined earnings of all U.S. corporations dwarf even the federal budget of the United States (Robbins 2002:123).

Because of campaign financing structures and media access considerations, potential legislators in both Mexico and the United States must demonstrate allegiance to the corporate sector before entering the ritual arena of democracy. Both Adam Smith and Karl Marx seem to have been wrong, the first in believing that an invisible hand would mitigate the influence of corporations, the second in his optimistic forecast that internal contradictions would magically lead to capitalism's undoing. Truly, there has been a slow withering away of the state, as Marx predicted, but it has come in the form of capitalism's triumph rather than its fall.

The cultural imperialism thesis tends to naturalize the nation-state and treat international systems of power as unnatural impositions. Indeed, global markets and corporate institutions are imposed, as are all forms of power; but they are no more natural or unnatural than the family, tribe, church, empire, or nation-state. All are imagined communities with specific histories and trajectories.

Most Mexica commoners could not have imagined any other system than the Triple Alliance; nor could the typical seventeenth-century neophyte think outside the hegemony of theocratic New Spain. Similarly, most people today cannot conceive of a world outside the disciplinary labor patterns, values, and beliefs within which they have been socialized and enculturated. Today and for the foreseeable future, most political debate and cultural life takes place within the hegemonic parameters of capitalism.

In the same way, most of us purchase the bulk of our culture from corporations without thinking about alternative possibilities. Therefore, contemporary popular culture is the result of an ongoing dance between cultural producers and consumers within a global capitalist framework, mediated by the culture industries, which are in turn part of a global capitalist system.

Mexico is inordinately influenced by the culture of its continental neighbor the United States and culture industries based there. However, it is important not to forget the point made earlier: that Mexican cultural industries are thriving and have a robust representation throughout the world, particularly in the rest of Latin America. According to the Bertelsmann Music Group (BMG), Mexico was the tenth largest market in the world for music in 2000. A large percentage of that market is supplied by Mexican artists. To see Mexico's vital popular culture as simply a borrowed commodity is to miss its nuances, hybridity, resiliency, and creativity.

Granted, much of Mexican pop does represent a commodified form of acculturation, called "Latinization" by Celeste Olalquiaga (1992:82). In such a world, Christina Aguilera, Ricky Martin, and Thalia become signifiers of that which is "Latin" to both Anglo and Latin American audiences, despite the fact that they are more similar to their Anglo pop counterparts than they are different. They are the "Latin" face of global pop. In fact, much of Mexican pop fits that description.

As opposed to pop, however, a fair percentage of Mexican rock falls into a very different category, what Olalquiaga refers to as "postindustrial pop" (1992:82). In that mode, "[p]arody and role inversion" allow performers and audiences to "resist colonial practices to the advantage of marginalized cultures." Postindustrial pop is "a more dynamic mode of acculturation than that of Latinization," based on more "spontaneous practices in which consumption is either secondary or dully displayed as consumption" (1992:82). Postindustrial pop is a form of critical and clever "appropriation" rather than the more mass-mediated acculturation taking place in much of "Latin" pop. Mexican rock groups like Café Tacuba, Lost Acapulco, and less well-known groups like Fucktotum consciously appropriate global cultural symbols to enact meaningful politics and art. They resist rather than reproduce the power of global capitalism, much as critical corridistas combated dictatorship, the jarabe musicians fought colonial censorship, and unknown musicians must surely have subverted Mexica hegemony long before that.

Whereas pop icons are more often appropriated to sell a commodified version of "Latin-ness" to audiences, Mexican rock does the reverse. Groups like Café Tacuba have appropriated pop and put it to postmodern purposes. For example, the group suddenly breaks into a bolero-style lament during the rock song "La ingrata," a parody of mexicanidad that serves as a nod and a wink to their core Chilango audience. Rather than simply selling itself to a broad transnational audience, the group is reinforcing its links to a knowledgeable home base that understands the more specific cultural and political meanings of its message. That message includes support for the Zapatistas and neocolonial critique. Conversely, many "cross-over" artists, interested mainly in sales, practice a sort of banal translation or cultural dilution in order to market pop-Latin music externally. Their music becomes deterritorialized, allowing it to flow more easily over cultural boundaries.

TRÍO AND THE ORIGINS OF MEXICAN POP MUSIC

Mexican pop music is often dismissed as derivative or artificial. Yet distinctly Mexican pop traditions persist. I do not simply mean popular music. Instead, I am referring to a specific musical style that for several decades has been referred to as *pop* in Mexico. Some of the best-selling Mexican pop acts, such as Lucero, Mijares, Ana Gabriel, and Fey, are not associated with any single pop genre or subcategory (grupera, cumbia, ranchera, bolero, salsa, etc.). The music played by these musicians is generally covered by the term *pop*, music that is defined partly by its lack of clear fit into those other style categories, partly by high sales. To complete the tautology, pop is what is popular.

Unfortunately, Mexican pop is generally dismissed as a derivative of U.S. Top Forty or the diminution of more artful Mexican forms. However, much remains to be done in terms of examining Mexican pop music as a cultural form in its own right. No style of music that is wholly mimetic or bastardized could possibly attain the great national and even global appeal of Mexican pop music, which contains intrinsically Mexican elements. In order to understand that, one must look at the ways in which Mexican pop not only borrows from foreign sources but continues past musical traditions as well.

The bolero was perhaps the most significant influence in the development of contemporary pop. The trío form of the bolero, in particular, had a significant influence on its early development, and vestiges of the bolero remain in evidence today. The bolero continued to evolve throughout the twentieth century. By mid-century trío troubadours had largely replaced the cabaret-style, piano-based bolero acts described in Chapter 10, at least in the record stores and on radio. The new tríos featured subtle guitar accompaniment rather than piano, violin, and orchestra. In many ways, trío marked a return to the string-based Yucatecan tradition from which Mexican bolero first sprang. Featuring classical guitar arpeggios and simple vocal harmonies, the trío conjuntos modernized the bolero while resurrecting deep-rooted guitar traditions.

The trío tradition was born with Los Panchos, a Mexican group that got its start in the United States. After finding fame in the United States, Los Panchos brought their melodic string-based boleros to radio station

Trío Los Tres Ases. Photo by Carlos Franco.

XEW in 1948, setting off a trend that competed with the ranchera and early rock for popularity throughout the 1950s. Such tríos (often made up of more than three musicians) carried the bolero into the second half of the century. The trío form continues to have strong appeal throughout Mexico.

Contemporary Mexican pop continues certain trío tendencies. Foremost among these is the emphasis on romantic balladry. Granted, the romantic pop ballad is common throughout the world. In Mexican pop, however, it is the absolute standard. As is true of postrevolutionary bolero, trío, and ranchera alike, contemporary Mexican pop emphasizes romantic love, loss, and longing to a much greater degree than in U.S. and European pop music. Mexican pop performances, also following tradition, tend to be more emotive, expressive, and extreme in their emotional range. In the U.S. pop world, there is somewhat of an ascetic onus, a need to be "cool." Not so in Mexican pop. Pop artists in Mexico tend to be unabashedly expressive and emotional.

VIRGIN SACRIFICE

Ultimately, the search for cultural origins and precedents fails, as do all attempts to extend national patrimony to specific cultural forms. Culture is fluid. Ideas, musical and otherwise, have been exchanged across social boundaries for millennia. Although the speed and intensity of cultural flow has increased (Appadurai 1996:27–85), it is not a new phenomenon.

Attempts by modern states and their patriots to thwart foreign influence have almost always been confounded by the unwillingness of cultural flows simply to remain at the border or, conversely, to remain at home.

Nor can culture simply be managed from above. Anne Rubenstein presents a textbook or perhaps "comic book" case of how Mexican cultural conservatives have largely failed in their attempts to censor popular discourse (1998; see also Hinds and Tatum 1992). In her provocative book *Bad Language, Naked Ladies, and Other Threats to the Nation: A Political History of Comic Books in Mexico,* Rubenstein shows how censorship has been used as a political tool against local as well as foreign media in Mexico (1998:148). While such governmental tactics may momentarily blunt the penetration of foreign cultural flows, ultimately the censors must bow to market pressure.

One of the problems for gatekeepers is determining where the foreign ends and national begins. A musical example demonstrates this difficulty. Consider the case of Mexico's major national icon, La Virgen de Guadalupe. The Virgin remains a vital icon in modern pop and rock music, as she has been in Mexican music since the Revolution of Independence. For example, in 1997 Mexico City rock group El Tri dedicated an entire song, album, and concert tour to La Virgen. The album *Cuando tú no estás* leads off with the song "Virgen morena," and her image appears on the album cover, emblazoned on lead singer Alex Lora's T-shirt. Countless other pop and rock bands have used La Virgen as a symbol of their patriotism and religious reverence (only a few iconoclasts have used her for satirical purposes). The Mexican pop diva who fails to reference La Virgen is a rarity indeed.

The Virgin goes by several names, indicating her extreme importance to Mexico. *La Morenita* (the Dear Little Brown Woman) is a favorite. Relatively tall, white performers metaphorically genuflect at the altar of La Morenita, perhaps as a means of legitimating themselves to the wider Mexican audience. The distance between these light-skinned urban elites and the larger mestizo population is perhaps reduced through their ritual reverence for La Morenita, Mother of Mexico.

When performed in the context of pop music, is this cult of the Virgin evidence of resistance or hegemony? Are these conspicuous references to the Virgin signs of cultural conservatism or cultural appropriation? A look at one dimension of the question — race — shows how complex and contradictory the rhetorical use of La Virgen is in contemporary pop. Despite eighty years of official recognition of mestizaje, *la raza cósmica,* the cult of whiteness continues unabated in Mexico. This is obvious from city billboards emblazoned with blonde women (the latest being gigantic images of Britney Spears drinking Pepsi) and pale television news anchors to the constant and not-so-subtle associations made between *belleza* (beauty) and whiteness throughout Mexican society. The latter is sometimes signified through references to blonde hair (*rubia*), but more direct, positive references to white skin are not at all uncommon.

This cult of whiteness goes back to the Conquest, of course, and the caste system instituted soon thereafter. However, the postcolonial literature continues to indicate an association between whiteness and beauty. Marieta Albini, a nineteenth-century opera sensation, was considered remarkably beautiful; her skin was described as "white like milk" (Madame Calderón de la Barca in Carmona 1984:26). Henriette Sontag, the countess of Rossi, was admired not only for her singing voice but also for her "marble" skin (Carmona 1984:62). Similarly, the majority of contemporary Mexican pop icons and telenovela stars are conspicuously white in comparison to their audiences.

There is an incredible disjuncture between mass-mediated Mexico and the face-to-face version(s). Mexican television actors and pop stars are generally drawn from the relatively small, predominantly white upper class; and nepotism is rampant, as it is in politics and other business sectors. Cultural, political, and economic privilege is largely inherited according to class. As in the United States, there is much greater class inertia than interclass mobility. However, in Mexico the inheritance of class privilege is more obvious, more directly acknowledged, and less ideologically obfuscated at the cultural level. One's social rank is more clearly marked by clothing and behavior, and the rules of engagement are more overt. In such a social milieu, ritual references to La Morenita take on an interesting ideological role.

La Morenita has played an ideological role for centuries. For example, hymns to the Virgin were used by *los americanos* (the Spanish word for the criollos of New Spain) to challenge *los gachupines* (the derogatory nickname given the Spanish in return). The Virgin was an icon of resistance for los americanos. It was their primary means of identification with the mestizo and indigenous masses of Mexico. This allowed the criollos to challenge the power of the Spanish while increasing their own. Today the Virgin continues to work for both purposes. As a media icon, the Virgin can be seen as a marker of nationality and recognition of Mexico as a mestizo nation. Yet, at the same time, this is a commodified image, held up by white elites as a means of instant legitimation.

No better example can be found than the telenovela *El alma no tiene color* (The Soul Has No Color), starring pop singer and actress Laura Flores. Flores plays the protagonist, a blonde, blue-eyed beauty persecuted for giving birth to a black child. Unbeknownst to the blonde protagonist, her real mother, and thus the grandmother of the black child, is an Afrocaribbean caretaker, played by salsa great Celia Cruz. The persecuted blonde mother often prays to an image of La Morenita, a metaphor linking her persecution with that of the Madre de Dios and not too subtly associating it with the plight of the nation's indigenous and downtrodden.

La Morenita is a recurrent media reference, particularly in telenovelas featuring white female protagonists—which is to say, the majority of them. Many such protagonists are also pop singers in both telenovelas and "real life." In addition to Flores, the list of telenovela pop stars includes Thalia, Lucero, Patricia Navidad, and many more. The Virgin serves as a ritual interlocutor between these white media goddesses and their mostly mestizo audiences.

"FUCK THE USA"

Contemporary Mexico: 1968–2002

Although many of my references lump pop and rock, they are clearly two different things. In fact, pop and rock are even more distinct in Mexico than in the United States. As mentioned earlier, Mexican pop is extremely romantic and largely dominated by women performers. Pop has been the darling of the Mexican media monopoly, Televisa. Conversely, the testosterone-driven world of Mexican rock is extremely political and has been largely locked out of local media. Although there are certainly liminal pop-rock performers—Alejandra Guzmán, Gloria Trevi, and Paulina Rubio come to mind—the two styles are in most ways polar opposites. This section explains the historical development of rock as well as current political and cultural implications.

Rock in Mexico began as a borrowed style (Stigberg 1985). Mexican rockers tended to imitate the music of gringo and British rock stars. As such, there was largely a one-way flow of pop music into Mexico during the 1950s and 1960s. "Elvis Presley overshadowed Agustín Lara" in the 1950s, Victor Roura notes (1985:17). The Mexican rock groups of the 1950s and 1960s mainly covered hits by U.S. and British groups, in what was viewed as the authentic language of rock: English. Even groups that would later pioneer *rock en español* started this way, including the Dug Dugs and Three Souls in My Mind (who later became El Tri).

Rock made the transformation from an imitative foreign import to a full-fledged part of Mexican musical culture in the late 1960s and early 1970s, propelled by its connection with student political movements. Violent overreactions on the part of Mexican authorities both focused and deepened the development of rock in the capital. The student movement was violently attacked and driven underground after the massacre at Tlatelolco in 1968 (the same site where Mexica warriors put up their final resistance to Cortés). Meanwhile, the Mexican rock movement was further marginalized by official state censorship and tacit media collusion.

A major turning point for Mexican rock took place at the Avándaro Festival, a Woodstock-like concert that drew 200,000 fans in September 1971. Avándaro marked the apex of the early rock movement or *la onda chicana*. Backlash from both the Left (who viewed rock as an artifact of imperialism) and the Right (who viewed it as immoral) split rock apart after Avándaro, leaving a smaller core of fans to take it into the uncertain 1970s. An excellent analysis of Avándaro, and Mexican rock as a whole, is provided by Eric Zolov in *Refried Elvis: The Rise of the Mexican Counterculture* (1999).

As was true in the Golden Age of the bolero, the early rock movement was largely led by youth. However, state repression, censorship, and corporate appropriation conspired to greatly limit rock's influence in those early years (Durán and Barrios 1995). Police repeatedly attacked rock concerts and festivals in the early 1970s (Roura 1985:61–75). Meanwhile, a media smear campaign painted all rockers as drugged-out degenerates. As a result of the repression, rock became a far more rebellious act in Mexico than it ever was in the United States.

Although state repression greatly limited the spread of rock, it also increased its subcultural appeal and political content. Mexican rock became the music of political rebellion. Alex Lora, lead singer of El Tri and the "father of Mexican rock," argues that "true rocanrol is 100% a rebel music" (Lora in Durán and Barrios 1995:9). El Tri has led the way with songs about governmental corruption and U.S. imperialism, not to mention popular urban anthems like the song "Chilango" and "Pobre soñador." Other bands forged in the 1970s, like Botellita de Jérez, prefer to create less political lyrics but are engaged in other creative political work, including caricature and political theater (Durán and Barrios 1995:13).

In the 1970s rock mainly stayed underground, in *hoyos fonquis* (funky pits). However, by the 1980s rock was exploding in popularity. State-supported media, including the massive Televisa corporation, maintained a de facto blackout on subversive rock; but this only heightened its subcultural appeal, particularly among Mexico City youth. The word *chilango* almost automatically conjures up rock and roll associations.

As in the United States, Mexico City youths project rock identities in order to demonstrate allegiance to a world of imagined compatriots somewhere "out there" in the world. Rock is the language of globalization. British punks, Japanese rockers, and Chilango rocanrolleros share a sense of collective alienation that is both a reaction against global capitalism and evidence of its hegemonic success.

Making fun of those who view rock as a purely foreign imposition, Thelma Durán and Fernando Barrios joke that rock, for the "Anglosaxon Barbarians," was itself the product of a clash between progressive youth and cultural conservatives (1995:73). As Durán and Barrios indicate, rock is no more or less natural in the United States than in Mexico and stems from the same basic impulses. Furthermore, Mexican music has had a direct influence on many of the U.S. forms that originally gave rise to rock (Lewis 1991). Throughout its development, rock has been a transcultural phenomenon rather than the exclusive domain of one nation.

In the 1980s Mexican rock began to take on more local themes. Rocker Brenda Martín talks about how Mexican music "says a lot about the problems of the city, and about us, the youth" (in Gaitán Cruz 1988:39). Betsy Pacanins adds that "this music demands energy, rebellion, liberty, and sincerity" (in Gaitán Cruz 1988:39). Café Tacuba is the consummate Chilango band, as represented in its theme, "Chilanga banda," a song so thick with local slang that most Spanish speakers unfamiliar with Mexico City cannot understand it. Café Tacuba sings about the subway, streets, cars, markets, bars, and other urban scenes, presenting the city with critical yet whimsical insight. Much of Mexico City rock is similarly part of a "reflective subculture" existing "outside the main culture, while illuminating central features of it" (Levine and Stumpf 1983:433).

The transition to local themes made Mexican rock more appealing both in Mexico City and internationally. Experimentation with Mexican elements created interesting new hybrid sounds. The music resonated better with local sensibilities while creating something distinctively new for foreign consumption. Having escaped its derivative stage, Mexican rock became an export item throughout Latin America, the United States, and Europe in the 1980s.

This surge in popularity has caused concern that other styles of music will be replaced. Mexican rock musician Jaime López disagrees, arguing that "the best way to preserve a tradition is to contradict it" (in Durán and Barrios 1995:36). As López indicates, the preservationists' panic over rock is probably misplaced. As with similar fears concerning the late colonial waltz, nineteenth-century opera, and twentieth-century bolero, rock does not so much replace previous forms of music as supplement and extend them into the present. Musicians like López are creatively redefining and reinvigorating Mexican popular music by experimenting in the liminal space where Mexico meets the outside world.

In the words of Mexican rockers Santa Sabina, "rock makes us recognize ourselves" (in Durán and Barrios 1995:38).

Pato, the lead guitarist of Maldita Vecindad (Bad Neighborhood), makes the point in cogent fashion (Durán and Barrios 1995:55):

The work of Maldita Vecindad is not that of rescuing Mexican culture, because the culture has not died, nor has it been lost; instead we are retaking it. However, to use that term is very rhetorical, because you cannot retake that which is part of the life inside you. All of the members of Maldita come from the *barrios populares* [poor and working class neighborhoods] and all of our lives have been an involuntary mixture of many cultures; we are a hybrid and a reflection of our nation.

Rock continues the musical tradition of Mexico, if not Latin America as a whole. Coriún Aharonián explains that "there is music of the conquered in Latin America and music of the conquerors, of conquerors conquered and the conquered who conquer . . . there is a permanent invading presence of the music of the metropole" and, as he concludes, an ongoing struggle to remake it (1994:203–204). Ultimately, rock music is not something alien to Mexican culture but an integral part of it. This paradox is particularly profound in the case of Mexico City, which is central to cultural production in Mexico yet peripheral to the global system. Mexico City is both producer and product, conquered and conqueror.

The Chilango and Chilanga thrive in that liminal space, and their musical rituals continue to demonstrate a heightened sense of both marginality and centrality. Performance artist Guillermo Gómez-Peña, a self-defined "Chico-lango" (half Chicano and half Chilango), describes the "Chilango" as "a hegemonic Mexico City hipster who happens to believe that Mexico City is the center of the continent — even if it is true" (1996:241). Critical performers like Gómez-Peña and those in the Mexican rock movement present a serious challenge to simplistic models of cultural imperialism. They show that Mexican audiences are not simply passive consumers and victims of foreign imposition. Mexico City's musical culture thrives through the constant appropriation and incorporation of new musical forms.

Rock is both a modern and increasingly postmodern phenomenon, combining such seemingly disparate elements as Zapatista rhetoric, precortesian symbols, and punk style with political critique of NAFTA and capitalist globalization. Perhaps the best example is Tijuana No's song and video "Transgresores de la ley." The song lauds the struggle of the EZLN, while the video places the struggle in the context of five hundred years of resistance. Similarly, Tijuana No's "La migra" protests the abusive behavior of border police. Not wanting to be misunderstood, they end the song in English, with the exclamation: "Fuck the USA!" A Mexican culebra compilation ends with that same song and epithet. Mexican rockers are perhaps the most openly anti-imperialistic musical community in Mexico.

EL TRI AND CAFÉ TACUBA

It is obligatory to mention at least two groups when discussing contemporary Mexican rock: El Tri and Café Tacuba. Both have large and fiercely loyal followings. I have witnessed both in concert and can think of no other performances that matched these in terms of audience enthusiasm.

I saw El Tri in concert at the Mexico City Hard Rock Café, a large concert facility separated from the restaurant. The concert was remarkable in many ways, not the least of which was the wide-ranging ages of the audience members. Although a lot of "old" fans were present, a great number of teenaged and twenty-something rockers were there as well. After thirty-four years and thirty-three albums, El Tri continues to be popular with a youthful, core rock audience.

Songwriter, lead singer, and guitarist Alex Lora is a musical legend in Mexico. El Tri and Lora in particular are famous for their leftist politics. Whole albums and many additional songs have been dedicated to various political causes and strident critiques of the PRI. In a song recorded for the *Juntos por Chiapas* compilation, "Epidemia," Lora repeatedly refers to "the fucked ones who have left the country in ruins" equating the PRI with "rats" and "traitors."

Lora is famous for his vulgar language. In a country that has invented several unique curses—the most famous being variations of the verb *chingar* (fuck)—Lora is considered a particularly articulate curser. Mexican rock brings colloquial speech into the public ritual space, a direct affront to bourgeois cultural norms.

El Tri is also a fiercely nationalist band. In addition to engaging in the Virgin discourse discussed earlier, the members of El Tri literally drape themselves in the Mexican flag, seeing themselves as heirs of an unfinished Revolution. "What use was the Revolution of Hidalgo and Zapata?" they ask rhetorically in "Epidemia," implying that the Revolution has not yet achieved its goals. At the Hard Rock Café concert, Lora shouted, "Let's have some applause for those Chavos who brought the Mexican flag." He also extolled the virtues of Che Guevara during the concert, demonstrating his allegiance to the internationalist Left. El Tri, like many Mexican rock bands, has been a stalwart supporter of the Zapatistas.

Lora and most of the rock subculture of Mexico City detest pop music. At the concert in question, Lora referred to Ricky Martin as a *puto*, which officially means "a man who practices sodomy" (*Diccionario Porrúa*) but in sociolinguistic practice is often applied to male prostitutes, effeminate men, and those who "suck up" or sell themselves for personal gain. Lora slammed both Guzmáns as well, 1960s pop-rocker Enrique and 1980s pop-rock princess Alejandra. The intensity of Lora's ire is not simply a matter of taste or even politics but also a deeply personal animosity born out of his exclusion from corporate media in Mexico. Media monopoly Televisa has consistently censored meaningful rock acts, no matter how popular, and instead favored apolitical pop acts like the Guzmáns. As Televisa gives way to competing sources, Lora remains embittered by decades of exclusion. After singing "Slave to Rock and Roll," a tribute to rock purity, he went into "Chicos de Televisa," a satirical critique. Lora stated that he would like to "celebrate the retirement of Raúl Velásquez," a Televisa MC who consistently barred political rockers from his weekly musical variety show.

Televisa generally did the ideological bidding of the PRI throughout the twentieth century. The collusion between the PRI and Televisa went to the level of an interlocking directorate that refused to allow dissenting groups meaningful access to the airwaves. Although meaningful critique is still rare on broadcast television, just as it is rare in the United States, there have been significant openings lately. The Televisa monopoly has been severely challenged by the rise of competing networks and the political success of the PAN and PRD. Even El Tri has found its way onto the local airwaves recently.

After completing their critique of Televisa pop, El Tri played "Fácil," a song dedicated to the disabled. Showing their approval, fans held cigarette lighters aloft, a time-honored rock ritual. Later inflated condoms were bounced around the crowd, a more recent addition to the ritual.

El Tri played several of the songs that made the group famous. Most of these are connected to the Federal District and have become "folk" anthems in the city. They deal with local news events, themes, and places. "Metro Balderas" (about a subway station) was one such tune played in the Hard Rock concert. Lora presaged the song with a joke about the "passing air" of the subway, a double-entendre concerning the foul smells of the subway and the brisk breeze pushed ahead by arriving trains. The subway is a major feature of social life in the city. Subway references have found their way into many local rock songs. Another is Café Tacuba's "El metro," a song about a lovestruck man who rides for "three or four months" in the same metro car, eating nothing but candy purchased from passing vendors.

Roura captures the spirit of El Tri's music: "Every song is a testimony, a contemporary corrido" (1985:52). Like the corrido, Chilango rock is a testament to urban lives and communal experiences. Nearly everyone rides the same subway, reads the same newspapers, and experiences the same foul air. Such songs validate and elevate the pedestrian aspects of urban existence.

The Hard Rock Café concert was special because it was the first following El Tri's nomination for a Grammy. A great deal of attention was given to the nomination. Mexican musicians have long criticized their exclusion from the Grammys or, as Lora refers to them, the "Gremlins." He acknowledged the honor of the nomination at the concert, stating that he was pleased to see "increasingly greater space, public recognition, here and internationally" for Mexican rock. He also saw the nomination as vindication. "For those intellectuals who say rock en español does not exist," he added, "you are a bunch of putos."

Lora saved several classic El Tri anthems for last, including "Chilango," "Siempre" (a Chilango love song), and "Piedras rodantes" (Rolling Stones). A night of rock and roll without the Stones, shouted Lora, is "like a garden without flowers." Of course, an encore followed the main set. Before leaving the stage for the final time, Lora did the Mick Jagger jump, shouting, "¡Viva México!"—to which the audience responded, "¡Que viva!"

Many critics fear that globalization will produce "at best . . . a predominately one-way flow of cultural expressions and an inaccurate, narrowed vision of the world" (Riggio 1986:19). I share that concern and would certainly do away with global corporate control if given a vote on the matter. However, groups like El Tri indicate that it may sometimes be repression itself that gives rise to the most interesting art. As both "fantasy" and the "attempt to imagine alternatives" (Roura 1985:7), rock thrives on repression.

There are also fears that global monopolization will lead to less cultural diversity (Riggio 1986:29). While monopoly can narrow the bandwidth for creativity and distribution, as Televisa demonstrates, new technologies and audience differentiation have at the same time led to greater musical diversity. In fact, profit maximization requires creativity and genre-splitting into new niches. This provides a "market niche" for critical acts. Multinational giant BMG, for example, has made a point of producing local acts through its Culebra label, many of which are decidedly critical of globalization, neoliberalism, and mainstream politics. Artful Mexican groups like La Lupita and Maldita Vecindad have prospered, despite (or perhaps due to?) their connections with global distributors.

Of course, as Roura first stated in 1973, corporate popular culture is an "industry of diversion that knows too well how to exploit the alienation and stupidity of the masses" (1985:58). Although I disagree with the contention that people are stupid, it is clear that the marketing apparatus of rock does a masterful job of exploiting feelings of alienation. Yet Mexican rock has maintained a politics of dissent, the direct sort of dissent that is hard to bend to polysemic interpretation, mass marketing, and commodification. Groups like El Tri have helped fuel creative dissent for over three decades.

RITUALS OF CHAOS

As noted earlier, Carlos Monsiváis is one of the most insightful analysts and critics of popular culture in Mexico. His book *Los rituales del caos* (Rituals of Chaos, 1995) provides a useful framework for understanding popular music in the modern metropole. Rock is nothing if not carnivalesque, a place where the order and discipline of the city is reproduced, subverted, celebrated, and challenged all at the same time.

I witnessed several rock rituals that illustrate the Monsiváis thesis. For example, during the mid-1990s I watched the punk group Technopal tossing political challenges in the direction of the National Palace. The fans would join in, combining concert celebration and protest in one ritual act. In the early twenty-first century, groups of fans gather in the zócalo to witness a one-man rock act, The Rollos and Rock and Roll (The Rolls and Rock and Roll). The act plays in the gap between the Metropolitan Cathedral and the National Palace. The crowd consists of an odd mix of scuffed-up young rockers, school kids in uniforms, and other onlookers. School kids untuck their shirts and blouses in order to dance on the edge of the performance space. For them, rock is release. The rock ritual is a space where mundane disciplines can be forgotten for the moment.

No other musical performance, however, achieves the emotional intensity of a Café Tacuba concert. This small band of brothers packs every venue, often choosing relatively small clubs like Rockotitlán over the big auditoriums it can easily fill. Their concerts are performances of controlled chaos. Unlike the mosh-pit violence of U.S. punk concerts, the packed-in audiences at Mexican rock clubs jam together and flow to-

The Rollos and Rock and Roll, playing in the zócalo. Photo by author.

Contemporary Mexico: 1968–2002

gether more than slam into each other. I have witnessed several injuries and serious anger at concerts in the United States but have never seen that sort of thing develop at a Mexican rock concert.

The crowd erupts when Café Tacuba breaks into "La ingrata" (The Ungrateful One). Sweat pours, and many fans seem to reach an almost transcendental state. Once again the inhibitive element of "cool" is largely missing. Mexican rock is a distinct urban subculture held together by common ideals. Despite its maturation, Mexican rock is still centered around rebellion and iconoclasm. Conversely, rock has diffused in the United States, taking on everything from the leftist rap of Rage against the Machine to the racist punk of the Oi movement. Rock in the United States now consists of a diversified set of loosely related subgenres rather than a single discernible cultural movement. Mexican rock, however, has retained its ritual intensity and political focus.

Among the rituals of chaos that Monsiváis describes is a concert by Gloria Trevi. Born in 1970, Trevi is a pop rocker from Monterrey, Mexico. She claims to have been inspired by Janis Joplin, Cindi Lauper, and other women rockers when growing up. Mislabeled the "Mexican Madonna" in U.S. newspapers and magazines, Trevi has been much more challenging and controversial than the "U.S. Trevi" could ever hope to be. She preaches the merits of premarital sex, masturbation, and sexual freedom for teens in both her songs and interviews. Her song "Virgen de las vírgenes," for example, cites a friend who has "done it with something like ten," yet remains "the most virgin of the virgins."

Monsiváis refers to the "scandal" of Gloria Trevi in *Los rituales del caos* (1995:166–167). By that he means the scandal provoked by Trevi's music and sexually laden performances, which include taking the pants off men who leap onto the stage with her. Interestingly enough, the Monsiváis book accidentally presaged a much greater Trevi scandal that came to light many years after its publication. Several young women charged Trevi, her ex-manager, Sergio Andrade, and backup singer María Raquenel Portillo with luring them into sexual slavery through promises of stardom. Trevi sought refuge from these charges in Brazil. At the behest of the Mexican courts, however, the Brazilian government and courts in 2001 indicated that they would extradite Trevi to Mexico. To complicate matters, Trevi became pregnant in the Brazilian prison (Brazilians cannot be extradited, a right usually extended to their mothers as well). Her cellmate claims that it was Trevi's intent all along and that her pregnancy was a ploy to skirt extradition. In November 2002 Trevi suddenly decided to stop fighting the extradition order. She and her child, Angel Gabriel, were flown to Chihuahua, where the pop diva would stand trial for charges of rape, kidnapping, and corruption of minors. As of January 1, 2003, no verdict had yet been reached. Like a telenovela, the Trevi saga continues.

The Mexican government and church organizations had long accused Trevi of moral transgression. Following the disclosures of sex crimes, their attempts at censorship seemed justified. The real target of the censors was her public message, however, not these alleged hidden acts (Rubenstein 1998:1–3). Trevi's pretense of sexual liberation for girls and political ambitions (she wanted to become president) have probably both been destroyed by the scandal. Her hyped career and sudden fall from grace might have damaged Mexican rock, and particularly the image of women in rock, if she had not always been seen as an outlier. Like the Sex Pistols, her performance was more a rock and roll "swindle" than an act that fans and critics took seriously. Yet, at the same time, nothing is more deadly serious than pop frivolity. Trevi's catchy pop-rock tunes hit the top of the charts, and her revealing calendar was one of the top-selling publications in Mexico. Trevi drew tens of thousands to her concerts. All of that may ultimately have had little to do with the creative work of a teenaged girl, however; it may have involved the effective puppetry of Sergio Andrade, her manager.

There is an element of puppetry in all popular music. Pop and rock in particular imbue liminal adolescents with a feeling of individual efficacy. Rock is a rite of passage. With songs of teenaged angst and rebellion like "Hoy me iré de casa" (Today I'm Leaving Home), Trevi gave teenaged Mexican girls a sense of individual empowerment. She also presented an ideal image for young men. What would any young man want more than a teenaged girl who believes liberation can be found primarily, perhaps exclusively, through sex? Trevi is a contemporary Aventurera.

Trevi's public decline into sexual decadence and crime, like Aventurera's, was watched by millions. They delighted in her transgression, only to turn on her in the end when she went too far. Also like Aventurera, Trevi appears to have been both the abuser and abused. She is victim and traitor, Virgin and whore, Malinche and Guadalupe. Assumedly about liberation, Trevi's performances were mostly about ensconced misogyny. She was fulfilling a cultural tradition, rather than rebelling against it.

Fortunately, Trevi's pop-rock is far from the only example for women in Mexican popular music. As outlined in Chapter 11, women represent a growing proportion of new composers and performers. In addition to artists like Eli Guerra and Julieta Venegas, there are a number of other female rock acts challenging the male-dominated rock world, such as the all-woman band Aurora y la Academia and mix-gendered groups like Santa Sabina and El Tri. Several of these artists have taken on the question of gender and sexuality directly. They have done so in a more authentically subversive vein, however, in ways that could potentially increase women's interests rather than further identify and stigmatize them as sexual objects. One heroine in that struggle is Guerra, a rock artist who has purposely produced her work through independent labels in order to maintain artistic integrity. She has done so partly to combat corporate handlers who wanted to promote her primarily as a sexual object.

A NEW SONG

Unlike Mexican rock, members of the nueva canción movement have tended to eschew "political rhetoric in their lyrics" for sake of "new ideas and values" (Behague 1986:46). Rather than being propaganda, nueva canción represents "a search for political, economic, and cultural identity in order to counteract widespread cultural stereotyping, economic domination by transnational corporations, and political manipulation by North American policy" (Tumas-Serna 1992:139). Nueva canción artists, led by a Cuban vanguard, have continued Simón Bolívar's quest to forge a pan–Latin American identity through cultural exchange. Nueva canción has failed to gain a major audience in Mexico. Nevertheless, it continues to hold the attention of a relatively small yet extremely devout audience.

Nueva canción has had an interesting parallel life in the United States. An alternative musical economy has been constructed, driven by folk romanticism and fascination with Latin American politics. Groups like Los Folkloristas receive significant support from U.S. liberals, leftist intellectuals, and others intent on "preserving a culture" against the ravages of the popular (Heath 1987). The foreign supporters of this music see themselves in solidarity with folk who are bravely combating the effects of U.S. media imperialism and other forms of oppression.

Meanwhile, back in Mexico, most nueva canción and *música protesta* performers in Mexico have ceased working directly under those titles, for fear of being stereotyped. The box was too narrow to allow artistic, and perhaps even political, creativity. Nevertheless, several musicians primarily associated with nueva canción have maintained significant followings. Among them is Oscar Chávez, who has recorded over 100 songs, ranging from huapangos to boleros. One of his most interesting efforts is *Parodias neo-liberales* (volume 1, 1997). The album includes satiric ballads as well as norteña, alabado, and bolero songs, all aimed at the neoliberal excesses of Carlos Salinas and his PRI allies. "Se vende mi país" (They Are Selling My Country) is a protest against what Chávez sees as the selling out of his country's natural resources, environment, culture, and history to foreigners. "I won't sell, no, because I love it," he sings. "I won't sell, no, better that I die."

Another artist associated with Mexican nueva canción is Tania Libertad. Peruvian by birth, but Mexican by popular adoption, Libertad has built a remarkable career mixing the popular and political, commercial and folkloric. An eclectic, she is particularly expert at integrating Afro-Peruvian sounds and rhythms into her Mexican repertoire. Performing in a less ironic mode than her fellow art singer, Eugenia León, Libertad has built a successful career with a powerful, clear voice, artistic creativity, and political drive. At one concert I attended, she encouraged people to sign a petition for "peace in Chiapas." Performing at the site of the National Palace, Libertad demonstrated the political fearlessness for which she is famous.

Many Mexican musicians are driven by the belief that art can inspire resistance. While overtly political folk, pop, and rock concerts have become rare in the United States, popular artists in Mexico—especially those performing rock, rap, nueva canción, and música protesta—consider political critique integral to the artistic process. However, Mexican concerts, like those the world over, are not just about rebellion; they are also about consumption, fashion, and escape. Musical rites cannot simply be reduced to exercises of power, on the one hand, or acts of resistance, on the other. They are full of contradictions, paradoxes, and conundrums. That is what makes popular ritual so interesting, both as an object of study and as subjective experience. No matter how well scripted the rite, there is always room for improvisation, uncertainty, danger, and negotiation. Performers and audiences alike are sparked by the knowledge that each concert, each ritual event, will provide not only the conservative catharsis of liturgy but also the potential to invent something new, to feel something different, to transcend the present.

> *We can close our eyes to poverty and marginalization; we can live with a little more crime, less clean drinking water, fewer forests, air that is a little more polluted. We can pretend that we do not see corruption, ignorance, illiteracy, and unemployment. If we did so, we would be betraying those who have fought for change.*
> —VICENTE FOX, INAUGURAL ADDRESS

17 Conclusion

Each set of chapters in this book has focused on the music of a specific era. However, the musical ritual landscape of Mexico City is not so neatly segregated. Every sound and performance is an intertextual mix of past and present.

Take the voladores of Papantla, a ritual performed daily for crowds outside the National Museum of Anthropology (Chapter 3). The voladores practice an ancient Mesoamerican ritual. The original ritual was designed as a sign of reverence for the Mesoamerican gods and the natural world, but new meanings have been added over the centuries. For example, the sign of the cross is performed at the beginning of each ceremony to bless the rite and protect the flyers. Clearly, colonial religion left its stamp on the ritual, even though rites like those of the voladores were suppressed during Spanish rule.

The voladores' ritual was reborn as a symbol of national pride after the Revolution for Independence. It took on yet another set of meanings after the Revolution of 1910, when Mexico began to discover the international marketing appeal of its cultural traditions. Today the voladores shout, "Five minutes to the next show!" when whipping up interest among milling crowds outside the museum. They also refer to their sacred performance as a "spectacle." The ritual has become a show for sale to tourists. The voladores earn their living by selling pipe-and-drum sets and other souvenirs to spectators. Like all contemporary performances, the rite of the voladores is now commodified.

In sum, the ritual of the voladores is Mesoamerican, colonial, national, and capitalist. It is all of these and more. Layers of meaning have accreted, new laid over old. What we experience today as the voladores is very different from what the people of Papantla knew, yet the "original" rite is still there. It has changed along with its performance context, yet it remains a fascinating, meaning-laden ritual for performers and spectators alike.

Even some of the newest music can contain ancient intertextual influence. Take the opening refrain to Aurora y la Academia's 1997 rock album *Horas*:

Guadalajara en un llano	Guadalajara on a plain
México en una laguna	Mexico in a lagoon
me he de comer esa tuna	I have to eat this prickly pear
aunque me espina la mano.	Even though I might get pricked.

These lines are lifted from a Mexican folksong, "Guadalajara en un llano," which incorporates both colonial and precortesian terms. Among the Mesoamerican words used in the folksong is *aguatarse* (to prick oneself), a hispanicized version of a Nahuatl verb. The final line was originally sung as "aunque me *aguate* la mano" (Soler Arechalde 1991:233). The folksong also makes reference to a Mesoamerican delicacy, the *tuna* (prickly pear).

The song is a metaphoric reference to man's sexual "conquest" of woman, urging him to persevere "even though [he] might get pricked" (Soler Arechalde 1991:234). When the song leads off an album by an all-woman rock band, however, the meaning is radically transformed. The narrative of androcentric conquest is turned into a gynocentric challenge.

Note that this new meaning can only be constructed and communicated if the old meaning retains popular currency. The listener needs to know at least two basic pieces of information for this to make sense: (1) that the original refrain is a sexual metaphor, and (2) that Aurora y la Academia are attempting to recode the old sexual metaphor ironically. To decode that information, the listener must know something about Mexican folk music and understand that rock is an ironic genre.

Oscar Chávez does similar work in "México es una letrina," a song based on the melody of "Guadalajara en un llano." He ditches the original folksong's lyrics and replaces them with PRI satire. For decades the PRI has promoted a folkloric definition of Mexican identity. It has elevated such folk forms to sacred status through ideological promotions of mexicanidad. Chávez reappropriates the public poetry, however, and turns it against power. The creative reinterpretations of Aurora y la Academia and Oscar Chávez illustrate how musical ritual is a war of definitions, a battle over whose realities will prevail in the collective space.

All songs, as cultural texts, are intertextual. Every song or ritual draws on past texts in order to make sense in the present, as in the above examples. Yet the present has its say as well. Histories lead to the present, but social dynamics and dialectics in the present also remake history. How we think about the past is largely a function of who, what, and where we are now.

Nevertheless, the chronological format of this book might imply an evolutionary framework: first this happened, then that, and so on, leading ultimately to the present. This is partly intentional, in the sense that cultural forms do accrete and evolve. Independent Mexico did follow New Spain, both in time and in form. In fact, any understanding of contemporary Mexico is incomplete without knowledge of its historical antecedents.

There are indeed patterns to ritual development, many of which correspond to wider patterns of historical change. For example, population density has greatly increased over time, as have the intensity and nature of economic production, energy use, and technological change. Social roles have multiplied, diversified, and stratified. Furthermore, local, national, and global institutions have become increasingly integrated over time, to the point that a Mexico City resident is now instantaneously connected to many of the same cultural images and sounds experienced by billions of others around the planet. Each of these social patterns is mirrored in music and musical ritual. Music has become more diversified and specialized at the same time that control over production and distribution has coalesced under the aegis of fewer, ever larger, institutions.

However, the present is not simply an evolutionary result of the past. Cultural reality comes not only from narrative (i.e., history) but also from drama (i.e., society). The interactions of people, institutions, environments, and systems in the present are creative in their own right and are never simply determined by historical inertia. The musical rituals of any era relate in some way to the dominant social contexts and structures within which they are performed in the present. Therefore, just as surely as the past informs the present, the present remakes the past. Through social drama we rewrite the historical narrative. Once the past is recoded in the present, made into a "new past" via ritual, we can never again imagine the past "as it really was." To use the "Guadalajara en un llano" example, it is fruitless to try to segregate the distinct Nahuatl, Spanish, and modern Mexican contributions to each new iteration of the song. At each stage, they have been recongealed to form a new song whose cultural sum is greater than its historical parts. In other words, ritual is both a creative and destructive process. Ritual both remakes and erases the past.

History is remade through social activity in the present. Time and text, narrative and drama, history and society, all maintain a dialectical relationship with the other. The following, and concluding, ritual vignette provides an excellent case in point. Hundreds of years of Mexican history were remade through musical ritual on December 1, 2000, a landmark day of political transition in Mexico.

700 YEARS OF MEXICAN RITUAL IN ONE DAY

On December 1, 2000, thousands gathered in the zócalo, awaiting the arrival of Vicente Fox, their new president. They were there for the Verbena, a popular celebration traditionally held as part of a daylong ritual, the Cambio de Poder (change of power).

Mexican leaders have been declaring themselves to the populace in this very same location for almost 700 years, since the founding of the great city of Tenochtitlán in A.D. 1325. From Aztec emperors and Spanish viceroys to nineteenth-century dictators and twentieth-century presidents, the star of each regime has been heralded through some form of ritual performance in the heart of Tenochtitlán/Mexico City.

Despite the antiquity of the ritual, however, the 2000 Cambio de Poder was noted more for its novelty than for adherence to tradition. After all, it was the first time since the great Revolution that a candidate from a party other than the PRI or its institutional forbears had gained the presidency.

Cognizant of his historic role, Fox faithfully completed the customary elements of the Cambio, including the oath of office before Congress, a military review, the Verbena, and a formal dinner with dignitaries to cap off the day. Each of these events included appropriate musical accompaniment, from military marching bands to mariachi ensembles. The day-long Cambio included representation of nearly 700 years of Mexican music.

However, Fox also modified the ritual significantly. The most significant breaks with tradition included eating breakfast with "street children" and attending Mass. First, he attended Mass at the Basilica de Guadalupe with his family, a taboo practice for PRI inaugurees. He then ate breakfast in the impoverished neighborhood of Tepito while Conchero dancers, street performers, and mariachis competed for the crowd's and cameras' attention.

The Mass and carnivalesque breakfast were not the only deviation from protocol. Fox also ad-libbed during the sacred Protesta, the oath or "profession" of national responsibility that each new president recites before the Mexican Congress. The new president expressed his interest in helping the "poor and marginalized." Fox's improvisation infuriated many members of Congress, who felt that he was acting like a demagogue, an ironic criticism coming from the PRI.

Fox's evening Verbena was also distinct. It was a pop-music affair, more akin to a concert than a traditional political festival. Many political commentators were put off by the pop theatrics. Ritual is serious business in Mexico, just as it is everywhere. The ritual specialist, whether priest or president, must be careful to adhere to time-honored tradition. Yet he or she must also infuse tradition with marks of distinction that will reflect favorably on the office and political sponsors. It would seem that Fox erred on the side of innovation, at least from the critics' perspective.

The presidency of Vicente Fox was announced to the nation through a succession of rituals, each targeting a different sector of the population. These sectors included Catholic parishioners and impoverished rockenrollero youth in the morning, military brass and political leaders during the mid-day Protesta, middle class PANistas at the early evening Verbena, and finally, an odd mix of foreign elites (e.g., Fidel Castro, Madeleine Albright) and corporate overlords (e.g., Bill Gates) who gathered at Chapultepec Castle to conclude the day's events.

A niche-specific ritual and musical soundtrack was provided for each target audience. The Tepito breakfast with street kids involved a carnivalesque mélange of rock, Azteca, and mariachi. The political and military classes were met with traditional march music, of course. The evening Verbena included a mix of ranchera and pop. Finally, a classical score was offered for the exclusive endgame. At times the Fox soundtrack emphasized ranchera, underscoring his image as a charro firebrand, while at other times he used pop music to demonstrate how his pulse beats to the rhythm of Mexican youth. Fox, the Coca-Cola Cowboy (he was president of Mexican operations for Coca-Cola), is the perfectly postmodern president, all things to everyone.

PRAYER AND POLITICS

The day began very early. Fox attended a special morning Mass at the Basilica de Guadalupe. It was just enough to communicate faith to his followers but not so much as to alarm the rest. Nevertheless, the Mass was viewed as a major symbolic break with the past. Generations of PRI leaders had made a point of distancing themselves from the Catholic church even if they were in secret devout Catholics. From its outset, the postrevolutionary PRI undertook a forceful campaign to secularize Mexico's political system. Only after a mid-century rapprochement between the PRI and the church could the party faithful dare admit to harboring religious sentiments. In fact, not until Fox has any postrevolutionary president dared to include a religious observance as part of inauguration day. His incorporation of religion into the rite of succession raised fears that the sleeping dragon of religion, and specifically the church, might awaken to thwart secular rule.

The Mass was an act of genuflection to PAN party faithful. The conservative PAN used religion as one tool for recruiting rank-and-file members, appealing to devout Catholics who had been alienated by the secular PRI. Yet in other ways this symbolic act merely repaired a historical breach. The religious and political order had been one and the same for the great majority of Mexican and Mesoamerican history. Every inauguration ritual performed by the Mexica and Spanish viceroys demonstrated to the Mexican people that their leader represented heaven's authority. By visiting the basilica, Fox was doing what hundreds of emperors and viceroys before him had done: bow before the temple, rise before the people. Fox "kept looking up at the Virgin," noted one observer, impressed with his reverence for the Holy Mother.

FOOD FOR THE PEOPLE

The next ritual act, a breakfast with homeless children, was designed to assuage the fears of critics who see Fox as a puppet for global capital. Critics paint the PANista president as an uncaring ogre who would sell off Mexico's resources to the highest foreign bidder, taking food from the mouths of babes. Fox appeared as anything but that, serving up tamales to street kids in Mexico City's rough Tepito district.

As Fox doled out *atole* (a boiled drink made of corn flour and sweetened water or milk) and tamales to his young friends from the streets, a carnival atmosphere prevailed. Clowns slapped noisemakers while mariachis belted out their musical laments and "Aztec" dancers circled to the beat of the huehuetl in the background.

Meanwhile, Fox and a few boys sat in the middle of the carnival eating tamales. As a further demonstration of his noblesse oblige, Fox let one of the boys at his table play with a high-tech miniature radio monitor that he was using to communicate with security. The boy, wearing a Chicago Bears jacket, marveled at the technology. The cameras focused in tightly on the symbolic exchange. Next Fox listened to a woman explaining her woes over a public address system. He matched her tear for tear.

Following the quick breakfast, Fox left the Tepito scene, harassed by a few mismanaged youth in the crowd. After his departure, the children continued eating (however, the tamales ran out and were replaced with hotdogs). Headlines the next day exclaimed: "He Ate Tamales with Street Kids" (*El Universal*, December 2, 2000, A6). The Left condemned the Tepito breakfast as an act of ritual posturing and demagoguery. Critics sarcastically tagged their new president Santa Fox, equating Fox with Santa Claus.

Despite the press criticism, Fox was more popular than ever after the inauguration. The majority of people I spoke to were favorably impressed by his actions on inauguration day. The breakfast made the greatest impact. "We have been waiting for a change," explained one man I spoke with on the zócalo. "There is a lot of poverty, so maybe this [meeting with the street children] means that there will be more respect for people's rights and the law." Fox was successful at turning anti-PRI sentiment into support for himself. Ironically, that support has allowed him to continue and accelerate many of the PRI's basic neoliberal policies. Ritual has played no small part in that political alchemy.

THE POLITICAL CLASS

Fox ducked into a house in Tepito where a new wardrobe awaited. He quickly donned a presidential suit and was off to meet with Mexico's political and military leaders. He appeared before the Congress of Deputies to take the oath of office. Many PRI deputies booed Fox vociferously, as opposition deputies had done to them for decades. Later he would in turn administer an oath of office to cabinet members at the National Auditorium. Fox required his cabinet members to swear that they would avoid corruption and dishonesty, a clear ritual stab at the PRI.

After taking the oath, Fox made an obligatory appearance before the military to the bold accompaniment of marching brass. Mexico is rather remarkable in the Latin American context for the relatively low profile of its military class. The same was true on inauguration day. The military element was greatly downplayed compared to the political, cultural, and economic components of the ritual.

After reviewing the troops, Fox was ceremoniously whisked down Avenida Cinco de Mayo in a convertible. A shower of tickertape (actually small white note cards) rained down upon the new leader. Repeating the route of conquerors past, Fox drove down what had once been the Tacuba causeway. Protesters took on the police near the Alameda Park but were beaten back at the intersection of three broad streets: Juárez, Madero, and Cárdenas. Fox continued on to the zócalo, the center of Mexico City–Tenochtitlán.

THE POP PRESIDENT

The evening of December 1, 2000, was unusually brisk. That did not stop a large crowd from gathering in the zócalo. Loudspeakers boomed ranchera versions of "La Adelita" and other folk standards to the gathered masses. Approximately three-quarters of the giant zócalo was covered with citizens awaiting word from their newly anointed leader. Just as whistles of impatience started to sound, Fox walked onto the balcony overlooking the giant square.

Still wearing the tricolor sash bestowed upon him at the congressional Protesta, Fox swore to be a president for all the people, shouting that "no one can throw a bucket of cold water on this revolution of hope!" People in the crowd mouthed his campaign slogans, turning the present-tense "¡Si se puede!" (Yes, it can be done!) into a celebration of success: "¡Si se pudo!" (Yes, it could be done!).

Next the pop star Mijares, also standing on the president's balcony above the zócalo, belted out the Mexican national anthem. Jaime Nuno's hymn was reborn as a pop anthem. Fox took off his suit coat and sash and claimed that he was about to sing and "one-up" Mijares. He did not do so, however. Instead, the presidential party withdrew from the balcony. As the announcer proclaimed, "A president among his people!" Fox and friends emerged from the massive front gates of the palace, marched down a long walkway, and came onto a stage jutting out into the assembled crowd. A mariachi fanfare accompanied the coterie on their march to the zócalo dais. Fox was flanked by two pop stars, Mijares and Eugenia León, along with a small contingent of family and citizens.

What followed was perhaps the greatest ritual gaff of the day. A young girl was paraded out to make a speech to the people. "From the mouths of babes . . ." Unfortunately, the little girl was so nervous that she could only emit shrill monosyllabic shrieks for several embarrassing minutes. The loudspeakers amplified each utterance, causing all of us gathered there to cover our ears and wince. What was at first a sense of sympathy for the girl soon turned to anger as she insisted on squeaking out more and more shrieks, assaulting the crowd's ears with her failed attempts to launch into her speech.

Fox walked out to the girl to calm her. Her embarrassment turned to anger. She angrily condemned the microphone and sound system for distorting her voice. Fox retired, his efforts appreciated by the crowd. Next an unidentified woman got up to talk to this little girl who had hijacked the Verbena. With the woman's help, the girl was able to turn her piercing screams into comprehensible words and sentences. She then gave an overly long speech, harshly condemning past leaders as "caciques" (the term *cofradías*, a reference to traditional political fraternities, was also often used during the Cambio de Poder). Fox would be different, according to the girl.

Despite the PANista composition of the crowd, many reacted fairly negatively to the girl's speech. By the time she had arrived at the obligatory "¡Que viva México!" a man in front of me was answering, "¡Viva!" in squeaky, broken falsetto, making fun of the girl's awkward screeching. The bald melodramatic ploy of having a little girl give such a speech went beyond the fairly broad parameters of ritual etiquette. The crowd seemed "turned off." The rock and roll flow of the pop ritual had been broken.

Ritual flow was partly repaired in the next act. Mijares and Eugenia León sang an anthem written expressly for the new administration by Alex Slucki and Antonio Calvo. Entitled "Nacerá" (It Will Be Born), the song describes the new day the Fox victory would bring:

Nacerá la esperanza	Hope is born.
germinará la nueva luz.	A new light germinates.
El 2 de julio fue la opción	July 2 was the chance to
transformar nuestra visión	Transform our vision
de un México distinto	Of a distinct Mexico
que hoy podemos	That today we can
vislumbrar.	Begin to see.

It was intended as an inspirational pop ballad, using all the obligatory techniques of the form. Starting with spare accompaniment, each vocalist sang his or her part in solo fashion. Then León and Mijares united in harmony for the chorus. In the final iterations of the chorus, the full force of the pop ensemble was brought to bear: drums, guitar, and synthesizer, all arranged within a Disneyesque formula.

The inclusion of Eugenia León in the event was surprising. She is best known for her critical performances as part of the Bar Hábito group. Working with Liliana Felipe and other leftist critics, León has performed masterful critiques of the political order. As discussed in Chapter 11, she and Felipe have refitted the normally apolitical forms of bolero and danzón to carry charged political messages against sexism, class domination, imperialism, and the government's role in all three. This hardly makes her a likely candidate for singing the Fox pop anthem—with a pop icon like Mijares, no less. However, León explained that she did not see it as an anthem for Fox but rather as a representation of hope for Mexico in general. No matter whose purposes the song served, it was well received. The crowd was brought back into the ritual moment and applauded vigorously at its conclusion.

Ritual damage undone, the true spectacle began. A series of historic visual images was projected on two giant water screens and the colonial buildings ringing the zócalo. The soundtrack was provided by music and sounds representing every major era of Mexican history. Originally crafted for a celebration of the city earlier in the year, it was instead offered as part of the Verbena.

The spectacle began with the sound of a conch shell trumpet played to the four cardinal directions. Next the huehuetl beat its rhythmic boom. Amplified through a wall of speakers held aloft by giant cranes, the effect was overpowering. The woofer reverberated, and jaws dropped. Montezuma-Fox was enacting ritual magic, at the same time beautiful and horrific.

Next came the rasping sound of stick on bone, whistles and flutes, teponaztlis, and the complete Calmecac conjunto. Images of Mesoamerican artifacts were projected onto the water screens: colossal Olmec heads, the parrot of Colima, and other Mesoamerican artworks, gigantic yet ephemeral as they appeared on the translucent sheet of water.

The mantra-like spell of the Mesoamerican music was broken by ringing alarms. An imposing image of the ships of Cortés appeared on the National Palace, to the east of the zócalo. A mask of Tezcatlipoca was projected on the palace as well. The message presumably is that the Mexica trickster-god, the Black Tezcatlipoca (one of his four manifestations), conjured up Cortés as another manifestation of himself—the White Tezcatlipoca or Quetzalcóatl—to come back from the East and retake his kingdom. The Conquest was simply part of Tezcatlipoca's mischief. The monstrous sound of horses then mixed with clashing steel swords, as Bernal Díaz del Castillo narrated the Mexica sacrifice of his Spanish comrades. In clever juxtaposition with Díaz del Castillo's narration concerning Mexica "noise," the sound of riotous colonial bells and an overpowering pipe organ blasted over the speaker. An image of the twelve missionaries arriving in Mexico marched along the palace toward the Metropolitan Cathedral on the north end of the zócalo. A new order was installed in Mexico.

The spectacle continued, celebrating the colonial era as a time when Mexico's cultural diversity and mestizaje were born. The narrative and images illustrated the ethnic diversity of the era, highlighting the interracial encounters that colonial officials worked so hard to thwart. In addition to traditional liturgical polyphony, sprightly villancicos played as part of the soundtrack.

Images of Sor Juana Inés de la Cruz and artifacts from the seventeenth century were then projected along the cathedral and palace. Next red gels were used to project fire on all sides of the square. The date "1692" was frozen onto the water screen. As discussed in Chapter 4, 1692 was a year of famine and popular rebellion. However, this was largely lost on the crowd. More than one person standing near me quizzed friends to discover the meaning of the date, and none that I spoke with after the show knew its significance. In that sense, this was very much a didactic ritual aimed at educating the participants as much as entertaining them.

As the referenced events and music got closer and closer to the present, the sense of popular resonance grew. The crowd came alive when Mexico's independence was announced. This was the beginning of relevant time for many of them. Wood and iron doors could be heard closing, perhaps representing Inquisition cells or maybe doors shielding the colonial conspirators, whose whispers were also audible on the soundtrack.

The Revolution succeeded. Everything went black, except for laser streams drawing the audience's attention to the flagpole at the center of the zócalo. To the sound of the national hymn, a giant flag was slowly raised. Hardly an eye was dry or mouth silent as the crowd began to chant, "¡México! ¡México!" Even cynical youth now stood in reverent awe, joining the chorus: "¡México! ¡México!" They then sang Nuno's hymn, their national anthem, with great vigor.

It is in such collective ritual acts that nations are made and remade. Although the brunt of such work is no longer mediated face-to-face, as in the case of the Fox Verbena, such mediated catharses continue to be the bedrock upon which national sovereignty is cemented. The "creation of a new nation," explains David Kertzer, "requires a massive effort at symbolic construction, of creating a sense of unity, of identification with a new, abstract entity, the nation" (1988:178).

The maintenance of nationhood requires almost as much ritual energy, particularly in a nation as fractious as Mexico. Whereas the organic institutions of nationhood in the United States (e.g., government and corporation) and their ideological concomitants (e.g., the vote) function to provide efficient hegemonic collectivity, the Mexican nation is forged somewhat more mechanically, through constant and spectacular reference to nationhood. To be draped in the flag is still somewhat embarrassing for many in the United States, viewed as an act of arrogance as much as collective identity. Conversely, in Mexico such patriotic acts continue to be viewed, at least on the surface, as collective arguments for the national interest. There is still a sense of newness to ritual performances of the Mexican national anthem, a feeling that the ritual act has not yet been fully consummated and that the promise of the nation has not yet been realized. The United States has long passed from a nation that needed to worry about foreign usurpation, whereas in Mexico there is a palpable feeling that the enemies are still at the gate. Therefore, the national anthem remains, in part, an act of collective resistance.

Charged with new emotion, the audience members were converted from ritual spectators to full participants. After the independence interlude, jets blasted water back into the sky and images from the nineteenth century danced around the zócalo. Fittingly, salón piano music played to underscore visions of modernization, such as the steam train and ship. Juxtaposed with these images of progress were photos of impoverished peasants and their children running next to a train. These were *los olvidados*, the forgotten ones of the Díaz regime. Such images presaged the next great Revolution. And so it came, signified by a photo of Zapata and Villa sitting at the Sanborns' lunch counter in Mexico City. "La Valentina" played, signifying the middle and end of the Revolution.

Next came a jumble of postrevolutionary images, including a lingering slide of bolerista Agustín Lara and renowned tenor Pedro Vargas, accompanied by Lara's classic "Mujer." Once considered a malinchista, Lara is now part of the cultural canon and a Mexican icon.

The show ended with the rumbera era, with no reference to the politically turbulent 1960s, the economic crises of the 1970s, 1980s, and 1990s, the oil boom and bust, the Salinas brothers, NAFTA, Zapatistas, Colosio, Zedillo, Fox. It is as if history ended at mid-century. The water cannons shut down, and a fireworks display exploded into the air. One missile exploded on the ground. Fortunately, no one was hurt. A final barrage was then unleashed, but not before the flow had once again been broken. Showered in ashes, the members of the largely PANista crowd looked at each other in surprise as the streetlights suddenly popped back on.

The rockenrollero ritual was not carried to its logical conclusion. There was no clear send-off, no "Fox has left the zócalo" or other end punctuation for the event. The president hugged León and others in his group and then led the group offstage. "He left without saying good-bye," yelled one man after the firework finale, feigning hurt feelings. The surrounding crowd laughed, sharing his sense of ritual discontinuity.

The milling crowd seemed uncertain what to make of the Verbena and its abrupt end. The high-tech program was awe-inspiring, yet the rest seemed a bit too disconnected from their immediate desires as Fox supporters. Many in the crowd wanted to receive collective recognition of their efforts in getting Fox elected. This was their victory, and they wanted to share in it more completely. After all, the Cambio de Poder Verbena, like the annual Independence Day celebrations on September 16, is supposed to be "the real fiesta of and for the people" (Fernández Tejedo and Nava Nava 2001:3).

Parents took their children by the hand and led them off, and the zócalo soon returned to its normal state. The awkward ending was not the only mismanaged aspect of the event. A phalanx of spotlights shone straight into the eyes of the crowd during the balcony speech and stage events, leading a heckler to yell, "Let me see!" Nevertheless, the spectacle probably achieved its intended effect. After all, it was not really intended for the live audience but rather for millions of others watching at home. The obtrusive lights were intended to demonstrate to the home audience that this was indeed a popular celebration. The crowd existed to provide verisimilitude. Whether the live crowd could actually see or not was secondary to the requirements of ritual and political mass mediation. Having served its purpose, the crowd was dismissed and the cameras turned off as Fox was whisked to the next and final stage of his ritual gauntlet.

DIALECTICS

After the Verbena was dispatched, Fox was off to the Castillo de Chapultepec for dinner and an evening of glad-handing with international dignitaries and corporate captains (who must have been pleased, knowing that one of their very own CEOs had achieved the highest office in Mexico). The corporate captains spoke of Mexico's future while dining on shrimp aspic, cream of artichoke soup, duck with truffles, and wild rice. They washed it down with French champagne and Mexican wine. How far Fox had come from the atole and tamales he started the day with in Tepito!

For each class there is an appropriate means of ritual mediation. Having connected with the popular and dispatched with the political, Fox was now directly parlaying with power. A local Communist newsletter, *Machete Arte*, lampooned the event and the president, referring to him as "Foximiliano" (December 2000:1). However, no detailed reporting of the event was allowed. It was, in every sense of the term, a private affair.

Not to be outdone completely by the Fox niche-specific spectacles, the PRDistas in control of city government staged their own counter-concert, called Baile, Música y Canto de Iberoamérica. The political intent of the counter-concert was spelled out on a banner featuring the city seal and a slogan: *El corazón de México late a la izquierda* (The heart of Mexico City beats on the left). The slogan is a double double-entendre. "México" is popularly employed to refer to both Mexico City and the nation. "The left" refers both to the location of the heart and, metaphorically, to the political Left, the PRD. The PRD was trying to ritually reappropriate the political and geographic center of Mexico, while warning Fox that Mexico City, as the nation's capital, would not be ignored. At the same time, the concert promoters were highlighting Mexico City's distinctive identity in relation to the rest of the nation, celebrating the city as a leftist enclave. Fox was now living in PRD territory.

Not surprisingly, the PRD concerts would attract a very different crowd than the Verbena. In fact, they brought in several different crowds. For example, the middle-aged Left turned out for Tania Libertad and Chavela Vargas, while young rockenrolleros came onto the scene for Eli Guerra and Julieta Venegas.

Conclusion

There is a sense of drift among the Mexican Left at the moment, as leftist nationalism has yet to be replaced by anything with the power to contest the neoliberal designs of Santa Fox. As collectively dreamed since Tlatelolco, the PRI is clearly crumbling. Unfortunately for leftist leaders, it is not the Left but rather a new, even more conservative nightmare that has arisen to replace the old one.

Capital is much harder to contest than corruption. Capital sets parameters and provides spectacle. Capital funds public relations, produces virtual realities, and flows with ease over international boundaries. Capital is at home everywhere, omnipresent yet ideologically obfuscated by mass-mediated ritual spectacle and target marketing. Unlike the legitimating rituals of the Mexica, the Spanish Crown, or later secular nationalists, capital works more through obfuscation than through direct legitimation. A Coca-Cola CEO in ranchero guise takes the reigns of a state ever more incorporated into the global system. The rituals of Conquest have moved from human sacrifice to Tepito's tamales, from the Spaniards' Requirement to much more subtle, yet spectacular, rituals of consumption. What is not said has become much more important than what is said in the public space.

During his inaugural speech in 1993, William Clinton swore that he would act as the "environmental president" and then, practically with his next breath, committed himself to strong economic growth for U.S. corporations worldwide, as if there would be no contradiction between the two. George W. Bush has enacted similar ritual politics. It has become the era of the polysemic president. Similarly, Fox, corporate CEO by day, cowboy by night, friend of Mexico City street children and international capitalists alike, has successfully used the ritual power of target marketing to appeal to multiple constituencies. If at some point he ceases to function effectively as a ritual frontispiece for capitalism, he too will be removed, just as surely as hundreds of previous caciques, viceroys, presidents, and parties were deposed when they ceased to achieve the ritual exigencies of their respective empires. Another leader, another party, another system, and another song will emerge in due time, only to be contested in turn.

Music and melodrama spark passion and draw people to ritual. Editorialists in opposition newspapers lamented that people only turned out at the Fox Verbena for the spectacle. It is an old complaint. Colonial officials complained that Mesoamerican Indians were drawn by the pageantry of the Mass, not by the religious message they were hoping to communicate. Aztec rituals, liturgical ceremonies of New Spain, and all other successful political ceremonies before and after were, and are, compelling spectacles of sight, smell, movement, and sound.

Nothing is more essential to the ritual spectacle than music. People participate in the musical rituals of power for the same basic reasons they take part in any musical event: escape, pleasure, transcendence, catharsis, rapture, solace, among myriad other motivations. Perhaps above all, people are drawn to musical ritual because it offers the collective promise of communion with other souls. We dance, we rave, we pray, we sing, we drink, and we cry together. We pay the piper and play our part, guided but not fully controlled by power. Why don't we simply opt out of the ritual life of power? To quote Carlos Monsiváis, we applaud the beast because "the most atrocious nightmare is the one that excludes us completely" (1995:250).

Appendix 1. Theory and Methodology

I have placed this more explicit theoretical and methodological discussion in an appendix rather than in the introduction and conclusion, where it is normally presented in academic works. While some readers may want this additional theoretical explication, others may not. Some readers might find the questions raised here too much like "inside baseball," discussions of more interest to social theorists and music researchers than to those concerned with Mexican musical history in more general terms. Those interested in additional theoretical and methodological context, however, should read on.

MUSICAL RITUAL AS THE PEDAGOGY OF POWER

Ritual is collective "symbolic behavior that is socially standardized and repetitive" (Kertzer 1988:9). Ritual is the means through which cultural cosmology is put into actual practice. It makes myth real and meaningful. Ritual incorporates individual bodies and disciplines them toward the collective ends more abstractly represented in myth. Therefore, the most affective rituals act throughout the body, presenting a complete sensorium of touch, site, smell, taste, and sound. The multisensory nature of ritual allows it to produce a profound transformative catharsis in the ritual participant.

Musical ritual performs a pedagogical function. Through ritual we not only reach an understanding of a text, creed, or ideology: we actually come to believe in it. Rather than reaching a negotiated agreement, in intellectual terms, ritual compels us to incorporate—literally, to "embody"—the pedagogy of power through a holistic appeal to our senses. The ritual sensorium takes its students well beyond the dry teaching of formal education into more transformative terrain. Ritual is one of the most effective forms of pedagogy, because it is an affective form of pedagogy.

Whether one lives in a band society or consumer capitalist metropolis, ritual is where we learn to become what a larger collective force would make of us. Through ritual, an elite Mexica youth learned what it meant to be a warrior in the mold of

Huitzilopochtli, a criolla of New Spain was instructed on what it meant to be a sacrificing mother in the image of La Virgen, a rural mestizo of nineteenth-century Mexico City was impelled to fight for the (secularized) patria, and a postrevolutionary girl of the 1930s learned how to be "La mujer divina," both modern consumer and that which is consumed. In the modern state, "rituals of a civic nature are the basic means through which the state presents itself to society" (Pérez Rayón E. 2001:141). Ritual is a primary site of social instruction.

Ritual instructs not only at the level of intellect, as is the case with classroom pedagogy, but also at the level of the soul. Ritual, as a sensorium, produces catharsis. This catharsis of mind, body, and spirit, when successful, is a much deeper sort of pedagogy than the term "learning" normally implies. Ritual goes well beyond mere socialization; it is a form of enculturation. Through ritual, one not only learns how to behave in society (socialization) but is also provided with a symbolic map to orient oneself to the world. That symbolic matrix will not only guide behavior but also construct a world and make it meaningful (enculturation). In other words, ritual is an essential site of semiotic construction, a place where cultural reality is created and naturalized.

Ritual is, therefore, a primary site of contact between self and society, a place where our individual selves are transformed into collective selves. We gain cultural identity through the ritual process. Yet in so doing we also lose something of our potential selves. Through our incorporation into a collective set of beliefs and practices (i.e., culture), we sacrifice something of our potential individuality. In other words, ritual is sacrifice. For example, through rituals of "blood sacrifice," nations "organize killing energy by committing devotees to sacrifice themselves to the group" (Marvin and Ingle 1996:767). We sacrifice much of our potential selves in order to become that which other people and other things (e.g., groups, organizations, and nations) would make of us.

Where does music fit into the ritual equation? In this book I have adopted Carol Robertson's definition of music. She defines music "not merely as a score or even as a complex of meaningful sounds but rather as a gestalt that embraces sounds, texts, history, human interaction, and all the dimensions of value and belief that are embodied in performance" (1988:10). Robertson's definition captures not only the technical and structural aspects of music but also the essential question of cultural meaning. Such semiotic definition is useful for thinking about music as part of ritual life.

Music is more than just accompaniment to the dramatic rite; it is a central part of the ritual catharsis. Although the silent, contemplative ritual moments are often the most powerful, even these demonstrate music's motivating power. Ritual silences are an aural punctuation empowered by the conspicuous absence of sound. They are made that much more meaningful by the expectation on the part of the participants that ritual should be filled with sound, filled with music. As musicologist Lourdes Turrent demonstrates in her book *La conquista musical de México*, music is a "social language" (1996:186). As such, music is one means through which we develop individual identities in relation to a social group and cultural world.

RITUAL AS IDEOLOGY

When I use the term "ideology," I specifically mean that which "serves the function of legitimizing and justifying the existing order" (Broda, Carrasco, and Matos Moctezuma 1987:6). This is not to say that all ideas serve power (not all ideas are ideology); nor by using this definition am I claiming that power consists solely of ideas that originate from and benefit the elite. There is more to power than ideology. There is also more to culture than ideology. That is the reason I have adopted Johanna Broda's definition for use in this book, so that the concept may retain a specific, and thus useful, meaning.

Social hierarchy has nothing natural about it; it must be developed and nurtured through cultural education, institutional reproduction, and ideology. Ritual can do such work directly, by presenting an argument for the moral correctness of power — as in the case of the theocratic state — or through obfuscation — by distracting attention from the real workings of power, often through the production of alternative narratives. Of course, most realities of power exist somewhere between the poles of simple legitimation, at one extreme, and sophisticated obfuscation, at the other. For example, Horatio Alger narratives in the United States legitimate the power of the rich, by implying that they have gained their power through inordinate effort, while obfuscating the fact that the great bulk of wealth and privilege is inherited (thus class inertia is more common than downward or upward movement).

Power is never completely external, something that merely acts upon us. It also acts through us. We are all active agents of power, regardless of our relative privileges or dispossessions. Power is not just "a force that says no" (Foucault and Rabinow 1984: 61) but also a result of dialectical struggle and negotiation among various social forces (e.g., social classes, audiences, institutions) and related discourses (e.g., ideologies and cultural metaphors). For example, the gender hierarchies involved in the Mexican danzón (Chapter 10) are not simply the patriarchal production of a group of men acting upon women but a set of metaphoric and practical possibilities, actively engaged in by women, providing certain social potentials and limitations to all of its participants. In the words of feminist critic Jean Bethke Elshtain, "we can never fly free for that would be not to exist in culture as an embodied being, hence one who will always confront, and be constituted by, constructions of gender" (1989:134). The same can be said of most basic identities. We are all the products of ideological construction. What is important for us as students of culture is that we become more aware of the power of ideology.

Unfortunately, it is easier to see the power of ideology from a distance, whether that distance is chronological or spatial. For example, people in the United States are often unwilling to recognize that they have been trained and operate under the influence of capitalist ideology. This is despite the fact, or perhaps because of the fact, that they have been raised in a consumer capitalist society. Yet the same people who most actively deny their own susceptibility to ideological enculturation often readily accept the idea that people living in other societies — feudal principalities, nomadic tribes, chiefdoms, dictatorships, socialist states, and so on — are the product of ideological training and influence. In other words, only others have ideology. We, conversely, are free-thinking individuals. Ironically, in making such claims we demonstrate our ideological training, rather than effectively contesting it.

After all, contesting ideology is difficult. The ruling ideologies of any historical moment by definition effectively reflect the system or systems of power dominant at the time. Quite simply, ideology supports power and the powerful. While ideologies are contested, remade, and sometimes even undone, they are by definition effective means of social control. Although I have delved into the various contradictions and complexities of Mexican musical ritual, I continually return to that basic premise.

Because it is an effective and affective ideological medium, musical ritual is intimately linked to ideological enculturation. "Enculturation" refers to the means through which we are taught to function in a given culture. That is a basic thesis of this work—one that I invite the reader to consider and one that I beg the reader to contest. After all, I would like to be wrong. Although I believe that musical ritual is a fundamental tool of power, I would rather this was not the case. If only the beautiful ritual performances documented here were somehow outside the touch of power, enriching our lives while serving no direct function of power. Like students who believe critical analysis will "ruin" a good concert, movie, or other "fun," I, too, wish that it were possible simply to revel in the spectacle without analyzing its meaning and function.

However, I suspect that both positions, pleasure and critique, are possible at one and the same time. Musical ritual provides incredible aesthetic pleasures, while at the same time functioning as a system of ideological reproduction. Musical ritual evokes the pleasure of community, while enabling the terrors of exclusion. For example, Disney films allow us to examine virtual worlds much better than this one. They are beautiful, awesome assemblages of sight and sound, drawing millions into the ritual space of the theater. Meanwhile, in places like Haiti and China, tens of thousands of Disney assembly workers produce Disney film-theme toys for extremely low wages, living in shanties and working without democratic redress. Disney, like all popular culture, is a mass of contradictions. Such contradictions are the soul of social existence. We would not partake in the rituals of power if at some level we did not ourselves find pleasure in them and if power were not, at some level, a part of us. Like muralist Juan González Camarena's Mexica warrior indistinguishably enmeshed in battle with a Spanish conquistador (*The Fusion of Two Cultures*), it is not always easy to determine where power ends and resistance begins.

In the same vein, sixteenth-century Mexican indigenous peoples found both succor and persecution in the church. Similarly, the colonial celebration of Corpus Cristi was at one and the same time a pleasurable feast and an ideological tool for maintaining exploitation. To read such rituals simply as ideological imposition, at one extreme, or communal celebration, at the other, is to miss the point. Rituals of power transcend the ambiguities of our profane, daily lives. These and all vital rituals are experiences of heightened contradiction and ambivalence, pleasure and pain, ecstasy and terror, incorporation and dismemberment. Ameliorating oppression does not require that we lose the sense of awe and pleasure the popular arts can inspire. Ritual life, like political life, is a matter of engaging contradictions.

Perhaps nowhere are the heightened contradictions of ritual more clearly represented than in the person of the sacrificial victim. In the hands of the Mexica priest, such men and women became the ultimate losers in the cosmic drama, knowing a pain and loss so keen that the word "torture" barely suffices. But they also became the most exalted of Mesoamericans, transformed into sacred messengers to the gods. At the sacrificial moment, the murdered slave or warrior occupied both the bottom of the social hierarchy and the top of the moral order, experiencing a range of pleasure and pain few others could ever know. The sacrificial victim was drawn from the margins of society yet absolutely central to the state's ritual needs. Such is the relationship between the powerful and powerless in all hierarchical societies.

Although outside of normal time and space, ritual is a primary means for making the vagaries of myth and ideology part of lived practice. It is through ritual that the abstractions of ideology are transformed into practice, enacted in real time and space. The abstract truths of myth and ideology are made manifest through theatrical structure and liturgical performance. We may think that "virtual reality" is something new. We lament the fact that people seem to find cinematic fiction more real than historical fact, yet this has been the case for as long as narrative exists. We cannot truly conceive of a world without such dramatic structures. As a result of the human predilection for fiction, those who most effectively produce such narratives, be they village elders or media conglomerates, will exert an inordinate level of cultural power over others.

Musical ritual is, therefore, particularly central to ideological enculturation. Through musical rituals we incorporate the lessons of power, feel them, embody them, perhaps even grow to love and need them. However, I do not want to reduce ritual's complex sensorium of sight, sound, touch, and smell to mere politics. I am sympathetic to Gerald Behague's warning that an "analytical approach that argues for explanations of the development of musical languages as the primary result of sociocultural struggle and conflict is inevitably loaded with a-priori assumptions that may not be cross-culturally accurate or applicable" (1986:42). Ritual, like music, involves much more than political struggle.

Here I have chosen to focus on those musical rituals that clearly are connected to "socio-cultural struggle." In other words, I make no claim that these musical forms are ideological in and of themselves—there is nothing intrinsically ideological, or even meaningful, about the aesthetic structures of sound in the abstract. It is the placement of music in ritual that makes it an inextricable part of social contests over meaning and therefore power. There is no question that the musical rituals sponsored by the Mexica, Spain, the Roman Catholic Church, the Mexican state, and contemporary global corporations involve larger social struggles over representation, wealth, and power. Powerful institutions would not commit resources for public rites if such rituals did not in some way reflect, reconstruct, and reinforce their ideological worldview and goals. Yet such performances, because they must involve various publics and contesting institutions to be truly popular, always present new possibilities. There is an element of contradiction, polysemy, and potential subversion in every popular rite.

Another reason for ritual's polysemy, beyond competing interests, is the issue of interpretation. Although ritual specialists—be they priests, politicians, or concert promoters—have a preferred reading in mind when they enact a given rite, the participants are not beholden to them. What a ritual means depends largely on who is interpreting it, when it is being interpreted, and for what purposes. As a gringo, for example, my own cultural lens filters how I interpret and write about the rituals in question, no matter how much I try to ferret out what these rituals mean to those more directly and emotionally involved in them. I have attempted to be honest and self-reflexive about that process rather than work under the pretense that mine is somehow a purely objective eye or ear. To the contrary, this should be read as the impressions of someone from the United States. The results are, therefore, different from that which a Mexican author would produce.

Furthermore, cultural study involves more than textual interpretation alone; it is a question of interpreting interpretations. Conducting cultural study is not unlike walking into Salón México's "Hall of Mirrors": one must make sense of reflected images. Culture is composed of layers of symbols, interpretations of interpretations, reflections of reflections that make the definition of one authoritative and objective reality impossible. That is what makes cultural study so difficult. It is also what makes it interesting.

RITUAL AND RESISTANCE

Although ritual is an essential pedagogy of power, rites of power are never simply a matter of active instruction and passive learning. The student resists, contests, and remakes knowledge, both individually and as part of a larger collective body. The tributary states of Mesoamerica fought against the brutal ritual acts of the Mexica. Likewise, indigenous musicians, black poets, and mestizo parishioners of New Spain adopted and reshaped liturgical pedagogy to serve their own needs outside the direct reach of the church. Culture is constantly contested and remade in this way.

Furthermore, ritual pedagogy goes well beyond simple vertical contests of power and resistance. Social contestation takes places horizontally as well as vertically. This is clearly reflected in the case of musical politics. Groups relatively equal in terms of social power—such as workers and peasants—constantly use each other as foils for forming their own cultural identities and staking political claims.

Indeed, every act of internal allegiance and inclusion is at some level also an act of external differentiation and exclusion. One gains identity X partly based on the fact that one is not Y. For example, one is identifiably Protestant by virtue of being "not Catholic." Such rituals of opposition operate horizontally and vertically. The axes of differentiation and struggle cut in multiple directions in the social hierarchy. Therefore, power is never a simple matter of opposition, assimilation, and control.

No matter how entrenched a system of domination may seem, it will be subject to change. The dialectics of desire will always undermine politics of domination. The cultural process can only be guided to a certain degree. For example, Mexico City is a megalopolis with as many as 20 million inhabitants, projected to reach 22 million by 2010 (Ward 1998:54). It is a beast that simply cannot be controlled—directed, maybe, but never controlled, at least by human agency alone. It is a superordinate entity that within environmental limits acts more upon individuals than they could ever hope to act upon it. As Bruce Nord (1995) explains, the hegemony of Mexico City is itself contested and conditioned by larger national, regional, and global forces. We can dream of resistance, and perhaps even score unlikely victories toward a more humane and pleasurable collective existence, but such plans must inevitably contend with matrices of power that far exceed the power of our ability to comprehend and control them. As Monsiváis (1995) indicates, even the most ordered system of collective expression is ultimately a ritual of chaos.

BEYOND TAXONOMY

If ritual practice and cultural identification make music political, what makes it popular? For the purposes of this book, I have considered any type of music "popular" if a lot of people listen to it. In other words, I am using the colloquial English definition of the term, employing it as an adjective rather than a noun. This is opposed to typical classificatory schemes in both the Anglophone and Mexican academic literature, where music is more often classified into categories based on who produces it, when it is produced, where it is produced, and to what end. I am more interested in determining who listens to it, where, and why.

Typical academic taxonomic distinctions include high vs. low culture, popular vs. folk, and art vs. popular. However, all of these classificatory schemes require an a priori evaluation. While such "etic" (from a researcher's point of view) cultural taxonomies are interesting as objects *of* anthropological study, they are not useful as categories *for* anthropological analysis. For example, many cultural researchers would assume that the most salient differences among the Mexican corrido, bolero, and classical music are (1) that the corrido is anonymously authored and performed in person, thus a "folk" form; (2) that the bolero is primarily communicated by mass media and is therefore a "popular" or "low-brow" type of music; and (3) that because classical music is authored for and by those who have received advanced training in institutionalized Western musical traditions, it is a form of "art" music or "high culture." From the perspective of a cultural researcher, these classifications are interesting as subjects of study (i.e., it is interesting to study the political means through which music comes to be defined as greater or lesser, associated with certain classes, etc.) but not very useful as categories for study if one is interested in learning how music actually functions in society. In other words, rather than assuming that one type of music is art and another is not, or that one type of music represents the true feelings of "the folk" or not, both a priori value judgments, it is more useful to explore the ways music is performed and the social functions it fulfills.

Nevertheless, as mentioned above, such classificatory schemes are interesting as subjects of anthropological study. For example, it is useful to study the ways in which one strain of musical tradition accrues cultural capital, while others become stigmatized as lesser forms. This is usually a reflection of the audiences who produce and listen to a given type of music or attend a given type of cultural event. Lawrence Levine's study of Shakespearean performance in the United States (1988), for example, illustrates how the same text can be ascribed very different social positions, moving from high to low culture or the reverse as it becomes performed for, and associated with, different audiences.

The same is true of music. While there are certain standards of quality within musical traditions, there is no intrinsic means of judging the relative quality of entirely different musical types and styles. For example, one can judge the relative merits of various postrevolutionary symphonies, but there is no universal and essential value system that would allow us to judge the comparative merits of postrevolutionary symphony vs. postrevolutionary bolero. There is nothing intrinsically better about a symphony than a bolero, corrido, or Mexica percussion performance, from a cultural viewpoint. Only by ethnocentric application of the standards of evaluation designed to evaluate pieces within one form can a style outside a given form be judged as lesser. For example, corridistas judge the relative merits of their genre through assessments of lyrical detail, dexterity, and clarity. If these particularistic criteria were mistaken for universal musical criteria, the classical music of Europe would be viewed as artistically inferior to the corrido. However, musical disciplines do not allow for such cross-disciplinary comparisons of artistic value.

Therefore, such comparisons of relative merit are not used in this book. In fact, there is very little evaluation of quality in this work. I am neither qualified to carry out such criticism nor interested in doing so. As an anthropologist, I am more interested in applying cultural relativism. My goal is to gain a better understanding of each musical form as developed, practiced, and understood by those who produce and consume it. While more evaluative critique has a place in the internal study of styles and genres, it fails as a cultural research tool.

In other words, I share Carlos Monsiváis' view that it is important to "transcend the schematic and almost always classicist visions between mass culture and elite culture, vanguard and kitsch, high culture and popular culture" (in Jiménez de Báez 1992:467). Rather than creating ranked systems based on relative differences between musical audiences or perceived differences in the intrinsic artistic merit of a musical style or piece, I have dealt with each genre and style as a meaningful cultural phenomenon and studied each within its relevant social context.

That also means that I have not paid particular attention to distinctions between "folk" and popular forms, except to the extent that the folk discourse influences the actual production and consumption of music. Folk music is viewed, often inaccurately, as that created by and for a community. Music given the "folk" appellation is assumed to be more authentic. People believe that it is a more sincere expression of community interests. Conversely, music assigned the "popular" label in Anglophone literature or "mass music" is viewed as something alien to the community, imposed by mass media rather than developed more organically.

I am suspicious of several elements of this dichotomy between folk and popular music. First, it strikes me as being a product of urban modernity rather than a critique thereof. I am skeptical about such idyllic images of "community" as a mythical place where collective beliefs, actions, and spirit are, or were, played out unmitigated and unmediated by struggles for power, ideology, or the impositions of larger social entities. The folkloricists seem to imagine a place and time when such communities existed outside of power, as if electronic mass media represented the first imposition of state domination on folk society. From Chapter 2 onward it should be clear that state mediation has been taking place for centuries if not millennia. Thus, in this book I have tried not to romanticize "traditional" or folk music or unduly stigmatize mass-mediated forms. Like the division between high and low cultures, the distinction between folk and popular is overly simplistic and misleading.

This is not to say that all forms of music are equally mediated. Some music does more closely link musical producers and consumers in face-to-face communities, while others may be mediated over great spatial, social, and technological distances. Theodore Solís provides a useful way of thinking about the relationship between music and mediation without falling into a simplistic folk (authentic) vs. popular (inauthentic) dichotomy. In reference to the marimba music of southern Mexico, Solís notes: "The middleman's hand becomes heavier in direct proportion to the amount of money involved, and the presence or absence of his influence is an important criterion in differentiating, if at all possible, 'popular' from 'folk' music" (1980:40). He goes on to explain that the least enfranchised marimba musicians are given greater autonomy in the musical production process than their more popular colleagues. Only a few marimba ensembles are able to gain recording contracts, and in so doing they often lose creative control.

It is a Faustian bargain. Musicians gain media access only to lose creative autonomy. It also shows, however, that folk musicians are allowed such creative space because mass media and mass audiences ignore them. This demonstrates the tautology and contradictions of the folk/popular distinction: folk is folk because it is not popular (or is it "not popular" because it is folk?). That causes a severe contradiction within the folk discourse. How is folk music the authentic expression of the people if most people are, in fact, listening to something else? Conversely, why is popular music considered inauthentic if so many people actually listen to it? The answer for many folkloricists, which I find both compelling and problematic, is that mass-mediated music is "imposed on the public by a commercial oligarchy" (Reuter 1981: 12). Unfortunately, rather than being argued, this position is more often simply asserted, leaving the aforementioned contradiction in play. Conversely, Solís' work is a rare case where connections between folk and mass-mediated music are carefully drawn, rather than assuming that there is an intrinsic division between the two. In most studies of folk music, popular music is simply denied, dismissed, or derided as an evil, adulterated form of cultural expression.

Further confusing any discussion of popular culture is the fact that many ethnomusicological, anthropological, and historical works use the term "popular" or "the popular" in reference to music that is authentically connected to "the people," a use that is very different from the one critiqued above. In such a framework, the "popular" can include folk and more mass-mediated forms, as long as it has some sort of authentic connection to people's interests.

I am also skeptical of such conceptions. For one thing, this conception of the popular, as noun rather than verb, assumes that there is some mythical mass disconnected from or outside the state. Moreover, such "invocations of 'the people,' 'the popular,' and so on" overly romanticize the subaltern (Joseph and Nugent 1994:10). As Gilbert Joseph and Daniel Nugent explain, these ideas have been a central part of the modern ideological project of the Mexican state at least since the Revolution of 1910 (1994:10). A great deal of ideological damage has been done in the name of "the popular." While pretending to be a socialist government "of the people," for example, the Partido Revolucionario Institucional (PRI) has instead used such conceptions of the popular to obfuscate and legitimate a form of state capitalist government that has benefited only a relatively small sector of the nation.

In truth, there is no "people." States are composed of many different populations, none of which can be defined as some sort of authentic subaltern. Nor, as argued earlier, can we simply lump all marginalized populations together and assume that they share common interests, even if they are equally disenfranchised. This is further reason why I have tended not to use the term "popular" as a noun in this work, as in the all-too-common anthropological references to "the popular." That usage reifies popular culture, as if it were some identifiable thing out there waiting to be cataloged and studied. Instead, I have attempted to identify and differentiate the specific groups and performances in question, leaving such taxonomic distinctions of authenticity to others.

Furthermore, I do not place "the popular" solely within the ranks of the subaltern. For me the term "popular," as adjective, designates any performance or text that is widely in play, be it among marginalized classes or moving across class and caste lines. The latter is more often the case, because neither popular culture nor resistance is isolated in the working classes. It would be unhelpful, for this analysis, to assume that resistance automatically resides in the oppressed or that the oppressed automatically harbor resistance. From the tributary caciques of the Mexica and criollo hacendados of the colony to the rural clerics of the nineteenth century's restored republic and middle-class urban nightclub dancers of the postrevolutionary era, the relationship of power, people, and music is much too complicated to reduce to simplistic dichotomies of subordinate vs. elite practices. Repeatedly in Mexican history relatively elite groups have taken part in musical resistance along with more oppressed classes. For example, all colonial classes practiced cultural subversion through the villancico. Relatively enfranchised elites have played lead roles in cultural resistance throughout the history of Mexico, from the criollo rebels who plagued the reign of New Spain to the upper-class intellectual leaders who dogged the PRI in the twentieth century. These resistant elites have struggled within and against the paradoxes of power, working as agents of both hegemony and resistance, often at the same time.

In sum, one cannot assume that resistance automatically resides in the lower classes or that the upper classes are totally devoid of subversive elements. Because of such baggage attached to popular culture as a theoretical subject, I tend to speak more often in reference to "culture," period. When I do slip into discussions of "the popular" as a noun, therefore, I have attempted to present it in situational contexts, as does Figueroa Hernández when he refers to "las(s) cultura(s) popular(es)" (1996:11).

The concept of "tradition" needs to be considered in a critical light as well. Traditional music, according to most folklorists, is transmitted from one generation to the next, mouth-to-mouth. While this does indeed differentiate different musical styles and eras, it is also much too simplistic a division. Electronic mediation is not the unnatural ideological syringe that traditionalists would lead us to believe; nor is traditional, mouth-to-mouth music unmediated by social technology and power. Even if a form of music is at some point transmitted in person (what type of music is not?), there is always a cultural matrix of myth, ritual, and ideology mediating that transmission. In turn, that mediation, whether via road or wire, is always conditioned by its relationship to power. There is nothing magic about the mouth or generational communication that automatically places such forms of communication outside the bounds of cultural mediation and power. In fact, the long-term maintenance of a cultural tradition is often as emblematic of its connection to the sustaining force of social power—imperial, colonial, national, or capital—as it is evidence of the unmediated survival of community spirit and local interests. The power of cultural tradition is its ability to adapt to, and negotiate, the symbolic relations of power (Knight 1994:398–399).

This is the only point on which I would critique the otherwise brilliant analysis of Lourdes Turrent in her exceptional book *La conquista musical de México* (1996). After she illustrates the process of social translation, mediation, and negotiation of music between the Spaniards and indigenous Mexicans, she falls back in the end on the traditionalist critique of modern popular music. She complains that mass media are now fundamentally "undermining" more "authentic" forms of Mexican music (Turrent 1996:193):

Currently, 100% of the Mexican population has electric services; everyone can hear the radio and view television. Unfortunately, these means of communication are now the totality of the sound expression of youth and therefore undermine and continue slowly undermining the language of sound of Mexico, which has been conserved in varied and rich form from 1521 to our day.

This is an extremely common critique in the musicological literature. Similarly, Jas Reuter dismisses the urban music of Mexico as "mass culture" that is the product of "the means of communication that manipulate the masses" (1981:9). This assumes that the "authentic" rural historical traditions have not been mediated by anything "artificial," while dismissing urban culture as somehow unnatural. Even these authors, who make the study of intercultural influences on folk music their major means of analysis, fall into this contradictory contagion critique when assessing modern, electronic mass media and music.

Although I, too, am highly critical of the capitalist infrastructure through which social thought is expressed today, the folkloricist critics' orientation appears to me to be more the product of modernity than a criticism thereof. The moderns imagine an edenic, traditional world before the fall and understand their modern world to be a corruption of natural human life. Armed with such a vision of the present, moderns like Diego Rivera optimistically imagined a totalizing and futuristic project, such as techno-communism. Other moderns, including folkloricists, look mainly to an imagined time before the fall, viewing cultural preservation as the route back to the garden. They view the present as a time when "much of the communal wealth of traditional culture is being lost" (Reuter 1981:9). Both visions are more a product of modernity than meaningful critiques of its ideological power. Power, foreign and domestic, has always influenced the development of popular music. While the qualities and scale of external influence may change over time, there is nothing distinctive about electronic mediation in that particular regard.

Another problem with the traditionalists' worldview is their inability to define the particular moments and styles that would constitute this seemingly authentic "traditional" assemblage of community music. Given the continual and dynamic changes within any musical style over time, there is no way of fixing a definite cultural mode or moment as authentic.

Conversely, systems of power are often fairly conservative, as demonstrated by the three-century reign of New Spain. One of the best places to look for continuity in culture, therefore, is within the rituals of power rather than outside them. In other words, musical forms often have long traditional trajectories not because they are connected to the subaltern interests of local communities but because they are supported by powerful institutions and ideologies. Each regime is like a cultural engine. Once the regime dies, so does the cultural infrastructure that propels its dominant musical forms. Therefore, to lament the death of popular music in folkloric fashion is also to lament the death of kings.

The process of cultural development that folkloricists see as imposed by the mass media is simply a more rapid and complex version of a musical dialectic that has been in force for centuries. In the case of Mesoamerica, Mexica musical ritual was a cultural mélange produced via social dialectics, intercultural clashes, and the mediation of power. The same can be said of all music everywhere and at all times and is particularly true in the case of Mexico's varied and rich musical history. Just as "European melodies transformed until becoming purely Mexican" (Reuter 1981:54), mass-mediated music is remade in local guise. Mexican rock, for example, the favorite target of the traditionalists, is filled with musical and lyrical *mexicanismos* that are missing in many other Mexican styles and genres. In other words, mass-mediated music is not simply representative of foreign domination but is rather the continuation of this creative process wherein cultural forms are appropriated, mediated, negotiated, and contested. All cultural traditions in Mexico, indeed in the world, are the result of intercultural exchange and creativity. In fact, all of the traditions that the folkloricists seek to preserve—villancico, *son*, corrido—are themselves the hybrid progeny of empire. Traditions survive not through static preservation but because they are adaptive.

In sum, as is true in Henry Schmidt's study of the Mexican lyric, traditional "disciplinary qualifications are not essential to my purpose" (1988:296). It is important to think outside the accepted taxonomies (popular, folk, art, high, low, etc.) in order to understand the cultural dimensions of music.

CULTURAL THEORY AND MUSICAL AUTHENTICITY

Throughout the book I have argued against essentialism, the philosophy underlying claims for cultural authenticity. No culture contains an immutable essence, no matter how much cultural nationalists would like to believe otherwise. There is comfort in essentialism but little veracity. All cultures are multiple, made up of many subcultures. All cultures are recombinant, heavily influenced by external forces. Culture lives through exchange. Therefore, culture is better thought of as a process than a thing, a matrix of symbols with some coherence but little solidity.

Folkloricists and musicologists often deal with musical rituals as if they represent basic, unchanging spiritual truths in contradistinction to the polluting effects of other, more contemporary, less authentic forms. This often propels such scholars into a search for origins, seeking to anchor the authenticity of a form by finding its linkage to past traditions.

Richard Stark provides a glimpse into the frustrations such a search can cause. Stark traveled to Spain in order to find the regional roots of the New Mexican alabado, certain he would find his answer there. "Your alabado has Spanish roots but it has changed," one of his informants suggested. "Have you thoroughly searched Mexico?" (1983:126). As all of Stark's informants tell him, the New Mexican alabado has changed much too greatly to forge definite evolutionary links to any single Spanish region. As a reflective and critical scholar, Stark rightly concludes that he will not find his answer to the origins of the New Mexico alabado in Spain. Nor would he find a simple answer in his search for origins were he to scour Mexico for clues. Spain has changed, Mexico has changed, the alabado has changed, and musical history has changed.

Stark's thoughtful piece teaches the musical researcher an important and humbling lesson. Another scholar, less willing to explore the limits of evolutionary reasoning, might argue that the New Mexican alabado originated in X region as demonstrated by Y declension. More than one study bears the mark of such ad hoc reasoning. Unfortunately, important musical qualities are often ignored in order to fit a piece or style into such simple evolutionary taxonomies post hoc. Musical creativity is denied and cultural meanings flattened in that sort of evolutionary analysis.

Stark presents a useful allegory for all who would seek the meaning of musical forms in their historical origins. Certainly, the history of a musical form tells us a great deal. I have learned invaluable information about Mexican culture from reading the musical histories cited here. Knowing how and why the trumpet was added to the mariachi ensemble enriches my understanding and enjoyment of the music. Learning how the bolero evolved over time and space deepens my listening and performing experience. However, origins are not everything. Meaning is established by synchronic (contemporaneous) social dynamics as much as by diachronic (historical) developments. As Carmen de la Peza argues, "the song does not exist beyond concrete realizations, which are always different" (2001:31). "Variations in use," she continues, "are not accidental, but rather necessary" in determining the meaning of a song.

Societies quickly adopt new forms, and cultural memory is short. Texts that appear foreign to cultural critics and analysts may seem entirely authentic to those who adopt them. Whether one is speaking of colonial liturgy or rock, people have an endless capacity to incorporate new influences and make them their own. New influences can be quickly naturalized and may sometimes even become "time-honored tradition" in very short order. For example, it took the bolero less than a century to evolve from a foreign artifact to a deeply felt Mexican tradition.

That which is widely considered a tradition is a tradition, no matter how recently it has entered into social practice. For "those who sing, recite, and tell traditional genres," explains Mercedes Díaz Roig, "the texts are as much their own as those created in their community, and they feel absolutely free to use them and to vary them as they choose" (1987:616). That is true of all musical practice. That which first seems foreign can be quickly adopted, naturalized, and transformed beyond recognition. No nation has shown greater skill in that regard than Mexico. In fact, as the world finally comes to grips with globalization, I believe there is much to be learned from Mexico's history of musical mestizaje.

Music, like culture, changes or it dies. Meaning is established through human interaction, performance, conflict, mediation, negotiation, and other acts of creativity. Although some people believe ritual and music carry essential qualities with them—core values that remain unchanged by history and time—the cultural researcher can find no empirical evidence for that position. There is no clear relationship between signifier and signification. Meanings change as social practices change. Therefore, traveling back to cultural origins is more a mythic journey than an academic enterprise.

Theory and Methodology

Musicologist Vicente Mendoza has studied a wide range of Mexican music, and his brilliant work reflects a thoughtful balance between historical and sociological analysis. He does not just look for the historical continuities in Mexican music but also explores disjuncture and change. For example, Mendoza has described the ways in which Spanish music "flourished" and "transformed itself" over time to become something new in Mexico (1953:5). He gives us a model of how we can appreciate both the changing and continuous dimensions of music, the foreign and the familiar.

Many judge musical performance based on how accurate it is in relation to some (arbitrarily chosen) historical origin point. For some this might mean that an authentic mariachi conjunto cannot include brass instruments (the influence of early radio), or that they should only play traditional songs, or that they must wear the charro costume we have become accustomed to seeing them in (which is highly influenced by film). To make such folkloric judgments, one must choose an arbitrary assemblage at an arbitrary point in time to fix as the "original" form, the essential archetype that all others must mimic.

I am not entirely unsympathetic to essentialist views; for even though they are based on mythical origins and arbitrary archetypes, such ideologies of authenticity often lead to the highest aesthetic standards. It is unlikely, for example, that historical or cultural relativism could ever motivate the sort of aesthetic perfection inspired by "classical" mariachi or "authentic" *son* conceptions.

The concept of authenticity can be defended on other grounds as well. As Néstor García Canclini has demonstrated, cultural artifacts are often alienated from both creators and consumers (1993:105–114). Culture, like labor, can be appropriated and exploited by those in positions of privilege and even used against those who most directly create and consume it. Essentialism can anchor cultural patrimony to cultural producers in positive ways, while relativist positions can be used to legitimate cultural appropriation.

Perhaps musical production should be evaluated on the same grounds that García Canclini proposes for Mexican crafts. The more authentic music is that which provides the greatest rewards and is the most meaningful to those who produce and consume it. A Mexican neophyte forced to learn and sing "Non nobis Domine" at Mass may constitute a less authentic performance than a requiem sung at his cousin's gravesite. In that same sense, a rock concert sponsored by Coca-Cola may be less authentic than a garage band jam session, which is more participatory, more creative, and, in the end, more rewarding.

Yet even in this application of authenticity I am imposing what is, from a strictly analytical point of view, an arbitrary standard. I am making the claim that individual lives and interpersonal encounters are somehow more real and truthful, thus more "authentic," than the actions of larger groups, institutions, and social systems. By the same token, this argument for authenticity contends that egalitarian relations are inherently better than inequitable ones. Authenticity in that sense is, ultimately, a humanistic ideology, a value judgment rather than an analytical observation or purely logical supposition.

Although I am aware of the dangers and bias inherent in such evaluations, I nevertheless strongly agree with García Canclini that cultural aesthetic practices should be evaluated based on how well they are connected to the pleasures and profits of those who most directly create and consume them. A mariachi Mass in a Mexican village is more authentic, in that sense, than a mariachi concert for tourists arriving at the Sheraton; a Café Tacuba concert is more authentic than a pop simulation; and so on.

However, no musical ritual ever represents an unadulterated lens into the beliefs or nature of an entire people. Music remains a vital part of social life largely because of its polysemy. In other words, musical rituals survive largely because they are *not* the stuff of consensus. The Mass serves not one single need, that of church or penitent, but rather multiple and often conflicting needs of multiple churches, penitents, parishioners, priests, and even those who never step foot inside the sanctuary. Within the Mass a battle is waged over whose meaning(s) will dominate. As a result of that battle, the Mass is modified and survives. Therefore, the Mass of today is a far different thing than it was five centuries ago, and the Mass of a wealthy Mexico City suburb is greatly different from that of a poor barrio in Los Angeles. Therefore, to seek the essential spirit at the heart of any ritual or cultural practice is to look in the wrong place. Musical rituals are successful and meaningful not for the sake of consensus but because of their potential to incorporate diversity.

Given this complexity, the cultural spirit of musical ritual cannot be saved through folkloric preservation. It is useful to remember the "absurd cultural protection decree of 1799," through which Spanish authorities attempted to plug the dyke of a dying culture by banning all foreign influence (Moreno Rivas 1989:55). Not only do such reactions represent a paranoid distraction from the fundamental causes and contexts of social unease, but they are also doomed to fail. The genius of Mexican music is its ability to mix multiple influences into new wholes, a mestizaje of sound that responds to ever changing cultural environments.

Rather than look at music in terms of "loss," therefore, perhaps we should instead look at the productive aspects of both old and new forms. "Contrary to that which many believe," explains Yvette Jiménez de Báez, "collective celebrations are flourishing" in contemporary Mexico (1992:493). "Some are created and others are revived," she explains, "and certainly all are transformed" (1992:493). As Díaz Roig adds, a "traditional genre possesses two principle characteristics: its power of conservation and its power of variation" (1987:616). It is the "power of variation" that explains how a cultural form can exist long enough to become a "tradition" in the first place. Therefore, musical ritual is best viewed as a creative, changing, and vital process.

METHODOLOGY

In 1992 I began attending musical events in Mexico City. What was first an informal interest had developed into a full-scale research project by 1997. I started attending as many public musical events as possible, talking to fellow audience members, taking field notes, occasionally conducting formal interviews, and examining lyrics and other musical texts. My ethnographic work in Mexico City was designed to supplement the extensive reading I have been doing for the last five years on the topic and my enthusiastic consumption of Mexican music, film, and television over the last decade.

The layout of this book mirrors the organization of my research. I conducted research concerning the general history of musical ritual in Mexico City while working toward an understanding of the way in which music is manifested in ritual performance. I used interdisciplinary methodology, combining ethnography, historical research, and intertextual analysis (examining how musical texts relate to one another and other cultural texts).

As is already apparent, I make no significant distinction between ritual and performance. There is no ritual that does not include performance. It is fair to say, however, that there are performances that do not meet all the requirements of ritual. Some performances are not terribly meaningful, entail little investment from participants, do not repeat, and/or have nothing resembling a liturgical order. Nevertheless, I believe many more contemporary performances meet the requirements of ritual than one might think at first glance. Take the rock concert, a performance many would dismiss as a meaningless act. To the contrary, rock fans invest themselves deeply in the event, rock performances are extremely structured, the concerts are sponsored by dominant social institutions (e.g., corporations), and both rock texts and performances reflect, enact, and negotiate central cultural myths. When having to operationalize these twin terms — "performance" and "ritual" — I found little need to distinguish between them. Searching out the essential musical rituals, past and present, I naturally found myself analyzing performance as well.

I attended a diverse array of musical performances (about one hundred formal performances and hundreds of informal musical events), taking notes, talking to fellow spectators and musicians, and on a few occasions conducting formal interviews. Whenever possible, I purchased recordings of the events. This was possible for a great many performances. As a result, I decided not to make field recordings. In most instances, field recording would have been redundant, unethical, illegal, and/or inappropriate. Instead, I purchased concert or studio recordings directly from the performers or, in the case of popular ensembles, bought them in the local record stores.

Whereas my earlier ethnographic project involved hundreds of formal taped interviews (Pedelty 1995), I decided that formal interviews would be counterproductive for this research. I instead used my time to view as many different performances as possible and talked to fellow audience members as the occasion arose, in a more natural fashion. Only a few formal interviews were conducted and are cited as such in the text.

I hope that I have not overstated the connections among various cultural scenes I encountered in the ethnographic research. Urban anthropology involves a profound paradox. The anthropologist is asked to produce a holistic understanding of culture, one that demonstrates the ways in which culture is connected to and manifested in "the imponderabilia of actual life" (Malinowski 1922:24). Such integral visions of culture come out of village studies, however, not urban anthropology. It is impossible to develop such a complete picture of a modern metropolis. To present an accurate and holistic view of the heterogeneous world of the city, one must provide a profound sense of the diversity and variance present in a large metropolitan center rather than act as if all these disparate worlds and subcultures are seamlessly connected into a communal whole. Therefore, adequately representing a cosmopolitan city like Mexico City requires that one not overstate continuities from subculture to subculture and connections between them. Instead, it is important to emphasize the incredible discontinuities, multiplicity, fluidity, diversity, and dynamism that make up the urban cultural landscape.

The two types of analysis, historical and ethnographic, are intended to complement each other in this regard, rather than one dominating the other. Individuals within a social collective act in varied and often unpredictable ways (as represented in the ethnographic chapters) even though as a mass and over time they will produce fairly predictable and discernible patterns (as is clear in the historical chapters).

The historical component of the research was based on secondary texts, by necessity and design. It would be impossible to cover the range of periods represented here with archival research, even if one had twenty or thirty years to complete such a project. Such work would certainly not leave time for ethnographic efforts. Furthermore, that exercise would be redundant, given the concerted efforts of the many historians cited here, historical researchers who have studied specific Mexican eras through the analysis of primary historical texts. Therefore, the historical component of this project represents a synthesis of the work of numerous music historians, musicologists, ethnomusicologists, archaeomusicologists, and anthropologists whose work has focused on specific periods in Mexico's musical history. I am indebted to their efforts.

Finally, I attempted to complement the ethnographic research and historical synthesis with textual and intertextual analyses. Intertextual analysis involves studying the relationship between various texts and social contexts. For example, such analysis was conducted on the song, film, and play versions of *Aventurera* in Chapters 10 and 11 in order to understand the relationship of music, film, and cultural life during the postrevolutionary era and the present.

The term "intertextual" was first used by literary critic Julia Kristeva (1969), who applied the concept to the work of Mikhail Bakhtin. While most intertextual studies have examined the relationship between a given text and its antecedents (Cancalon, Spacagna, et al. 1994), other authors have expanded the meaning of intertextuality to include textual representations of historical events and figures. An example of the latter is Kirsten Nigro's intertextual analysis of Fuentes' *Orquídeas a la luz de la luna* (Orchids in the Moonlight) (Fuentes 1986; Nigro 1989). Some people working with intertextual methodology have examined the ways in which contemporary texts represent, reproduce, and recode past texts (Worton and Still 1990), while others add the element of "real" human interaction with fictional texts. Examples of the latter range from studies of international relations as intertextual encounters (Der Derian and Shapiro 1989) to an examination of tabloid-driven conversations in the supermarket checkout line (Bird 1987).

Marsha Kinder's work with Saturday morning television is another example of society-and-text interaction research. Kinder has carefully examined textual transfers between film and television and the consumption practices of child viewers (1991: 39–86). She demonstrates very effectively how children become part of a larger mediated text of consumption. Intertextual analysis allows us to study the cultural matrices linking textual artifacts (phonograms, films, photographs), rituals (danzón, courtship, concerts), social settings (cabaret, Salón México, taxicab), plot narratives (romantic betrayal, peso devaluations), and the most essential anthropological element, people (Agustín Lara, María Félix, Aaron Copland, contemporary audiences). We all inhabit such intertextual worlds to some degree. While it is wise to keep in mind the distinction between fictional and factual elements of intertextual cultures, it is also important to recognize their nearly seamless integration. People draw from fictional texts to give new meanings to their lives, and "real life" greatly informs the production of fiction.

Yet, by definition, ritual acts are often accorded a truth-value far exceeding that of daily life. Ritual is a fictional reality, a "real" practice designed to provide sensual verification to cultural narratives, essentially making fact of fiction. The Christian church service, for example, places parishioners within its fantastical narrative through bodily disciplines patterned according to stories. From entering the sacred space to eating the flesh of God, the body politics of the rite function to embed cultural narratives into sensory experience. Therefore, any research into ritual experience must go beyond objectivism and reductionism. Here I have documented what I have seen, heard, and felt and have tried my best to understand how others experience it as well, but by no means do I contend that what I present here is *the* truth. It is *a* truth, subjective, specific, and, as with all truths, incomplete.

REFLEXIVE ANTHROPOLOGY

It is always important for a social researcher to clearly communicate how his or her beliefs and identities have influenced a project. Anthropologists refer to this as "reflexive research." I am an anthropologist and thus have a strong interest in cultural life, particularly in reference to questions of ritual, performance, power, and identity. As a U.S. anthropologist, I do not claim to have captured the essential soul of *México profundo*. Ultimately, no matter how much I have studied in and about Mexico, I remain a tourist. As an anthropologist, I am no better than any other "foreigner or intellectual" described by Jesús Flores y Escalante lurking awkwardly around the dance salon, hoping to experience the scene "in the flesh" (1993). As an anthropologist I attempt to gain a sense of the cultural insider's perspective on these questions through ethnographic methodology. However, what I present is inevitably colored, dominated really, by my own perspective as a cultural interloper.

I hope that, despite my deficits as a gringo anthropologist, I am still qualified to undertake the task of writing a book about musical ritual in Mexico City. That does not explain why I would actually want to write such a book. There are two basic reasons: professional and personal. The professional reason is that such a book is long overdue. Robert Stevenson was the first author to write an entire book in English solely devoted to the history of Mexican music (1952). Relatively few have been written since then. Furthermore, most studies have been dedicated to a very specific musical style rather than providing an analytical overview.

My personal motivations are also easy to explain. Like the people I met, interviewed, and befriended during my research in Mexico, I absolutely love Mexican music. My passion for it started developing in 1990, when I conducted ethnographic fieldwork in Central America. That fieldwork involved the study of war and journalism. Music, particularly Mexican popular music, became my pleasurable and privileged retreat. I made several extended trips to Mexico as part of that project, conducting interviews and surveys of the local press corps during the day, going to concerts, piano bars, and other musical venues at night. That pleasurable retreat eventually turned into this research project and this book.

As for my audience, I can only imagine who is reading this. Yet an author needs to create such an image in order to write a comprehensible text. Therefore, as I wrote this I imagined fellow scholars interested in Mexican music and cultural history, undergraduate students, and others interested in Mexico. By studying Mexico, we learn more about our neighbors and thus more about ourselves. In other words, the study of Mexico is a matter of critical, intercultural, and intersubjective exploration.

This book aims to fulfill the mission completed by other cultural histories, such as Jeffrey Pilcher's *Que Vivan los Tamales: Food and the Making of Mexican Identity* (1998) and Julia Tuñón Pablos' *Women in Mexico: A Past Unveiled* (1999), works that trace the development of a specific cultural issue over time. Such books have been of great use to me as an interdisciplinary scholar working in Mexico as well as to my students. I hope this book will fulfill a similar purpose for those interested in Mexican music and ritual.

I recognize that, at least in the initial printing of this book, I will mainly reach a U.S. readership. Therefore, I have placed intercultural questions in the foreground. However, I have attempted to avoid representing Mexico as the exotic "Other." It is all too easy to turn cultural modalities into cultural stereotypes. Likewise, I have tried not to fall into the opposite trap, that of denying cross-cultural difference altogether. Although nomothetic or at least transnational structures are embedded in much of Mexico's ritual life, a great deal of it is also unique to Mexico.

There are a number of potential dangers in any act of ethnographic writing, particularly when the writer is a citizen of the most powerful nation in the world, a country with a very spotty record as a continental neighbor. As a citizen of the nation that stole half of Mexican territory (and that continues to dominate Mexico through "free trade" policies), I cannot escape such contradictions and conundrums. I can only work within and through them. Therefore, I have tried to remain critical in reference to the dangers of intercultural research, while remaining open to the potential opportunities it offers us to invent something better than the present. Ethnography always takes place in the liminal space between cultures, the place where ethnographer and informant meet. Rather than deny that place, this book is all about it. After all, it is in that liminal borderland between territories, eras, classes, identities, and nations that culture is most clearly revealed.

The border is not only a revelatory space but also a creative space. Most of the musical and ritual performances described in this work were forged in geographic and metaphorical borderlands, the place where Aztec sacrifice encountered the Catholic Mass, where Mexican musicians encountered German polka, and where Frank Sinatra met Agustín Lara. When assessing my early work on Lara's life, anthropologist John Kelly advised me to seek out the topic's "gravity field." He suggested that Mexican music and ritual might contain "memories of violence," a cumulative record or at least a faint memory of the costs incurred by the people of Mexico City. It was excellent advice. Indeed, memories of violence are there in the music, sublimated and melancholy in Lara's poetry, vibrating subtly through the strings of Blas Galindo's "Poema de Pablo Neruda," proudly screaming out of Alex Lora's microphone, and pounding slowly and patiently out of a battered huehuetl each night at the edge of the zócalo.

Appendix 2. Timeline

MEXICA

1325	Founding of the island city of the Mexica, Tenochtitlán
1427–1440	Itzcóatl extends Mexica influence, connects Tenochtitlán to the mainland with three causeways
1428	Triple Alliance formed: Mexica, Texcoco, and Tlacopan
1440–1469	Moctezuma I greatly expands the empire, particularly to the south and east
1469–1481	Axayácatl expands the alliance's influence to the west and northeast
1486–1502	Ahuitzotl pushes Aztec influence farther south, into the Isthmus of Tehuantepec
1502–1519	Moctezuma II attempts to consolidate power in the south: Tarascans remain unconquered, Tlaxcalans and others continue to maintain various levels of resistance to the alliance

NEW SPAIN

1519–1521	Hernán Cortés, leading 550 men, conquers the Mexica
1523	First Franciscans arrive
1529	Juan de Zumárraga becomes the first bishop and archbishop of New Spain
1531	La Virgen de Guadalupe appears to Juan Diego at Tepeyac
1535	Don Antonio de Mendoza becomes first viceroy of New Spain
1565	Acapulco–Manila trade route established

	1566	Conspiracy against the Crown involving Martín Cortés is discovered and thwarted
	1572	First Jesuits arrive
	1651–1695	Life of Sor Juana Inés de la Cruz, poet, scientist, and philosopher
	1692	Famine and riots in Mexico City
	1767	Jesuits expelled from Mexico
	1780	Founding of Art Academy of San Carlos
	1784–1787	Widespread famine and pneumonia epidemic
	1810–1821	Revolution of Independence led by Miguel Hidalgo and José Morelos y Pavón

NEW NATION

1822–1823	Agustín de Iturbide rules as emperor
1824	Mexican Republic established
1833	General López de Santa Anna becomes president for first time
1836	Texas War and secession
1838	"Pastry War" with France
1846–1848	U.S.–Mexico War
1855	Liberal reform era led by Benito Juárez
1863–1867	French occupation
1867	Juárez reestablishes the republic
1876	Santa Anna dies, after serving as president eleven times
1876–1911	Dictatorship of Porfirio Díaz
1910–1911	Francisco Madero leads revolution to overthrow Díaz
1913	Victoriano Huerta leads coup against Madero and establishes dictatorship, supported by U.S. ambassador Henry Lane Wilson
1914	Huerta resigns, having been defeated by the efforts of Emiliano Zapata in the South and the Constitutionalist forces led by "First Chief" Venustiano Carranza and Generals Francisco Villa and Alvaro Obregón in the North; Carranza becomes president, supported by Obregón; Villa and Zapata lead a rebellion against Carranza
1915	Obregón defeats Villa at Celaya; United States officially recognizes Carranza
1916	Villa attacks Columbus, New Mexico; President Woodrow Wilson sends General "Black Jack" Pershing on a "Punitive Expedition" to get Villa, which fails
1917	Carranza swears an oath to Mexico's new constitution and is elected president
1919	Zapata assassinated by Carranza agents; Obregón declares candidacy for presidential elections of 1920

1920	Carranza attempts to install replacement; Obregón leads successful resistance; Carranza flees en route to Veracruz and is killed in escape; Obregón becomes president, the first in an eighty-one-year succession of presidents belonging to what would become the Partido Revolucionario Institucional (PRI); Villa agrees to lay down arms
1923	Villa assassinated

POSTREVOLUTIONARY MEXICO

1923–1924	Adolfo de la Huerta leads failed rebellion against Obregón
1924	Plutarco Calles becomes president
1926–1929	Cristero Rebellion led by Catholics upset by Calles' attempts to limit church influence
1934–1940	Presidency of Lázaro Cárdenas; nationalization of the oil industry
1940–1968	The "Mexican Miracle": period of relatively strong economic growth

CONTEMPORARY MEXICO

1968	Tlatelolco massacre: hundreds of protesting students killed by police and military
1976	Devaluation of the peso; economic crisis
1978–1982	Oil boom and staggering economic growth
1982	Oil bust; corruption and spending lead to debt crisis; President José López Portillo, in desperate move, nationalizes banks
1988	Carlos Salinas de Gortari elected president in election widely believed to have been stolen from Cuauhtémoc Cárdenas of the Partido de la Revolución Democrática (PRD)
1994	North American Free Trade Agreement (NAFTA) goes into effect; Zapatista National Liberation Army (EZLN) uprising begins in Chiapas
1997	Cuauhtemóc Cárdenas becomes mayor of Mexico City
2001	Vicente Fox of the Partido Acción Nacional (PAN) becomes president, ending the eighty-one-year reign of the PRI and its institutional predecessors

Appendix 3. Discography

Note: The following discography is not intended to be an exhaustive listing but rather a small selection of recordings related to the musical styles, pieces, and performances discussed in the text. They are listed by style and era. For example, most corrido compilations, even if contemporary, are placed in the "Revolution" section, as discussed in the text. The only exceptions are those artists and albums that cross style boundaries. All are available in CD form.

CHAPTERS 2–3. MEXICA

TEMAZCAL
1999 *Ritual Ceremonies of the Aztecs.* Obertrubach, Germany: Mariposa.

TRIBU
1990 *Mazeual: El hombre de este sol.* Mexico City: CADEMAC.

CHAPTERS 4–5. NEW SPAIN

CORO DE LA CATEDRAL DE MÉXICO
1993a *Música sacra de la colonia.* Guillermo López Nava, director. Clásicos Mexicanos. Mexico City: Spartacus Discos.
1993b *Villancicos de la colonia.* Guillermo López Nava, director. Clásicos Mexicanos. Mexico City: Spartacus Discos.

DÚO VILLEY-HINOJOSA
2000 *Miró Celia una rosa: Canciones profanas del México barroco.* Madrid: Plectrum.

NESH-KALA
1995 *La música prohibida por la Inquisición.* Mexico City: Radio Educación.

CHAPTERS 6–7. THE NINETEENTH CENTURY

CUARTETO LATINOAMERICANO
2001   *Valses mexicanos 1900.* Troy, N.Y.: Dorian.

FUENTE, HERRERA DE LA
2000   *Mexico clásico.* Mexico City: Prodisc.

HIMNO NACIONAL MEXICANO
1994   *Himno nacional mexicano.* Baruj Lieberman, Eduardo Llerenas, Enrique Ramírez de Arellano. Mexico City: Orfeón.
1994   *Antología del son de México/Anthology of Mexican Sones.* Mexico City: CORASON.

ZUK, EVA MARÍA
1998   *Composiciones de Ricardo Castro.* Mexico City: FONCA, Clásicos Mexicanos, distributed by Prodisc.

CHAPTERS 8–9. REVOLUTIONARY CORRIDOS

CHÁVEZ, OSCAR
1995   *Parodias neo-liberales.* Volumes 1 and 2. Mexico City: IM.

HERNÁNDEZ, GUILLERMO E.
1996   *The Mexican Revolution: Corridos.* El Cerrito, Calif.: Arhoolie.

LÓPEZ TARSO, IGNACIO
1995   *Leyendas.* Mexico City: Sony.

CHAPTERS 10–11. TWENTIETH-CENTURY BOLERO AND DANZÓN

ACERINA Y SU DANZONERA
1995   *Acerina y Su Danzonera.* Mexico City: Orfeón.

CAPO, BOBBY
1995   *Espérame en el cielo.* New York: BMG.

CÁRDENAS, GUTY
1993   *El ruiseñor yucateco.* Mexico City: Discos CORASON.

LANDÍN, MARÍA LUISA
1999   *Epoca de oro.* New York: BMG.

LARA, AGUSTÍN
1997   *20 éxitos.* Serie Platino. New York: BMG.

LEÓN, EUGENIA
1989   *Ven aca.* Mexico City: Polygram.
1996a   *Oh noche.* Songs by Liliana Felipe. Mexico City: El Hábito.
1996b   *Tirana.* Mexico City: Columbia.
2000   *Acércate más.* Mexico City: Universal.

LEÓN, EUGENIA, WITH DANZONERA DIMAS
1995   *Que devuelvan.* Songs by Liliana Felipe. Mexico City: El Hábito.

LIBERTAD, TANIA
1989   Mucho corazón. Mexico City: Sony.
MIGUEL, LUIS
1997   Romances. Miami: WEA Latina.
2001   Mis romances. Miami: WEA Latina.
NEGRA, TOÑA LA
1995   20 éxitos. New York: BMG.
SOLÍS, JAVIER
1995   Boleros del alma. Miami: Sony.
LOS TRÍO
1999a   Mi gloria, eres tú. New York: BMG.
1999b   Nuestro amor. New York: BMG.
VARGAS, CHAVELA
1995   Boleros. Mexico City: Orfeón.
VARIOUS ARTISTS
1996   Historia musical de los grandes tríos. Mexico City: Orfeón.

CHAPTERS 12–13. TWENTIETH-CENTURY CLASSICAL

CHEN, HSUAN-YA
1999   The Piano Works of Carlos Chávez. Riverdale, Md.: Elan.
FRENK, MARÍA TERESA
1997   El siglo XX en México: Antología pianística (1900–1950). Mexico City: FONCA, UNAM.
ORQUESTA FILARMÓNICA DE LA CIUDAD DE MÉXICO
1993   Música mexicana. Volumes 1–8. London: AVS.
ORQUESTA SINFÓNICA NACIONAL DE MÉXICO
1997   Revueltas: La coronela. Mexico City: Spartacus.

CHAPTERS 14–15. TWENTIETH-CENTURY MARIACHI AND RANCHERA

BELTRÁN, LOLA
1994   20 éxitos. Serie Platino. New York: BMG.
Fernández, Vicente
2000   Historia de un ídolo. Volume 1. Mexico City: Sony.
INFANTE, PEDRO
2000   Rancheras del siglo. Mexico City: Orfeón.
JIMÉNEZ, JOSÉ ALFREDO
2001   Los 100 clásicas. Volumes 1–2. New York: BMG.
MARIACHI VARGAS DE TECALITLÁN
1997   Mi historia. New York: Polygram.

NEGRETE, JORGE
1996   20 éxitos. Serie Platino. New York: BMG.

ROJAS, NYDIA
1999   Si me conocieras. Hollywood: UNI.

CHAPTER 16. POPULAR MUSIC TODAY

Contemporary Tropical

CONTROL
2001   Fuera de control. Mexico City: EMI.

PARAÍSO TROPICAL DE DURANGO
1999   Pa'la pachanga. Mexico City: Sony.

Contemporary Norteño and Banda

BANDA MAGUEY
2001   Canciones de mi pueblo. New York: BMG.

BÁRBARA, ANA
1998   Hacia el milenio con 21 éxitos. Van Nuys, Calif.: FONOVISA.

BELTRÁN, GRACIELA
1994   Tesoro. Hollywood: Capitol.

LOS HURACANES DEL NORTE
1999   Norteño 2000. Van Nuys, Calif.: FONOVISA.

PRISCILA Y SUS BALAS DE PLATA
1999   Todo por ti. Van Nuys, Calif.: FONOVISA.

LOS TEMERARIOS
1996   Camino del amor. Van Nuys, Calif.: FONOVISA.

Contemporary Art and Avant-garde

HADAD, ASTRID
1995   Corazón sangrante. Mexico City: Cabaret.

LEÑERO, CARMEN
1997   Almuerzo en la hierba. Mexico City: Producciones Carmen Leñero.

LIBERTAD, TANIA
1995   Amar amando. Mexico City: Circo.

VARIOUS ARTISTS
1999   Mexican Divas. Rohnert Park, Calif.: Candela.

Contemporary Rock

AMORES PERROS
2000   Amores Perros Soundtrack. Mexico City: SURCO Records.

AURORA Y LA ACADEMIA
1997 *Aurora y La Academia.* New York: Polygram.
CAFÉ TACUBA
1994 *Re.* Mexico City: Warner.
1996 *Avalancha de éxitos.* Mexico City: Warner.
GUERRA, ELI
2002 *Lotofire.* Malibu, Calif.: Higher Octave.
TIJUANA NO
1993 *No.* New York: BMG.
EL TRI
1993 *El Tri 25.* Burbank, Calif.: Warner.
1996 *Hoyos en la bolsa.* Mexico City: Warner.
VARIOUS ARTISTS
1996 *Alternativo-Culebra.* New York: BMG.
1997 *Juntos por Chiapas.* Mexico City: Serpiente Sobre Ruedas.
VENEGAS, JULIETA
1997 *Aquí.* Mexico City: BMG.

Contemporary Pop

GABRIEL, ANA
1991 *México.* Miami: Sony.
1994 *Ayer y hoy.* Miami: Sony.
1995 *Joyas de dos siglos.* Miami: Sony.
1997 *Con un mismo corazón.* Miami: Sony.
1998 *En la Plaza de Toros, México.* Miami: Sony.
LUCERO
1997 *Piel de ángel.* Miami: Universal.
2001 *Solo pienso en ti.* Van Nuys, Calif.: FONOVISA.
MÁRQUEZ, EDITH
2000 *Caricias del cielo.* Mexico City: Warner.
ROMO, DANIELA
1997 *Daniela Romo . . . 97.* Mexico City: Melody.
RUBIO, PAULINA
2000 *Paulina.* Mexico City: Universal Music Mexico.
THALIA
1997 *Amor a la mexicana.* Mexico City: EMI.
TREVI, GLORIA TREVI
1991 *Tu ángel de la guarda.* New York: BMG.
1992 *Me siento tan sola.* New York: BMG.
VARIOUS ARTISTS
1999 *Sexo, pudor y lágrimas.* Mexico City: EMI.

Bibliography

Agrasánchez, Rogelio, Jr. 2001. *Cine Mexicano: Posters from the Golden Age, 1936–1956.* San Francisco: Chronicle.
Aharonián, Coriún. 1994. Factores de identidad musical latinoamericana tras cinco siglos de conquista, dominación y mestizaje. *Latin American Music Review* 15 (2): 189–225.
Alcaraz, José Antonio. 1996. *Carlos Chávez: Un constante renacer.* Mexico City: Instituto Nacional de Bellas Artes.
Anderson, Benedict R. 1991. *Imagined Communities: Reflections on the Origin and Spread of Nationalism.* New York: Verso.
Appadurai, Arjun. 1996. *Modernity at Large: Cultural Dimensions of Globalization.* Minneapolis: University of Minnesota Press.
Aura, Alejandro. 1990. *La hora íntima de Agustín Lara.* Mexico City: Cal y Arena.
Azuela, Mariano. 1996. *Los de abajo/The Underdogs.* New York: Signet Classic.
Baldwin, Kate. 1995. Montezuma's Revenge: Reading *Los Ricos También Lloran* in Russia. In *To Be Continued: Soap Operas around the World,* edited by R. C. Allen, 285–300. New York: Routledge.
Bantjes, Adrian A. 1994. Burning Saints, Molding Minds: Iconoclasm, Civic Ritual, and the Failed Cultural Revolution. In *Rituals of Rule, Rituals of Resistance: Public Celebrations and Popular Culture in Mexico,* edited by W. H. Beezley, C. English Martin, and W. E. French, 261–284. Wilmington, Del.: Scholarly Resources.
Barwick, Steven. 1994. Mexico. In *The Early Baroque Era: From the Late Sixteenth Century to the 1660s,* 349–360. Englewood Cliffs, N.J.: Prentice-Hall.
Beezley, William H. 1987. *Judas at the Jockey Club and Other Episodes of Porfirian Mexico.* Lincoln: University of Nebraska Press.
Behague, Gerard. 1979. *Music in Latin America: An Introduction.* Englewood Cliffs, N.J.: Prentice-Hall.
———. 1986. Popular Music in Latin America. *Studies in Latin American Popular Culture* 5: 41–68.

Bierhorst, John. 1985. *Cantares Mexicanos: Songs of the Aztecs.* Stanford, Calif.: Stanford University Press.

Bird, Elizabeth. 1987. Media and Folklore as Intertextual Communication Processes: John F. Kennedy and the Supermarket Tabloids. *Communication Yearbook* 10: 758–772.

Bliss, Katherine. 1999. The Science of Redemption: Syphilis, Sexual Promiscuity, and Reformism in Revolutionary Mexico City. *Hispanic American Historical Review* 79 (1): 1–40.

Bonfil Batalla, Guillermo. 1996. *México Profundo: Reclaiming a Civilization.* Translated by P. A. Dennis. Austin: University of Texas Press.

Britton, John A. 1995. *Revolution and Ideology: Images of the Mexican Revolution in the United States.* Lexington: University of Kentucky.

Broda, Johanna. 1987. Templo Mayor as Ritual Space. In *The Great Temple of Tenochtitlán: Center and Periphery in the Aztec World,* edited by J. Broda, D. Carrasco, and E. M. Moctezuma, 61–123. Berkeley: University of California Press.

Broda, Johanna, David Carrasco, and Eduardo Matos Moctezuma. 1987. *The Great Temple of Tenochtitlán: Center and Periphery in the Aztec World.* Berkeley: University of California Press.

Bruschetta, Angelina. 1993. Yo lo vi nacer al amor y a la fama. In *Todo lo que quería saber sobre Agustín Lara,* edited by G. Mendizábal and E. Mejía, 43–54. Mexico City: Editorial Contenido.

Burnett, Robert. 1996. *The Global Jukebox: The International Music Industry.* New York: Routledge.

Burr, Ramiro. 1992. Mariachi! Mexico's Romantic Tradition. *Sing Out! The Folk Song Magazine* 37 (1): 28–34.

Butzer, Karl W. 1991. Spanish Colonization of the New World. *Erkunde* 45 (3): 205–219.

Cabello Moreno, Antonio. 1975. *Panorama musical de la Ciudad de México.* Mexico City: DDF.

Cancalon, Elaine D., Antoine Spacagna, and Florida State University. 1994. *Intertextuality in Literature and Film: Selected Papers from the Thirteenth Annual Florida State University Conference on Literature and Film.* Gainesville: University Press of Florida.

Cardon, Hugh. 1991. Twentieth-Century Mexican Art Songs. *NATS Journal* 47 (3): 15–20.

Carmack, Robert M., Janine Gasco, and Gary H. Gossen, eds. 1996. *The Legacy of Mesoamerica: History and Culture of a Native American Civilization.* Upper Saddle River, N.J.: Prentice Hall.

Carmona, Gloria. 1984. *La música de México: Período de la Independencia a la Revolución.* Vol. 3 of *La música de México.* Edited by J. Estrada. Mexico City: UNAM.

Carrasco, David. 1987. Myth, Cosmic Terror, and the Templo Mayor. In *The Great Temple of Tenochtitlán: Center and Periphery in the Aztec World,* edited by J. Broda, D. Carrasco, and E. M. Moctezuma, 124–162. Berkeley: University of California Press.

Carrasco, Pedro. 1994. La sociedad mexicana antes de la conquista. In *Historia general de México,* 165–288. Mexico City: El Colegio de México.

Carredano, Consuelo. 1992. *Felipe Villanueva.* Mexico City: CENDIM.

Castellanos, Pablo. 1970. *Horizontes de la música precortesiana.* Mexico City: Fondo de Cultura Económica.

Catalyne, Alice R. 1976. Manuel de Zumaya (ca. 1678–1756): Mexican Composer for Church and Theater. In *Festival Essays for Pauline Alderman: A Musicological Tribute*, edited by B. L. Karson, 101–123. Provo, Utah: Brigham Young University Press.

Chamorro, Arturo. 1982. Chirimías: Sondeo histórico de un modelo islámico en América Hispana. *Latin American Music Review* 3 (2): 165–187.

Claro, Samuel. 1970. La música virreinal en el nuevo mundo. *Revista Musical Chilena* 109/110: 7–31.

Cockcroft, James. 1990. *Mexico: Class Formation, Capital Accumulation, and the State*. New York: Monthly Review Press.

Cornyn, John Hubert, ed. 1931. *The Song of Quetzalcóatl*. Yellow Springs, Ohio: Antioch Press.

Curcio-Nagy, Linda A. 1994. Giants and Gypsies: Corpus Christi in Colonial Mexico City. In *Rituals of Rule, Rituals of Resistance: Public Celebrations and Popular Culture in Mexico*, edited by W. H. Beezley, C. English Martin, and W. E. French, 1–26. Wilmington, Del.: Scholarly Resources.

Davis, Diane E. 1994. *Urban Leviathan: Mexico City in the Twentieth Century*. Philadelphia: Temple University Press.

Davison, Phil. 1996. Mexico's Battling Peasants Keep Spirit of Zapata Alive. *Independent*, April 16 (Tuesday), 11.

De la Peza, Carmen. 2001. *El bolero y la educación sentimental en México*. Mexico City: Porrúa.

De María y Campos, Armando. 1962a. *La Revolución Mexicana a través de los corridos populares*. Vol. 1. Mexico City: Biblioteca del Instituto Nacional de Estudios Históricos de la Revolución Mexicana.

———. 1962b. *La Revolución Mexicana a través de los corridos populares*. Vol. 2. Mexico City: Biblioteca del Instituto Nacional de Estudios Históricos de la Revolución Mexicana.

Der Derian, James, and Michael Shapiro. 1989. *International/Intertextual Relations: Postmodern Readings of World Politics*. Lexington, Mass.: Lexington Books.

Diamond, Jared. 1997. *Guns, Germs, and Steel*. New York: Norton.

Díaz Castellanos, Guadalupe. 1996. El goce de ser Eugenia León. *Fem* 20: 13–15.

Díaz del Castillo, Bernal. 1956. *The Discovery and Conquest of Mexico*. New York: Farrar, Straus, and Cudahy.

Díaz Roig, Mercedes. 1987. The Traditional Romancero in Mexico: Panorama. *Oral Tradition* 2 (2–3): 616–632.

Doty, William G. 1986. *Mythography: The Study of Myths and Rituals*. Tuscaloosa: University of Alabama Press.

Dryden, John. 1667. *The Indian Emperour, or the Conquest of Mexico by the Spaniards*. London: H. Herringman.

Dueñas, Pablo. 1993. *Bolero: Historia documental del bolero mexicano*. Mexico City: Asociación Mexicana de Estudios Fonográficos (AMEF).

Dultzin Dubin, Susana, and José Antonio Nava Gómez Tagle. 1984. La música en el panorama histórico de Mesoamérica. In *La música de México: Período prehispánico*, edited by J. Estrada, 17–34. Mexico City: UNAM.

Durán, Thelma G., and Fernando Barrios. 1995. *El grito del rock mexicano*. Mexico City: Ediciones del Milenio.

Elshtain, Jean Bethke. 1989. Cultural Conundrums and Gender: America's Present

Past. In *Cultural Politics in Contemporary America*, edited by I. H. Angus and S. Jhally, 123–134. New York: Routledge.

Engelman, Ralph. 1996. *Public Radio and Television in America: A Political History*. Thousand Oaks, Calif.: Sage.

Escorza, Juan José. 1987. La música en la conquista espiritual de México. *Pauta* 22: 55–59.

———. 1990. Apuntes sobre el jarabe mexicano. In *Jarabes y fandanguitos: Imagen y música del baile popular*, 6–23. Mexico City: Museo Nacional de Arte.

Esparza, María José, and Mirella Lluhi. 1990. El jarabe: La representación plástica del baile popular. In *Jarabes y fandanguitos: Imagen y música del baile popular*, 24–31. Mexico City: Museo Nacional de Arte.

Esposito, Matthew D. 2000. Death and Disorder in Mexico City: The State Funeral of Manuel Romero Rubio. In *Latin American Popular Culture: An Introduction*, edited by W. H. Beezley and L. A. Curcio-Nagy, 87–103. Wilmington, Del.: Scholarly Resources.

Estrada, Jesús. 1973. *Música y músicos de la época virreinal*. Mexico City: Secretaría de Educación Pública.

Farnsworth, Paul, and Robert H. Jackson. 1995. Cultural, Demographic, and Economic Change in the Missions of Alta California. In *The New Latin American Mission History*, edited by E. Langer and R. H. Jackson, 109–129. Lincoln: University of Nebraska.

Fernández Tejedo, Isabel, and Carmen Nava Nava. 2001. Images of Independence in the Nineteenth Century: The Grito de Dolores, History and Myth. In *Viva México! Viva la Independencia!: Celebrations of September 16*, edited by W. H. Beezley and D. E. Lorey, 1–41. Wilmington, Del.: Scholarly Resources.

Fesperman, John. 1984. The Mexican Legacy of Organs. *Musical Times, Great Britain* 125 (February): 107–109.

Figueroa Hernández, Rafael. 1996. *Salsa mexicana: Transculturación e identidad*. Xalapa, Veracruz: ConClave.

Flores, Chava. 1994. *Relatos de mi barrio*. Mexico City: Ageleste.

Flores, Richard R. 1992. The Corrido and the Emergence of Texas-Mexican Social Identity. *Journal of American Folklore* 105 (416): 166–182.

Flores y Escalante, Jesús. 1993. *Salón México: Historia documental y gráfica del danzón en México*. Mexico City: Asociación Mexicana de Estudios Fonográficos.

Foppa, Alaíde. 1993. Mujer divina. In *Todo lo que quería saber sobre Agustín Lara*, edited by G. Mendizábal and E. Mejía, 121–139. Mexico City: Editorial Contenido.

Foucault, Michel, and Paul Rabinow. 1984. *The Foucault Reader*. New York: Pantheon Books.

Fox, Elizabeth. 1997. *Latin American Broadcasting: From Tango to Telenovela*. Luton: University of Luton.

Fuentes, Carlos. 1986. Orchids in the Moonlight. In *Latin America: Plays*, edited by G. W. Woodyard and M. P. Holt, 143–186. New York: PAJ.

Gaitán Cruz, Ernestina. 1988. Las mujeres en el "rock." *Fem* 12 (70): 38–39.

García, Gustavo, and Rafael Aviña. 1997. *Época de oro del cine mexicano*. Mexico City: Clio.

García Ayluardo, Clara. 1994. A World of Images: Cult, Ritual, and Society in Colonial Mexico City. In *Rituals of Rule, Rituals of Resistance: Public Celebrations and Popular Culture in Mexico*, edited by William H. Beezley, C. English Martin, and William E. French, 77–93. Wilmington, Del.: SR Books.

García Canclini, Néstor. 1993. *Transforming Modernity: Popular Culture in Mexico.* Translated by Lidia Lozano. Austin: University of Texas Press.
———. 1995. *Hybrid Cultures: Strategies for Entering and Leaving Modernity.* Translated by Christopher L. Chiappari and Silvia L. Lopez. Minneapolis: University of Minnesota Press.
Garfias, Robert. 1983. The Marimba of Mexico and Central America. *Latin American Music Review* 4 (2): 203–228.
Garza de Koniecki, Ma. del Carmen. 1992. Los corridos del maldición. In *Estudios de folklore y literatura dedicados a Mercedes Díaz Roig*, edited by Garza Cuarón and Y. Jiménez de Báez, 591–640. Mexico City: El Colegio de México.
Gasca, Yolanda. 1993. Mi vida con un genio. In *Todo lo que quería saber sobre Agustín Lara*, edited by G. Mendizábal and E. Mejía, 31–41. Mexico City: Editorial Contenido.
Geijerstam, Claes af. 1976. *Popular Music in Mexico.* Albuquerque: University of New Mexico.
Gelpí, Juan. 1998. El bolero en la Ciudad de México. *Cuadernos de Literatura* 4 (7–8): 197–211.
Gil, Carlos B. 1992. Lydia Mendoza: Houstonian and First Lady of Mexican American Song. In *Chicano Border: Culture and Folklore*, edited by José Villarino and Arturo Ramírez, 181–193. San Diego: Marin.
Gómez-Peña, Guillermo. 1996. *The New World Border: Prophecies, Poems, and Loqueras for the End of the Century.* San Francisco: City Lights.
González Cruz Manjarrez, Maricela. 1996. *La polémica Siqueiros-Rivera: Planteamientos estético-políticos 1934–1935.* Mexico City: Museo Dolores Olmedo Patiño.
Gordillo, Mercedes. 1995. *Luna que se quiebra.* Managua: Nueva Nicaragua.
Gradante, William. 1982. "El Hijo del Pueblo": José Alfredo Jiménez and the Mexican Canción Ranchera. *Latin American Music Review* 3 (1): 36–59.
Guillermoprieto, Alma. 1994. *The Heart That Bleeds: Latin America Now.* New York: Knopf.
Gutmann, Matthew. 1996. *The Meanings of Macho: Being a Man in Mexico City.* Berkeley: University of California Press.
Guzmán Bravo, José Antonio. 1984. Glosario de instrumentos prehispánicos. In *La música de México: Período prehispánico*, edited by J. Estrada, 170–220. Mexico City: UNAM.
———. 1978. Mexico, Home of the First Musical Instrument Workshop in America. *Early Music* 6 (3): 350–355.
———. 1986. La música instrumental en el virreinato de la Nueva España. In *La música de México: Período virreinal (1530–1810)*, edited by J. Estrada, 75–145. Mexico City: UNAM.
Guzmán Bravo, José Antonio, and José Antonio Nava Gómez Tagle. 1984a. Calendario ceremonial mexica. In *La música de México: Período prehispánico*, edited by J. Estrada, 113–169. Mexico City: UNAM.
———. 1984b. La música mexica. In *La música de México: Periodo prehispánico*, edited by J. Estrada, 89–112. Mexico City: UNAM.
Harris, Max. 2000. *Aztecs, Moors, and Christians: Festivals of Reconquest in Mexico and Spain.* Austin: University of Texas Press.
Harrison, Frank L. 1988. The Musical Impact of Exploration and Cultural Encounter. In *Musical Repercussions of 1492: Encounters in Text and Performance,*

edited by C. E. Robertson, 171–184. Washington, D.C.: Smithsonian Institution Press.

Heath, Alice. 1987. Los Folkloristas: Preserving a Culture. *Sing Out!* 33 (1): 16–20.

Heller, George. 1979. Fray Pedro de Gante, Pioneer American Music Educator. *Journal of Research in Music Education* 27 (1): 20–28.

Hernández, Antonio Avitia. 1989. *Corridos de Durango*. Mexico City: INAH.

Hernández, Guillermo E. 1986. La punitiva: El corrido norteño y la tradición oral, impresa y fonográfica. *Heterofonía* 19 (3): 46–64.

Herrera-Sobek, María. 1990. *The Mexican Corrido: A Feminist Analysis*. Bloomington: Indiana University Press.

Hess, Carol. 1995. El Salón México: Chávez, Copland, and American Music. *Sonneck Society for American Music* 21 (2): 5–8.

Hinds, Harold E., and Charles M. Tatum. 1992. *Not Just for Children: The Mexican Comic Book in the Late 1960s and 1970s*. Westport, Conn.: Greenwood.

Inés de la Cruz, Sor Juana. 1997. *Poems, Protest, and a Dream*. Translated by M. Sayers Peden. New York: Penguin.

Ivey, Jean Eichelberger. 1966. Mexico's Music. *Inter-American Music Bulletin* 55: 4–10.

Jara Gámez, Simón, Aurelio Rodríguez, and Antonio Zedillo Castillo. 1994. *De Cuba con amor . . . el danzón en México*. Mexico City: Consejo Nacional para la Culturas Populares.

Jáuregui, Jesús. 1990. *El mariachi: Símbolo musical de México*. Mexico City: Banpais.

Jiménez, Armando. 1992. *Cabarets de la Ciudad de México*. Mexico City: UNIcornio.

Jiménez de Báez, Yvette. 1992. Décimas y decimales en México y Puerto Rico: Variedad y tradición. In *Estudios de folklore y literatura dedicados a Mercedes Díaz Roig*, edited by Garza Cuarón and Y. Jiménez de Báez, 467–493. Mexico City: Colegio de México.

Johns, Michael. 1977. *The City of Mexico in the Age of Díaz*. Austin: University of Texas Press.

Johnson, Allen, and Timothy Earle. 1987. *The Evolution of Human Societies: From Foraging Group to Agrarian State*. Stanford, Calif.: Stanford University Press.

Joseph, Gilbert M., and Daniel Nugent. 1994. Popular Culture and State Formation in Revolutionary Mexico. In *Everyday Forms of State Formation: Revolution and the Negotiation of Rule in Modern Mexico*, edited by G. M. Joseph and D. Nugent, 3–23. London: Duke University Press.

Kandell, Jonathan. 1988. *La Capital: The Biography of Mexico City*. New York: Henry Holt.

Kay, June. 1964. *Las siete vidas de Agustín Lara*. Mexico City: El Universal Gráfico.

Kertzer, David I. 1988. *Ritual, Politics, and Power*. New Haven, Conn.: Yale University Press.

Kinder, Marsha. 1991. *Playing with Power in Movies, Television, and Video Games: From Muppet Babies to Teenage Mutant Ninja Turtles*. Berkeley: University of California Press.

Knight, Alan. 1994. Popular Culture and the Revolutionary State in Mexico, 1910–1940. *Hispanic American Historical Review* 74 (3): 394–444.

Koegel, John. 1993. Spanish Mission Music from California: Past, Present and Future Research. *American Music Research Center Journal* 3: 78–111.

Kristeva, Julia. 1969. *Semeiotike: Recherches pour une sémanalyse*. Paris: Editions du Seuil.

Krooth, Richard. 1995. *Mexico, NAFTA, and the Hardships of Progress: Historical Patterns and Shifting Methods of Oppression.* Jefferson, N.C.: McFarland and Company.
Kuss, Malena. 1988. Identity and Change: Nativism in Operas from Argentina, Brazil, and Mexico. In *Musical Repercussions of 1492: Encounters in Text and Performance*, edited by C. E. Robertson, 299–335. Washington, D.C.: Smithsonian Institution Press.
Lafayette Boilès, Charles. 1982. A Paradigmatic Test of Acculturation. In *Cross-cultural Perspectives on Music*, edited by Robert Falck and Timothy Rice, 53–78. Toronto: University of Toronto Press.
Langer, Erick, and Robert H. Jackson, eds. 1995. *The New Latin American Mission History.* Lincoln: University of Nebraska Press.
Leclerc, Jean-Marc. 1966. Misa Tepozteca: Desarrollo de la música litúrgica en Tepoztlán, México. *Sondeos* 16: 1–177.
Lemmon, Alfred E. 1989. New Orleans Popular Sheet Music Imprints: The Latin Tinge Prior to 1900. *Southern Quarterly* 27 (2): 41–57.
Leñero, Vicente. 1999. Don Juan en Chapultepec. In *Dramaturgia terminal: Cuatro obras*, 77–117. Mexico City: Colibrí.
León de Infante, María Luisa. 1961. *Pedro Infante en la intimidad conmigo.* Mexico City: Editorial Comaval.
León-Portilla, Miguel. 1963. *Aztec Thought and Culture: A Study of the Ancient Nahuatl Mind.* Norman: University of Oklahoma Press.
———. 1990. *The Broken Spears: The Aztec Account of the Conquest of Mexico.* Boston: Beacon Press.
Levine, Harold, and Steven Stumpf. 1983. Statements of Fear through Cultural Symbols: Punk Rock as a Reflective Subculture. *Youth and Society* 14 (4): 417–435.
Levine, Lawrence W. 1988. *Highbrow/Lowbrow: The Emergence of Cultural Hierarchy in America.* Cambridge, Mass.: Harvard University Press.
Lewis, George H. 1991. Ghosts, Ragged But Beautiful: Influences of Mexican Music on American Country-Western and Rock 'n' Roll. *Popular Music and Society* 15 (4): 85–103.
———. 1992. La Pistola y El Corazón: Protest and Passion in Mexican-American Popular Music. *Journal of Popular Culture* 26 (1): 51–67.
Llerenas, Eduardo, Enrique Ramírez de Arellano, and Baruj Lieberman. 1993. *Anthology of Mexican Sones.* Mexico City: Música Tradicional.
Lockhart, James. 1991. Care, Ingenuity, and Irresponsibility: The Bierhorst Edition of the *Cantares Mexicanos*. *Reviews in Anthropology* 16 (1–4): 119–132.
Long, Haniel. 1939. *Malinche.* Santa Fe: Writers' Editions.
López, Ana. 1993. Tears and Desire: Women and Melodrama in the "Old" Mexican Cinema. In *Mediating Two Worlds: Cinematic Encounters in the Americas*, edited by J. King, A. López, and M. Alvarado, 147–163. London: BFI.
Maehder, Jürgen. 1992. The Representation of the "Discovery" on the Opera Stage. In *Musical Repercussions of 1492: Encounters in Text and Performance*, edited by C. E. Robertson, 257–298. Washington, D.C.: Smithsonian Institution.
Malinowski, Bronislaw. 1922. *Argonauts of the Western Pacific: An Account of Native Enterprise and Adventure in the Archipelagoes of Melanesian New Guinea.* New York: Routledge.
Malzárraga, Javier Ramos. 1993. El último día feliz de Agustín Lara. In *Todo lo que*

quería saber sobre Agustín Lara, edited G. Mendizábal and E. Mejía, 19–28. Mexico City: Editorial Contenido.
Markman, Robert, and Peter Markman. 1992. *The Flayed God: The Mythology of Mesoamerica*. New York: HarperCollins.
Martín-Barbero, Jesús. 1993. *Communication, Culture, and Hegemony: From Media to Mediations*. Newbury Park, Calif.: Sage.
Marvin, Carolyn, and David W. Ingle. 1996. Blood Sacrifice and the Nation: Revisiting Civil Religion. *Journal of the American Academy of Religion* 64: 767–780.
Matos Moctezuma, Eduardo. 1987. The Templo Mayor of Tenochtitlán: History and Interpretation. In *The Great Temple of Tenochtitlán: Center and Periphery in the Aztec World*, edited by J. Broda, D. Carrasco, and E. M. Moctezuma, 15–60. Berkeley: University of California Press.
———. 1988. *The Great Temple of the Aztecs: Treasures of Tenochtitlán*. London: Thames and Hudson.
McKeever Furst, Jill Leslie. 1995. *The Natural History of the Soul in Ancient Mexico*. New Haven, Conn.: Yale University Press.
Melhuus, Marit, and Kristi Anne Stolen. 1996. *Machos, Mistresses, Madonnas: Contesting the Power of Latin American Gender Imagery*. New York: Verso.
Mendizábal, Guillermo, and Eduardo Mejía, eds. 1993. *Todo lo que quería saber sobre Agustín Lara*. Mexico City: Editorial Contenido.
Mendoza, Vicente T. 1953. La música tradicional española en México. *Nuestra Música* 8 (29): 5–50.
———. 1954. *El corrido mexicano*. Mexico City: Fondo de Cultura Económica.
———. 1997. *El romance español y el corrido mexicano*. Mexico City: UNAM.
Miranda-Pérez, Ricardo. 1990. Muros Verdes and the Creation of a New Musical Space. *Latin American Music Review* 11 (2): 281–285.
Monsiváis, Carlos. 1977. *Amor perdido*. Mexico City: Biblioteca Era.
———. 1993a. Mexican Cinema: Of Myths and Demystifications. In *Mediating Two Worlds: Cinematic Encounters in the Americas*, edited by John King, Ana M. López, and Manuel Alvarado, 139–146. London: British Film Institute.
———. 1993b. Serenata con trío en un cementerio de rockolas. In *Todo lo que quería saber sobre Agustín Lara*, edited by G. Mendizábal and E. Mejía, 113–120. Mexico City: Editorial Contenido.
———. 1995. *Los rituales del caos*. Mexico City: Ediciones Era.
Mora, María Elvira, and Clara Inés Ramírez. 1985. *La música de la colonia a la independencia*. Mexico City: Comisión Nacional para las Celebraciones del 175 Aniversario de la Independencia.
Moreno, Daniel. 1985. *Batallas de la revolución y sus corridos*. Mexico City: Editorial Porrúa.
Moreno Rivas, Yolanda. 1989. *Rostros del nacionalismo en la música mexicana: Un ensayo de interpretación, vida y pensamiento de México*. Mexico City: Fondo de Cultura Económica.
Morgan, Tony. 1994. Proletarians, Politicos, and Patriarchs: The Use and Abuse of Cultural Customs in the Early Industrialization of Mexico City, 1880–1910. In *Rituals of Rule, Rituals of Resistance: Public Celebrations and Popular Culture in Mexico*, edited by W. H. Beezley, C. English Martin, and W. E. French, 151–171. Wilmington, Del.: Scholarly Resources.
Mull, Dorothy S. 1987. Contemporary Mexican Villains in Story and Song: The Pop-

ular Representation of Durazo and Caro Quintero. *Proceedings of Pacific Coast Council on Latin-American Studies* 14 (2): 61–75.

Murphy, Yolanda, and Robert Francis Murphy. 1985. *Women of the Forest*. 2d ed. New York: Columbia University Press.

Nelson, Diane M. 1999. *A Finger in the Wound: Body Politics in Quincentennial Guatemala*. Berkeley: University of California Press.

Nigro, Kirsten. 1989. Pop Culture and Image Making in Two Latin American Plays. *Latin American Literary Review* 17 (33): 42–49.

Nord, Bruce. 1995. *Mexico City's Alternative Futures*. Lanham, Md.: University Press of America.

Olalquiaga, Celeste. 1992. *Megalopolis: Contemporary Cultural Sensibilities*. Minneapolis: University of Minnesota Press.

Oropreza, Deborah. 1996. The Franciscans in Sixteenth-Century Mexico: Painting, Music, and Theater as Instruments of Evangelization. Master's thesis, University of Texas, Austin.

Orovio, Helio. 1991. *300 Boleros de oro: Antología de obras cubanas*. Mexico City: Instituto Nacional de Arqueología e Historia.

Orta Velázquez, Guillermo. 1981. *El corrido*. Mexico City: Manuel Porrúa.

Paredes, Américo. 1958. *With His Pistol in His Hand: A Border Ballad and Its Hero*. Austin: University of Texas Press.

———. 1976. *A Texas-Mexican Cancionero: Folksongs of the Lower Border*. Austin: University of Texas Press.

Pareyón Torreblanca, Roberto. 2001. *La época romántica de México*. Mexico City: Self-published.

Parker, Robert. 1984. Carlos Chávez y la música para el cine. *Heterofonia* 17 (1): 13–27.

———. 1994. Carlos Chávez's Orchestral Tribute to the Discovery of San Francisco Bay. *Latin American Music Review* 15 (2): 177–188.

Paz, Octavio. 1985. *The Labyrinth of Solitude*. New York: Grove Press.

Pedelty, Mark. 1995. *War Stories: The Culture of Foreign Correspondents*. New York: Routledge.

———. 2000. Mexican Popular Culture as Development Discourse: An Intertextual History of Agustín Lara's "Aventurera." In *Redeveloping Communication for Social Change: Theory, Practice, and Power*, edited by K. Wilkins, 119–134. Lanham, Md.: Rowman and Littlefield.

Peña, Manuel. 1985. *The Texas-Mexican Conjunto: History of a Working-Class Music*. Austin: University of Texas Press.

Pérez Rayón E., Nora. 2001. The Capital Commemorates Independence at the Turn of the Century. In *Viva México! Viva La Independencia!: Celebrations of September 16*, edited by W. H. Beezley and D. E. Lorey, 141–166. Wilmington, Del.: Scholarly Resources.

Pilcher, Jeffrey. 1998. *Que Vivan los Tamales: Food and the Making of Mexican Identity*. Albuquerque: University of New Mexico Press.

Pineda, Adela. 1990. La evolución del bolero urbano en Agustín Lara. *Heterofonia* 21 (102–103): 4–23.

Pulido Silva, Esperanza. 1983. Mexican Women in Music. *Latin American Music Review* 4 (1): 120–131.

———. 1986. Diversos aspectos del nacionalismo de Manuel M. Ponce. *Heterofonia* 18 (3): 43–54.

Rafael, Hermes. 1983. *Origen e historia del mariachi*. Mexico City: Editorial Katun.

Ramírez, Juan. 1995. *Remembranzas de un hombre del Bajío*. Mexico City: Litografía Helio.

Ramos, Raymundo. 1993. Notas para una rapsodia. In *Todo lo que quería saber sobre Agustín Lara*, edited by G. Mendizábal and E. Mejía, 85–111. Mexico City: Editorial Contenido.

Rawcliffe, Susan. 1988. Complex Acoustics in Pre-Columbian Flute Systems. In *Musical Repercussions of 1492: Encounters in Text and Performance*, edited by C. E. Robertson, 35–64. Washington, D.C.: Smithsonian Institution Press.

Redfield, Robert. 1930. *Tepoztlán, a Mexican Village: A Study of Folk Life*. Chicago: University of Chicago Press.

Reding, Andrew, and Christopher Whalen. 2003. Multinational Monitor. www.multinationalmonitor.org/hyper/issues/1993/10/mm1093_05.html.

Reuter, Jas. 1981. *La música popular de México: Origen e historia de la música que canta y toca el pueblo mexicano*. Mexico City: Panorama Editorial.

Revueltas, Silvestre. 1989. *Silvestre Revueltas por el mismo*. Mexico City: Era.

Riggio, Annette. 1986. The Gate Keepers of Popular Music in Mexico: National and Transnational Record Producers. *Studies in Latin American Popular Culture* 5: 19–31.

Rivera Ayala, Sergio. 1994. Lewd Songs and Dances from the Streets of Eighteenth-Century New Spain. In *Rituals of Rule, Rituals of Resistance: Public Celebrations and Popular Culture in Mexico*, edited by W. H. Beezley, C. English Martin, and W. E. French, 27–46. Wilmington, Del.: Scholarly Resources.

Robbins, Richard H. 2002. *Global Problems and the Culture of Capitalism*. Boston: Allyn and Bacon.

Robertson, Carol E., ed. 1988. *Musical Repercussions of 1492: Encounters in Text and Performance*. Washington D.C.: Smithsonian Institution Press.

Robles-Cahero, José Antonio. 1989. El vals en Tlalpan, 1815. *Heterofonía* 100–101: 41–48.

Romero, Jesús C. 1987. *Verdadera historia del himno nacional mexicano*. Mexico City: Talleres Gráficos de la Nación.

Ross, John. 1998. *The Annexation of Mexico*. Monroe, Maine: Common Courage Press.

Rostas, Susanna. 1996. The Production of Gendered Imagery: The Concheros of Mexico. In *Machos, Mistresses, Madonnas: Contesting the Power of Latin American Gender Imagery*, edited by M. Melhuus and K. A. Stolen, 207–229. New York: Verso.

———. 1998. From Ritualization to Performativity: The Concheros of Mexico. In *Ritual, Performance, Media*, edited by F. Hughes-Freeland, 85–103. New York: Routledge.

Roura, Victor. 1985. *Apuntes de "rock": Por las calles del mundo*. Mexico City: Nuevomar.

Rubenstein, Anne. 1998. *Bad Language, Naked Ladies, and Other Threats to the Nation: A Political History of Comic Books in Mexico*. Durham, N.C.: Duke University Press.

Ruiz Ortiz, Xochiquetzal. 1994. *Blas Galindo: Biografía, antología de textos y catálogo*. Mexico City: CENIDUM.

Saavedra, Leonora. 1989. Los escritos periodísticos de Carlos Chávez: Una fuente para la historia de la música de México. *Inter-American Music Review* 10 (2): 77–91.

Sahagún, Fray Bernardino de. 1950–1982. *Florentine Codex, General History of the Things of New Spain* (originally written 1575–1577; 12 books). Edited and translated by Arthur J. O. Anderson and Charles E. Dibble. Santa Fe/Salt Lake City: School of American Research/University of Utah Press.
Sahlins, Marshall. 1981. *Historical Metaphors and Mythical Realities.* Ann Arbor: University of Michigan.
Salazar, Jaime Rico. 1988. *Cien años de boleros.* Bogota: Centro Editorial de Estudios Musicales.
Saldana, Hector. 1997. Nydia Rojas, Mariachi Music's Teen Savior. *Austin American-Statesman*, May 19, E2.
Saldívar, Gabriel. 1934. *Historia de la música en México (Epocas precortesiana y colonial).* Mexico City: SEP.
———. 1937. *El jarabe: Baile popular mexicano.* Mexico City: Talleres Gráficos de la Nación.
Schmidt, Henry C. 1988. History, Society, and the Popular Lyric in Mexico: A Study in Cultural Continuity. *Mexican Studies* 4 (2): 295–318.
Seed, Patricia. 1995. *Ceremonies of Possession in Europe's Conquest of the New World, 1492–1640.* Cambridge: Cambridge University.
Serrano Martínez, Celedonia. 1973. *El corrido mexicano no deriva del romance español.* México City: Centro Cultural Guerrerense.
Sevilla, Amparo. 1990. *Danza, cultura y clases sociales.* Mexico City: INBA.
Simmons, Merle E. 1957. *The Mexican Corrido as a Source for Interpretive Study of Modern Mexico (1870–1950).* Bloomington: Indiana University Press.
Simonett, Helena. 2000. Popular Music and the Politics of Identity: The Empowering Sound of Technobanda. *Popular Music and Society* 24 (2): 1–23.
Smith, Michael E. 1996. *The Aztecs.* Malden, Mass.: Blackwell.
Soler Arechalde, María Angeles. 1991. Nahuatlismos en algunos refranes de la lírica popular mexicana. *Estudios de Cultura Náhuatl* 21:231–235.
Solís, Theodore. 1980. Muñecas de Chiapaneco: The Economic Importance of Self-Image in the World of the Mexican Marimba. *Latin American Music Review* 1 (1): 34–46.
Sordo Sodi, Carmen. 1982. La música mexicana en la época del Presidente Benito Juárez. In *Die Musikkulturen Lateinamerikas* (in Spanish), edited by R. Gunther, 299–325. Regensburg: Gustav Bosse.
Stanford, E. Thomas. 1984a. Rasgos de la música precolombina. In *La música de México: Período prehispánico*, edited by J. Estrada, 79–86. Mexico City: UNAM.
———. 1984b. *El son mexicano.* Mexico City: Fondo de Cultura Económica.
Stark, Richard. 1983. Notes on a Search for Antecedents of New Mexican Alabado Music. In *Hispanic Arts and Ethnohistory in the Southwest: New Papers Inspired by the Work of E. Boyd*, edited by M. Wiegle, Claudia Larcombe, and Samuel Larcombe, 117–127. Santa Fe: Ancient City.
Stevenson, Robert. 1952. *Music in Mexico: A Historical Survey.* New York: Thomas Y. Crowell.
———. 1964. Secular Music in Colonial Mexico. *Inter-American Music Review* (39): 1–3.
———. 1968. *Music in Aztec and Inca Territory.* Berkeley: University of California Press.
———. 1979a. Baroque Music in Oaxaca Cathedral. *Inter-American Music Review* 1 (2): 179–205.

———. 1979b. Mexico City Cathedral: the Founding Century. *Inter-American Music Review* 1 (2): 131–179.
———. 1980a. Jaime Nuno after the Mexican National Anthem. *Inter-American Music Review* 2 (2): 103–116.
———. 1980b. The Latin Tinge, 1800–1900. *Inter-American Music Review* 2 (2): 73–103.
———. 1982a. Chopin in Mexico. *Inter-American Music Review* 4 (2): 31–46.
———. 1982b. Haydn's Iberian World Connections. *Inter-American Music Review* 4 (2): 3–30.
———. 1986. La música de México de los siglos XVI a XVIII. In *La música de México: Período virreinal (1530–1810)*, edited by J. Estrada, 7–74. Mexico City: UNAM.
———. 1987. Mexico City Cathedral Music, 1600–1675. *Inter-American Music Review* 9 (1): 75–114.
Stigberg, David. 1985. Foreign Currents during the 60s and 70s in Mexican Popular Music: Rock and Roll, the Romantic Ballad and the Cumbia. *Studies in Latin American Popular Culture* 4: 170–184.
Summers, William J. 1980. Orígenes hispanos de la música misional de California. *Revista Musical Chilena* 149–150: 34–48.
Taibo, Paco Ignacio. 1984. *La música de Agustín Lara en el cine*. Mexico City: Filmoteca de la UNAM.
———. 1985. *Agustín Lara*. Mexico City: Ediciones Jucar.
Taussig, Michael. 1987. *Shamanism, Colonialism, and the Wild Man: A Study in Terror and Healing*. Chicago: University of Chicago.
Taylor, Julie. 1998. *Paper Tangos*. Durham, N.C.: Duke University Press.
Tello, Aurellio. 1992. *Sonido y ciudad*. Mexico City: Instituto Nacional de Bellas Artes.
Tenenbaum, Barbara. 1994. Streetwise History: The Paseo de la Reforma and the Porfirian State, 1876–1910. In *Rituals of Rule, Rituals of Resistance: Public Celebrations and Popular Culture in Mexico*, edited by W. Beezley, C. E. Martin, and W. French, 127–150. Wilmington, Del.: Scholarly Resources.
Thomas, Hugh. 1993. *Conquest: Montezuma, Cortés, and the Fall of Old Mexico*. New York: Simon and Schuster.
Thomas, Lewis. 1857. *Cortez the Conqueror: A Tragedy*. Washington, D.C.: B. W. Ferguson.
Tovar, Juan. 1970. *Las adoraciones*. Mexico City: Editorial Diógenes.
Trejo, Angel. 1992. *¡Hey, familia, danzón dedicado a . . . !* Mexico City: Plaza y Valdés.
Tumas-Serna, Jane. 1992. The "Nueva Canción" Movement and Its Mass-Mediated Performance Context. *Latin American Music Review* 13 (2): 139–157.
Tuñón Pablos, Julia. 1999. *Women in Mexico: A Past Unveiled*. Translations from Latin America Series. Austin: University of Texas Press/Institute of Latin American Studies.
Turrent, Lourdes. 1996. *La conquista musical de México*. Mexico City: Fondo Cultural Económica.
Vázquez Santa Ana, Higinio. N.d. *Cantares mexicanos: Canciones, cantares y corridos mexicanos*. Mexico City: Ediciones León Sánchez.
Velazco, Jorge. 1991. Antonio Gomezanda y el nacionalismo romántico mexicano. *Latin American Music Review* 12 (1): 65–72.
Villarino, José (Pepe). 1992. La Masacre en San Ysidro: Text and Context. In *Chicano Border: Culture and folklore*, edited by J. Villarino and A. Ramírez, 236–250. San Diego: Marin.

Viquiera Albán, Juan Pedro. 1999. *Propriety and Permissiveness in Bourbon Mexico.* Translated by S. Lipsett-Rivera and S. Rivera Ayala. Wilmington, Del.: Scholarly Resources.
Wald, Elijah. 2001. *Narcocorrido: A Journey into the Music of Drugs, Guns, and Guerillas.* New York: Rayo.
Ward, Peter M. 1998. *Mexico City.* New York: Wiley.
Warkentin, Larry. 1981. The Rise and Fall of Indian Music in California Missions. *Latin American Music Review* 2 (1): 45–65.
Waxer, Lise. 1994. Of Mambo Kings and Songs of Love: Dance Music in Havana and New York from the 1930s to the 1950s. *Latin American Music Review* 15, no. 2: 139–176.
Worton, Michael, and Judith Still. 1990. *Intertextuality: Theories and Practice.* New York: Manchester University Press.
Zolov, Eric. 1999. *Refried Elvis: The Rise of the Mexican Counterculture.* Berkeley: University of California Press.

Index

"Adios Mamá Carlota," 97
Agrasánchez Jr., Rogelio, 154
Aguilar, Pepe, 245
Aguilera, Christina, 257
Aharonían, Coriun, 265
alabado, 75, 302
Alcaraz, José Antonio, 206
anarchism, 80, 226
Aura, Alejandro, 167
Aurora y la Academia, 276, 319
"Aventurera," 155–160, 179, 183–188, 272
"Ay Jalisco no te rajes," 232
Aztec. *See* Mexica

Bach, Johann Sebastian, 96–97
banda, 107–115, 252, 318
Banda de Tlayacapan, 111–114
Bantjes, Adrian, 204
baroque, 58
Beezely, William, 100
Behague, Gerard, 69, 95, 204, 233, 272, 295
bel canto, 102, 231
Beltrán, Graciela, 252, 318
Beltrán, Lola, 231, 317
"Bésame," 243
"Bésame mucho," 152
Bierhorst, John, 21
Bliss, Catherine, 178

bolero, 60, 102, 139–202, 225, 231, 232, 258–259, 316
Bonfil Batalla, Guillermo, 35, 139, 150, 203
Britton, John, 144
Broda, Johanna, 9–10

Caballos de Vapor, 206
Café Tacuba, 81, 255, 257, 264, 266–270, 319
capitalism
  commodification, 175–176, 209, 253–258
  rituals of, 80, 204–205, 236–237, 288–289
  transformations toward, 87, 97–100, 160–161, 211–212
  See also globalization
Cárdenas, Guty, 147, 316
Cárdenas, Lázaro, 204, 210, 235
Cárdenas Solórzano, Cuauhtemóc, 114, 186
Carmona, Gloria, 90, 207
Carranza, Venustiano, 40
Carrasco, Pedro, 6
Castañeda, Daniel, 22
Castellanos, Pablo, 44
Castro, Ricardo, 102
Catalyne, Alice Ray, 69

cathedrals
    Mexico City, 57, 65, 71–74, 81, 221, 284–285
    Oaxaca, 54, 61
Catholicism
    conversion, 39–56
    Corpus Cristi, 63–65
    Mass, 39, 58–59, 67, 71–76, 78, 279–280, 304
    missions, 47–51
censorship, 52–53, 67–69, 260, 271
Chamorro, Arturo, 52
Chávez, Carlos, 167, 203, 205–215, 217
Chávez, Oscar, 133, 273, 276, 316
Chiapas, 35–36, 73, 80, 113, 186, 251, 273, 319
"Chilanga banda," 264
"Chilango," 263
chirimía, 51–52
choral music, 51, 53, 58, 61, 76–79, 217, 219, 315
"Chuchumbé," 67, 80–81
Claro, Samuel, 68
classical music, 144, 203–224, 237
"Combates de Celaya," 162
Concheros, 32–33, 39, 278
Copland, Aaron, 149, 173, 206
corrido, 103, 121–135, 162–163, 169, 170, 316
"Corrido de Juan B. Galindo," 124
Cortés, Hernan, 6, 11, 39–40, 42–43, 56, 122, 263, 284
Cristero War, 124, 204, 236
Cruz, Sor Juana Inés de la, 60, 65–66, 68, 285
Cuba, 145–147, 151
cumbia, 145, 252–253
Cura de Espantos, 28–32
Curcio-Nagy, Linda, 63–64

dances and dance styles
    danzón, 96, 139–202, 316
    el huapango, 61, 213
    El rubí, 78
    Guelaguetza, 79–80
    jarabe, 87–88, 213
    la bamba, 61
    La llorona, 78
    los Chinelos, 114
    salsa, 145, 252
    waltz, 68, 89, 316
Día de los Muertos, 107, 196
diaspora, 250
Díaz, Porfirio, 40, 94, 97–98, 101, 120, 286
Díaz del Castillo, Bernal, 11, 17, 40, 284
Díaz Roig, Mercedes, 103, 303, 305
Dueñas, Pablo, 148, 151, 155, 172, 180
Dug Dugs, 262
Dultzin Dubin, Susana, 19
Dúo Arcaraz, 222
Dúo Villey-Hinojosa, 78–79, 315

Earle, Timothy, 10, 44
Ejército Zapatista de Liberación Nacional (EZLN), 35–36, 73, 81, 186, 251, 257, 265, 267, 286
"El amor acaba," 132
"El metro," 268
"El pan de manteca," 67
"El perico," 102
El Tri, 251, 253, 255, 260, 262–263, 266–269, 272, 309, 319
"El último adiós," 240
"Epidemia," 266
Escorza, Juan José, 58–59
Estrada, Jesús, 48, 66
ethnicity and race
    African-Americans, 61–63, 90, 145, 203, 252–253, 255, 261–262
    criollos, 63, 67, 69, 99, 105
    indigenismo, 94, 143–144, 150, 203–215
    indigenous, 63, 69, 70, 74, 112–114, 203, 210–211, 228 See also Mexica
    mestizos and *mestizaje*, 59–61, 67, 69, 70, 203, 204, 211, 254, 260
    vagabundos, 59, 67
    whites, 70, 260–261

"Fácil," 267
Felipe, Liliana, 190, 283
Félix, María, 149, 158
film genres
    cabaretera, 144, 149, 153–160, 235
    charro, 226–227, 232–235
Flores, Chava, 133–134

Flores, Ricardo, 130
Flores Urbán, Mario, 35
Flores y Escalante, Jesús, 178–179
folk music, 191–192, 205, 237, 267, 272–274, 297–305
Foppa, Alaide, 169–170
Fox, Vicente, 77, 185, 192, 275, 278–289
France
   intervention of, 40, 87, 88, 91, 92, 94–96, 98, 110–111, 228
   musical and cultural influence of, 69, 89, 103, 108, 227–229
Franco, Hernando, 65, 71
Frenk, María Teresa, 217, 317

Gabriel, Ana, 134, 193, 240, 253, 319
Galaz Chacón, Enrique, 160, 174
Galindo, Blas, 210, 217, 219–220, 309
Gante, Pedro de, 47–51, 54, 59, 64, 66
García Canclini, Nestór, 144, 198, 304
Garza de Koniecki, María del Carmen, 130
Gelpí, Juan, 152, 174, 180
gender,
   and education, 14, 95
   and sexuality, 90, 162, 267, 270–272, 276
   ritual, 12, 14, 65–66, 200, 233, 241
   roles and identities, 126–128, 163, 167–172, 191, 196–202, 217–218
Gil, Alfredo, 232
globalization, 181, 209, 253–260, 263–266, 268–269, 277, 288, 303
Gómez-Peña, Guillermo, 265
Gordillo, Mercedes, 141–142
Gradante, William, 89
Graniceros, 30–31
"Gregorio Cortez," 123
Grever, María, 152, 172, 199–200
"Guadalajara en un llano," 276
Guelaguetza, 31
Guerra, Eli, 199–200, 272, 288, 319
Guillermoprieto, Alma, 239
Guzmán, Alejandra, 262, 267
Guzmán Bravo, José Antonio, 46, 52, 145

Hadad, Astrid, 134, 190, 318
Harris, Max, 114

Hernández, Figueroa, 151
Herrera-Sobek, María, 123, 126–128, 156, 160, 169, 170
Herz, Henri, 85–86
"Himno nacional," 86, 91–94, 109–110, 282, 285, 316
"Hoy me iré de casa," 271–272

Infante, Pedro, 231, 317
Instituto Nacional de las Bellas Artes (INBA), 208
Italian influence, 96, 102, 103

Jiménez, Armando, 152
Jiménez, José Alfredo, 231, 317
Jiménez de Baez, Yvette, 304–305
Johnson, Allen, 10, 44
Juárez, Benito, 96, 97, 102, 107, 108, 189
"Júrame," 152, 199–200

Kahlo, Frida, 165, 166, 169–170, 206, 214, 237
Kandell, Jonathan, 20
Kelly, John, 309
Kertzer, David, 25, 285, 291
Knight, Alan, 125, 143, 172, 177–178, 235–236
Kristeva, Julia, 306

"La Adelita," 121, 127, 129, 159, 174, 282
"La ingrata," 257, 270
"La migra," 266
"La noche de los Maya," 214
Lara, Agustín, 139, 147–148, 154–156, 160, 162–179, 192–193, 237, 262, 286, 308–309, 316
"Las mañanitas," 75
Leñero, Vicente, 110
León, Eugenia, 190–191, 273, 282–284, 316
Libertad, Tania, 134, 273, 288, 317, 318
Lockhart, James, 21
López, Ana, 147, 156, 158
Lora, Alex, 266–267, 309
Los Bukis, 250
Los Panchos, 232
Lost Acapulco, 257
Los Temerarios, 250–251, 318

Los Tigres del Norte, 135, 250
Lucero, 193, 240, 258, 262, 319

"Madrugal," 81
Maldita Vecindad, 265
Malinche, 55, 158, 159, 170, 228, 272
"María Bonita," 173
Mariachi Juvenil de América, 243–245
Martin, Ricky, 257, 267
Martín-Barbero, Jesús, 155, 157, 158, 171, 187
mass media
  film industry, 144, 175, 178, 214, 232–233
  radio, 150, 153–154, 160, 179, 230–231, 253
  recording industry, 129, 151, 160, 174, 230, 233, 254, 298–299, 301
  television, 154, 223, 229, 254, 261–262, 267, 287
Melhuus, Marit, 201
Mendoza, Vicente, 22, 124, 303
methodology, 305–309
"Metro Balderas," 267
Mexica
  dualism, 15–16, 55–56
  gods
    Cihuacóatl, 55
    Coatlicue, 5, 10–11, 12, 159
    Coyolxauhqui, 5, 10, 12, 15, 20, 41, 55, 159
    Huehuetéotl, 14
    Huitzilopochtli, 5, 10–11, 12, 15, 39, 41, 159
    Ometéotl, 20
    Quetzalcoatl, 6–7, 20, 29, 40, 284
    Tezcatlipoca, 9, 14, 20, 39, 284
    Tlaloc, 15, 71
    Tlaltecuhtli, 8, 12, 170–171
    Tonantzín, 45–46
    Tonatiuh, 12, 18, 20
    Xilónen, 20
    Xipe Tótec, 20, 73
    Xochipilli, 205
  Great Temple, 15, 30, 40–41, 57
  instruments, 17–23, 26–27, 39–41, 52, 284, 309
  migration, 5
  poetry, 5, 7, 21, 24, 40
  rituals
    New Fire, 8–9
    sacrifice, 7–8, 10, 17, 19, 22, 35, 159
    Snake Dance, 14
    Tickle Dance, 55
    Toxcatl, 9, 39
Mexico City Philharmonic Orchestra, 220–222, 317
Miguel, Luis, 193, 241, 317
Mijares, 193, 258, 282–284
"Mi novia," 140, 177, 188
Moctezuma, Matos, 11, 15, 41–42
Monsiváis, Carlos, 140, 145, 147, 155, 174, 177, 193, 232, 235, 269, 270–271, 289, 298
Morelos, José Antonio, 91
"Morena mia," 151
Motecuhzoma Xocoyotzin, 6, 7, 56
"Mujer," 167, 286
musical instruments
  manufacture of, 85
  percussion, 61, 249, 253
  piano and organ, 52, 96–97, 148, 164, 217–218, 220–221, 222, 249, 258, 286
  strings, 51, 61, 79, 88, 148, 225, 229, 232, 249, 258
  winds, 43, 52, 74–75, 91, 107–115, 223, 225, 230, 249, 252
  See also Mexica
music education, 13–15, 44, 46, 47–51, 59, 68, 76, 78, 95–96, 207, 212, 214, 216–217, 222

"Nacerá," 283
Nacional Conservatory of Music, 95, 96, 208, 216
National Palace, 57, 273, 284
Nava Gomez Tagle, José Antonio, 19, 46
Negra, Toña la, 155, 172, 317
Negrete, Jorge, 231, 317
Nelson, Diane, 111
Nezahuacóyotl, 21, 47
"Noche de ronda," 141, 193
norteño, 249–251, 318
North American Free Trade Agreement (NAFTA), 110, 180–181, 186–187, 190, 220, 286

nueva canción, musica protesta and, 133, 272–274
Nunó, Jaime, 91–92, 282, 284

Olalquiaga, Celeste, 257
Olmos, Carlos, 183–188
Opera, 102, 104, 105, 261
Oropreza, Deborah, 49
Orovio, Helio, 151
Orozco, José Clemente, 203, 206, 215
Ortega, Aniceto, 102

"Pan de jarabe," 67
Paredes, Américo, 123, 130
Partido Acción Nacional (PAN), 183, 185, 199, 267, 278–289
Partido de la Revolución Democrática (PRD), 114, 183, 186, 199, 226–227, 267, 287–288
Partido Revolucionario Institucional (PRI)
  corruption, 178
  decline, 199, 278–281, 288
  musical sponsorship, 76, 113
  resistance to, 81, 114, 133, 184–186, 266–267, 273, 276
  ritual and ideology, 143, 159, 233–236
Paz, Octavio, 231
Peña, Manuel, 130
Peralta, Angela, 95
"Perfidia," 172–173
Peza, Carmen de la, 140, 253, 302
Pilcher, Jeffrey, 14, 308
Pineda, Adela, 172, 173–174, 234
"Pobre Soñador," 263
"Poema de Pablo Neruda," 219–220
Ponce, Manuel, 88, 154, 205, 214, 217

"Que devuelvan," 190
quínceañeras, 243

Rafael, Hermes, 228
Ramírez, Juan, 139, 229
Ramírez Berg, Charles, 154
Ramos, Raymundo, 146, 149, 155
ranchera, mariachi and, 225–245, 317–318
Rawcliffe, Susan, 21–22
Redfield, Robert, 122, 124–125, 133

Revolution for Independence, 87–88, 99, 101–102, 204, 285
Revolution of 1910, 99, 119–130, 143, 232–234, 266, 316
Revueltas, Silvestre, 213, 217
Rivera, Diego, 166, 170, 175, 203, 206, 218, 237
Rivera Ayala, Sergio, 67–68
Robertson, Carol, 292
Robles-Cahero, José Antonio, 89
rock, pop and, 197, 198, 199–200, 249, 253–272, 282–284, 286, 318–319
Rollos and Rock and Roll, 269–270
romances, musical, 122–123
romanticism, 105
"Rosa," 168
Rosas, Juventino, 87, 96
Rostas, Susanna, 32–34
Roura, Victor, 262, 269
Rubenstein, Anne, 260
Rubio, Paulina, 240, 262, 319

Saavedra, Leonora, 208
Sahagún, 23, 54
Sahlins, Marshall, 6, 15
salsa, 145
"Santa," 154
Santa Anna, Antonio López de, 91–92
Schmidt, Henry, 62, 144, 211, 301–302
Seed, Patricia, 43
Serrano Martínez, Celedonia, 122–123
Sinfonía india, 205
Siquieros, David Alfaro, 167, 171, 203
Smith, Michael, 7, 8
"Sobre las olas" (Over the Waves), 96
socialism, 80, 176, 203–204, 209, 211–212, 226, 236–237
"Solamente una vez," 140, 151, 173
son, 61–62, 78–79, 89–91, 108, 146, 212, 230, 316
"Sones mariachi," 210
Sordo Sodi, Carmen, 95, 105
"Soy de San Luis Potosí," 232, 243
Spain
  Bourbon reforms, 53, 65, 67–69, 86, 99, 101, 304
  conquest, 39–46, 122, 125, 284
  Council of Trent, 52–53, 74, 75
  cultural influence and legacy, 88, 103

Stanford, E. Thomas, 22, 228
Stark, Richard, 75, 302
Stevenson, Robert, 17, 19, 104, 163, 307–308
Stolen, Kristi Anne, 201

Taibo, Paco Ignacio, 165, 168, 175
tango, 148, 194–196
Taylor, Julie, 199
Tello, Aurellio, 214
Thalia, 257, 262, 319
theater, 16, 55, 56–57, 59, 68–69, 78, 110–111, 145, 183–188
Tijuana No, 265, 319
"Tirana," 67
"Tom Mix, Buck Jones, Bill Boyd, Tim McCoy," 133
tonadilla escénica, 103
Tovar, Juan, 59
"Transgresores de la ley," 265–266
Trejo, Angél, 145, 149
Trevi, Gloria, 262, 270–272, 319
Tribu, 26
trío, 232, 258–259
"Triste recuerdo," 194
tropical music, 249, 252–253, 318
Tumas-Serna, Jane, 272
Tuñon Pablos, Julia, 308
Turrent, Lourdes, 12, 48, 292, 300–301

United States
  corporations, 80, 114, 133, 254–258, 279, 288
  intervention and war, 40, 60, 88, 91, 93, 94, 111, 233
  Manifest Destiny, 56
  Mexican musical influence in, 152, 172–173, 208–209, 231, 250, 272–273
  musical influence in Mexico, 69, 103–104, 115, 152–153, 187, 251, 253–258
Universidad Nacional Autónoma de México (UNAM), 26, 28–31, 217, 219–220
Urbán, Victor, 220–221
Urreta, Pilar, 30–32

"Valentín de la sierra," 134
Vallen, Mark, 35
Vasconcelos, José, 167, 203
Venegas, Julieta, 200, 272, 288, 319
Villa, Francisco, 121, 129, 139, 162, 166, 204, 286
villancico, 60, 315
Villanueva, Felipe, 87, 96, 216
Viquiera Albán, Juan Pedro, 78
Virgen de Guadalupe
  as gender role model, 127, 159, 168, 170, 188
  and racial politics, 259–262
  ritual, 73–74, 107, 271–272, 279–280
  as symbol of resistance, 59, 91
  syncretism, 45–46
"Virgen de las vírgenes," 270
"Virgen morena," 260
voladores, 27–28, 184, 275–276

Wald, Elijah, 134–135

Xochipilli, 205

Zapata, Emilano, 121, 125, 128–129, 139, 286
Zedillo, Ernesto, 79–80
Zolov, Eric, 263
Zuk, Eva María, 218, 316
Zumárraga, Juan de, 49
Zumaya, Manuel de, 68–69, 71

www.ingramcontent.com/pod-product-compliance
Lightning Source LLC
Chambersburg PA
CBHW060940230426
43665CB00015B/2011